Technocrats in Turmoil

As the economy became more financialized, the politics of money considerably changed after the late 1970s. American and European central bankers first allied with conservative forces to fight inflation in the 1980s; then, that alliance unraveled after the 2008 financial crisis. Many observers gloss over this change because they see central bankers either as stewards of financialization, or as economists dedicated to economic stability. Nicolas Jabko shows how changing alliances between central bankers, economists, and politicians led to momentous shifts in monetary regimes. He argues that central bankers are technocrats who navigate and powerfully shape three overlapping arenas – their own internal monetary policy committees; the economics profession; and the broader public arena. Steeped in a machine-assisted analysis of central bank archives, *Technocrats in Turmoil* thus reveals the key role that the Fed and the ECB played in the waxing and waning of technocratic neoliberalism.

Nicolas Jabko is a professor of political science at Johns Hopkins University. A transatlantic scholar at heart, he has spent most of his life and career between the United States and Europe.

Technocrats in Turmoil

The Fed, the ECB, and the Changing Politics of Money

NICOLAS JABKO
Johns Hopkins University

CAMBRIDGE
UNIVERSITY PRESS

CAMBRIDGE
UNIVERSITY PRESS

Shaftesbury Road, Cambridge CB2 8EA, United Kingdom

One Liberty Plaza, 20th Floor, New York, NY 10006, USA

477 Williamstown Road, Port Melbourne, VIC 3207, Australia

314–321, 3rd Floor, Plot 3, Splendor Forum, Jasola District Centre, New Delhi – 110025, India

103 Penang Road, #05–06/07, Visioncrest Commercial, Singapore 238467

Cambridge University Press is part of Cambridge University Press & Assessment, a department of the University of Cambridge.

We share the University's mission to contribute to society through the pursuit of education, learning and research at the highest international levels of excellence.

www.cambridge.org
Information on this title: www.cambridge.org/9781009727440

DOI: 10.1017/9781009727488

© Nicolas Jabko 2026

This publication is in copyright. Subject to statutory exception and to the provisions of relevant collective licensing agreements, no reproduction of any part may take place without the written permission of Cambridge University Press & Assessment.

When citing this work, please include a reference to the DOI 10.1017/9781009727488

First published 2026

Cover image: GrafikLab / DigitalVision Vectors / Getty Images

A catalogue record for this publication is available from the British Library

A Cataloging-in-Publication data record for this book is available from the Library of Congress

ISBN 978-1-009-72744-0 Hardback
ISBN 978-1-009-72745-7 Paperback

Cambridge University Press & Assessment has no responsibility for the persistence or accuracy of URLs for external or third-party internet websites referred to in this publication and does not guarantee that any content on such websites is, or will remain, accurate or appropriate.

For EU product safety concerns, contact us at Calle de José Abascal, 56, 1°, 28003 Madrid, Spain, or email eugpsr@cambridge.org

To Franck

Contents

List of Figures		*page* ix
Preface		xi
1	Fallen Conservative Heroes	1
2	Political Economy versus Economics	11
3	Economists with Power	24
4	The Waxing of Technocratic Neoliberalism in the United States	41
5	The Waxing of Technocratic Neoliberalism in the European Union	74
6	The Waning of Technocratic Neoliberalism in the United States	104
7	The Waning of Technocratic Neoliberalism in the European Union	137
8	Beyond Neoliberalism?	168
9	Technocrats, Neoliberalism, Keynesianism, and Democracy	186
Appendix A Natural Language Processing (NLP) Methodology and Results		191
Appendix B Correspondence with the ECB Executive Board		203
References		211
Index		231

Figures

2.1	Schematized political economy perspective on economic evolution (since 1945).	*page* 13
2.2	Schematized (macro)economics perspective on economic evolution (since 1945).	14
4.1	Disagreement at the FOMC, 1979–1987.	45
4.2	Volcker Fed dissents, 1979–1987.	46
4.3	GDP in the United States.	59
5.1	Disagreement on the Committee of Governors, 1980–1989.	78
5.2	Disagreement on the Delors Committee, 1988–1989.	80
6.1	Disagreement at the FOMC, 2008–2017.	110
6.2	FOMC dissents, 2000–2019.	123
6.3	Frequency of terms "headwind," "drag," and "downside risk" from 2000 to 2018.	130
7.1	Eurozone public deficit as percentage of GDP.	140
7.2	Eurozone public debt as percentage of GDP.	140
7.3	ECB overnight deposit interest rate.	141
7.4	Eurosystem assets, in millions of euros.	141
7.5	News items about Eurozone governance.	146
7.6	References to "transmission mechanism" in ECB speeches, 2008–2019.	152
7.7	References to "transmission mechanism" and "redenomination" in ECB speeches, 2008–2019.	159
8.1	FOMC dissents, 2020–2024.	170
8.2	Federal Reserve's federal funds rate, July 2019–July 2024.	175
8.3	ECB deposit facility rate, August 2019–July 2024.	176
A.1	Disagreement at the FOMC, 1979–1987.	197

A.2	Disagreement at the FOMC, 2008–2017.	198
A.3	Disagreement on the Delors Committee.	199
A.4	Disagreement on the Committee of Governors.	200
B.1	Author's letter to ECB.	204
B.2	ECB's letter to author.	206

Preface

This book took much longer to write than I would have hoped when I first started studying the politics of central banking in the early 2000s. The global financial crisis of 2008 and its long aftermath profoundly changed what central banking was about. As it happened, 2008 was also the year when I started work on a research project (funded by France's Agence Nationale de la Recherche) about the return of the nineteenth-century "liberal state" theorized by Karl Polanyi in the 1940s, despite the progress of democracy after the Second World War. That project aimed to explain a contemporary phenomenon: the increased power of central bankers and other state actors that had prioritized low inflation and successfully encouraged a host of market-friendly policies. Paul Volcker and Alan Greenspan, or even the leaders of the young European Central Bank (ECB), had become household names at the helm of remarkably powerful institutions.

As the financial crisis and its aftermath unfolded, however, I often watched the news in disbelief. I soon realized that the liberal state of the twenty-first century was much more elusive than I had initially thought. The leaders of the Fed, the ECB, and other central banks were in many ways just as powerful as before 2008, but they were acting quite differently. As I later found out when I read transcripts of their committee deliberations, the world was also turned upside down for many central bankers. This book is thus, in part, my attempt to make sense of a twice-transformed landscape of political economy.

Two personal experiences especially struck me. First, I found myself writing papers that went against the grain of a growing scholarly literature on austerity and on central bankers' endorsement of fiscal conservatism, especially in Europe. I did not really know what central bankers' endgame was, but I quickly realized that the ECB was not just carrying out neoliberal austerity policies – even though I recognized that it certainly did that, too. As I saw it, neoliberalism not only triggered but also morphed into various kinds of populist movements fueled by a broad anger about economic crises. In the United States but also in the European Union (EU), this development clearly shook the usually polite worldviews of central bankers. Economic crisis, neoliberalism, and populism are thus the backdrop of this book's story about central bankers and the politics of money.

Second, I was struck when some of my undergraduate students who took courses in economics reported to me that radical free-market policies had been discredited. At a time of deep austerity and growing rage against the "deep state," that seemed odd to me. Either my colleagues in the economics department did not pay much attention to politics, or they knew something that I did not know. In reflecting as a political scientist about the perspective of economists, I increasingly focused on the economics profession's autonomy from real-life politics. This autonomy is paradoxical, since economists are much more present in policymaking circles than any other social scientists. Most importantly perhaps, they populate central banks. The Federal Reserve or the European Central banks are public institutions that wield considerable influence over economic policies and yet enjoy considerable autonomy from governments.

Ultimately, this book tries to make sense of two major economic slumps from the vantage point of central bankers and their relation to the economics profession and to the public more generally. As I read detailed transcripts of their meetings and began to better understand them, I also realized that eulogies of or attacks on central bankers often essentialize their position in unproductive ways. Abundant archival evidence points first to their remarkable yet often awkward proximity to conservative politics in the 1980s, and secondly to their estrangement from that sphere in the 2010s. As central bankers and economists became increasingly united around Keynes' ideas and their "moderately conservative" implications, their direct influence on conservative politics paradoxically declined. This is something that few scholars understand very well. If my readers become better aware of the peculiar role of economic technocrats and economists in the politics of capitalist democracies, I believe this book can serve the public debate.

*

Let me now say a few words about the many debts, intellectual as well as institutional, that I have incurred while working on this book.

A faculty fellowship at Harvard University's Warren Center for the Study of American History in the academic year 2022–2023 enabled me to complete a full first draft of the manuscript. The workshop's theme was "Capitalism's Hardwiring: Money, Credit, and Finance in a Globalizing World, 1620-2020." Christine Desan and Kenneth Mack were great workshop leaders, and I am also grateful to them for enabling me to engage in productive cross-disciplinary conversations with other money geeks – especially Ann Daly,

Devin Fergus, Pierre Fink, Trevor Jackson, Sohaib Khan, Andrew Konove, Rebecca Lossin, Simon Middleton, Ellen Nye, and Christopher Todd. While at Harvard, I also benefited from conversations with Frank Dobbin, who invited me to present my project at the Harvard-MIT seminar on economic sociology, as well as with Amel Ahmed, Peter Hall, Perry Mehrling, Quinn Slobodian, and Daniel Ziblatt.

Two stays in Europe immediately before and after that Warren Center workshop enabled me to develop the framework of my manuscript. I started my research on central bank minutes and transcripts in the fall of 2021, as a research fellow at the LawFin Center of Goethe Universität Frankfurt. I presented the project at the weekly LawFin seminar and benefited from conversations with Rainer Haselmann, Elsa Massoc, and Tobias Tröger. Then in September 2023, I benefited from a visiting appointment at the École des Hautes Études en Sciences Sociales-Paris School of Economics, where I presented drafts of several chapters. I especially enjoyed conversations with Jérôme Bourdieu, Eve Chiapello, Pierre-Cyrille Hautcoeur, Sébastien Lechevalier, Éric Monnet, and Thomas Piketty.

In the summer of 2023, I was able to present my work in progress at two book workshops on both sides of the Atlantic, for which scholars read the entire manuscript and gave me precious feedback. At Johns Hopkins, I am grateful to my colleague Steve Teles for hosting a book workshop at the Hewlett Center for Economy and Society, with Gerry Berk, Jacquie Best, Peter Conti-Brown, and Marion Fourcade. In addition to his workshop participation, Gerry Berk deserves a special accolade for his friendly mentoring and generous feedback on countless proposals and drafts over many years. At Sciences Po Paris, I am grateful to Benjamin Braun and Matthias Thiemann for hosting a parallel European book workshop, with Mark Blyth, Elsa Massoc, and Laurence Scialom.

For their support and friendship during the maturation of this book, I am especially grateful to my colleagues at Johns Hopkins University and in the Baltimore/Washington area. I learned so much from so many conversations, joint teaching stints, and co-authoring experiences on topics of shared interest related to this book. I am especially grateful to Yuen Yuen Ang, Larry Ball, Jane Bennett, Angus Burgin, Bill Connolly, Sam Chambers, Dick Katz, John Krakauer, Nils Kupzok, Meghan Luhman, Kate McNamara, Monica Prasad, Sebastian Schmidt, Adam Sheingate, Steve Teles, Nicolas Véron, and so many others; it would be tedious to cite them all here, but they will recognize themselves. For the natural language processing component of this project, I thank Hritamber Chakraborty and Jimena Guallar-Blasco for their research assistance, Kenton Murray for his feedback and advice, and the Johns Hopkins Center for Economy and Society for its financial support. I also thank Henry Clayton for his research assistance in preparing the book's index.

I benefited from many conferences and conversations where I was able to discuss my work in progress or related papers and ideas. I am especially grateful to Mark Blyth, Stefan Eich, and Leah Downey for organizing a recurring online Central Banking Salon, and to all salon participants for regular and lively conversations on this theme, throughout and after the worst of the pandemic. I thank Benjamin Braun and Björn Bremer for inviting me to a workshop on the politics of central banking at the Max Planck Institute in Cologne. And I thank Amandine Crespy, Tiago Moreira, and Vivien Schmidt for organizing a workshop at the Université Libre de Bruxelles, where Nils Kupzok and I presented a paper on green central banking.

For patiently telling me about their experiences of the Fed, the ECB, and other central banks, I am grateful to the numerous economists, central bankers, and other public officials who granted me confidential interviews. I am forever indebted to Philippe Martin, a longtime friend who taught me a lot of what I know about economics and economists.

At Cambridge University Press, I thank Robert Dreesen and his team for their constant support, as well as two anonymous reviewers for their thoughtful feedback.

Last but not least, I thank Franck-Olivier Boëcasse for his patience and emotional support, and also for his help in designing the cover of this book.

1

Fallen Conservative Heroes

After the global financial crisis of 2008, central bankers ceased to be the conservative heroes that they had become since the late twentieth century. In the 1980s, conservatives praised Paul Volcker's Federal Reserve for its unwavering focus on fighting inflation, while the orthodox German Bundesbank was held as a model for the future European Central Bank (ECB). At the turn of the twenty-first century, Alan Greenspan, the then-chair of the Fed and once a follower of libertarian guru Ayn Rand, was widely acclaimed as the "maestro" of America's economic stability and prosperity. Meanwhile, Jean-Claude Trichet, the head of the young ECB, vaunted the merits of low inflation, balanced budgets, and structural reforms. Less than a decade later, Tea Party protesters and their Republican allies called to "end the Fed" and to "tar and feather" Greenspan's successor Ben Bernanke. In Germany, the new right-wing party AfD gained visibility by demanding more austerity in the European Union's periphery, and a tabloid caricatured Trichet's successor Mario Draghi as a "Count Draghila" sucking on the blood of German savers. In a strange role reversal, new grassroots protest movements now demanded tight money and market discipline against central bankers who favored accommodative policies. Central bankers apparently no longer conformed to their long-standing image of conservative technocrats fending off spendthrift politicians.

Conservative cheers and later assaults on central banks exposed crucial but largely submersed changes in the politics of money. Based on a machine-assisted analysis of central bank archives, I demonstrate that Fed and ECB policymakers not only navigate but also powerfully shape three arenas traversed by latent contests – their own internal monetary policy committees; the economics profession; and the broader public arena. Thus, American and European central bankers were at the forefront of important changes in monetary and economic governance during the late twentieth century, and again after the global financial crisis of 2008. As I argue, central bankers are economic technocrats who were key players in both the waxing and the waning of what I call *technocratic neoliberalism*. That broad economic governance regime first waxed in the 1980s, then waned after the global financial crisis of 2008. In both cases, central bankers entered new alliances that cut across different organizational, professional, and public arenas. In the 1980s, central bankers' turn to tight-money policies accelerated political change within each of these arenas, which caused the waxing of technocratic neoliberalism. In the 2010s, however, the alliances that had long supported neoliberal policies unraveled. At that point, the Fed's and the ECB's turn to monetary easing led to the waning of technocratic neoliberalism. Thus, both in the 1980s and in the 2010s, the changing politics of money produced broad watersheds in monetary and political-economic regimes.

This argument challenges the ways in which central bankers are usually portrayed in political economy or economics. Scholars of political economy in various academic disciplines typically see central bankers as stewards of financialization. For example, political scientists Lawrence Jacobs and Desmond King indict the US Federal Reserve for wielding its power in such a way that "finance wins."[1] In such readings, central banks cater to an increasingly finance-driven economy, itself fueled by mutually reinforcing trends – the rise of neoliberal ideology and market-friendly policies in the 1980s, the structural shift of advanced capitalist democracies from manufacturing to services, and the decline of the Left's old manufacturing working-class base. The strident post-2008 attacks on the Fed and the ECB thus appear as a broad populist backlash against bankers and finance. By contrast, mainstream scholars of economics who discuss central banks and monetary policy generally avoid bringing up financialization or neoliberalism. Instead, they underscore central bankers' responses to strictly economic problems, such as the "Great Inflation" of the 1970s or the "Great Recession" of the 2010s. As Princeton economist (and former Fed vice chair) Alan Blinder puts it, central bankers are "technocrats, mostly economists" who act on "economic considerations."[2] They are primarily focused on managing the money supply in response to a changing economy, unlike politicians whose motivations are primarily political. In this reading, denunciations of central bankers are usually misguided but understandably ideological.

While such broad or focused interpretations make sense in their own terms, they are often so strangely truncated that the role of central bankers remains opaque. Although central bankers are anything but anti-establishment rebels, they cultivate their aura as independent public servants and seek to avoid the charge that they serve privileged interests. Neither are they merely economists who can afford to be attentive only to the economy and to economic theories.

---

[1] Jacobs and King 2021.   [2] Blinder 2022: 3, 391.

As technocrats, central bankers always maneuver in different arenas at the same time. Their role in multidimensional contests about money is therefore not well captured by typical disciplinary portrayals.

To make sense of central bankers' puzzling rise and fall as conservative heroes from the 1980s to the 2010s, we must examine the changing positions that they adopted in various arenas. Once we do this, their crucial role in building and later partially dismantling a technocratic form of neoliberal *status quo* also becomes clearer. The support of central bankers was key to Reagan's conservative revolution as well as to the European Union's integration around a single market and the euro, and thus to the emergence of a transatlantic neoliberal governance regime. That regime then waned after the financial crisis of 2008 when central bankers on both sides of the ocean retreated from it. Beyond the central bankers' rise in favor and later fall from grace among conservatives, this book's examination of their role in a changing politics of money therefore illuminates the waxing and waning of technocratic neoliberalism over several decades.

1.1 WHEN UNORTHODOX CENTRAL BANKING BECOMES ORTHODOX

The main turning points of central banking history in the late twentieth and early twenty-first centuries are well-known and relatively uncontroversial. In the decade that followed the oil shocks of the 1970s, central bankers in the United States and in Europe increasingly turned to what was then an unorthodox approach. In the turmoil of persistent inflation, "monetarist" policies had gained traction, especially after University of Chicago economist Milton Friedman received the Nobel Prize in 1976. In the 1980s, however, central bankers became increasingly wary of the damaging effects of monetarist policies on growth and employment. They therefore moved away from strict monetarism, while continuing to advocate fiscal discipline and market liberalization to keep inflation at bay. The 2008 global financial crisis ushered in another period of turmoil. Once again, central bankers adopted unorthodox policies, such as quantitative easing, this time to restore financial stability and to spur growth. Central bankers progressively incorporated these new tools into their policy toolbox, before quickly rolling them out in the face of a global pandemic.

Twice over four decades, therefore, new and previously unorthodox monetary policies became orthodox. Not coincidentally, a technocratic form of neoliberal regime initially became prevalent, and later declined. As this book will show, the waxing and waning of technocratic neoliberalism were the outcomes of multidimensional contests across different organizational, professional, and public arenas. To explain these outcomes, I will zoom in on the world's two leading independent central banks in times of drastic monetary policy regime changes, first in the 1980s and then in the 2010s. I mobilize a large body of primary sources – above all, the troves of monetary policy committee records released by central banks. These publicly available, easily accessible archives of internal deliberations and communications form relatively homogenous datasets of texts. I leverage a machine-assisted detection of contentious speech patterns in these texts, at the service of a qualitative analysis of central bankers' disagreements and conflicts about money.[3] In addition to central bank transcripts and minutes, I also rely on policymakers' memoirs, interviews, hearings, and other primary and secondary sources.

Based on a historical comparison of the Federal Reserve and the ECB, I demonstrate how central banks first overtly supported and later increasingly resisted neoliberal policies. Far from being bound by a stable orthodox doctrine, central banking was remarkably syncretic and evolved considerably over time. In the 2010s, conservatives were reacting to a departure from the orthodox kind of central banking to which they had become accustomed since the late twentieth century. And if we go back to the 1980s, we can see that criticisms coming from the Left were a reaction to central bankers' break with the status quo ante, in which central bankers often deferred to politicians' concerns about employment. In each case, how central bankers started to view previously unorthodox policies as orthodox is not a simple story. As technocratic organizations, central banks strive to apply state-of-the-art economic knowledge and, at the same time, they operate in a political environment. Economic ideas and the broader political context do not evolve in lockstep, however. The actions of central bankers change in ways that are not well captured by linear narratives of shifts in macroeconomic paradigms or in the political-economic status quo.

1.2 THE POLITICS OF MONEY

It is possible to historically document the politics of money, both within and outside central banks. How money is governed constitutes the focus of contests not only in the conventional sphere of "politics" – that is, among elected officials or in the public – but also within central banks and within the economics profession. Within the monetary policy committees of central banks, policymakers of different backgrounds and opinions coexist. Often labeled as "hawks" or "doves," these central bankers deliberate and debate, form coalitions and voting blocs, and compete for policy leadership. Within the economics profession, different subfields and schools of thought are also in competition. Some are more successful than others in securing positions in academe and in satellite organizations, including central banks themselves. The economics profession is thus sociologically characterized by a "hierarchical" social structure, "expert interventions," and distinctive "ways of

---

[3] For a presentation of the natural language processing (NLP) element of this book's research design, see Appendix A.

thinking."[4] Last but not least, central bankers act within a public arena traversed by political cleavages that are the bread and butter of political science. Through the dynamics of appointments, parliamentary testimonies, and other public venues, central bankers are immersed in everyday contests within and between governments, parties, and interest groups. Although central bankers must preserve an aura of neutrality to protect their independence, they also cannot completely ignore these public contests.

Organizational, professional, and public contests over monetary governance are worth studying together because they are tectonic forces that drive change in monetary regimes but also, more broadly, in political-economic regimes. Not all monetary regime changes lead to broader political-economic regime changes; but some do, and they are the focus of this book. Actors who navigate several interacting arenas can engage in "creative action" and produce "emergent" institutional constellations.[5] While the emergence of such multidimensional institutional regimes is impossible to predict, it can be explained after the fact through a close historical analysis of these interactions.

As I will show, central bankers exert considerable agency in regime change by carefully positioning themselves in contests over monetary governance across different arenas. Within the organizational arena of central banks, contestation is real but structurally limited, which enables central bankers to present a relatively united front. The internal hierarchy of central banks, along with their ethos of collegiality and deliberation, tends to mute internal dissent. Within the professional arena of economists, central bankers typically side with the most high-status ("mainstream," or "orthodox") economists. Thus, central bankers marginalize their critics among economists and contribute to reinforce and, in fact, to define the mainstream. Finally, within the broader public arena, central bankers typically aim for middle-of-the-road positions with respect to the main cleavages – between Republicans and Democrats in the United States, or between member governments in the European Union. Although such centrist positioning does not deter all political detractors, it often succeeds in making their criticisms appear as immoderate, and thus in discounting them as "partisan," "extreme," or "populist."

1.3 THE WAXING AND WANING OF TECHNOCRATIC NEOLIBERALISM

An examination of central bankers' actions across these three different arenas casts light on long-standing objects of scholarly debate, namely, "neoliberalism" and "regimes." After the global financial crisis of 2008, there has been

---

[4] Fourcade 2009; Eyal and Buchholz 2010; Popp Berman 2022.
[5] Berk and Galvan 2009; Herrigel 2010; Sabel and Zeitlin 2010; Padgett and Powell 2012; Berk, Galvan, and Hattam 2013; Fligstein and McAdam 2015; Jabko and Sheingate 2018; Ansell and Boin 2019; Gross, Reed, and Winship 2022.

renewed interest in neoliberalism as a broad form of political order.[6] Historians and political theorists have often conceptualized neoliberalism as an essentially technocratic project originally carried by elite circles around the Mont Pelerin Society and its key figures, including Friedrich Hayek and Milton Friedman. In this reading, advocates of neoliberalism wanted to safeguard capitalism at the international level, and they allied with conservative as well as center-left politicians.[7] Instead of studying neoliberalism as a normative project, other social scientists have often focused on economic governance regimes supported by policy communities and political coalitions. The concept of regime has a distinguished pedigree in political economy.[8] It has often been applied to money, but also to taxes, production, welfare, inequality, or, most recently, growth.[9]

Rather than choosing one approach or the other, the concept of technocratic neoliberalism is intended as a bridge between them. Technocratic neoliberalism, as I define it, is a broad regime of political economy centered around a new monetary governance regime of low inflation administered by independent central banks. Although that political-economic regime emerged in the late twentieth century context at a time when the neoliberal project was ideologically prominent, its changing fortunes cannot be simply explained by normative shifts or electoral realignments. Technocratic neoliberalism is a complex assemblage with deep and tangled roots, whose consolidation required durable political support from cross-cutting alliances. To explain the waxing and later the waning of technocratic neoliberalism, this book starts from an archive-based analysis of contests among central bankers. As we will see, contests within the organizational arena of central banks are related, but cannot be reduced, to contests in the professional arena of economics or in the broader public arena.

Both in the United States and in Europe, technocratic neoliberalism crystallized in the 1980s around a new politics of money, characterized by new alliances that cut across different arenas. Within the professional arena of economics as well as in the public arena, a new policy agenda became ubiquitous. While the Chicago School reached the peak of its influence among economists, Margaret Thatcher and Ronald Reagan led a transatlantic neoliberal crusade against inflation, high taxes, welfare spending, and government restrictions on markets. For both US and European central bankers, therefore, being mainstream and middle-of-the-road now meant something different than before.

---

[6] The scholarship on neoliberalism is huge, but Michel Foucault's lectures on this topic have become a common point of reference since their English-language publication in 2008 (Foucault 2008).

[7] Burgin 2012; Mirowski and Plehwe 2015; Brown 2015; Cooper 2017; Phillips-Fein 2017; Slobodian 2018; Mudge 2018; Plehwe, Slobodian, and Mirowski 2020; Gerstle 2022.

[8] The scholarship on regimes (or systems, or models) of economic governance is equally huge, going back in a sense to the origins of political economy in the eighteenth and nineteenth centuries.

[9] For a seminal article on "growth regimes," see Baccaro and Pontusson 2016. For a recent critical survey, see Hall 2024.

After they defeated inflation, central bankers increasingly attracted support not only on the right but also on the center left. Central bankers were now able not only to assert their independence as monetary policymakers, but also to set the tone for fiscal policy as well as many other government policies. In Europe as well as the United States, neoliberal policies became more entrenched. When European governments planned the euro, they tasked the ECB to fight inflation, but they also made a collective commitment to fiscal discipline.

By the 2010s, however, technocratic neoliberalism waned due to another complete turnaround in the politics of money. After the 2008 financial crisis, central bankers shifted to unorthodox policies that gained the support of most economists concerned about the "Keynesian" problem of unemployment and anemic growth. Yet they were also immersed in a public arena traversed by contradictory trends. While the global financial crisis dented the neoliberal faith in deregulated finance, the neoliberal political-economic regime that policymakers had assembled over decades was still standing. A new kind of populist attacks erupted, however, coming from conservatives committed to neoliberal ideology. In the United States, the Tea Party and their Republican allies blamed the Fed and the Obama administration for illegitimately interfering with markets. In Northern Europe, right-wing parties blamed the ECB, the European Union, and their own governments for bailing out banks and undeserving southerners.

In sum, the close identification of neoliberalism with technocracy was upended. An important rift opened in the 2010s between conservatives who favored austerity and central bankers who increasingly retreated from all-out neoliberal policies. Yet the evolution of cross-cutting alliances between central bankers, economists, and politicians has attracted little scholarly attention – perhaps because central banks, the economics profession, and partisan politics are the subjects of largely separate bodies of scholarship. While the advent of a new monetary regime did not go unnoticed, scholars of political economy have typically stressed the continuing "financialization" of the economy or the "strange non-death of neoliberalism" after the global financial crisis.[10] To be sure, the prevailing neoliberal regime of political economy did not suddenly collapse. But the regime that emerged in the 2010s sharply differed from late-twentieth century technocratic neoliberalism. Central bankers who conducted easy-money policies met virtually unprecedented conservative criticisms in the name of market discipline. At that point, the heyday of technocratic neoliberalism was over.

1.4 REGIMES AS OUTCOMES OF ORGANIZATIONAL, PROFESSIONAL, AND PUBLIC CONTESTS

The waxing and waning of technocratic neoliberalism reveal the importance of different but interrelated processes at play in the political economy of advanced

[10] Krippner 2011; Crouch 2011.

capitalist democracies. Regimes of political economy generally encompass heterogenous elements – including epistemic elements – that constantly evolve and interact. Instead of assuming that these elements either cohere as a system or evolve independently from each other, we should follow the advice of science studies scholars and strive more agnostically to "reassemble" them.[11] In the case of technocratic neoliberalism, changes in the professional arena of economics and in the organizational arena of central banks interacted with broader changes in the public arena. Although contests among central bankers and economists obviously did not take place in a political vacuum, they cannot be simply reduced to politics-as-usual.

In the late twentieth century, central bankers became the technocratic ush-erers of neoliberalism, when they asserted their independence from elected officials in the fight against inflation. Contests within central banks as well as within the economics profession interacted with political contests to produce this powerful emergence of central bankers in the public arena. After the global financial crisis of 2008, however, these different organizational, professional, and public arenas continued to evolve each according to its own logic. Central bankers continued to assert their independence, but this time to conduct easy-money policies to offset fiscal austerity. As a result of these different yet interacting processes, the long-standing association between central bankers and neoliberalism loosened considerably.

Thus, a new and understudied populist recombination of the neoliberal project became more visible. Scholars of neoliberalism who see it as inherently technocratic tend to ascribe the rise of all populist movements to a societal reaction against a neoliberal elite. Yet they often gloss over the increasingly important populist strand of neoliberalism, or they downplay the fact that technocrats considerably pulled back from neoliberal policy prescriptions over time. By contrast, conservative politicians doubled down on their support of neoliberalism by taking up the defense of fiscal austerity and sound money, and they increasingly accused central bankers of betraying the people. Thus, the apparent resilience of neoliberalism concealed its progressive transformation from a technocratic into a populist project.

By conceptualizing technocratic neoliberalism as a regime of political economy that waxed and waned, this book therefore contributes to our understanding of neoliberalism and of its association with different governance regimes. Regimes of political economy such as neoliberalism often wax and wane one element at a time – which can evidently produce an impression of fuzziness. Neoliberalism is, in this sense, similar to democracy or authoritarianism.[12] Like these political-constitutional regimes, political-economic regimes rarely emerge

---

[11] Latour 2007.
[12] Scholars have shown, for example, that democracy is often built (or dismantled) "one institution at a time," and that "hybrid" regimes can emerge. See Capoccia and Ziblatt 2010: 945; Levitsky and Way 2010.

or collapse all at once. More often, they wax and wane, or sometimes mutate over time – and their evolution is equally worth studying. As we will see, changes in alliances that cut across different arenas are central to the evolution of political-economic regimes. In the 2010s, central bankers renounced their late-twentieth century role at the core of a broad crusade against inflation, thus signaling their retreat from technocratic neoliberalism. Although neoliberalism persisted when its organizational and professional dimensions receded, that regime ceased to be evidently technocratic.

1.5 BOOK OUTLINE

The next two chapters develop the book's methodology and theoretical argument.[13] Chapter 2 shows the existence of a discrepancy between scholarly portrayals of central bankers as independent economists or as stewards of a financialized economy, and then it presents a methodology for resolving that discrepancy. Chapter 3 reflects on how central bankers seek allies in the face of economic and political turmoil and, more broadly, on the central role of money and its changing politics in the successive waxing and waning of technocratic neoliberalism. It highlights a changing politics of money not only in the public arena outside central banks – as many studies of the political economy of central banking have done – but also within central banks themselves, and within their main reference group, namely the economics profession.

The first empirical part of the book documents the waxing of technocratic neoliberalism in the late 1970s and 1980s. Chapter 4 analyzes the politics of the Volcker Shock and its aftermath. A Carter appointee, Paul Volcker sought support from Milton Friedman, an influential economist in Republican circles, and discovered ways to lead a divided Federal Open Market Committee (FOMC) while building bipartisan support. As a result, the Fed under Volcker became considerably more powerful, and better able to throw its weight behind fiscal as well as monetary conservatism. Chapter 5 highlights the paradoxical influence of the German Bundesbank's anti-inflationary policies on other European states. In the context of recurring exchange rate crises, European leaders mandated a committee of central bankers, chaired by European Commission president Jacques Delors, to plan for an economic and monetary union. Despite important cleavages and heated debates, Europe's central bankers produced the basic design for an inflation-focused ECB, which later became the staunchest advocate for neoliberal policies in the European Union.

The book's second part then turns to the waning of technocratic neoliberalism in the 2010s. Chapter 6 shows how the Fed under Ben Bernanke and then Janet Yellen shifted to unorthodox crisis-time policies that were progressively

---

[13] Chapters 2 and 3 can be skipped by readers who do not care to delve deeply into the book's methodology and contribution to existing scholarship on central banks, economic ideas and policies, and political economy.

incorporated into the Fed's policy toolbox. This incorporation not only placed FOMC hawks in the position of permanent dissenters, but it also counteracted fiscal austerity in a way that antagonized conservative economists and politicians. Chapter 7 shows how the ECB under Jean-Claude Trichet and especially under Mario Draghi initially sided with and then increasingly alienated monetary and fiscal hawks. The ECB shifted to unconventional policies of monetary expansion that progressively marginalized hawkish – often German – central bankers, and it came to support fiscal accommodation despite the opposition of German political leaders.

The book's third and last part considers how far the argument can be generalized, and what it says about the status of economic expertise in democracies today. Chapter 8 takes stock of the distance traveled since the 1980s by examining the Fed's and the ECB's responses to the pandemic in the early 2020s, and it reflects upon the parallel trajectories of technocratic neoliberalism at the IMF, the Bank of Japan, and the Bank of England. Chapter 9 concludes by addressing some questions of truth and power raised by the special status of economics and economists in contemporary economic governance, as well as the implications of technocratic power in a democracy.

2

Political Economy versus Economics

Scholars of political economy and of economics typically view contemporary economic governance from rather different perspectives. Two of the most cited books of political economy in the 2010s attributed conservative economic policies in and beyond the United States to a "winner-take-all-politics" that led up to a "neoliberal shift" in the 1970s and 1980s.[1] Whether they call it "neoliberalism," "financialized capitalism," or a "second gilded age," most scholars of political economy in political science and other disciplines concur that the late twentieth century marked a shift toward a new political and economic order. After the global financial crisis of 2008, many then puzzled over the "strange non-death of neoliberalism," despite its responsibility in fueling the crisis, unemployment, and inequalities[2] – except during a brief "rediscovery of Keynes" in 2009.[3]

Since the late twentieth century, however, prominent members of the economics profession, including those in senior policymaking positions, have increasingly identified themselves as "neo-Keynesian." Ben Bernanke, a Princeton economist who served as chair of President George W. Bush's Council of Economic Advisers and then as chair of the Federal Reserve from 2006 to 2014, explains in his memoirs how he came to adopt a "modernized Keynesianism" that "undergirds the thinking of most mainstream economists today."[4] N. Gregory Mankiw, a Harvard economist and author of a best-selling textbook who also chaired Bush's Council of Economic Advisers before Bernanke, also describes himself as a neo-Keynesian proponent of "counter-cyclical stabilization policies that [Milton] Friedman thought were fruitless."[5] These are not isolated views. While mainstream economists often endorsed

---

[1] Hacker and Pierson 2010; Blyth 2013: 45. [2] Crouch 2011. See also Helleiner 2014.
[3] Blyth 2013: 83. [4] Bernanke 2015: 29–30. [5] Mankiw and Reis 2018: 91.

many of the policies that led to the global financial crisis, a majority of them deplored and disowned the pro-cyclical austerity policies of the 2010s.

In this chapter, I make the case that different disciplinary perspectives tend to produce different readings of economic evolution from the late 1970s through the 2010s, and I elaborate a comparative case study research design to evaluate these readings. From a political economy perspective, the Keynesian policies of the early post-World War II era gave way to neoliberal policies and a financialized economy after 1980. Political economy scholars therefore debate why the global financial crisis failed to discredit neoliberalism and to provoke a durable shift to Keynesian policies. From an economics perspective, by contrast, Keynesian ideas became ever-more dominant among mainstream economists after the 1980s. Most economics scholars rarely address neoliberalism, which they see as a political or ideological rather than an economic label. While they usually recognize the influence of Milton Friedman's "monetarist" ideas in politics, they often note that monetarism lost ground among economists after the 1980s. In the rest of this chapter, I first outline these different interpretations and their implied portrayals of central bankers. Then, I select four critical cases where these baseline portrayals can be tested against the available record of central bank archives. Finally, I delineate a method for analyzing the Fed's and the ECB's internal deliberations in the 1980s and the 2010s.

2.1 TWO CONVENTIONAL PERSPECTIVES ON ECONOMIC EVOLUTION

Scholars tend to cluster around two contrasting visions of the contemporary evolution of advanced Western economies since the end of the Second World War. On the one hand, many scholars of political economy outside the economics discipline (especially in political science, sociology, or history) often characterize that evolution in similar broad terms – moving from an era of "embedded liberalism," "Keynesianism," and "Fordism," to an era of "neoliberalism" or "financialization." On the other hand, scholars of economics often characterize that evolution from the more focused perspective of the economics discipline's macroeconomic mainstream – moving from a period of increasingly unstable growth through a period of "Great Inflation," followed by a period of "Great Moderation" that ended in 2007–2008, and then a slow recovery from the "Great Recession" that followed the global financial crisis.

As schematized in Figure 2.1, scholars of political economy often view economic evolution since the Second World War as a succession of two broad political-economic regimes.[6] The first regime, under the auspices of "embedded

---

[6] Although this periodization is most conventional, it is often questioned, from various perspectives, by scholars of political economy. For example, intellectual historians generally trace neoliberalism back not to its heyday in the late 1970s and 1980s, but to its roots in the 1940s (Burgin 2012; Mirowski and Plehwe 2015; Slobodian 2018).

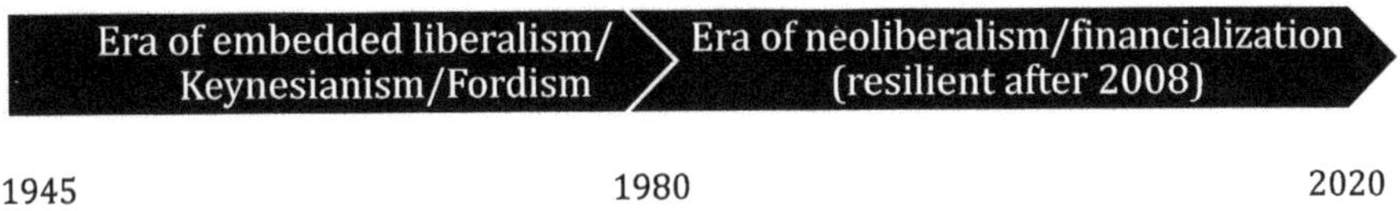

2.1 Two Conventional Perspectives on Economic Evolution

| Era of embedded liberalism/ Keynesianism/Fordism | Era of neoliberalism/financialization (resilient after 2008) |

1945   1980   2020

FIGURE 2.1 Schematized political economy perspective on economic evolution (since 1945).

liberalism," is typically defined as a compromise between free-market liberalism and Karl Polanyi's view that the economy is always and must remain "embedded" in society.[7] This was also a Golden Age for "Fordist" economic development – industrial wages supported mass consumption; labor gained strength in a context of full employment; and modern welfare policies were built. Because of the long-lasting influence of British economist John Maynard Keynes over this period of "embedded liberalism," scholars have often also called it the "Keynesian era."[8] Then, in the 1970s, increasing inflation spelled trouble for "Keynesian" policies, and the electoral victories of Margaret Thatcher and Ronald Reagan marked the beginning of a new "neoliberal" era.[9] Scholars today often characterize "neoliberalism" in terms of its adoption of the market as a norm of political as well as economic order, and its rejection of discretionary government intervention in the economy.[10] Independent central banks were now empowered to fight inflation and restore monetary stability, even at the cost of greater unemployment. Enabled by a "reemergence of global finance" after the 1960s, the new era was also characterized by "financialization" – a process by which finance increasingly imposed its logic on the entire economy.[11] To varying degrees, advanced economies experienced the offshoring of manufacturing industries and the rise of service sectors; the fragmentation of the working class and the decline of labor unions; a decline of the public sector and its penetration by financial logic. For many scholars, this era of neoliberalism and financialization also continued into the 2010s. Far from triggering a radical reorientation of economic policies, the global financial crisis of 2008 initially led to a revitalization of neoliberalism and financialization. The "strange non-death of neoliberalism" was perhaps most evident in the form of fiscal "austerity" policies in the 2010s, paving the way for a reassertion of "monetary austerity" in the face of post-pandemic inflation.[12]

Many scholars of economics often refer to a somewhat different chronology of economic evolution, focused on changing monetary regimes – with different

---

[7] The term "embedded liberalism" was coined by Ruggie (1982). See also Polanyi 2001.
[8] Hall 1989; Hall 2013.   [9] Blyth 2002; Harvey 2007; Hall 2013.   [10] Foucault 2008.
[11] Helleiner 1996; Krippner 2005, 2011; Van der Zwan 2014. The focus on financialization, rather than neoliberalism, generally highlights structural rather than ideological evolution. Although scholars tend to privilege one or the other phenomenon, they often adopt a similar periodization with a turning point around 1980.
[12] Blyth 2013; Cooper 2024; Blyth and Fraccaroli 2025.

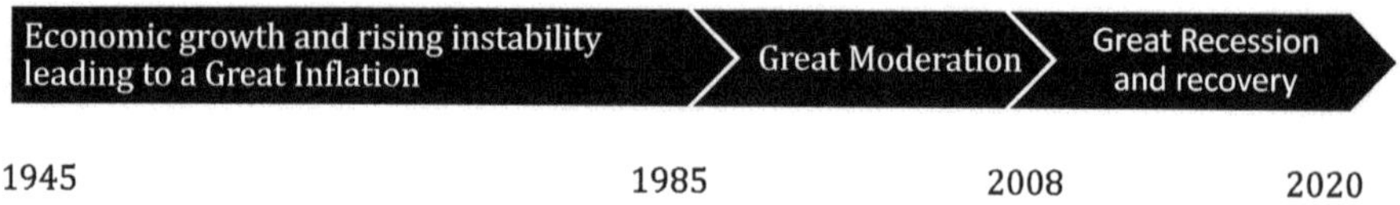

| Economic growth and rising instability leading to a Great Inflation | Great Moderation | Great Recession and recovery |

1945   1985   2008   2020

FIGURE 2.2 Schematized (macro)economic perspective on economic evolution (since 1945).

periods and labels, schematized in Figure 2.2. Standard textbooks, surveys of the macroeconomics field, and the Fed's website disseminate a widespread narrative, with three defining periods rather than two.[13] First, the United States and Europe returned after 1945 to peacetime economic growth, under the auspices of modern macroeconomics. That field was soon dominated by a theoretical "synthesis" – led in the United States by Paul Samuelson – that combined the neoclassical norm of market equilibrium with a managerial approach to the business cycle as advocated by Keynes. Yet economists also see that period as one of rising economic instability, leading up to the "Great Inflation" of the 1970s. More than a decade before the move away from Keynesianism in the conventional political economy narrative, Milton Friedman's 1967 influential presidential address to the American Economic Association stressed the importance of market expectations and criticized "simple-minded Keynesianism" for dismissing the role of monetary policy.[14] The second period starts around 1985, after the Volcker Fed's successful fight against inflation. Economists often refer to it as the "Great Moderation," since it combined relative economic stability and low inflation. That period is also marked by the reconstruction of a "neo-Keynesian" perspective – alias "new consensus," or "new neoclassical synthesis."[15] After the mixed results of the Volcker Fed's experiment with monetarism in the early 1980s, Keynesian ideas regained ground within the economics profession, without, however, supplanting the neoclassical emphasis on market actors' expectations and "microfoundations." Finally, a third period starts with the global financial crisis of 2008. It is marked by a "Great Recession" and an almost decade-long economic recovery. During that period, the Bernanke Fed is usually credited for completing the rehabilitation of the Keynesian idea that market instabilities must be addressed via active and evidence-supported macroeconomic policies[16] – a legacy continued by Fed chairs Janet Yellen and Jerome Powell.

---

[13] Samuelson 1955: 212; Blanchard 2009; Mankiw 2020. To be sure, "heterodox" and "post-Keynesian" economists often dispute this conventional narrative, and especially the Keynesian credentials of mainstream "neo-Keynesian" macroeconomists.
[14] Friedman 1968: 5; Mankiw and Reis 2018: 82, 87.
[15] Goodfriend and King 1997; Goodfriend 2007; Blanchard 2009.
[16] Bernanke 2015: 29; Mankiw and Reis 2018: 91. Even though Bernanke was first appointed by George W. Bush, a Republican president with a neoliberal agenda, his adoption of Keynesian tenets clearly comes across in his memoirs (Bernanke 2015, esp. ch. 2) and, as we will see, in the

2.1.1 Two Portrayals of Central Bankers

At first glance, the discrepancies between the conventional economics and political economy perspectives seem to reflect incommensurable differences in disciplinary focus. Economists pay attention mostly to the evolution of markets and macroeconomic conditions, whereas scholars of political economy are considerably more focused on politics. There are important areas of overlap between economics and politics, however. Central banks are a case in point. In the late twentieth century, central bankers developed strong ties to the economics profession and increasingly asserted their independence from elected officials. At the same time, central banks remained policymaking organizations, ever more essential to the machinery of modern government. At the turn of the twenty-first century, the US Federal Reserve and the young ECB increasingly set the tone for how modern capitalist economies should be governed. This historical development raises the question of what drives central bankers' actions, and from which scholarly perspective these actions are more usefully understood.

As it happens, the different scholarly perspectives of economics and political economy produce sharply contrasting portrayals of central bankers. Economists generally view central bankers in terms of their roles as economic experts.[17] They debate monetary policy primarily in economic terms, by discussing the relative merits of different assumptions and policies in response to new economic developments and problems. Central bankers make mistakes, of course, but they can learn from their mistakes – with the help of the economics profession. In fact, monetary regime change often takes place when central bankers learn from their failures. In the 1970s, central bankers were faced with a situation of rising inflation and economic stagnation. As Friedman's 1967 warnings sounded increasingly prophetic, monetarism and Chicago-style "freshwater" thinking spread within the economics profession at that time.[18] If we listen to prominent economists today, however, American central bankers since the end of World War II have more consistently followed Keynes' ideas than Friedman's.[19] As it turned out, the Fed's monetarist experiment of the early 1980s produced higher-than-expected unemployment and was short-lived. In the face of lower inflation after that, central bankers generally adopted lower policy rates – a form of Keynesianism "in deed though not in word."[20] After the global financial crisis of 2008, central bankers soon realized that they faced a risk of deflation, rather than

---

positions he took as Fed chair. Another important trend often cited by economists is the empirical effort to better identify different policies' macroeconomic effects. See Nakamura and Steinsson 2018.

[17] Bernanke 2015, 2022; Krugman 2021; Blinder 2022.
[18] Hall 1976. Mankiw and Reis (2018: 88) call the 1970s stagflation "one of the greatest successes of out-of-sample forecasting by a macroeconomist."
[19] Krugman 2021; Blinder 2022; Bernanke 2022.   [20] Blinder 2022: 244.

inflation. To get the economy out of its slump, they increasingly turned to Keynesian recipes of monetary accommodation.

In the eyes of many economists, central bankers often play the part of Cassandras vis-à-vis governments. To the extent that central bankers rely on and sometimes are themselves professional economists, they can figure out what must be done to ensure economic stability and prosperity. But they are often held back or overruled by political calculations or by ideologies that stem from misguided or outdated economic ideas. As Keynes famously said, policymakers are often the "slaves of some defunct economist" – or, as Paul Krugman puts it, "zombies."[21] Thus, in the 1970s, President Nixon and many European governments resisted central bankers' inclination to tighten money in the face of inflationary pressures. Governments then appeared to go by what Milton Friedman called "simple-minded Keynesianism," by accepting inflation as a price to pay for lower unemployment. By the 1980s, many economists concluded that central bankers needed to be more "conservative" – meaning, more inflation-averse – than governments.[22] Central bankers should accommodate growth if and only if inflation was under control. American central bankers thus experienced Greenspan's two-decade leadership as a goldilocks period of low inflation and moderate interest rates, dubbed the "Great Moderation."[23] After the 2008 financial crisis, however, ideological factors and political pressures prompted a "hard right turn" toward austerity, which inhibited central bankers from immediately providing sufficient stimulus.[24] Again resisting the advice of most mainstream economists – this time, by being too conservative, rather than too accommodating – politicians took the economy to the brink of deflation and made the recovery excruciatingly slow.

By contrast, scholars of political economy typically adopt a broader and often more critical perspective on central bankers. They generally recognize the importance of deeply entrenched policy "regimes" that are "sustained over time by supportive coalitions that have transcended and outlasted any specific electoral majority."[25] After 2008, many chipped away at the "myths" of central banks' independence and neutrality, the "catechism" that depicts the US Federal Reserve as a "benevolent social planner," or the "technocratic view" of central banks concealing their true nature as "political institutions."[26] Instead of envisioning central banks as bastions of economic experts besieged and thwarted by politicians, scholars of political economy thus tend to depict them as pillars of a broad and slowly changing political-economic status quo. In this sense, central bankers are often wedded to conservative policies – not because of the inherent nature of central banks' tasks, but because they cater to the interests of the wealthy and the powerful. In addition, their insulation from

---

[21] Krugman 2020. See also Quiggin 2012.   [22] Rogoff 1985.
[23] Stock and Watson 2002; Bernanke 2004.   [24] Eichengreen 2015: 7, 9.
[25] Hacker and Pierson 2014: 652.
[26] Adolph 2013; Binder and Spindel 2017; Jacobs and King 2021; Moschella 2024.

electoral politics enables central bankers to pursue unpopular economic policies. This is the case *a fortiori* when they operate at the international level, as the ECB does. Central bankers may see the shortcomings of conservative policies, but they generally aim to preserve "authority"[27] – at least until powerful new political coalitions form on behalf of new ideas and interests.

Accordingly, scholars of political economy often attribute an important part to central bankers in the defense of "financialization" or "neoliberal" policies. They portray central bankers as flag bearers of the "Washington consensus" or the "Brussels-Frankfurt consensus."[28] In narratives that stress financialization, central banks became, in the late twentieth century, the main stewards of an increasingly finance-oriented regime of political economy. That new regime served central bankers' bureaucratic interests, insofar as they were able to assert their technocratic priorities – not only central bank independence, but also price stability and balanced budgets.[29] It also served the interests of market actors, who experienced a boost in the value of their financial assets.[30] Scholars have highlighted various explanations for this pro-finance bias, including the increasing proportion of central bankers with a professional background in finance, the centrality of financial actors in economic and political structures, or the role of financial corporations in central banks' open market operations.[31] In narratives that stress neoliberalism, technocrats have acquired considerable power to resist democratic impulses. The insulation of central banks, as well as international economic organizations such as the IMF or the WTO, explains why Hayek and his Mont Pelerin Society consistently pinned their hopes on technocrats and on "globalism."[32] Noting that central bankers continued to defend the status quo after 2008, scholars of political economy often gloss over or dismiss the "neo-Keynesian" turn within the field of macroeconomics and among central bankers.[33] Adam Tooze, for example, has made the case that new Keynesian economists' inclination for technocratic fixes embodies what he calls "actually existing neoliberalism."[34] Many also note that new Keynesian economists, unlike post-Keynesians and other heterodox economists, discount politics and reason in terms of the microeconomic "foundations" of macroeconomic policies.[35] From this perspective, a neoliberal logic may still dominate central banking, even under a new Keynesian label.

---

[27] Farrell and Quiggin 2017; Matthijs and Blyth 2017.
[28] McNamara 1998; Schäfer and Streeck 2013; Jones 2013; Blyth 2013; Schmidt and Thatcher 2013; Matthijs and Blyth 2017; Streeck 2017; Hopkin 2020.
[29] McNamara 2002; Best 2025.
[30] Krippner 2011; Blyth 2013; Dietsch, Claveau, and Fontan 2018; Braun and Gabor 2020; Jacobs and King 2021.
[31] Adolph 2013; Culpepper and Reinke 2014; Woll 2014; Braun 2020; Massoc 2022; Wansleben 2023.
[32] Mirowski and Plehwe 2015; Slobodian 2018.
[33] There are exceptions, however. See, for example, Mann 2017, ch. 13; Shenk 2023.
[34] Tooze 2021. [35] Baccaro, Blyth, and Pontusson 2022.

2.1.2 Four Cases of Central Bankers in Turmoil

Which of these two stylized scholarly portrayals of central bankers better describes how they act? If we compare them side by side, we see an especially visible discrepancy in the 1980s as well as in the 2010s. These were moments when policymakers on both sides of the ocean addressed similar economic challenges – economic stagnation and persistently high inflation in the 1980s; a persistent economic slump in the 2010s, but without inflation. As became clear in hindsight, both situations led central bankers to carry out monetary regime change. In the 1980s, central banks shifted toward tight-money regimes to lower inflation, whereas in the 2010s, they veered toward easy-money regimes to reflate the economy. From a methodological perspective, these two moments lend themselves especially well to the comparative case study method. First, they are amenable to a comparison of how policymakers made decisions in the 1980s and the 2010s – in other words, within and across two historical cases of monetary regime change. Second, they also lend themselves to a comparison of how the Fed and the ECB, the independent central banks of the world's two largest advanced economies, responded to parallel economic circumstances. Such a "similar-case comparison" is useful because it facilitates the identification of causal mechanisms. In sum, it is possible to build a rigorous comparative historical research design to investigate the mainsprings of central bankers' actions in four cases of major monetary regime shifts.

The typical economics and political economy portrayals of central bankers generate competing benchmarks of hypotheses about the actions of American and European central bankers – first in the 1980s, and second in the 2010s. If we consider things from an economics perspective, the main problem for central bankers in the 1980s was the "Great Inflation" that had started in the 1970s. Central bankers therefore implemented monetarism, the rising monetary theory of the day, to tighten monetary policy. The Volcker Fed adopted monetary targets in the fall of 1979 and pushed through disinflation, ushering in a durable low-inflation monetary regime. Likewise, in Europe, the success of Germany's Bundesbank in fighting inflation led central bankers to design an independent ECB focused on fighting inflation.

By contrast, the political economy perspective grants greater weight to specifically political factors in causing changes in monetary regimes and in broader political-economic regimes. In the United States, financialization and the political tide of neoliberal ideas enabled Paul Volcker to gain support for the Fed's monetarist experiment and for the assertion of the Fed's power. Meanwhile, the influence of neoliberal ideas and the leverage of Germany in European negotiations enabled the creation of the euro and of an EU monetary and political-economic regime centered around an independent ECB devoted to low inflation and other neoliberal policies.

If we fast-forward to the 2010s and we apply the same two perspectives, we also find two competing sets of hypotheses. From an economics perspective, central bankers at the Fed and the ECB faced in the 2010s a very different situation than in the 1980s – not inflation, but a chronic weakness of demand. They used state-of-the-art (new) Keynesian economics to diagnose and confront the problem with increasing accuracy. They were often held back, however, by forces mostly external to economics. Ideologically motivated advocates of tight fiscal and monetary policies held disproportionate influence and enabled austerity. This led to policy failure in both the United States and Europe in the early 2010s – before central bankers were able to provide much-needed monetary accommodation.

From a political economy perspective, however, austerity was influenced by central bankers concerned about their authority, and the modalities of central banks' shift to easy money manifested the continuing grip of neoliberal ideas and financialization. Central bankers balked at fiscal expansion, especially in the European Union, where "ordoliberals" were dominant. Although their "unconventional policies" evidently broke with the strictly anti-inflationary doctrines of the 1980s, quantitative easing purposefully relied on the same "repo" markets and risk management tools that had enriched financial actors before the 2008 crisis.

2.2 A TERRAIN FOR EMPIRICAL INVESTIGATION

It is possible to empirically investigate central bankers' actions and thus to critically assess their conventional scholarly portrayals. Fortunately, there is now a huge trove of data about central bankers' policy decisions in various historical contexts. In the United States, the Fed has undergone a "quiet revolution" of greater transparency in central banking.[36] After considerable prodding by the US Congress in the early 1990s, the Fed made minutes of FOMC decisions, including voting records, available after a few weeks, and it has published verbatim transcripts of FOMC deliberations after five years. In Europe, the archives of the European Committee of Governors, a body that was established in 1964 and later became the Governing Council of the ECB, are only available after thirty years. The contrast with the US rule on the publication of Fed transcripts after five years therefore remains quite stark. Nevertheless, the thirty-year delay means that transcripts are now available for the 1980s

---

[36] Blinder 2004.

and early 1990s. Even for more recent years, the ECB has not completely escaped the "quiet revolution" of transparency. In 2015, the ECB started to publish "accounts" of its Governing Council's deliberations, which eerily resemble the Fed's published minutes except that they do not contain records of committee votes at the end. These de facto minutes are useful but not nearly as revealing as transcripts, due to their brevity and their dual nature as an exercise of both transparency and public relations, which inherently tends to underplay disagreements among central bankers.

2.2.1 The Empirical Approach of this Book

In an effort to make the data about central bankers' deliberations in the United States and the European Union more homogenous and therefore more easily comparable, I submitted two "requests for documents" to the ECB, in 2016 and 2022, to obtain "monetary policy accounts" or excerpts of minutes before 2015. In my first request, I made the case that the ECB should follow the example of the Fed after a similar disclosure in 1993 and should publish its minutes retrospectively. The ECB gave me a negative response, arguing that "monetary policy accounts" were not minutes, and that such accounts did not exist before 2015. In 2022, I attempted to obtain mere excerpts of ECB Governing Council minutes for only four meetings in the early 2010s. When that request was denied, I then appealed it to the ECB Executive Board. The ECB Board again gave me a negative response, justified by the legally binding EU Treaty provision on the confidentiality of its deliberations – but without addressing my remark that the ECB had partly lifted this confidentiality, as the Treaty allows, with the publication of ECB minutes after 2015 (see Appendix B). Despite my inability to obtain ECB Governing Council minutes before January 2015, the minutes available after that date still enable readers to get a sense of ECB debates – especially if there are recurring disagreements over several meetings. In addition, scarce publicly available data on central bank deliberations can also be complemented by reporters' accounts, as well as by confidential author interviews with central bankers.

When full transcripts are available – as is the case for three of my four case studies – the archival record is as rich in data as it gets for any executive decision-making process. Reading a transcript feels almost like being present at the meeting. Everything that central bankers say gets transcribed – including jokes and laughter, hesitations and unfinished sentences, or when the FOMC sings happy birthday to Ben Bernanke. The only missing indications are body language and voice intonations that may have been important cues for in-person participants. Of course, the committee transcripts do not allow us to read into the central bankers' minds. The committee meetings are not freewheeling, informal one-to-one conversations of the type that central bankers can have in

2.2 A Terrain for Empirical Investigation

the privacy of an office. The meetings are highly formal, with structured deliberations that are largely based on central bankers' prepared and often well-rehearsed statements. At the Fed, there is also evidence that the formality of FOMC meetings has increased since the 1993 decision to publish transcripts after five years.[37] Even though the central bank committee meetings are not immediately made public, they are occasions for individual as well as collective performances. Committee members, especially the chair, often express strategic positions to move the deliberation in particular directions. Yet because of their duration and their collegial and deliberative ethos, these meetings also leave room for open-ended exchanges and a degree of improvisation. Central bankers often change their views over time, sometimes even during a single meeting. The transcripts, therefore, enable outside observers to reconstruct the terms of debates and the lines of cleavage, when applicable, to locate rather precisely different individual central bankers' positions within these debates, and the evolution of these positions; and to retrace the ways in which they articulate their positions and express agreement or disagreement with their colleagues.

From a scholarly perspective, the minutes and transcripts are a rich source of data that lend themselves to various methods of machine-assisted analysis. The transcripts of FOMC meetings, for example, are routinely more than 200 pages long, whereas the minutes are summaries of deliberation and only a few pages long. Sociologists, historians, political scientists as well as economists have increasingly used transcripts as sources of evidence, at various levels of granularity. Since my qualitative investigation spans two decades of debates in two central banks, I have developed a particular method to approach minutes and transcripts without getting drowned in them. I have read available minutes of the 1980s and of the 2010s as a way to get a sense of the debates and orient myself onto the most relevant committee transcripts – except for the European Union in the 2010s, for which transcripts remain sealed. For the 1980s, I have also used secondary literature and interviews not only as sources of evidence but also to help me sort out important meetings and their transcripts. In both the minutes and transcripts, I have paid special attention to debates between central bankers on macroeconomic "fundamentals" with the greatest impact on monetary policy decisions, such as economic growth, inflation, and unemployment, as well as fiscal policies. Whenever I surmised an interesting debate, or in some cases where other scholars have identified interesting transcripts, I have referred myself to the full transcripts as primary sources. Then I tried to assess the causal dynamics of the decision-making process against benchmarks of conventional expectations among economics and political economy scholars.

As will become clear in the empirical chapters, this book will constantly zoom in and out of crucial or particularly revealing monetary committee meetings. When I zoom in, I will primarily mobilize transcripts and minutes

---

[37] Meade and Stasavage 2008.

as primary sources, as well as interviews and secondary sources. When I zoom out, I will rely primarily on secondary sources, including scholarly literature, memoirs, journalistic accounts, and other (so-called) gray sources. Even though I was not able to study ECB transcripts for the 2010s, due to the embargo on transcripts, the historical and geographical coverage of my comparison was very extensive. To mitigate possible selection biases in my analysis of Fed transcripts, I have built on the recent progress of large language models like ChatGPT and their improved detection of language patterns in such "text as data." It has become possible to use automated natural language processing to detect the most contested meetings and even contentious individual statements across hundreds of thousands of pages of central bank transcripts (see Appendix A). On that basis, I have engaged in a fine-grained analysis of transcripts or transcript sections that stood out as especially contentious and that might not have caught my attention otherwise.

2.2.2 The Added Value of a Comparison of Central Banks in Turmoil

An empirically grounded comparison of the Fed and the ECB is useful for several purposes. Most immediately, it can help to resolve the discrepancy between the disciplinary perspectives of economics and political economy scholars, and to clarify the link between monetary regimes and broader political-economic regimes. Economists tend to analyze central banks' actions through the prism of their own debates, such as "monetarism" versus "Keynesianism"; they typically attribute the political backlash against central banks' "unconventional" responses in the 2010s slump to ideologically motivated politicians. Conversely, scholars of political economy usually analyze central banks from an external political perspective, and they often highlight the central bankers' continued support to neoliberal policies or financialization. An empirical examination makes it possible to test, and possibly to question, truncated disciplinary assumptions about central bank policies in terms of relatively narrow monetary regimes or in terms of broad political-economic regimes.

More concretely, a systematic Fed-ECB comparison can show how central bankers navigate economics and politics – a question that should be of interest not only to scholars but also to a broader audience. As Alan Blinder recalls, most Americans "paid no attention whatsoever to the Federal reserve" when he joined its Board in the early 1990s and before the Fed was lionized under Greenspan: "one of the incumbent governors joked to me that most Americans thought the Federal Reserve was a national forest."[38] At that point, the ECB and the euro did not exist; most national European central banks – and, actually, most of the world's central banks – were seen as stolid government agencies. Things have obviously changed since then. Central banks today

---

[38] Blinder 2022: 206.

2.2 A Terrain for Empirical Investigation

hardly seem boring – at least, judging from the amount of media attention that they attract. Economists and central bankers themselves often note that independent central banks have acquired considerable policy clout.[39] Political economy scholars generally concur, although they are more likely to be critical of the nondemocratic aspects of neoliberalism and central banking.[40]

In this regard, an important question is whether there is a natural congruence between technocracy and neoliberalism. Although Hayek advocated the rise of international technocracy as a bulwark against domestic protectionist tendencies, other neoliberal luminaries were ambivalent about technocratic power. Milton Friedman, for example, suspected independent central bankers of prioritizing self-aggrandizement at the expense of good monetary stewardship.[41] In fact, the actions of electorally insulated technocrats deserve an empirical and a priori agnostic examination. Central bankers may well have favored the triumph of neoliberal policies and financialization in the 1980s and beyond, but a genealogical understanding of neoliberalism should also alert us to the possibility that neoliberalism can change with changes in its historical context.[42] In particular, the advent of "populism" may have inflected the trajectory of central banking. This would not be for the first time. According to Karl Polanyi, the rise of modern central banking was essentially a way to "buffer" societies against the unequal effects of falling prices under the gold standard, which often became a focus of strident class conflict in the nineteenth and early twentieth centuries.[43] In the 2010s, central bankers' former conservative allies clearly veered toward right-wing forms of populism.[44] To understand the consequences of this shift for the broader neoliberal political-economic regime, we need to suspend strong a priori assumptions and observe how central bankers coped with a new kind of populist politics.

---

[39] Crow and Meade 2007; Tucker 2018; Blinder 2022: 206.
[40] Eich 2022; Cooper 2024; Downey 2025.   [41] Friedman 1962: 62.   [42] Foucault 2008.
[43] Polanyi 2001, ch. 16.   [44] Brandes 2019; Slobodian 2025.

3

Economists with Power

To make sense of central bankers' actions, it is useful to start from the observation that they are, in a broad sense, *economists with power* – aka technocrats. On the one hand, the economics narrative of central-bankers-as-independent-economists does not sufficiently recognize the fact that *central bankers have power*. While legally independent and thus above the fray of electoral politics, central bankers are nonetheless also immersed in the public arena.[1] They routinely interact with politicians and other public officials, as well as with other economists and bankers. In the 1980s, conservatives in the United States and Europe heaped praise on central bankers' disinflationary policies. By the 2010s, many conservatives withdrew their support and moved to the forefront of central bankers' critics. This rift, in turn, carried major consequences for the public arena within which central bankers operated. On the other hand, the political economy narrative of central-bankers-as-stewards-of-financialization does not sufficiently delve into the fact that central bankers navigate politics *as economists*. Many central bankers are often professional economists, with PhD-level credentials; some have other professional backgrounds, usually in public service or private finance. In all cases, however, they lean on the expertise and legitimacy of the economics profession to assert their independence and to manage the economy.[2] In the 2010s as well as the 1980s, central bankers adopted policies that deviated from the then-prevailing status quo and yet – not coincidentally – met the approval of leading members of the economics profession.

The fact that central banks have increasingly become bastions of power for professional economists has profound implications. Because of their legally guaranteed independence, central banks are an archetype of the "highly

---

[1] Adolph 2013; Conti-Brown 2016; Binder and Spindel 2019; Moschella 2024.
[2] Holmes 2014; Fligstein, Brundage, and Schultz 2017; Abolafia 2020.

consequential" forms of organized governance that have been "effectively removed" from electoral contestation.³ While Ronald Reagan's and Margaret Thatcher's electoral victories certainly mattered, historians and historical sociologists have shown that the growing power of economic technocrats in domestic policymaking and international organizations was crucial to the transatlantic shift toward neoliberal policies in the 1980s.⁴ In particular, the Volcker Fed's crusade against inflation is often identified as a decisive event in the transition to a new "age" of American capitalism.⁵ Building on these insights, my own account notes that independent central bankers in the United States and also in the European Union have become key actors in economic governance. Yet it departs from both the political economy and the economics scholarship that considers "politics" as an arena *external* to central banks. As scholars of science studies underscore, professional and scientific discourse is characterized by contests that are never fully settled yet shape conventional terms of expertise about reality.⁶ Accordingly, I will consider how central bankers navigate a politics of money that is also *internal* to their own organizations, as well as to the economics profession to which many of them belong.

As this book will argue, central bankers cultivate *cross-cutting alliances* with economists and politicians, which in turn enable important regime shifts. Their participation in a multidimensional politics of money thus gives them considerably more agency than their narrowly assigned mandates would suggest. Over the course of four decades, central bankers first contributed to the waxing and later to the waning of *technocratic neoliberalism* – namely, a broad political-economic regime premised on a technocratic prioritization of low inflation. Central bankers argued over various policy options within their internal organizational arenas, and these contests enormously mattered for the advent of technocratic neoliberalism in the 1980s. At the same time, central bankers' network ties with economists also gave contests in the professional arena of economics an outsized importance. Last but not least, central bankers were attuned to changes in the broader public arena. In sum, shifts in monetary regimes toward tight or easy money were only the tip of the iceberg. Both the waxing of technocratic neoliberalism and its waning in the 2010s were tumultuous processes of political-economic regime change along multiple dimensions – much like historical processes of political-constitutional regime change studied by scholars of democracy and authoritarianism. It took a decade for actors inside and outside central banks to assemble crucial elements of technocratic neoliberalism, and another decade to disassemble them. Both decades signaled momentous changes in America's and Europe's broad political-economic regimes.

---

[3] Hacker, Hertel-Fernandez, Pierson, and Thelen 2021: 8.
[4] Babb and Kentikelenis 2018; Offner 2019; Popp Berman 2022.
[5] Levy 2021. See also Stein 2010; Rodgers 2011. [6] Pickering 1995; Latour 2007.

This chapter outlines how changes in monetary regimes have led to broader shifts in political-economic regimes since the late 1970s. Its objective is to theorize central banks' agency and the effects of changes in their cross-cutting alliances with economists and politicians. First, I discuss the way in which central banks produce monetary regime change. I highlight the rarely conceptualized fact that there is a politics of money *inside* central banks and *inside* the economics profession. Expanding on a large scholarship in economic sociology, I make the case that economics is inherently a contested repertoire, and that this is especially important for central banking. Like economists, central bankers often disagree over what is happening in the economy and which policies are more appropriate. To explain how monetary regime change takes root, we must therefore consider contests among central bankers and economists, and their resonance with broader contests in the public arena. Second, I turn to the effects of changing alliances that cut across these three arenas on broader political-economic regimes. When central banks implemented tight-money policies in the late 1970s, the result was the emergence of that new regime of political economy. Central bankers, the mainstream of the economics profession, and many center-left as well as conservative politicians now prioritized sound money, but also fiscal discipline and market liberalization. By contrast, the 2010s saw a partial defection of central banks from the very policies that had led to their ascendance. Central bankers' decisions to embrace easy money triggered the waning of technocratic neoliberalism as a regime of political economy.

3.1 HOW CENTRAL BANKS PRODUCE MONETARY REGIME CHANGE

Central bankers' tasks and practices are complex, technical, and somewhat obscure to most people. They speak a language best understood by economists and close observers of central banks. When he was once congratulated on the clarity of a Congressional testimony, Fed chair Alan Greenspan half-jokingly replied: "If I seem unduly clear to you, you must have misunderstood what I said."[7] Central banks can be analyzed as organizations that carry out specific tasks and that innovate over time. At the same time, they are arenas of sustained debate between central bankers, as central banks' archival records reveal. Because independent central banks' internal debates are predominantly cast in economic language, they are also directly related to debates that take place in the professional arena of economics.

3.1.1 Central Banks as Organizations

Central banks' most important tasks are to set monetary policy – that is, they regulate the supply of money in the economy – and to supervise banks and the

---

[7] See Mallaby 2016: 476.

3.1 How Central Banks Produce Monetary Regime Change

financial sector. To carry out monetary policy, they intervene through various "open market operations" – that is, purchases or sales of securities such as government bonds. Central bankers also sometimes experiment with policies that do not conform to established practice, especially in times of turmoil. When confronted with resilient inflation in the 1970s, central bankers turned to "monetary targeting" techniques that were largely untested until then. After the global financial crisis of 2008, central bankers started to experiment with tools such as "quantitative easing," "forward guidance," and "zero" (or even negative) interest rates that became quite common but that were initially unfamiliar.[8] In addition, their massive recourse to "unconventional policies" arguably blurred the boundaries between monetary policy and fiscal policy, insofar as it effectively channeled financial resources to financial actors, homeowners, or local governments.

In other words, central banks are sites of organizational innovation – a process that has been abundantly studied by scholars of organization theory and psychology.[9] Like all organizations, central banks resort to and slowly develop baseline analytical frameworks and operational tools. They typically exercise "bounded" rather than comprehensive forms of rationality.[10] They generally eschew revolutionary thinking in favor of "muddling through."[11] There are times when such incremental change in habits is insufficient, however. Central bankers then start to collectively reflect on what went wrong, and they typically argue back and forth to experiment different ways to "make sense" of a new situation.[12] In the sense of pragmatist social theory and political science, they are "skilled" or "creative" actors.[13] Technocrats are a bit like trained musicians, for whom deciphering a musical score is an effortless habit: "A glance at the musical hieroglyphs, and the pianist's fingers have rippled through a cataract of notes."[14] Although central bankers' policy baseline of models and tools restricts the space of feasible choices, it also paradoxically makes change more manageable. When their habitual policies fail to produce desirable results, central bankers experiment with actions that do not conform to their conventional models. If that experimentation is successful, it can lead to durable shifts in monetary regimes and policy frameworks – to the point that unconventional policies no longer appear so outlandish.

The respective roles of rational deliberation and other factors in causing monetary regime shifts are difficult to disentangle, however. Perhaps because

---

[8] Perry Mehrling (2011) argues that the Fed reconnected with an old "money view" of central banking when its purchases of large amounts of financial assets made it into a "dealer of last resort" on capital markets.
[9] Simon 1947; Lindblom 1959; Kahneman 2011. [10] Simon 1991. [11] Lindblom 1959.
[12] Weick 1995; Abolafia 2020.
[13] Berk and Galvan 2009; Herrigel 2010; Sabel and Zeitlin 2010; Herrigel 2010; Berk, Galvan, and Hattam 2013; Jabko and Sheingate 2018; Ansell and Boin 2019; Gross, Reed, and Winship 2022.
[14] James 1890: 114.

central banks are legally independent and apolitical, many scholars portray them as acting coherently upon systematized data, models, or ideational paradigms. Yet even Peter Hall, the author of a seminal political economy article on "policy paradigms," acknowledged that, "like subatomic particles, ideas do not leave much of a trail when they shift."[15] Controlled experimental evidence on central bankers' cognitive processes, which many social scientists consider as the highest standard of causal inference, is likely unattainable. Observers of central bankers should nonetheless listen to scholars of organization and psychology, who generally agree that actors rarely act on rationally coherent models, especially in crises. As Daniel Kahneman puts it, "fast" intuitive thinking is most important in decision-making, whereas "slow" analytical thinking is "a supporting character who believes herself to be the hero."[16] When it comes to the practice of economics, we should also heed science studies scholars' warnings against strong assumptions of paradigmatic coherence. Andrew Pickering, for example, describes scientific culture as a "mangle of practice" characterized by its "disunity, its patchiness and scrappiness."[17] When the going gets rough, there are thus many reasons to think that paradigms are not necessarily the most reliable practical guide – for trained economists as well as for most people.

3.1.2 The Internal Politics of Central Banks

Despite its complexity, the process by which central bankers make decisions about monetary regimes is not a complete black box. Archives of central bankers' meetings and decisions are an irreplaceable trove of observational data. Even though it is impossible to get into central bankers' heads, areas of agreement and disagreement over a central bank's discourse and policies are relatively easy to document, after the fact, in the archival record. That record enables social scientists to follow the advice of science studies scholars, who point out that "reassembling the social" involves "following the actors themselves," instead of making heroic assumptions about collective rationality or the power of concealed social forces.[18] Archival analysis can also illuminate how monetary regimes relate to broader political-economic regimes. In steering the economy via their monetary policies, central bankers orient the decisions of myriads of economic as well as political actors. "The economy" is, in fact, an assemblage that brings together many heterogenous actors and forces – an

---

[15] Hall 1993: 290. Peter Hall (1993: 279, 290) called monetarism a "policy paradigm," – that is, "a framework of ideas and standards [...] taken for granted and unamenable to scrutiny as a whole" – and argued that the "policymaking process can be structured by a particular set of ideas." Hall's concept of policy paradigm spurred a large scholarship on the role of ideas in political economy and public policy. For a review and critique, see Jabko and Schmidt 2021.
[16] Kahneman 2011: 31.   [17] Pickering 1995: 94.   [18] Latour 2007.

3.1 How Central Banks Produce Monetary Regime Change

instance of what science scholars and political theorists call "distributed agency."[19] Because of this heterogeneity, the economy does not always behave in the way central bankers hope it will. When central bankers encounter inertia, adversity, or unintended consequences, they deliberate over the possibility of modifying their policies. These debates and actions sometimes result in new monetary regimes, or can even lead to broader change in political-economic regimes.

A large corpus of central bank archives is publicly available, and yet scholars rarely investigate in depth the politics that takes place *inside* central banks. Most seem to assume that the most important politics that impacts central banks takes place primarily outside of them – either because central bankers are independent, according to the conventional economics view, or because central bankers are dependent on external political support, in the conventional political economy view. As we will see, however, contestation inside central banks cannot easily be reduced to politics-as-usual in the broad public arena. What I call the politics of money is therefore not just these outside political pressures – even though those pressures exist and central bankers cannot completely ignore them. The politics of money also has an important organizational dimension – *inside* central banks – as well as a professional dimension – *inside* the economics profession, to which many central bankers have important ties.

Central bankers constantly debate the policies most appropriate for carrying out their mandate and for steering the economy. They consider economic conditions, the state of the art in economics, but *also* the audiences they address – including each other. In other words, central bankers' actions are a contested terrain. Central bankers think and deliberate about their own policies and practices, but at the same time jockey for advantage. There is a large and varied scholarship, in political science and sociology, about the importance of ambiguity and contestation for social, institutional, and political change.[20] Insofar as this insight is applicable to central banking, it suggests the evolution of central bankers' practices does not follow a logic of frontal opposition between successively dominant paradigms. More likely, we can expect this evolution to result from practical debates, mutual manipulation, and coalition building. Ultimately, these contests among central bankers and their interactions with professional and public contests are worth studying because they are important engines of change.

3.1.3 Economics as the Discursive Repertoire of Central Banking

When it comes to the substance of contests among central bankers, any reader of central banks' archives quickly realizes that they are primarily cast in the

---

[19] Latour 2007; Hardie and MacKenzie 2007; Bennett 2010; Connolly 2013; Delanda 2016.
[20] Steinberg 1999; Best 2005; Jabko 2006; Schneiberg and Clemens 2006; Wiener 2007; Berk and Galvan 2009; Herrigel 2010; Thelen 2010; Ayoub 2015; Fligstein and McAdam 2015; Widmaier 2016.

language of economics. Economics is the common mode of reasoning that central bankers use in their deliberations, to make sense of their actions, both among themselves and vis-à-vis the outside world. The centrality of economics as the discursive repertoire of central banking therefore requires that we consider not only contests as strictly internal to central banks. Contests among central bankers often rehearse and prolong contests, however subdued, within the broader economics profession.

Within economics as in any scholarly field, there are cleavages between various schools and theoretical as well as methodological orientations. The most well-known theoretical divides – for example, between neoclassical, Keynesian, or Marxist economists – have been important in the historical development of economic thought. Overlapping with this first cleavage, there is a second and sociologically important divide between "mainstream" economists and "heterodox" economists.[21] Mainstream economists dominate top-ranked economics departments at US universities and beyond, in an increasingly internationalized yet largely US-centered academic community. They practice a type of economics often labeled as "orthodox" by those economists who are considered "heterodox" and therefore not part of the mainstream. In the late twentieth and early twenty-first centuries, mainstream economists have tended to identify as neoclassical or neo-Keynesian, whereas heterodox economists include Marxist economists and also some ("post"-) Keynesian economists. Since the 2000s, there has also been a noticeable turn toward more empirical work and away from such theoretical labels, but sociological and methodological cleavages remain important.

The cleavage between mainstream and heterodox economists is also a hierarchy – both within the field of economics and, crucially, in the world of policymakers. From a sociological perspective, the economics profession is characterized by a remarkably hierarchical social structure and culture.[22] Mainstream economics is labeled as such not only because it has been vetted by the high-status segment of the economics discipline within academe, but also because its practitioners have successfully peddled it to the policy world as a reliable form of expertise. Although the authority of economists has been increasingly challenged, this "crisis of expertise" has taken place in advanced liberal societies that rely on policy experts more than ever before.[23] For central banks, one attraction of mainstream economics is its vocal claim to science-based, apolitical expertise. For example, "new Keynesian" economics is a body of knowledge with "moderately conservative" implications – as Keynes himself described his theory.[24] Not surprisingly, most central bankers also find "new Keynesian" economics more appealing than, say, "post-Keynesian" economics. They typically downplay critical aspects of Keynes' theory that post-Keynesian

---

[21] Colander, Holt, and Rosser 2004; Lawson 2006.
[22] Fourcade 2009; Eyal and Buchholz 2010; Popp Berman 2022.   [23] Eyal 2019.
[24] Keynes 1964: 377.

economists often stress, such as his "skeptical" view about a "merely monetary policy" or his critique of "large disparities" in the distribution of wealth and income.[25] Mainstream economists' claim to apolitical expertise and central bankers' claim to independence mutually support each other.

Central bankers thus represent and, indeed, contribute to define mainstream economics. The influence of mainstream economics on central bankers is therefore not a one-way street. Central banks influence what is or is not considered mainstream, especially through the funding of economics research and the practice of hiring of economists. Perhaps the most vivid illustration of central bank influence on defining the economics mainstream is the Nobel Prize in economics, created and funded by Sweden's central bank.[26] Academic economists, many of whom have ties to central banks, often aim for policy relevance and adopt the viewpoint of central banks. Central banks regularly resort to economists as consultants, and have developed considerable in-house economics expertise.[27] For example, the Fed employs about 500 mostly PhD-level economists and the ECB's staff of economists is close to 400.[28] Although central banks make some efforts to diversify their recruitment, they hire mostly economists, mostly from top-ranked PhD programs in economics, where the weight of mainstream economics is preponderant. Except for the legal profession, other academic disciplines – including those that have subfields devoted to the study of political economy – have little if any representation. That lesser proximity probably contributes, in turn, to their more critical stance toward central banks.

Economics constitutes recognized expertise about the economy, but this expertise also shapes the economy insofar as economic ideas profoundly inform policymaking.[29] For the purpose of understanding how monetary policy is made, two aspects of economists' influence on the economy deserve to be stressed. First, only *mainstream* economists exert a clear and direct influence. In this sense, who among the – mainstream – "neo-Keynesians" and the – heterodox – "post-Keynesians" has a more accurate model of the economy is

---

[25] Keynes 1964: 164, 374.
[26] Offer and Söderberg 2016; Mirowski 2020. Although the Swedish central bank's motivations in this funding decision are subject to debate, the influence of that new Nobel Prize in shaping an increasingly global economics mainstream is beyond doubt.
[27] Claveau and Dion 2018. See also Thiemann, Melches, and Ibrocevic 2021.
[28] Author interviews and computations based on ECB and Federal Reserve Board websites. These numbers do not include the also considerable numbers of economists employed by district federal reserve banks in the United States and national central banks in the European Union.
[29] Sociologists debate the precise nature of the relationship between economics and the economy in terms of the "performativity" of economic ideas, the "authority" of economists, the "economic style of reasoning," or the "mutual constitution" of economic expertise and the economy. See: MacKenzie, Siu Leung-Sea, and Muniesa 2007; MacKenzie 2008; Çalışkan and Callon 2009; Fourcade 2009; Eyal and Buchholtz 2010; Holmes 2014; Jasanoff 2015; Konigs 2018; Wansleben 2018; Carruthers 2022; Popp-Berman 2022.

practically beside the point. The evolution of mainstream economics, especially within the field of macroeconomics, has shaped independent central bankers' practices. When central bankers claimed to follow "monetarist" economics – as they briefly did in the 1980s – or "New Keynesian" economics – as was increasingly the case after the 1990s – they were using these two theoretical frameworks to make sense of economic realities. Yet they were also participating in a professional discourse that defines legitimate terms of debate among economists. Although other heterodox (e.g., "post-Keynesian" or even "Marxist") forms of economic expertise also existed, they were not influential among elite segments of the economics profession. Heterodox economists – with few exceptions[30] – therefore had much less impact on central bankers' regular debates and practices.

A good first example of that influence of mainstream economists on central banking is the rise of the Chicago School of "new classical" economics, which has been traced back to a period shortly before and after the Second World War.[31] A longtime leader of the Mont Pelerin Society, Milton Friedman developed in his scholarly work a "monetarist" vision in which the proper role of central banks was to provide a "stable monetary framework," in contrast to what he saw as the arbitrariness inherent to government intervention.[32] At Chicago and within the economics profession at large, Friedman became also the leader of many economists who were highly critical of Keynesian ideas. His pronouncement in his 1967 presidential address at the American Economic Association that "there is no permanent trade-off" between inflation and unemployment progressively became axiomatic among economists[33] – especially after Friedman received the Nobel Prize in 1976. It also buttressed many central bankers' claim that, by independently focusing on price stability alone, they were making a technical decision. Rather than infringing on politicians' legitimate prerogatives and disregarding their concern with unemployment, central bankers' focus on price stability in the long run represented their best possible contribution to employment and growth. Central bankers who followed that theory could therefore claim that they could do nothing about the level of what Friedman called "natural unemployment," which was a result of other institutions and policies. As they saw it, fighting unemployment was just not their job.

While economic expertise shapes the real economy, the economy also shapes economics. Here, the renewed favor of (new) Keynesian theory among mainstream economists and central bankers in the late 1980s and 1990s provides a good second example of the economy not behaving as expected and then

---

[30] The clearest and most often cited (posthumous) exception is Hyman Minsky after the 2008 financial crisis, which Janet Yellen (2009) referred to as a "Minsky meltdown."
[31] Foucault 2008; Burgin 2012; Mirowski and Plehwe 2015; Slobodian 2018.
[32] Friedman 1962: 38, 51.   [33] Friedman 1968: 11.

shaping economics in return. In the early 1980s, severe anti-inflationary policies caused mass unemployment. Such steep recession had not been observed in decades, which diminished the authority of the Chicago School. Critics of Keynesian policies were still around, but increasing numbers of young economists now identified as "new Keynesian." As prominent new Keynesian economists tell the story, a central bank's adoption of stable rules of money creation was no guarantee that economic agents and the real economy would adjust seamlessly ("rationally").[34] The new Keynesians still accepted Friedman's tenet that the money supply could not be expanded beyond a "natural" level of employment at which inflation would start to accelerate. Yet the "stickiness" of prices and wages could cause unemployment to rise well beyond levels that could be assumed to be "voluntary." A central bank's task was therefore to achieve a "non-accelerating inflation rate of unemployment" (NAIRU).[35] That theory gained popularity among central bankers in the 1990s. It presented them not with a political choice, but again with a technical problem amenable to economic analysis – namely, the constrained optimization problem of maximizing employment under a constraint of low inflation.

In sum, the evolution of central banks' practices is related to the evolution of mainstream economics, but that relationship is not straightforward. This brings us to a second important aspect of economists' influence on central banking – namely, the fact that economics is a *contested* repertoire that can justify different expectations and actions.[36] As the discursive repertoire of central banking, mainstream economics encompassed a real, albeit limited, variety of perspectives. As we will see, inflections in central banks' policies often echo the ways in which contests in the professional arena of economics are typically settled. To buttress their claim to apolitical expertise, mainstream representatives of the economics profession face strong incentives to present a "consensus" to the outside world, even when they continue to have important disagreements and robust internal debates. For central bankers, a practical attraction of the economics profession's elastic conception of consensus is that it enables them to harness the authority of economics but also to hedge their bets and, if necessary, to change their policies relatively quickly – what pragmatist scholars refer to as "syncretic" action.[37] As in the 1950s, mainstream economists at the turn of the twenty-first century converged on a "synthesis"

---

[34] Bernanke 2015: 29. See also Clarida, Gali, and Gertler 1999.
[35] Ball and Mankiw 2002. NAIRU remained an object of debate, however, since it was difficult if not impossible to measure directly. See especially Galbraith 1997; Meyer 2004: xvi–xvii; Greenspan 2008: 170. For a recent overview of NAIRU debates at the Fed, see Arbogast, Van Doorslaer, and Vermeiren 2024.
[36] Critics of the concept of "performativity" in economic sociology also often point this out. See, for example, Beckert 2016; Rilinger 2023.
[37] Berk and Galvan 2009.

between what remained the two dominant – neoclassical and Keynesian – strands of mainstream macroeconomics in the United States and Europe. Not coincidentally, central bankers increasingly identified the "new neoclassical" *alias* "neo-Keynesian synthesis" as an appropriate framework to independently carry out their monetary policy mission.

The contests among central bankers thus appear to the outside as rather subdued. Even on the inside, discords are generally more latent than acute. Independent central bankers strive to project an external image of collegiality and professional competence. They take pride in making evidence-based decisions, using the data collected by their in-house research departments, as well as models and forecasts developed by economists within and outside their institution. They constantly revise their policies at the margin and, when existing policies fail, they experiment with new policies, which sometimes leads to rather drastic changes in monetary regimes. While they also recognize that governing money is a politically sensitive task, central bankers often stress the difference between contests among themselves and political contests. As they see it, conflicts among politicians about economic policies are about power and ideology. By contrast, central bankers strive to ignore those contests and to only debate fact-based expert assessments of the economy, with the help of professional economists.[38] Depending on the economic situation, monetary policy should be restrictive if the priority is to avoid inflation, or accommodative if the goal is to boost the economy. Where to place the cursor between monetary restraint and accommodation should be, in their eyes and for most mainstream economists, mostly a matter of independent expert judgment, rather than a political decision.

That is, of course, how mainstream economists and central bankers have presented the case for central bank independence since the late twentieth century. But central bankers also recognize that the economic situation can be difficult to read, and that even trained economists often disagree on what needs to be done. For that reason, there are contests on what central banks need to do, as will become evident when we examine their records. Central bankers' practices and actions result, in part, from an evolving balance of power, on the monetary policy committee, between advocates of different courses of action – often referred to as "hawks" and "doves." The economic situation and its assessment by economists obviously affect that balance of power. Different levels of inflation, unemployment, and growth may objectively call for different monetary policies at different times. If this could always be decided objectively, however, there would be no debate among economists and no contest among central bankers. But clearly, that is not the case. And that is where broader political factors come into the picture, however reluctant central bankers and mainstream economists may be to discuss them in public.

---

[38] Clarida, Gali, and Gertler 1999; Goodfriend 2007.

3.2 CROSS-CUTTING ALLIANCES AND POLITICAL-ECONOMIC REGIMES

The politics of money, for the purpose of this book, refers to interrelated contests over monetary governance that take place both within and outside central banks. As I will demonstrate, these contests periodically lead to changes not only in monetary regimes, but also in broader political-economic regimes. Central bankers draw from the discursive repertoire of mainstream economics, so their policies tend to conform to mainstream economists' understandings of the economic situation. But in and of itself, that is often not enough to determine their policies. At any given point, there are disagreements between central bankers with different inclinations; between mainstream economists who hold different views; and, between different political forces in the broader public environment of central banks. These disagreements are structured by long-standing cleavages in each of these organizational, professional, and public arenas. Central bankers are important players across all three arenas, however, and this leaves them significant room for agency. They enter informal alliances that cut across these arenas, thus shaping each arena but also the broader politics of money. Let us now unpack what this means and how it can result in regime change by considering each of these three arenas.

3.2.1 Three Arenas for the Politics of Money

First, a central bank's policies, and especially the odds of a sustained change in monetary regime, depend on the balance of power among central bankers. This in turn depends not only on the perceived gravity of the economic situation, but also on the composition of the central bank's main decision-making bodies – for example, how many "hawks" and "doves" sit on them, and how influential they each are. In other words, there is politics within the central bank, despite its legally protected independence from external politics. In fact, central bank independence magnifies the relative importance of central banks' internal politics. Central bankers decide, by majority vote at regular committee meetings, which policies they will pursue. When they consider a highly innovative change of monetary regime, this is often controversial. It is not rare that a minority of central bankers will oppose such moves, and they may express vocal dissent. That internal central bank politics, however, is removed from politics-as-usual among elected officials and in public opinion. The chair usually tries to build a consensus and to avoid having many dissenting votes, since entrenched contestation is seen as detrimental to collegiality, to public trust, and possibly even to the central bank's independence. This is obviously different from politics in law-making bodies, where a sizable and vocal opposition is normal in a democracy. But it is also different from expert judicial bodies such as the US Supreme Court.

The second arena in which the politics of money plays itself out is the economics profession. As it happens, the opinions expressed by leading professional economists outside the central bank also matter internally. These economists are credentialed experts, whose analyses of the economic situation are widely heeded. Economists in universities' economics departments sit at the apex of the profession, but leading economists can also be found in think tanks, the media, and in some economist-heavy organizations – including central banks themselves. When they offer opinions and policy advice on what central banks should do, prominent economists on the outside directly challenge central bankers on their own turf. This can become a problem for central bankers, especially in times of turmoil. Thus, Milton Friedman pilloried the Fed in the 1970s and early 1980s in the name of monetarism. Here was a Nobel Prize–winning economist questioning central bankers' technical claims in their own terms. So was Paul Krugman, another Nobel Prize winner and opinion leader in the 2010s. Krugman's *New York Times* columns often offered scathing criticisms of the ECB and – more rarely – of the Fed. Such prominent economists' critiques are bad publicity and provide ammunition for other critics of central banks, including politicians. Central bankers therefore cannot easily dismiss them. They have an institutional interest in courting leaders of the economics profession and in bringing them to their side, by coopting them as privileged interlocutors, or even as consultants.

Finally, a third arena matters for the politics of money – the arena of elected officials and public opinion that is most familiar to political scientists. That public arena can be permissive for central bankers, but it can also become constraining – especially when central bankers are challenged by prominent economists. From the early 1980s through 2008, central bankers mostly succeeded in playing their institutional role as apolitical, independent experts. In fact, they were so successful that they were increasingly able to assert their independence from elected officials and to translate that power over monetary policy into influence over other economic policies. Successive Fed chairs Paul Volcker (1979–1987) and Alan Greenspan (1987–2006) practically walked on water. Meanwhile, European governments made a treaty commitment in 1992 to grant independence to the future ECB and to their own national central banks, most of which were not independent at that point. Circa 2000, the global trend toward central bank independence, led by American and European central bankers, thus appeared as a path toward a more "scientized" and "depoliticized" central banking.[39] After 2008, however, the politics of money significantly changed. Conservatives, who had long been staunch supporters of independent central banks, now questioned both fiscal and monetary stimulus,

---

[39] On the spread of central bank independence, see McNamara 2002; Polillo and Guillen 2005; Crow and Meade 2007; Fernández-Albertos 2015; Mandelkern 2016. On the "scientization" and "depoliticization" (and later "re-politicization") of central banking, see Marcussen 2009; Krippner 2011; Riles 2018; Best 2025.

often vilified as "bailouts." Although central bankers had long endorsed fiscal conservatism, they became ambivalent about it in a context of deep recession. For the first time in decades, money thus became a highly politicized issue, and central bankers were caught in a political crossfire.

In sum, central bankers take active part in informal yet long-standing alliances that cut across the central bank itself, the economics profession, and the arena of "politics" as conventionally understood. Which strand of economics dominates is, in part, a political story – but not in the straightforward sense of being determined by politics external to the economics profession. In any given economic situation, there are contests among central bankers and economists about which model of the economy is more relevant. The economics profession is an arena where contestation echoes the contests internal to central banks, and conversely. These contests matter because their outcomes often shape policy and sometimes lead to monetary regime change. But such changes also occur in a broader political context, since even independent central bankers need a minimum of political support to consolidate the monetary regimes that they oversee. And because central bankers generally seek political allies to ring-fence these monetary regimes, the politics of money can produce not only changes in monetary regimes but also changes in broader regimes of political economy.

3.2.2 The Waxing and Waning of Technocratic Neoliberalism

American and European central bankers' adoption of anti-inflationary monetary regimes in the 1980s were crucial monetary elements in the waxing of a broader political-economic regime that I call technocratic neoliberalism. To conceptualize that political-economic regime, I draw inspiration from the political science scholarship on the evolution of political-constitutional regimes. Scholars of political-constitutional regimes today generally question any binary opposition between democratic and authoritarian regimes. Rather, "democracy is built one institution at a time";[40] in addition, different features of democracy and authoritarianism can coexist in "hybrid" regimes.[41] If political constitutional regimes are built (or dismantled) over time, then their various elements do not necessarily evolve all at once. Likewise, regimes of political economy should be conceived as concatenations of different elements that do not all necessarily evolve in unison, and that sometimes appear contradictory.

As we will see, technocratic neoliberalism knit together evolving realities that were heterogenous and not necessarily coherent. It brought together central banks and other technocratic organizations, the mainstream of the economics profession, and various political coalitions in the service of a distinctive

---

[40] Capoccia and Ziblatt 2010: 945. See also Ziblatt 2017; Ahmed 2025.
[41] Slater 2010; Levitsky and Way 2010.

market-friendly regime of political economy. From this perspective, central bankers' early 1980s adoption of tight-money disinflationary policies and their 2010s shift in the opposite direction toward easy-money policies therefore appear in a new light. Technocratic neoliberalism waxed and waned over time, as its different elements came together or came apart.

In the 1980s, central bankers' move to prioritize the concern with inflation over the goal of preventing unemployment ushered in a heyday of technocratic neoliberalism. For the Volcker Fed, monetary targeting served effectively to kill inflation, but also to rally support among economists and to minimize political opposition. For European central bankers, there was the economic concern with inflation, but also the problem of preserving pegged exchange rates between the different European currencies – a political as well as an economic imperative. After long debates, they agreed on the creation of a single currency and an independent inflation-focused central bank at the European level. On both sides of the ocean, the result was a durable transition to a low-inflation monetary regime, increasingly ring-fenced by other conservative economic policies. Central bankers worked not only to coopt economists but to assuage center-left politicians. In the United States, for example, Fed chair Alan Greenspan famously convinced President Bill Clinton to become a fiscal conservative. Circa 2000, many US and EU politicians had made their peace with a new division of labor. While central bankers delivered low inflation, center-left as well as conservative politicians pledged to reduce fiscal deficits and to liberalize markets.

In the 2010s, however, the alliance that had supported technocratic neoliberalism unraveled. The global financial crisis of 2008 contributed to destroy public confidence in many neoliberal policies that were already in doubt since the Asian financial crisis of 1997. To prevent economic collapse, central bankers first introduced "unconventional measures." As the threat of inflation clearly receded, they also became much more ambivalent toward disinflation and other neoliberal policies. After decades of ring-fencing technocratic neoliberalism, a complete and sudden reversal of all their policy priorities and an intransigent approach to finance were not in the cards. Unlike outspoken critics of economic orthodoxy, central bankers were not overtly advocating a radically alternative set of ideas and policies. In fact, they continued to profess mainstream economic views – which may explain why their progressive critics discounted their actions. Central bankers continued to ease monetary policy through most of the 2010s, however, and paid less and less attention to conservatives' concerns about inflationary risks that did not materialize during that decade. Their expansionary monetary policies were also increasingly designed to counteract the contractionary effects of fiscal austerity.

Over time, central bankers therefore became the targets of conservative attacks. They were accused of failing to prevent the financial crisis, and of funneling money in the direction of underserving people – not just bankers and financiers, but also irresponsible homeowners in the United States, and lazy

Southerners in the European Union. After decades of being lionized, central bankers' veneer of independence and technocratic rationality began to crack. Meanwhile, the public arena was marked by austerity politics – which goes a long way toward explaining what scholars of political economy, unlike economists, see as the resilience of neoliberalism. Many conservative politicians continued to advocate policies such as tax cuts, fiscal consolidation, welfare retrenchment, and deregulation. In doing so, these politicians claimed to defend "the people" against special interests and other politicians who would unduly tax their incomes, drive them deeper into national debt, and give away scarce public goods to undeserving groups. This political rhetoric was both neoliberal and populist. It also hinged on normatively favorable views of the market among the public – what political theorists call "neoliberal subjectivity."[42] Conservative politicians who engaged in this kind of neoliberal populist rhetoric were, however, not overly concerned with policy coherence. In part because they were much less closely aligned with economic technocrats than in the late twentieth century, they were also less committed to a full range of neoliberal policies. For example, some embraced trade protectionism, or moved opportunistically between pro-austerity and pro-deficits positions when that seemed politically expedient.

3.2.3 Neoliberalism as an Increasingly Populist Project

In sum, the populist element of the neoliberal project increasingly displaced its technocratic element. Over time, central bankers retreated from neoliberal policy prescriptions, whereas conservative politicians increasingly embraced them. Since most areas of economic policies remain the prerogatives of politicians, the prevailing political-economic regime remained broadly neoliberal in the 2010s, despite its waning technocratic element. Yet beneath the surface, the neoliberal political-economic regime that survived in the 2010s sharply differed from the technocratic neoliberalism of the 1980s. In both cases, central bankers decided to carry out important changes in monetary regimes to address problems that they diagnosed with the help of economists – in the 1980s to fight inflation, and in the 2010s to pull the economy out of a major recession. But in the 2010s, central bankers increasingly found themselves at odds with the austerity policies that conservative politicians continued to advocate despite changing circumstances.

This shift from technocratic to populist neoliberalism also provides an alternative explanation of the resilience of neoliberal policies, which helps to

---

[42] Foucault 2008; Connolly 2013; Brown 2015. Scholars in other fields also document similar attitudes, albeit with different names. For example, scholars of political behavior talk about "norms of fairness" that run against socially redistributive policies (Cavaillé 2023); sociologists often stress the spread of "moral values" that favor the "deserving" rich (Prasad et al. 2009); legal theorists speak of "everyday libertarianism" (Murphy and Nagel 2002).

resolve the contradictions between various scholarly perspectives on economic evolution. First, it steers us toward an explanation of why economic technocrats either gravitate toward, or deviate from, neoliberal polices. The gravitation takes place when central bankers take refuge in purely economic rationales for neoliberal policies. This technocratic style can shield them against political attacks, by attracting approval among their peers and in the economics profession. In the 1970s and 1980s, central bankers built on their reputation of expert neutrality to fight inflation, in relative insulation from political critics. But central bankers can also sometimes assert their independence by deviating from neoliberal policies, despite resilient political pressures in favor of such policies. This was increasingly the case in the 2010s, as central bankers invoked economic expertise to quietly resist many conservative politicians' calls for monetary or fiscal contraction.

Second, the populist element of the neoliberal project helps explain its durability, despite its liabilities, but also its mutations over time. Although technocrats were sometimes able to push for neoliberal policies as apolitical measures, there were limits to this technocratic style of policymaking. Market liberalization periodically spurred calls for protection from foreign trade and from unfair competition from cheap immigrant labor and minorities. In response to such calls, politicians on the Right increasingly ran on populist, anti-establishment platforms. They combined a neoliberal rhetoric with a platform of trade protection, immigration restrictions, law and order, and social conservatism. From this perspective, populist elements that already existed in Margaret Thatcher's and Ronald Reagan's neoliberal projects were greatly amplified in the platforms of the Tea Party and Donald Trump, as well as Germany's Alternative für Deutschland (AfD) and other European right-wing parties that combined neoliberalism and populism. Scholars often gloss over this populist element of neoliberalism, or they treat it as a logical contradiction. Yet, over time, it became crucial to an evolving neoliberalism that was increasingly detached from its long-standing base of support among economic technocrats. Neoliberalism thus survived as a populist project, rather than as a coherent technocratic policy platform.

4

The Waxing of Technocratic Neoliberalism in the United States

In the pantheon of central bankers, Paul Volcker occupies a special place. As chair of the US Federal Reserve from 1979 to 1987, he was lionized for slaying the inflation dragon of the 1970s. Today, he is remembered for ushering in a new era of low inflation and financial opulence, as well as economic instability and inequality. As Fed chair, Paul Volcker implemented restrictive monetary policies conducted with the narrow technocratic aim of taming inflation, even at the cost of a deep recession. The Fed appeared to espouse "monetarist" views that had long been peddled by University of Chicago economist Milton Friedman and his followers. Less well-known but perhaps more significant for the long term, Volcker increasingly asserted the Fed's preference for fiscal retrenchment and endorsed some key neoliberal economic priorities of the Reagan administration. According to a conservative folk wisdom that also came to be broadly accepted by many centrist politicians and voters, the Reagan-Volcker years moved the United States decidedly beyond a 1970s decade of inflation during which government had been too big, unions too powerful, wage growth too high, the Fed too submissive, and money too easy.

This chapter retraces the emergence in the United States under Reagan and Volcker of what I call technocratic neoliberalism – a broad political-economic regime centered around the Federal Reserve's shift toward extremely assertive anti-inflationary policies. To explain this development, I will highlight the changing politics of money in three arenas: the Federal Reserve itself, the economics profession, and the broader public arena of American politics. In an increasingly financialized economy, Fed central bankers who adopted anti-inflationary policies entered an uneasy alliance with politicians who embraced neoliberal policies. Under Volcker's leadership, the Fed gained an unprecedented role in the United States' late twentieth-century political economy, even though it supported policies that threatened elected officials with the political liability of persistently high unemployment. In previous decades, central bankers had often relented in their pursuit of monetary stability to support full employment – a politically crucial objective since the New Deal era, for Republicans as well as for Democrats. In the late 1970s and the 1980s, all this changed. Central bankers became increasingly identified with monetary but also fiscal conservatism, and they pushed all politicians – not just conservatives – to pursue neoliberal policies. In retrospect, the Volcker Fed was therefore much more than a support cast for Reagan's neoliberal policies. By making sound money central to the broader neoliberal agenda, the Fed shaped an ideology of monetary and fiscal conservatism that outlived not only the Reagan administration, but even the Fed's own commitment to it.

4.1 BEYOND THE VOLCKER FED'S MONOLITHIC IMAGE

In his 2018 memoirs, Paul Volcker expressed his conviction that the Fed's disinflation of the early 1980s was inevitable. While acknowledging that the Fed did a lot of damage in the process, he felt that the Fed had to do the dirty job of putting an end to a long period of uncontrolled inflation: "Did I realize at the time how high interest rates might go before we could claim success? No. From today's vantage point, was there a better path? Not to my knowledge – not then or now."[1] The second question is counterfactual, so Volcker's answer is, by definition, debatable. Yet the question obviously still matters for "today"– not only for the Fed's monetary policy, as Volcker himself clearly implied, but also because of its broader political-economic implications.

Decades later, the Volcker Fed remains a polarizing topic among scholars. On the one hand, the conventional perspective among economists tends to converge with that of Paul Volcker himself. The most positive judgments about the Volcker years have come from economists closest to the classical tradition in economics.[2] For many, the Volcker Fed had to engage in painful disinflation to make its pursuit of low inflation credible in the eyes of market actors.[3] In recent books that cover the Volcker period, economists and former Fed leaders Ben Bernanke and Alan Blinder nonetheless underscored that the mixed results of the Volcker Shock opened the way for "neo-Keynesian" macroeconomics.[4] As Bernanke puts it, the major recession that was caused by the

---

[1] Volcker and Harper 2018: 118.
[2] Fed historian Allan Meltzer (2009: 1018) praised the Fed's decision "to control monetary growth in order to control inflation, a position it had denied in the past." Meltzer himself happened to be advocating for this position at the time, as co-chair of a "Shadow Open Market Committee" of economists. See also the biography of Paul Volcker by economist William Silber (2012), subtitled *The Triumph of Persistence*.
[3] Orphanides 2004; Goodfriend and King 2005; Hetzel 2022: 402–423.
[4] Bernanke 2022: 35–36; Blinder 2022: 131–133. By the mid- to late 1980s, a majority of neo-Keynesian economists concluded that the Chicago School's assertion about the short-run neutrality of money was "unrealistic," and that the Fed's exclusive focus on fighting inflation could only come at the cost of high unemployment (Ball et al. 1988: 16, 68).

Fed's monetarist experiment was "a direct contradiction of New Classical Economics, which says that should not happen."[5] On the other hand, scholars outside the economics discipline have often adopted a broader political economy perspective on the Volcker Fed. Many highlight the Volcker Shock as marking the end of the "age of control," often dubbed "Keynesian," and the beginning of a new and more "chaotic" era of market neoliberalism.[6] According to sociologist Greta Krippner, the Fed "capitalized on crisis," as its pro-finance policies unwittingly attracted foreign capital to US bond markets and thus loosened the Reagan administration's budget constraint.[7] Historian Judith Stein highlighted the damage done by the Fed's tight-money policy on US manufacturing, thus "burning down the house to roast the pig" (as MIT economist Robert Samuelson once quipped).[8] Sociologist Mitchel Abolafia has showcased first Paul Volcker's "political judgment call" in 1979 to focus on the risk of inflation rather than recession, and the Fed's later negative assessment of monetary targeting in 1982.[9] Political scientists Jacqueline Best and Ben Clift have stressed American as well as British policymakers' unwillingness to recognize the "quiet failure of early neoliberalism," including "the hollowing out of monetarism."[10] Such accounts tend to vindicate earlier portrayals of Paul Volcker as a Fed chair willing to make a "pact with the devil," and who "bandwagoned with the monetarists."[11]

Among other things, the economics and political economy perspectives on the Volcker Fed disagree about the significance of the Volcker Schock for the subsequent evolution of monetary and political-economic regimes. Mainstream economists generally see the Volcker Shock as a relatively short monetarist parenthesis in the Fed's broadly "Keynesian" monetary regime since World War II. For example, Alan Blinder says that Volcker's policies after 1982 simply returned the Fed to normal monetary policy "along Keynesian lines" – a technocratic practice that continued under Greenspan, unlike fiscal policy where "politics rules the roost."[12] By contrast, political economy scholars tend to see it as the inauguration of a broader "neoliberal" political-economic regime increasingly characterized by what Greta Krippner called its "financialization."[13] Importantly, that regime was no longer "Keynesian" in the same sense as during most of the post-1945 period. Jacqueline Best thus reads the Fed's resort to "Keynesianism in reverse" as part of a broader pattern of "clever obfuscations" that surreptitiously but durably prioritized price stability at the expense of employment and shifted

---

[5] Bernanke 2015: 29.
[6] The expressions "age of control" and "age of chaos" are those of historian Jonathan Levy (2021: 597). Daniel T. Rodgers (2011), another historian, similarly calls the 1980s an "age of fracture."
[7] Krippner 2011. [8] Stein 2010, esp. ch. 10–11: 231. [9] Abolafia 2005, 2012.
[10] Best 2020; Clift 2018. [11] Greider 1987: 97, 105–106; Blyth 2002: 168.
[12] Blinder and Reis 2005; Blinder 2022: 3, 383. [13] Krippner 2005, 2011.

power relations and politics.[14] In sum, the economics perspective is focused on the Volcker Fed's inauguration of a new monetary regime that successfully tackled inflation in a modernized version of Keynesian economics, whereas the political economy perspective highlights the Volcker Fed's role in tilting economic governance toward a distinctly pro-market political-economic regime.

To resolve that discrepancy, I will highlight different but intersecting contests about monetary governance within and outside the Volcker Fed, which led to the emergence of a new and durable alliance across different arenas. Contrary to the image projected by Paul Volcker's towering figure, the Volcker Fed was anything but a monolith. While the economics perspective usefully highlights the professional arena of debate between different schools of economic thought, it often seems to assume that the Fed was primarily a site for that professional debate, protected by its independence from politics in the broader public arena. As for the political economy perspective, it generally focuses on that public arena and often overlooks contests specific to both the professional arena of economics and the organizational arena of the FOMC. To adequately explain the trajectory of both monetary and broader political-economy regimes, however, we need to consider all three arenas and their interactions in a changing politics of money.

Against considerable internal and external opposition, Paul Volcker led the Fed to undertake a daring experiment with monetary aggregate targets, and three years later operated not only an abrupt turnaround in the Fed's approach but also in the way he navigated a changing politics of money. While monetarism was quietly shelved, the Fed continued to assert its independence and also to set the tone for US economic policies quite differently than before the 1980s. Throughout the Volcker years, Paul Volcker and his allies at the Fed antagonized various constituencies – "doves" within the FOMC, who were greatly concerned about the effects of disinflation on growth and unemployment; professional economists who identified as Keynesian; and segments of the American public most likely to be harmed by tight money and rising unemployment, especially within the Democratic Party and among its voters. Ultimately, the Fed successfully asserted its independence but also its policy leadership role in an increasingly neoliberal US political economy. As we will see, this trajectory was not preordained. Under both the Carter and the Reagan administrations, the Volcker Fed faced considerable turmoil. Fed central bankers stood at the intersection of three arenas, each characterized by its own distinct cleavages.

First, the FOMC itself was an arena that was relatively prone to conflict, as even a cursory comparison between the number of conflicting statements in the 1980s and 2010s reveals (see Figure 4.1, and Appendix A). In comparison with his successors, Volcker also faced more vocal dissent within the Board of

---

[14] Best 2020: 612. See also Best 2022: 10.

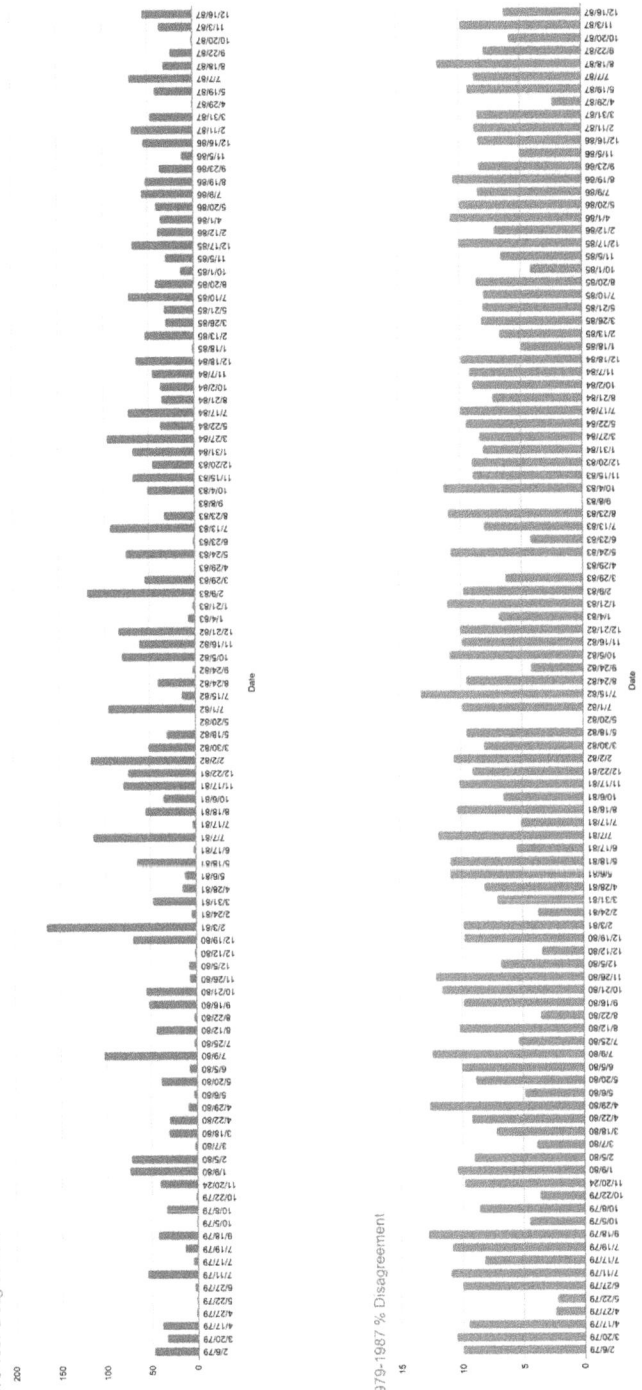

FIGURE 4.1 Disagreement at the FOMC, 1979–1987.

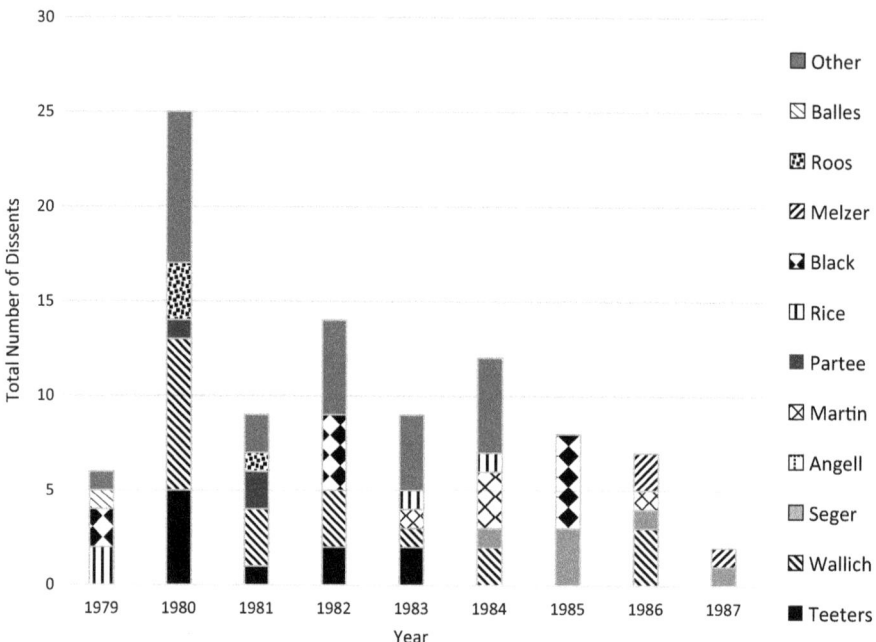

FIGURE 4.2 Volcker Fed dissents, 1979–1987.

Governors in Washington, DC, rather than among the presidents of Federal Reserve districts.[15] Dissenting votes by governors Nancy Teeters, Henry Wallich, or Martha Seger became a fixture of the Volcker Fed (see Figure 4.2).

When Paul Volcker became Fed chair in 1979, inflation had become a growing and seemingly intractable problem, especially in the face of two successive oil shocks that both raised prices and caused economic stagnation (*alias* "stagflation"). Paul Volker was widely known as an inflation "hawk" intent on fighting inflation above all. According to his memoirs, he had always believed that "price stability is the ultimate responsibility of the Federal Reserve."[16] Whether he would succeed in bringing the Federal Reserve's collegial governing bodies to focus on price stability rather than on maximum employment remained an open question, however. On the FOMC, inflation "hawks" coexisted with "doves," who were primarily concerned about rising unemployment. The two groups typically worked out compromises that fell within the Fed's existing policy habits. The Fed lowered interest rates when growth subsided and unemployment increased, and it raised them when economic growth and inflationary pressures picked up. Until 1979, the Fed had not forcefully reacted to the growing problem of inflation, for fear of raising

---

[15] Thornton and Wheelock 2014. [16] Volcker and Harper 2018: 106.

unemployment. American central bankers then hoped to just "muddle through," as students of public administration would see it. Like any policy community, they were disinclined to rock the boat if they could avoid it. Volcker therefore knew that any radically "hawkish" departure from the status quo would especially antagonize the Fed "doves" – but he took that risk.

Second, the Volcker Fed, by repeatedly changing its monetary approach, took positions in contests between "monetarists" against "Keynesians" within the professional arena of economics. In 1979, Volcker initially led the FOMC to try a monetarist approach to monetary policymaking. Monetarism was closely associated with the name of Milton Friedman, who had recently won a Nobel Prize in economics in 1976. Since the early 1980s, observers and scholars have often sought a simple answer to a simple question: Did Volcker personally believe in monetarist ideas, or did he use them to refocus the Fed on the fight against inflation? Put in such binary terms, the question assumes that Volcker had firm and constant – either positive or cynical – beliefs about monetarism. This is not the only possibility, however. As we will see, Paul Volcker led the Fed on the path of change, by convincing his colleagues to experiment with a yet untested policymaking method. As Volcker recalled a decade after the Volcker Shock, "the approaches that had been debated (and forgotten) within the Fed seemed worth looking at again."[17] Above all, Volcker had spent most of his career as a high-level federal public servant, and was therefore particularly adept at reading a political situation. The Volcker Fed's decision to adopt monetarism was not only a policy experiment, but also a political gamble. Volcker could count on influential figures within the economics profession to support the Fed's experiment – starting with Milton Friedman himself.

Third, the Volcker Fed also operated in a public arena where it took advantage of a favorable political context. By the late 1970s, a "panic at the pump" developed in the face of soaring oil prices and shortages, fueling a preexisting inflationary trend and producing a growing sense of intellectual as well as economic and political "crisis."[18] In that context, a Democratic president uncharacteristically appointed an inflation hawk as Fed chair. Volcker's aura as newly appointed chair helped him convince his dovish colleagues at the FOMC to initially suspend disbelief and follow his lead. The November 1980 election of President Ronald Reagan – who was informally advised by Milton Friedman – ensured the administration's continued support to the Fed's fight against inflation, despite the increasing economic and social costs of that approach. After three years and many mishaps, however, the Volcker Fed's monetarist experiment was terminated. Monetary targets proved too volatile to be used as a standard tool of monetary governance. Instead of incorporating

[17] Volcker and Gyohten 1992: 167. [18] Krippner 2011; Jacobs 2016; Eich 2022: 177–205.

them into its policy framework, the Fed therefore reverted in October 1982 to its previous practice of targeting interest rates. Professional economists in the administration and in academe soon noticed, but most people did not. That was not a coincidence. Despite its mitigated results and short duration, the Volcker Shock enabled the independent Fed to assert its power in shaping US economic governance.

In sum, the Volcker Shock was designed not just to kill inflation, but also to overcome FOMC dissent, to rally support among economists, and to minimize public opposition. It threw a wrench into a monetary regime that was legally and effectively designed for ensuring maximum employment as well as price stability. Fed leaders managed to break the deadlock inside and outside the Fed, but also to entrench the Federal Reserve's independence at the apex of America's political economy. While it was launched by a relatively narrow coalition of strange bedfellows, the Volcker Shock ultimately gave birth to a new political-economic regime that involved the Federal Reserve, the economics profession, and the American public. Volcker's legacy – the Fed's increased focus on price stability, advocacy of fiscal discipline, and endorsement of other neoliberal policies – endured for three decades. As we will see, however, there was no highly coherent paradigm underlying the Fed's actions and the new political-economic regime that it inaugurated. Rather, the key to the endurance of technocratic neoliberalism, despite its political liabilities, was the capacity of its advocates to recruit expanding circles of support. Technocratic neoliberalism's success initially rested on the support of central bankers, mainstream economists, and conservative politicians. Yet it also increasingly attracted center-left politicians and a remarkably large swath of the general public.

4.2 THE STRANGE BEDFELLOWS BEHIND THE VOLCKER SHOCK

Paul Volcker was appointed by President Jimmy Carter, after spending most of his career in government service. A Democratic appointee, Volcker was a priori an unlikely partner to Reagan's Republican administration and its staunchly pro-market, small-government ideology. Yet Paul Volcker carried out a shock therapy against inflation that garnered Reagan's support. That sudden change came after several years of accommodative monetary policies under Arthur Burns, a Republican Fed chair under Republican President Richard Nixon, who had also been Milton Friedman's academic mentor.[19] If there was to be a change of monetary policy at the Fed, one might have expected it to occur during the Nixon–Burns years. Although he was a proponent of a strong and independent Fed, the Nixon tapes revealed that Burns repeatedly gave in to President Nixon's focus on reelection and to his desire for monetary

---

[19] Wells 1994.

4.2 The Strange Bedfellows behind the Volcker Shock

accommodation.[20] After Burns stepped down in 1978, G. William Miller was equally unable to stem inflation during his brief tenure as Fed chair – before President Jimmy Carter appointed him as treasury secretary. Paul Volcker's appointment to replace Miller was widely seen as a victory of Wall Street. As president of the New York Fed, Volcker had repeatedly cast dissenting votes against the FOMC's majority. He was identified by the press as the leader of the "Volcker minority" in favor of greater monetary restraint.[21] He was the favorite of Wall Street and, at that point, a weakened President Carter did not seriously try to resist Volcker, to the dismay of his own advisers.[22]

4.2.1 The Volcker Fed before the Volcker Shock

Volcker's arrival as the head of the Fed was partly a product of historical contingencies – Miller's appointment as treasury secretary and the fact that Carter was weak and needed a Fed chair who would be acceptable to Wall Street. It took a widespread perception of crisis for that situation to occur, however. Seized by "panic at the pump," the American public had begun to question a political culture that took root at the time of Roosevelt's New Deal, in which the government ultimately ensured the welfare of citizens.[23] Grassroot popular challenges to government authority and the rise of anti-government attitudes can also be traced back to the 1960s, when the Left resented government repression and government-sponsored capitalism while the Right became wary of government regulations of capitalism.[24] Both the Left and the Right then started to embrace freedom as their motto – even though they had starkly different notions of freedom and policy remedies. By the late 1970s, most Americans considered inflation the country's number one economic problem, and increasingly distrusted the government to resolve economic problems. Ironically, this new context gave the Volcker Fed a license to fight inflation with unprecedented resolve – while often pretending to do nothing more than enabling the market to work its "magic" on the US economy.[25] Volcker could see that, in the face of persistent inflation, American politicians might be more willing to let him break the mold of past policies.

The moniker "Volcker Shock" underscores the depth but also the rapidity of a change that would retrospectively be seen as historic – between August 18, the first FOMC meeting after Volcker's appointment as the new Fed chair, and October 6, 1979, when Volcker announced in a post-meeting press conference that the Fed would now aim at controlling monetary aggregates rather than

---

[20] Conti-Brown 2016: 193.   [21] Silber 2012: 142.   [22] Greider 1987: 34–35, 46–47.
[23] Jacobs 2016.   [24] Harvey 2007.   [25] Levy 2021: 597–608.

short-term interest rates. Seen from within the Fed, the new policy was unorthodox insofar as it implied a break from "routine techniques" of US monetary policy that had failed.[26] Yet it also implied a clear prioritization of the fight against inflation, barely a couple of years after the US Congress adopted the 1977 Federal Reserve Reform Act's "dual mandate" of "maximum employment" and "price stability." That mandate itself was, according to scholars of the US Congress, a formalization of long-standing Keynesian practice, which the Democrats-dominated Congress feared the Fed might otherwise give up.[27] So what was at stake was not only a change in the FOMC's own practice, but also a radical change in the ways the Fed related to the economics profession and to American politics more broadly. For Volcker's new approach to take hold required considerable and sustained attention to the politics of money across these various arenas.

In the arena of the FOMC, Volcker's colleagues understood that President Carter had appointed him to steer the Fed in a more hawkish direction. On August 18, Volcker was able to obtain a rate hike without too much controversy. He faced only two dissenting votes that day – one from Emmett Rice, another Carter appointee to the Board, who worried about the risk of deeper recession, but also a dissent on the hawkish side from Richmond Fed chief Robert Black, who faulted the FOMC's rate hike for not being sufficiently bold. Yet Volcker's grace period as Fed chair was quite short. On September 18, he tried to build a consensus at the FOMC in favor of another rate hike, also citing broad political support on Capitol Hill:

I share the view that has been widely expressed that this isn't the time for any easing, in the visible sense, of interest rates. (...) I also share the view that has been quite widely expressed that we have to show some resistance to the growth in money. I would note that that remains a source of political support for us. It's not every day that we get a letter from the leader of the Black Caucus [in the House] exhorting us to show more restraint on the money supply side. (...) As I listened, among the voting members of the Committee at least, I think there was a majority desire–but clearly not unanimous–to make a little move on the federal funds rate. So I would propose 11-1/2 percent on that at this point. (transcript, pp. 34–35)

In the end, however, Volcker faced four dissenting votes. San Francisco Fed president James Ball joined Rice on the dovish side, while Philip Coldwell, a Nixon appointee to the Board, sided with Black's hawkish dissent. According to our automated reading of disagreements, the September 1979 FOMC meeting was also among the two most contentious of the Volcker years, with 12.8 percent (forty-three) disagreeing statements. A manual reading of the transcript confirms the existence of two clearly demarcated camps: Nancy Teeters, David Eastburn, Frank Morris, and Charles Partee in addition to Balles and Rice

---

[26] Abolafia 2012: 104.   [27] Binder and Spindel 2017: 144–150.

on the dovish side; and Lawrence Roos, Henry Wallich, and of course Paul Volcker as a mediator but also clearly leaning toward the hawkish camp.

4.2.2 The Historic FOMC Meeting of October 1979

In the context of persistent inflation and market turmoil, Volcker called an unscheduled meeting of the FOMC on October 5–6, 1979. To preempt the risk of deadlock in the Fed's internal arena, Volcker adopted a different tactic than at the previous meeting. He still took on the role of honest broker, but this time he introduced the meeting with a bold proposal aimed at changing the terms of the deliberation. Volcker's proposal, which would alter the course of US monetary history, was to control the growth of the money supply rather than interest rates. That proposal took up monetarist ideas that had long been defended most prominently by Milton Friedman in conservative circles. Already at the September 1979 FOMC meeting, Lawrence Roos, the president of the St. Louis Fed and himself a former Republican elected official, had proposed to directly address the problem of "money growth," which he asserted was the market's main concern.[28] The Fed Board staff's response to Roos was noncommittal, if not dismissive:

MR. PARDEE. Well, the market is concerned about inflation however it is induced. There are some monetarists in the market who do follow closely the aggregates, but they are just one segment. There are others who worry about other things.[29]

Paul Volcker, however, had responded more positively:

My feeling would be that you're not out of order in raising that question, Mr. Roos. We would be out of order in having an extended discussion of it today, because I don't think we're going to resolve it. (...) But I think it is a very relevant question, which has come up from time to time, and I think we should be exploring it again in the relatively near future. And I would plan to do so.[30]

A month later, Volcker sided with the monetarist proposal. The Fed was now going to tailor its monetary policy in such a way as to reach money supply targets, rather than follow its normal practice of adjusting its short-term interest rates (the so-called federal funds rate). On the evening of October 6, Volcker summoned a press conference to announce the change. This post-meeting press conference was highly unusual for a time when the Fed – like other central banks – operated in relative secrecy and did not yet have a policy of communicating its decisions as transparently as possible.[31] The move was

---

[28] Meeting of the Federal Open Market Committee, September 18, 1979, transcript, pp. 1, 12.
[29] Meeting of the Federal Open Market Committee, September 18, 1979, transcript, pp. 1–2.
[30] Meeting of the Federal Open Market Committee, September 18, 1979, transcript, p. 14.
[31] Goodfriend 1986; Blinder 2004.

therefore designed to garner maximum media coverage of the Fed's new approach.

What led the Fed to Volcker's new approach remains an object of debate. At the time, it seemed like a straightforward victory of the monetarist worldview within the professional arena of economics. Yet recent histories of the Fed by former Fed leaders note that Volcker, far from accepting monetarist doctrine at its word, would have encountered considerable political pushback if he had more transparently set sky-high interest rates.[32] After the Fed ended its monetary targeting three years later, Milton Friedman himself accused Volcker of pretending to adopt monetarism simply as a pretext for raising interest rates through the roof: "There was no monetarist experiment and there was never an intent for a monetarist experiment."[33] Volcker himself later sometimes came close to acknowledging that ploy, citing as a "benefit of the new technique" the fact that he "would not have had much support for raising short-term rates that much."[34] In that vein, some scholars have interpreted the Fed's decision to target monetary aggregates rather than interest rates as an attempt to "de-politicize" monetary policy via "an attempt to present policy choices as arising automatically from market-generated fluctuations."[35]

The October 5–6 FOMC meeting transcripts obviously do not reveal what was in the hearts and minds of central bankers.[36] Yet they do shed light on the politics of the Fed's internal FOMC arena, and on Volcker's agility in steering the committee toward the new approach. Volcker evidently prepared the FOMC meeting of October 6 quite carefully. In a meeting by conference call the day before, he had announced that he wanted the FOMC to consider experimenting, on a strictly provisional basis, with a new approach that he had asked the Board staff to outline:

> The reason I think we should come together physically is that we have often discussed one way or another in the past. (...) I want to discuss tomorrow whether we want to adopt that approach, not as a permanent [decision] at this stage, but as an approach for between now and the end of the year, roughly, in any event.[37]

Volcker was also careful not to advocate a purist version of monetarism. There was no discussion of a commitment to a fixed rule of growth for monetary aggregates à la Milton Friedman. Volcker wanted to target the quantity of money in circulation, but he also wanted the FOMC to retain discretion over the choice of monetary targets:

---

[32] Blinder 2022: 126–127; Bernanke 2022: 35–36.
[33] That quote is reported in an article published in the *New York Times*, December 31, 1983, p. 29.
[34] Volcker and Gyohten 1992: 170.   [35] Krippner 2011: 108; see also Abolafia 2012.
[36] For that, we can only rely on their necessarily subjective retrospective accounts, including Volcker's (Volcker and Harper 2018: 104–108). See also the interviews that William Greider (1987: 105–106) quotes from his account of that October 1979 meeting.
[37] Meeting of the Federal Open Market Committee, October 5, 1979, transcript, p. 1.

4.2 The Strange Bedfellows behind the Volcker Shock

We are not – at least I am not – proposing that we go to a purely mechanical reserve targeting approach. (...) We are proposing an approach where somebody – some human being – will sit down and say: For the period ahead I'm making a new estimate of currency and allowing an adjustment for its impact on the total reserve base (...) There are all these elements of judgment that enter into the process.[38]

As Volcker presented it in a long introductory statement on October 6, his proposed new approach was above all a way for the Fed to regain the initiative and thereby stop losing "credibility" in the eyes of market participants – that is, to break the "market psychology" that, in his eye, fueled ever-renewed inflation:

[W]e are not dealing with a stable psychological or stable expectational situation by any means. And on the inflation front we're probably losing ground. In an expectational sense, I think we certainly are, and that is being reflected in extremely volatile financial markets (...) My feeling was that by putting even more emphasis on meeting the money supply targets and changing operating techniques [in order to do so] and thereby changing psychology a bit, we might actually get more bang for the buck. (...) I overstate it, but the traditional method of making small moves has in some sense, though not completely, run out of psychological gas.[39]

The word psychology (or psychological) appears a total of thirty-six times in that transcript, and the word credibility (or credible) eight times. In Volcker's own later recollection, "a change in our approach" was needed to get the Fed out of the "psychological trap" of "ineffectual baby steps" and convince the public and market actors that "we meant business."[40] Thus, the so-called Volcker Shock was purposefully designed as a shock that would disrupt widespread expectations of what the Fed was up to. Above all, Volcker refused to be like Arthur Burns and to accept that the Fed could do little to defeat inflation.[41] For that purpose, a monetarist approach was useful because it signaled a new resolve.

The transcript of October 6 clearly reveals the same two camps as in the previous two meetings. Roos was the FOMC member who was most enthusiastically in favor of a monetarist approach: "God bless you for doing this! [Laughter]"[42] Yet this time, the entire FOMC unanimously acquiesced to the new approach – including the long-standing doves. How Volcker was able to achieve this result is subject to some debate.[43] In Volcker's own recollection, he

---

[38] Meeting of the Federal Open Market Committee, October 6, 1979, transcript, p. 28.
[39] Meeting of the Federal Open Market Committee, October 6, 1979, transcript, pp. 6, 8.
[40] Volcker and Gyohten 1992: 166–167; Volcker and Harper 2018: 105–107.
[41] Volcker and Harper 2018: 107.
[42] Meeting of the Federal Open Market Committee, October 6, 1979, transcript, p. 24.
[43] According to an interview of Fed vice president Fred Schultz about that FOMC meeting: "'Paul was masterful,' Fred Schulz said. 'I knew exactly what he was doing. The others ended up arguing with him, talking him into doing it. By the end of the day, he had them fully committed.'" (Greider 1987: 123). According to other interviews with FOMC members, Volcker steered

was ardently advocating a radical change of approach, since he felt there was no other choice and market actors interpreted dissenting votes as signs that the Fed would not hold steady until inflation was defeated.[44] Volcker pointed out in his memoirs that the transcript does not convey "the nuance and the tone of voice."[45] Even so, the transcript definitely confirms that Volcker deftly steered the deliberation toward the decision that he favored from the start – but without being too overbearing. In the end, FOMC members all agreed to suspend disbelief on the new approach:

CHAIRMAN VOLCKER. There is quite clearly a great majority who want the new technique. Now let me ask the question slightly differently. How many feel strongly about this? I doubt that anybody thinks it's a matter of life or death but I just want to see how strong the sentiment is.
SPEAKER(?). I think it's big.
CHAIRMAN VOLCKER. Who has a strong preference for moving in the new direction?
MR. ALTMANN. 1, 2, 3, 4, 5, 6, 7, 8.
CHAIRMAN VOLCKER. You're in that camp, Nancy?
MS. TEETERS. I feel queasy about it. (...) I'm in.[46]

In retrospect, the Volcker Fed and the monetarist side of the economics arena were strange bedfellows. First, the monetarists were unlikely to support the Fed wholeheartedly. Milton Friedman, the father of monetarism, had long distrusted the Federal Reserve. Already in *Capitalism and Freedom* (1962), he had argued against the concentration of power in the hands of "an 'independent' central bank (...) money is much too serious a matter to be left to the Central Bankers."[47] In a congratulatory letter to Volcker after his appointment, Friedman doubted the Fed could exert the needed "monetary restraint" to quash inflation "without major changes in its methods of operation."[48] In response, Volcker then wrote a letter to Milton Friedman that invited his support: "[Y]ou know I will not be unhappy to have you preaching the doctrines of monetary rectitude as we move ahead."[49] Yet Friedman's opposition to Fed discretion continued under Reagan, at which point he wielded even greater influence. Friedman suggested that the Fed might be advantageously replaced by "a computer," and Reagan asked his entourage, "Do we really need the Fed?" – a question the president eventually put to Volcker himself.[50] Second, Volcker himself was clearly no big fan of Milton Friedman. Despite his belief in the importance of price stability, he also dismissed Friedman's "doctrinaire" monetarism and its plea in favor of a "hard and fast, almost

---

the FOMC discussion in ways that effectively discouraged dissent without strong-arming would-be dissenters. Silber 2012: 156–177.
[44] Volcker and Harper 2018: 118.   [45] Volcker and Harper 2018: 107.
[46] Meeting of the Federal Open Market Committee, October 6, 1979, transcript, p. 50.
[47] Friedman 1962: 62.   [48] Silber 2012: 148.   [49] Silber 2012: 149.
[50] Silber 2012: 194–195, 201; Mallaby 2016: 266.

mechanistic rule" that "essentially meant removing the Fed's human judgement."[51] Before the FOMC meeting that adopted the new method of monetary targeting, Volcker reportedly had one-on-one meetings with Fed Board members.[52] Fed Governor Henry Wallich's objection to monetarism was that "[i]t's a pact with the devil." Volcker then responded: "Sometimes you have to deal with the devil."

Scholars of political economy have often stressed that money supply targets gave Paul Volcker an excuse to continue to raise the Fed's interest rates beyond levels with which most politicians and, indeed, most Americans felt comfortable. Although there was clearly an element of obfuscation in Volcker's adoption of monetarism, it is difficult to conclude that this was a primary driver of the Volcker Shock. First, monetarism's political cover was only temporary and quite imperfect. At best, it bought time for the Fed. Congress increasingly grilled Volcker on the interest rate effects of monetary targeting. At a Senate testimony in the midst of the 1982 recession, Democratic Senator Jim Sasser accused Volcker of conducting policies that were the "chief cause of our economic problems" and leading the country into "bankruptcy."[53] While Volcker could count on the support of monetary targeting advocates in Congress, the veil of monetarism was really thin for anyone who tried to look through it. As Volcker himself put it to his FOMC colleagues on the eve of the Volcker Shock:

It's an easier political sale, and we are obviously moving into an area that is sensitive, to say the least. We do have a background of some Congressional thinking that puts great emphasis on the money supply targets. So, to the extent that we accept that emphasis one might argue that we will get more support. I think that it is a factor to be weighed, but there are those who would say: 'The hell with all this theorizing about where the targets are; when Congress sees the interest rate effects, that won't make any difference.' So it is not a black or white situation by any means but I think it is something we can take into account.[54]

Economic journalist William Greider's indictment of the Volcker Fed in his 1987 book *Secrets of the Temple* – without access to the transcripts – also underscores the limits of monetarism as a tactic for defusing political controversy.[55] Greider's plea in favor of "a governing structure in which the central bank was subservient to the elected government" as in "most other industrial nations" suggests that well-informed observers perceived the Volcker Shock as a politically radical move that would not have been adopted without a considerable degree of central bank independence. As we now know in hindsight, however, most industrialized nations traveled in the direction of America's model of central bank independence – not the other way around.

---

[51] Volcker and Harper 2018: 20, 32–33. See also Volcker and Gyohten 1992: 167.
[52] Greider 1987: 105–106. [53] Jacobs and King 2021: 216.
[54] Meeting of the Federal Open Market Committee, October 6, 1979, transcript, p. 8.
[55] Greider 1987. See also Best 2022.

Whether Volcker believed that monetarism would work, or whether he agreed with Chicago School economists that it would lead to a painless adjustment of actors' expectations, was in a sense beside the point. Volcker's tactic harked back not so much to Friedman's monetarist theory literally, but to Friedman's more generic call to heed market actors' expectations in his 1967 address to the American Economics Association.[56] His adoption of monetarism was anything but wholehearted and, in fact, his relationship with Milton Friedman and the monetarists was increasingly strained.[57] His biographer argues that Volcker's thinking paralleled that of the "rational expectations" school of economists around Robert Lucas, and that his actions "revealed an appreciation of rational expectations before that principle gained acceptance."[58] To be sure, Volcker's emphasis on "psychology" is reminiscent of the "Lucas critique" of government policies that are ineffective because market actors are able to rationally anticipate them. Yet Volcker was equally careful to steer away from Lucas' assertion that demand management policies were doomed to be ineffective: "I would not go so far, but I do think (...) that what people think and expect (...) is a fact of economic life that we cannot escape."[59] Alan Blinder, who also interviewed Volcker on his monetary beliefs, calls him "a bit cagey on this question."[60] As recalled by a former senior Fed staff official and close collaborator of the Fed chair, Paul Volcker was "remarkably hard to pin down."[61]

A consummate practitioner of American bureaucracy and politics, Volcker understood a general reality of statecraft – namely, that it can be best to refrain from making clear commitments in order to keep different clienteles on board and thus to effectively build power.[62] To gain and retain support in various critical arenas, Volcker thus cultivated ambiguity and aimed to retain as much flexibility as possible when he chose a particular course of action. To carry out disinflation without being thwarted by its opponents, he courted different constituencies – at the FOMC, among the economics profession, on Wall Street, and among inflation hawks at the White House and on Capitol Hill. For precisely this reason, however, Volcker's positions were influenced by the *Zeitgeist* of Chicago-style economics. In a later interview, Volcker confessed no specific recollection of economics scholarship about "time consistency" under "rational expectations," but distinctly remembered that one Fed advisor "made a big point about credibility and expectations, so I lapped that up because that mattered."[63] Thus, Volcker was not immune to the intellectual climate in the

---

[56] Friedman 1968. [57] Silber 2012: 231; Volcker and Harper 2018: 33, 109.
[58] Silber 2012: 3, 134–135. [59] Volcker 1976, quoted in Silber 2012: 135.
[60] Blinder 2022: 126. [61] Author interview, Cambridge, MA, April 26, 2023.
[62] Ansell and Padgett 1993.
[63] Schonhardt-Bailey 2013: 443–444. The classic reference in economics on the topic of time consistency is Kydland and Prescott 1977.

economics profession and to its emphasis on market actors' expectations of future Fed policies. The Volcker Fed's discussions largely echoed discussions that were going on in the broader economics profession at the time about the relative importance of Keynesian versus neoclassical understandings of how the economy worked, and how economic agents made decisions. FOMC members clearly cared about economists' opinions, in Chicago School circles and beyond, about their poor performance in taming inflation. As San Francisco Fed chief John Balles recounted a public meeting to his colleagues:

> It was by the economists that we really got blasted. They came from Stanford, Berkeley, the University of California at Davis, and from a number of major banks in town. Quite frankly, they were highly critical of what they called pro-cyclical Fed policy and the extreme swings in the growth rates of money and credit that they've witnessed over the past year.[64]

Volcker's and other FOMC members' attention and sensitivity to the opinions of economists can be understood when we think about the Fed's position vis-à-vis the economics profession. The Fed's job is to regulate financial markets and banks and this involves highly technical aspects that are topics of study for economists in academe and beyond. In the 1970s, Fed chair Arthur Burns, who was himself a former economics professor, had decided to beef up the analytical capacities of Fed staff by recruiting PhD economists.[65] The FOMC members who were credentialed economists were best able to speak the language of economics. They and the Fed staff influenced the discussion on what economists mostly cared about – and Volcker surely wanted to win them over. In addition, Volcker interjected a few more thoughts about how the Fed's decisions would be received on the Hill and at the White House:

> I should report to you that obviously I discussed the whole problem on the international side and inevitably on the domestic side with the Administration. I think I can say flatly that they are ready for a strong program; they would have no disagreement with that conclusion at all.[66]

Although ordinary Washington politics was not further discussed at that meeting, everybody at the FOMC understood that, even for the independent Federal Reserve, a modicum of political support would be needed to carry out a radical new method and to withstand the inevitable political attacks on the Fed's forthcoming monetary tightening. In sum, Volcker's rapid assertion of Fed power in adopting that method involved careful maneuvering in three arenas at the same time – the arena of the FOMC itself, the professional arena of economics, and the broader US public arena.

---

[64] Meeting of the Federal Open Market Committee, September 18, 1979, transcript, p. 24.
[65] Author interview with former Fed senior official, Cambridge, MA, April 26, 2023.
[66] Meeting of the Federal Open Market Committee, October 6, 1979, transcript, p. 9.

4.3 THREE BUMPY YEARS

The Volcker Fed's active use of monetary targets lasted between October 1979 and October 1982. To say that the experiment did not deliver all that it promised is an understatement. According to monetarist theory, there was "no permanent trade-off" between inflation and unemployment, and the Fed should stick to a fixed rule for the growth of money supply in the economy. The implication was that the Fed should remain strictly focused on fighting inflation and disregard spikes in unemployment, since the theory viewed these spikes as temporary and caused by factors other than monetary policy. Yet the increasingly apparent volatility of monetary aggregates, as measured by the Fed itself, led to stop-and-go monetary policy. Episodes of sharply rising interest rates were followed by drops in monetary aggregates as well as employment, which effectively forced the Fed to loosen its monetary policy.[67] These policy gyrations, in turn, long undercut the Fed's attempt to fight inflation via monetary targets. What the transcripts reveal is the tense contests, both within and outside the Fed, that led to the Fed's fateful decisions during that period.

4.3.1 A Period of Turmoil

After a brief truce between FOMC hawks and doves in late 1979 and early 1980, epic contests soon started to reemerge within the Fed's internal arena. The FOMC meeting on July 9, 1980 was one of the most contentious meetings of the Volcker period, as measured by ChatGPT. The most consistent critic of the Volcker Fed's tight-money policies on the FOMC was Nancy Teeters, the first woman to serve on the Federal Reserve Board and herself another Carter appointee (before Volcker). In the face of persistent inflation despite monetary targeting, she lashed out at the Fed's drastic monetary tightening as the economy went into serious recession. In late 1980 and early 1981, Teeters did not mince her words: "It seems unconscionable to raise interest rates when the economy is still going down."[68] "To take the few indications of reviving growth and use that as an excuse to tighten monetary policy seems to me totally unacceptable. We will create a double-dip recession (....)."[69] "I think it's well known that we could have gotten the same degree of restraint without having to go to 21-1/2 percent interest rates."[70] As Figure 4.3 indicates, Teeters' prediction of a double-dip recession proved exactly correct.

Another consideration was the Fed's external support in the public arena of American politics – especially since 1980 was an election year. FOMC

---

[67] For an in-depth and largely interview-based study of the Volcker Fed years by an investigative reporter, see Greider 1987. For Volcker's recollections, see Volcker and Harper 2018: 102–151.
[68] FOMC meeting, August 12, 1980, transcript p. 36.
[69] FOMC meeting, September 16, 1980, transcript p. 37.
[70] FOMC meeting, February 3, 1981, p. 53.

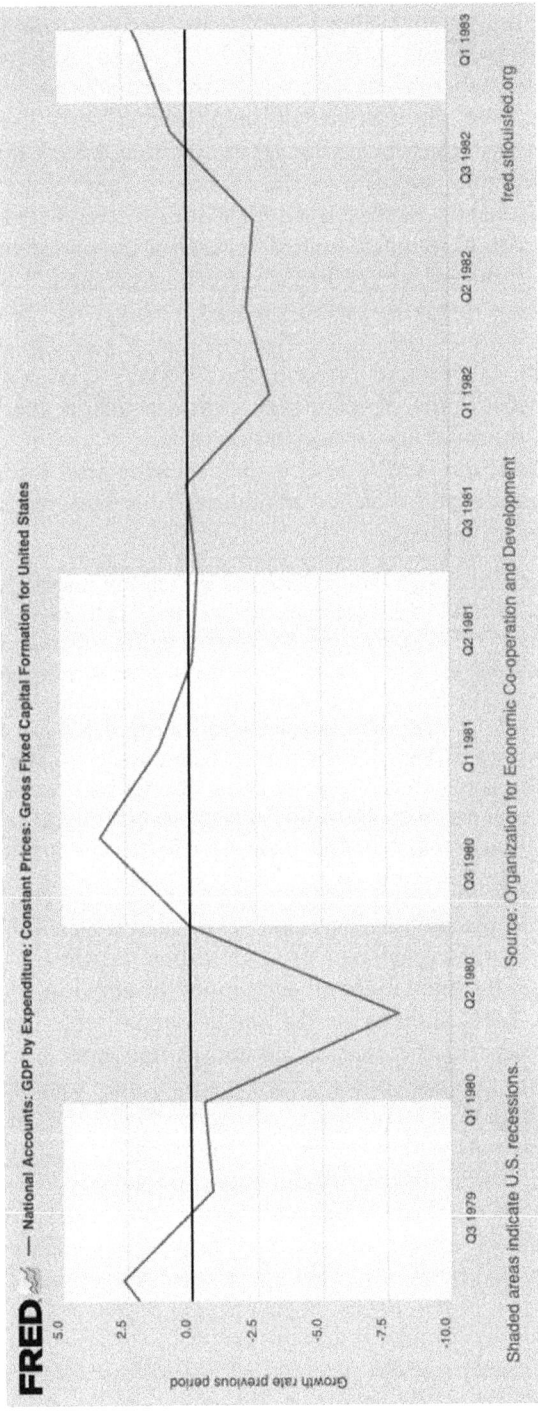

FIGURE 4.3 GDP in the United States.

transcripts clearly suggest that central bankers worried about the Fed's capacity to preserve its independence: "MR. GRAMLEY. (...) we just have to recognize that if we turn this economy around again and promote another decline in economic activity once the bottom has been reached, this country and the Congress may not have the tolerance to let us continue. I don't think it will."[71] After a drop in the money supply over the summer of 1980, Volcker pushed for tighter policy – against an increasing number of dissenting FOMC members – in the fall of 1980. In November, Jimmy Carter lost the presidential election – after a campaign during which the Fed's monetary tightening "certainly didn't help," as Volcker's memoirs acknowledged.[72] Later in November and December, Volcker nonetheless called two emergency meetings of the FOMC by conference call. In order to preserve the FOMC's chosen money supply targets, the Fed had to raise the caps that it maintained on interest rates as a safeguard against the volatility of monetary targets.

In February 1981, the FOMC held its first meeting after President Ronald Reagan's inauguration and Volcker summarized his sense of the mood on Capitol Hill for his colleagues:

CHAIRMAN VOLCKER. (...) I get this [criticism] all the time, of course, most specifically from the current Chairman of the Banking and Currency Committee. (...) He is in a mood where he says: "I don't give a damn where those money supply figures go, but you have too much volatility in interest rates." Now, that is one source of criticism. Everybody can unite on criticizing us on volatility. One group comes at it from the standpoint of instability in the money supply and another group comes at it from instability in interest rates. (But) you can't have it both ways, boys. You can criticize us for one or the other, but not both. Now, we know what the particularly monetarist oriented people are talking about. Mr. Garn has put it quite clearly, saying: "I'm sick and tired of all that monetarist business. I don't like these fluctuations in interest rates."[73]

That statement nicely illustrates the three main arenas that Volcker was considering. He had to placate the "monetarist oriented people." Here, Volcker referred to a group that gravitated around Milton Friedman, especially his circle within the professional arena of economics. In addition, Volcker had to worry about the Fed's support in the public arena. "Monetarist oriented people" were present in the Reagan administration and in Congress, but Volcker also had to consider public officials – including some Republicans – who were "sick and tired of all that monetarist business." And of course, Volcker had to navigate within the FOMC arena, where his colleagues were themselves also following debates about monetary targets and interest rates outside the walls of the Fed. While committed monetarists at the FOMC now wanted to double down on monetary targets, opponents to the Fed's tight-money policy, led by Teeters, strongly resisted that approach:

---

[71] FOMC meeting, September 16, 1980, pp. 37–38.   [72] Volcker and Harper 2018: 111.
[73] FOMC meeting, February 3, 1981, transcript p. 168.

4.3 Three Bumpy Years

MR. ROOS. If I may, Mr. Chairman, I'd like to go on record as favoring total elimination of the interest rate bands.

MS. TEETERS. Well, I find that hard to accept. (...) I think we're just abrogating our responsibility if we say we're not going to pay any attention at all to the interest rates.[74]

Meanwhile, the situation of the US economy continued to deteriorate. By the summer of 1981, there seemed to be little progress in the fight against inflation, and yet the economy was in deep recession. Although the Fed's internal discussions remained mostly focused on inflation, FOMC members were also clearly concerned about the continuing recession and the increasing difficulty of the manufacturing sector to compete with foreign manufacturers due to high interest rates and the US dollar's high exchange rate vis-à-vis other currencies.[75] This prompted a heated discussion about what the Fed should do:

VICE CHAIRMAN SOLOMON. Market people that I talk with feel that inflationary expectations are not down. That's a view among their clients as well as their own view. And, of course, that is corroborated by the long rates we see. So, I come back to a very pessimistic view. It seems to me that there's a good deal of likelihood that [the economy] will stay stagnant. (...)

MS. TEETERS. (...) I don't think we can live with these interest rates over that period of time without really causing a recession, the timing of which I'm uncertain about.

MR. WALLICH. (...) I think it would be surprising if we got out of this inflation without more sacrifice.[76]

At that meeting, the sacrificial view prevailed once again. Teeters was the sole FOMC member who cast a dissenting vote that day. Ultimately, the Volcker Fed implemented a painful disinflation, taking the US economy through major dislocation. Based on an analysis of transcripts, former Fed officials sympathetic to Volcker have argued that it took a remarkably long period of continuously tight policies for the Volcker Fed to establish its credibility – that is, to convince market actors that the Fed would stay the course despite the economic costs, rather than loosen its policy at the first sign of recession.[77] More critical accounts at the time have denounced "secrets of the temple" as undemocratic, and have more recently faulted the Volcker Fed for choosing "finance over factories" – aka "financialization."[78] What is beyond doubt is that manufacturing industries were decimated in America's Rust Belt, industrial unemployment skyrocketed, and economic inequalities increased. Even though employment was on par with inflation in the Fed's legal mandate, the Fed

---

[74] FOMC meeting, February 3, 1981, pp.54–55.
[75] Meeting of the FOMC, July 6–7, 1981, p. 10.
[76] Meeting of the FOMC, July 6–7, 1981, p. 28–31.
[77] Goodfriend and King 2005. On the importance of credibility as a topic of FOMC deliberations under Volcker, see also Schonhardt-Bailey 2013; Romer and Romer 2024.
[78] Greider 1987; Stein 2008; Krippner 2011.

remained laser-focused on price stability, which Volcker saw as "the ultimate responsibility of the Federal Reserve."[79]

4.3.2 The End of the Monetarist Experiment

By early 1982, inflation finally began to durably subside, but unemployment remained so high that FOMC members increasingly questioned the Fed's monetary targets. Nancy Teeters was at the forefront of that battle, against Lawrence Roos who was toeing Milton Friedman's line about the need to adopt a more purist version of monetarism:

> MS. TEETERS. I would say to Larry Roos that having gone to the reserve targeting and monetary aggregates targeting with a great deal of reluctance and skepticism, and having all the troubles and criticism that we have had, I am getting more and more to the point that I do not think it is the right way to conduct policy. (...) We have bounced this economy all over the mat for three years with no growth.
> MR. ROOS. Of course, Nancy, what disturbs me – and I say this with humility – is that I fear that what is being done may not produce the results we sought. Procedurally, I don't think we really are doing what ought to be done to conduct monetary policy in the way that those who wanted to target on reserve targets had sought initially. (...) And everybody, broad-brush, will say that the monetarist approach failed when I really do not think that we have conducted a true monetaristic experiment here. (...)
> MS. TEETERS. I have a much more practical point. I do not like what we have done to the economy in the past three years. I do not like 9 percent unemployment rates and I do not like interest rates in the 17 to 20 percent range.[80]

That battle within the organizational arena of the FOMC continued in the spring of 1982, even as the FOMC somewhat eased its money supply targets in response to lower inflation. Monetary easing was too fast for hawkish FOMC members like Henry Wallich, who were concerned about the risk of refueling inflationary expectations. But it was not fast enough for Nancy Teeters, who increasingly led the charge against monetary targeting: "[I]t seems to me utter foolishness to have 9.4 percent unemployment and a 15 percent federal funds rate (...) I've had it with the monetarist experiment."[81]

On October 5, 1982, the Fed abandoned money supply objectives and returned to its previous policy of defining interest rate objectives. The way it happened once again underscores Volcker's recourse to ambiguity as an instrument of leadership. Volcker first initiated a conversation about the severity of the recession in the United States – which would two months later cause a landslide midterm victory for the Democrats – and the difficult predicament of indebted countries. Well into the FOMC meeting, he then circulated a draft directive

---

[79] Volcker and Harper 2018: 106.   [80] FOMC meeting, February 2, 1982, transcript, p. 92.
[81] FOMC meeting, May 18, 1982, transcript p. 27. See also FOMC meeting, April 29–30, 1982, transcript p. 44.

4.3 Three Bumpy Years

without the usual monetary targets and asked members to react.[82] As the meeting progressed, it slowly dawned on FOMC members that Volcker was, in fact, proposing to end monetary targeting. Teeters immediately approved the move, while card-carrying monetarist Roos was clearly unhappy; others expressed concerns about credibility, but acknowledged that the recession was deep.[83] Volcker tried to reassure his committee – as he had done in 1979 – that the move would be "temporary" and was only intended to address "a one-quarter" risk that monetary targeting would force the Fed to raise interest rates in the midst of recession.[84] In the end, the FOMC approved Volcker's directive. The meeting was contentious, but not extraordinarily so. According to our automated count, the transcript contains eighty-one disagreeing statements, that is, 10.9 percent of all statements. Only three Fed district presidents dissented – but they objected to monetary easing rather than in defense of monetary targeting.

Beyond the organizational arena of the committee, there was also the question of how the Fed's move would be received by economists and by politicians. As FOMC vice chair – and former Treasury official – Anthony Solomon puts it: "I think this is a rather momentous FOMC meeting. (…) I recognize that there will be a good deal of questioning, not only in monetarist circles but more generally."[85] In part to assuage Roos and the monetarists at the FOMC and beyond, Volcker conceded that the Fed would "of course" continue its practice of publishing weekly M1 figures.[86] While minimizing the significance of the Fed's reversal, Volcker also highlighted the political stakes, namely the need for the Fed to protect itself against Congressional legislation that would diminish its independence:

I think we're also in a very critical period right now for all the reasons I suggested. (…) I don't think many people, if you take this out of the election atmosphere, are going to interpret this as a cave-in, in and of itself. Most people in the financial markets at least, to put it bluntly, think we've overstayed the course now. It gets into this great question of credibility that I suppose we're taking rather personally. At the risk of being misunderstood, following a mechanical operation because we think that's vital to credibility and driving the economy into the ground isn't exactly my version of how to maintain credibility over time.(…) But if one wants to put it in terms of risk to the institution: If we get this one wrong, we are going to have legislation next year without a doubt. We may get it anyway. (…) I'm not sure how it looks just in strict electoral terms, since that question has been raised, to sit here in some sense artificially doing nothing and then have to make a big move right after the election. I'm not sure that would wash very well in terms of anybody's opinion of our professional competence as an institution (…)[87]

---

[82] FOMC meeting, October 5, 1982, transcript, p. 29.
[83] FOMC meeting, October 5, 1982, transcript, pp. 40, 48.
[84] FOMC meeting, October 5, 1982, transcript, p. 31.
[85] FOMC meeting, October 5, 1982, transcript, p. 48.
[86] FOMC meeting, October 5, 1982, transcript, p. 41. According to Jacqueline Best, even US Treasury officials were not immediately sure that the Fed had abandoned monetarism (Best 2020: 608).
[87] FOMC meeting, October 5, 1982, transcript, p. 50–51.

To be sure, there were important practical reasons for the Fed's abandonment of monetary targets. The FOMC's decision to drop its practice of monetary targeting was due to shortcomings that were increasingly recognized by FOMC members. The Fed's timing was off, since it had adopted monetary targets at precisely the time when monetary aggregates had become more volatile due to financial deregulation – orchestrated, in part, by the Fed itself. The Fed was therefore unable to regulate the supply of credit: "[W]e were getting boxed in by money supply data," as Volcker himself later acknowledged in an interview.[88] The October 1982 FOMC transcript has been interpreted as a collective "sensemaking" exercise led by Volcker.[89] Yet after three years of sharp volatility and a major recession, the realization that monetary targets were not a panacea for monetary policy was hardly a scoop. In addition to a collective FOMC reckoning with their shortcomings, the abandonment of monetary targets that were now core to the Volcker Fed's brand required political work. What the transcripts clearly reveal is the changing internal as well as the external contests that contributed to that decision. These contests echoed the initial decision to adopt monetary targeting in 1979, but they played themselves out quite differently.

Just like the Fed's turn to monetarism, its abandonment of monetarism was a carefully crafted political exercise. By October 1982, Volcker was evidently concerned about his frequent spats with the Reagan administration and with Congress. This time, he wanted to avoid rocking the boat and thus further antagonizing politicians – unlike the Fed's October 1979 decision, when he had judged that the administration was "ready for a strong program."[90] In December 1982, the FOMC agreed on an innocuous open-ended statement, which later became a boilerplate for the published minutes: "In implementing monetary policy, the Committee agreed that substantial weight would continue to be placed on behavior of the broader monetary aggregates." In other words, monetary aggregates were no longer a key policy target, but they remained part of the Fed's policy framework. Only a decade later did Volcker's successor Alan Greenspan acknowledge that monetary aggregates had become irrelevant.[91] Since Volcker did not broadcast the failure of the monetarist experiment, the Volcker Fed's success in fighting inflation is often attributed to a successful monetarist strategy – even to this day.[92] As in his 1979 plea in favor of monetary targets, Volcker carefully navigated the FOMC's organizational arena, the arena of the economics profession, and most obviously the public arena of the Reagan administration and Congress. Yet that multidimensional politics of money is often overlooked both by scholars who stress either the continuing neoliberal and financialized external environment of Fed policies or the economic shortcomings of monetarist theory.

---

[88] Mehrling 2001: 450. See also Volcker and Harper 2018: 117–118.   [89] Abolafia 2005.
[90] Greider 1987: 540.   [91] Blinder 2022: 131.   [92] Best 2020: 597.

4.4 THE FED'S ADVOCACY OF FISCAL DISCIPLINE

An important ingredient in the 1980s rise of a powerful Fed was its support of fiscal discipline. That support is another signature legacy of the Volcker Fed – although less often recognized as such – and further justifies the common identification of neoliberalism as an inherently technocratic regime of political economy. In the 1980s, a new and uneasy tandem emerged between central bankers and conservative politicians on the question of fiscal policy. Even though the Federal Reserve has no power over fiscal policy, Volcker became a critic of the Reagan administration's fiscal deficits and an active advocate of fiscal as well as monetary conservatism. Volcker's advocacy thus caused a rift with the Reagan administration that also brought to light a rift between different neoliberal factions. This further underscored a reality that the politics of the Volcker Shock already illustrates. Far from being the seamless bloc that its advocates worked to present, the neoliberal policy regime that triumphed in the 1980s was thus actually a rather precarious assemblage of heterogenous elements, each with its own logic.

4.4.1 From the Volcker Shock to the Fed's Advocacy of Deficit Cutting

Volcker's memoirs mention a conversation with Reagan, shortly after the inauguration in 1981, during which "the conversation drifted off to [Volcker's] area of concern: the importance of getting the deficit under control."[93] Not coincidentally, that conversation occurred in response to Reagan's interrogation as to whether the Fed was "really needed." A few years later, after inflation was brought down, the Reagan White House's support to Volcker's tight-money policy began to wane. To understand this, we must observe what happened after the Volcker Shock. By 1982, even after the Fed managed to overcome high inflation and was able to lower the short-term interest rates that it charged to banks, long-term interest rates charged to private US borrowers remained high. For American central bankers, this was puzzling. Meanwhile, the combination of the Reagan tax cuts and increased military expenditures sent the federal budget deficit to the highest level since the end of World War II.[94] The FOMC started to seriously debate this issue in the summer of 1982.[95] At that point, Volcker expressed some understanding that Congress was unwilling to tighten the fiscal deficit as long as monetary policy remained tight.[96] In early 1983, FOMC members were increasingly worried that the fiscal deficit was "crowding out" private investment, because the government competed with private borrowers for a limited supply of capital.[97]

---

[93] Volcker and Harper 2018: 113.   [94] Blinder 2022: 151.
[95] FOMC meeting, July 7, 1982, transcript, pp. 92–97.
[96] FOMC meeting, July 7, 1982, transcript, p. 97.
[97] FOMC meeting, February 9, 1983, transcript pp. 17–19.

This discussion came to a head at a rather contentious meeting on July 13, during which FOMC members discussed a report from the Reagan administration's Treasury department that justified government deficits and downplayed their importance. Concerned as always about risks of inflation, Volcker asked his colleagues, "the policy question is whether we want to accommodate that."[98] At that meeting, the Fed decided to ease its monetary policy, but only slightly. Ever the hawk on the committee, Henry Wallich cast a dissenting vote because he wanted the Fed to tighten its monetary policy. He worried that the deficit created a credibility problem for the Fed in the eyes of market actors, since the Fed would be under pressure to lower its policy rates in order to ease borrowing conditions, instead of fighting inflation.[99] According to Wallich's reasoning, the high public deficit would fuel inflation through market fears that future deficits would be "monetized" – that is, financed by an excessively accommodative monetary policy, at the cost of greater inflation. But his concern about the fiscal deficit was widely shared among FOMC members. Even though Nancy Teeters ultimately cast a dissenting vote because she thought the Fed's policy remained too tight, she also worried about the deficit: "We haven't had deficits of this size as a long-term trend before."[100]

According to his biographer, Volcker then became convinced that long-term rates reflected market expectations that high budget deficits would sooner or later be monetized, and thus translate into more inflation.[101] In the fall of 1983, Volcker's desire to keep bringing inflation further down increasingly conflicted with what many on the FOMC saw as the threat of an "out of control" budget deficit.[102] In early 1984, the Fed started going public with its critique of the Reagan administration's budget deficit, issuing a press release that highlighted "the risks that unprecedented deficits in the federal budget posed for the sustainability of the economic expansion and the stability of financial markets, domestic and international."[103] By the summer of 1984, Volcker also took up this critique in his Congressional testimony – with encouragements from others on the FOMC:

CHAIRMAN VOLCKER. (...) I might say that as I look at the situation with the economy moving the way it is and the inflationary risks, yes, there's a possibility we might have to tighten.

VICE CHAIRMAN SOLOMON. Particularly since you guys aren't doing anything on the deficit!

CHAIRMAN VOLCKER. Particularly since anything on the deficit – and as I evaluate the great prospects for much easing. I might well.[104]

---

[98] FOMC meeting, July 13, 1983, pp. 37, 65.   [99] Greider 1987: 358, 360.
[100] FOMC meeting, July 13, 1983, pp. 37, 65.   [101] Silber 2012: 269.
[102] FOMC meeting, December 19–20, 1983, transcript, pp. 19, 23, 25, 30, 36, 38, 42, 43, 46.
[103] Federal Reserve, press release – record of policy actions, January 30–31, 1984, pp. 7–8. Throughout 1984–1985, many similar press releases expressed continuing Fed concerns about the budget deficit.
[104] FOMC meeting, July 16–17, 1984, transcript, pp. 70–71.

4.5 VOLCKER'S ROCKY RELATIONS WITH THE REAGAN ADMINISTRATION

The fact that, even after inflation abated, Volcker remained reluctant to ease monetary policy strained Volcker's relationship with the Reagan administration – especially with a looming presidential election in the fall of 1984. Volcker's memoirs characterizes as "cordial" his relationship with Reagan, who "understood the importance of our mission" and "the dangers of inflation."[105] Volcker was a Carter-appointed Democrat, but also, above all, a hawkish central banker. He was grateful for Reagan's firing of "thousands" of air traffic controllers and hailed their union's defeat as a "contribution to the fight against inflation."[106] Yet Volcker's memoirs also mention the White House's "reported grumblings about the Fed," as well as an "awkward meeting," in Reagan's silent presence, where Reagan's chief of staff Jim Baker told him: "The president is ordering you not to raise interest rates before the election."[107]

Scholars typically interpret the Volcker Fed's reluctance to ease and his advocacy of deficit cutting in two ways that are not necessarily incompatible – in terms of economics or in terms of political economy. According to Alan Blinder, Volcker reasoned in terms of the Fed's credibility as an inflation fighter, without taking into account the Fed's own tight-money policies in fueling high long-term interest rates.[108] In Greta Krippner's more political interpretation, partly based on interview evidence with former Reagan officials, Volcker continued to tighten money because he wanted to "force the administration back on the path of fiscal austerity" – until the administration was rescued by an unprecedented flow of foreign capital into US government bonds, which ended the "fiscal crisis of the state."[109] Although both interpretations make sense in their own terms, they shed little light on the politics of money, both internal and external to the Fed, that drove the Volcker Fed's remarkably strident support of fiscal conservatism and its later retreat from that advocacy.

Volcker's refusal to lower interest rates and his support of deficit cuts had earned him friends, not just enemies, in the public arena.[110] Within the Reagan White House, three factions quarreled over economic policy[111] – the monetarist faction, whose most extreme members thought the Fed should be abolished; the supply-siders who wanted to downsize the government and lobbied for tax cuts that would pay for themselves through higher growth (as justified by the "Laffer curve"); and the fiscal conservatives behind White House budget

---

[105] Volcker and Harper 2018: 113.   [106] Volcker and Harper 2018: 113.
[107] Volcker and Harper 2018: 118–119.   [108] Blinder 2022: 121, 184.
[109] Krippner 2011: 22, 96–97.
[110] Greider 1987: 556–569, 595–604, 607–609; Silber 2012: 207–215, 268–270; Prasad 2018; Blinder 2022: 133–151.
[111] Greider 1987: 364–368; Best 2020.

director David Stockman, who thought the deficit should be tackled by a combination of spending cuts and tax increases. Volcker's memoirs mention quarrels with Reagan's "staff of strong-minded monetarists and supply-siders, both critical of the Federal Reserve for their own reasons."[112] Milton Friedman, the leader of the monetarists, acted as informal advisor to Reagan, and as we saw created growing political difficulties for Volcker. So did the supply-siders, since they believed that fiscal deficits did not matter much. Yet Volcker had important allies among the fiscally conservative faction, especially David Stockman, the White House budget director.[113] In return for Stockman's support of the Fed's fight against inflation, Volcker supported Stockman's fiscal conservatism, especially against the supply-side faction within the administration. Although Reagan in principle supported the Fed's tight-money policies, fiscal conservatives progressively lost ground to supply-siders who favored tax cuts as well as increased government expenditures in some areas – usually military rather than social expenditures.[114] The supply-siders and other Fed critics judged that the Fed's continued high interest rates policies not only engineered the deep recession of 1982, but prevented a quick recovery and caused the fiscal deficit to increase. They faulted Volcker for playing a "game of chicken" with Reagan and thwarting his economic policies.

Over time, Volcker's aura declined inside the Reagan administration, but also within the Fed. In Reagan's close circle of advisers, Treasury Secretary Donald Regan and especially the White House chief of staff (and then treasury secretary) James Baker were dissatisfied with the Fed's tight-money policies. Volcker was accused of not being a good "team player" – a factor that weighed heavily in cabinet discussions about whether to reappoint Volcker for another term, first in 1983 and again in 1987.[115] After successfully taming inflation, Paul Volcker had a lot of political capital, so it was difficult for a conservative administration to openly disavow his action. Instead, the president appointed new Federal Reserve Board members who increasingly challenged Volcker's authority and tight-money policies. That became especially clear after the summer of 1984, when Martha Seger was appointed in June to fill the seat vacated in May by Nancy Teeters. Even though the Fed was already starting to ease in response to slowing economic growth, Martha Seger joined Preston Martin, the first Reagan appointee, in casting several stridently dovish dissents at the final FOMC vote tally.

The FOMC meeting of December 18, 1984 registers as relatively contentious with 9.9 percent contentious statements – bucking the Volcker Fed's trend line of declining contention over time. Seger even suggested that the Fed's policies were causing the economic slowdown: "I think the slowdown in the economy is real. That's all I'm saying. And I think there is some association between that

---

[112] Volcker and Harper 2018: 113.
[113] Greider 1987: 364–368, 515–516; Volcker and Harper 2018: 114.
[114] Greider 1987: 537–569.   [115] Greider 1987: 713–714; Silber 2012: 233.

4.5 Volcker's Rocky Relations with the Reagan Administration

and what happened to monetary policy (...)."[116] In early 1985, the internal battle continued. Volcker's ever-hawkish ally Henry Wallich then entered the fray: "We have no serious imbalances other than, of course, the terrible one – the budget deficit."[117] Wallich then engaged in a tense exchange with Preston Martin:

MR. WALLICH. Well, I don't see the setting of these targets as a means of accommodating the economy. We're setting the targets so as to shape the economy.

MR. MARTIN. I'd like to see us shape the economy with a 4 percent real growth rate, Henry.

MR. WALLICH. Well, that's not my objective.[118]

Powerful political and economic winds blew against Volcker and the FOMC's inflation hawks, however. In July, Volcker overtly deplored losing his main fiscally conservative ally in the Reagan administration: "CHAIRMAN VOLCKER. The comment made about the budget earlier is reinforced by the fact that I now read that Mr. Stockman has resigned as Director of the Office of Management and Budget. It's not encouraging to think that we'll have striking new vigor toward budget cuts."[119] Meanwhile, unemployment remained over 7 percent as the economy slowed down, and inflation below 4 percent no longer seemed as historically worrisome as in the early 1980s. Reagan appointees on the FOMC, especially Martha Seger, increasingly became vocal dissenters: "MS. SEGER. I guess I'm more concerned about the health of the economy than most of my colleagues. The sluggishness in some areas is actually almost to be described as a recession, if you look at certain parts of the industrial sector. And in Mr. Guffey's farm area I would almost call a depression. Looking at the strong dollar and the effect that it's having on the manufacturing sector, I would really like to push for something that is considered easing."[120]

By early 1986, two more Reagan appointees, Manuel Johnson and Wayne Angell, joined the Board of Governors. Reagan appointees were now a majority on the seven-member Board, and their conflict with Volcker quickly came to a head. In December 1985, Congress had adopted the Gramm–Rudman Act, which (optimistically) mandated a balanced budget within five years.[121] Coming straight out of Reagan's Treasury Department, Johnson immediately started downplaying the acuteness of the deficit problem: "Everybody has been waiting for this turning point on the budget situation, and I think we see it. (...) One of the major factors creating concern in the past was the potential for the budget and political environment to pressure this organization into partially monetizing the deficit and then inflation might result from that. I think some of

---

[116] FOMC meeting, December 18, 1984, transcript, p. 17.
[117] FOMC meeting February 12–13, 1985, transcript, p. 23.
[118] FOMC meeting February 12–13, 1985, transcript, p. 33.
[119] FOMC meeting, July 9–10, 1985, transcript, p. 18.
[120] FOMC meeting, July 9–10, 1985, transcript, p. 60.   [121] Blinder 2022: 177–179.

that pressure is starting to subside and I am fairly optimistic about that."[122] Wayne Angell, the other Board newcomer, made the case that declining energy prices signaled a weakening economy in which money was too tight. He claimed that the Fed should "let interest rates respond to economic forces," and he then framed an overt challenge of the Fed chair in the economics language of the "real" economy against Volcker's reference to "Keynesian" modeling:

MR. ANGELL. (...) If Messrs. Axilrod, Kichline and Prell can tell me that my concerns are unfounded and that the model really works – that the real growth occurs with no interest rate responses – I will feel much more at ease because I have a great deal of respect for their judgment.
CHAIRMAN VOLCKER. You may have less so for the Chairman's judgment. Let me say that I find the analysis of this oil situation a little ambiguous. (...)
MR. ANGELL. Well, would you explain to me what it is? I just don't understand. (...) The models that I have run and can think of – unless someone can point out another model to me – would suggest to me that the path toward expansion in the real sector is through a reduction in interest rates. (...)
CHAIRMAN VOLCKER. It depends upon your model. If you use a strictly Keynesian model, you get a big increase in purchasing power from the decline in oil prices.
MR. ANGELL. Well, I never use such models.[123]

Adding insult to injury, the "gang of four" Reagan appointees openly rebelled against Volcker at the Board meeting of January 24, outvoting him in favor of cutting the Fed's discount rate. After what he saw as a coup attempt, Volcker threatened to resign.[124] James Baker stepped in to avoid such disruption and convinced Volcker to stay. Shortly after that, Preston Martin resigned from the Board. The "gang of four" did succeed in ending Volcker's control of the Fed's agenda, however. After February 1986, there was barely any mention of the fiscal deficit at FOMC meetings. Volcker effectively became a lame-duck chair, especially after longtime Board members Henry Wallich and Emmett Rice resigned in December 1986. In the end, Volcker decided not to seek a third mandate, which was communicated as Volcker's "personal" decision. Paul Volcker was reportedly willing to serve again, however, but only under certain conditions.[125] Reagan's advisers pretended not to hear Volcker's "ultimatum," and were relieved when Volcker offered to resign. Evidently, Volcker's quasi-

---

[122] FOMC meeting, February 11–12, 1986, transcript, pp. 21, 54–56.
[123] FOMC meeting, February 11–12, 1986, transcript, pp. 54–56.
[124] Greider 1987: 700–701; interview with Manuel H. Johnson, Federal Reserve Board Oral History Project, June 15, 2010.
[125] Greider 1987: 713–714. Volcker's 2012 biography by William Silber and Volcker's 2018 autobiography do not echo this back-and-forth with Reagan advisers, however, and stick to the official story of "personal reasons."

heroic stature on Wall Street as well as Main Street made his exit a delicate matter for the Reagan administration.

4.6 THE VOLCKER LEGACY

In a sort of farewell statement to the FOMC at its July 1987 meeting, Paul Volcker articulated a few precepts that also help illuminate his legacy of an aggrandized Federal Reserve at the apex of US economic governance:

> I would certainly work on the budget deficit. There's not much we can do about it, but at least we get some protection on the growth of domestic consumption as well as on the financial side and interest rates. I worry about minimum wages and all that stuff. Now, when it comes to monetary policy, I would be cautious. I think it would be a big mistake not to be cautious.[126]

After his three-year inconclusive experiment with monetary targets, Volcker did not just return to the status quo ante. He built the Fed's reputation as a "cautious" inflation-focused institution. He was quite explicit about this in his memoirs: "Then, as now, we could not escape the fact that price stability is the ultimate responsibility of the Federal Reserve – and in my judgement of all central banks."[127] But he also did more than just refocus the Fed on the price stability side of its mandate. Even though Volcker's continued pressure on the Reagan administration to slash the budget deficit ultimately failed, fiscal conservatism won the moral argument. All US governments after the 1980s professed a desire to get deficits under control – even if they did not live up to that.

From an economics perspective, the Volcker Fed's unflinching focus on fighting inflation ushered in what economists later hailed as the "Great Moderation," a new monetary regime that combined low inflation and moderate interest rates. From a political economy perspective, and despite the failure of the monetarist experiment, the new monetary regime also went hand in hand with new economic policies. Attracted by high interest rates and a strong dollar in the early 1980s, investors flocked to US financial markets, including government bond markets. This influx was not without broader costs for the US economy, however. While US financial assets and services benefited from this capital inflow, many US manufacturing industries could not compete with foreign rivals. America's "sun belt" developed at the expense of its "rust belt" and at the cost of increased financial market volatility. Despite the Volcker Fed's responsibility in the recession of the early 1980s and in America's deindustrialization, its victory over inflation ultimately generated huge trust in and power for the Fed. The Fed-orchestrated pattern of finance-fueled growth continued beyond the Volcker years in the context of what Ben Bernanke later

---

[126] FOMC meeting, July 7, 1987, transcript, p. 43.   [127] Volcker and Harper 2018: 106.

called the "global savings glut," since foreign investors apparently had an unlimited appetite for US financial assets.

To secure his leadership and the Fed's new stature, Volcker carefully intervened in the organizational arena of the FOMC, in the professional economics arena, and in the broader public arena. Beyond their – blunt – usefulness in killing inflation, monetary targets also served to rally monetarist economists and to minimize political opposition. Once the monetarist experiment ended, Volcker had established that the Fed would be focused primarily on price stability and truly independent from the White House – unlike the Fed of the 1970s. Greenspan continued in the footsteps of Volcker and emerged as the "maestro" of the US economy.[128] Like Volcker in 1980 – when the Fed's rate hikes contributed to the electoral defeat of the president who had appointed him – Greenspan kept interest rates high through George H.W. Bush's reelection campaign in 1992.[129] And like Volcker vis-à-vis Reagan – although more successfully – Greenspan worked behind the wings to convince president-elect Bill Clinton to limit the extent of his fiscal stimulus.[130] His advocacy of fiscal conservatism also contributed to the Democrats' movement in that direction under Clinton. In this sense, Greenspan consolidated Volcker's legacy to further secure the Fed's broad aura of technocratic expertise.

4.7 CONCLUSION: THE FED'S SUPPORT OF NEOLIBERALISM

If we step back, we begin to see that the Volcker Fed oversaw the waxing of a novel regime of political economy that defies conventional political economy as well as economics perspectives. Political economy accounts often make it sound as if the Volcker Fed rode powerful financial and ideologically neoliberal forces that radically broke with the previous Keynesian regime. To adopt this perspective, however, is to reduce the Volcker Fed's role to that of a largely passive enabler of a new political-economic regime. It glosses over the fact that central bankers, starting with Paul Volcker himself, deftly navigated a thorny political as well as economic landscape. From an economics perspective, conversely, it is easy to dismiss "neoliberalism" as an inappropriate political label that does not reflect the failure of monetarism and the increasing influence of neo-Keynesian economic ideas at the Fed. Yet this perspective tends to reduce central banking to a primarily technocratic exercise and to downplay the Fed's participation in a multidimensional politics of money.

As I have argued, it took much more complex politics than is often recognized to put together the US version of technocratic neoliberalism. Volcker simultaneously sought allies at the FOMC, in the professional arena of economics, and of course in the public arena of "politics" conventionally

---

[128] Woodward 2000.   [129] Woodward 2000: 196.   [130] Blinder 2022: 187–188.

4.7 Conclusion: The Fed's Support of Neoliberalism

understood. When he became Fed chair, Volcker was inclined to tackle inflation in a hawkish manner, by prioritizing price stability above employment. But there were others on the FOMC who favored a more gradual approach against inflation. To outgun them, he initially allied with "monetarist" economists, and with conservative supporters in the public arena. That is when Volcker became a hero and burnished a durable conservative image for the Fed. Even though inflation was clearly a problem, the Fed's drastic turn to monetarist positions in contests over money was not overdetermined. In fact, it quickly ran into practical difficulties. After monetary targets proved hugely damaging for the economy, unreliable for the conduct of monetary policy, and potentially threatening for the Fed's independence, Paul Volcker changed his political tack to address these growing concerns. He lowered his guard against FOMC doves and quietly ended his alliance with the monetarists in the face of an increasingly hostile Congress and administration. Whether the Volcker Fed could have brought down inflation with different policies supported by a different alliance is impossible to know. What is clear is that the Volcker Fed's remarkably hawkish stance despite its growing costs, but also its willingness to quietly stand down, established the Fed at the helm of a durable alliance that entrenched a new and remarkably technocratic political-economic regime.

What the US politics of money in the 1980s clearly suggests, then, is that many truncated interpretations of the Volcker Fed's actions are ultimately misleading. In fact, the Fed's shifting alliances at the nexus of changing organizational, professional, and public arenas produced the emergence of a new and distinctive political-economic regime, which I have called technocratic neoliberalism. Under Paul Volcker, the Fed asserted itself as the leading policymaker in the US economy first by adopting and later by dropping monetary targets *and* by remaining focused on low inflation *and* by supporting fiscal conservatism. Insofar as it reverted to targeting interest rates without following a mechanistic rule, the Fed followed a discretionary practice of monetary governance that met the approval of mainstream Keynesian economists and thus can be legitimately understood as "Keynesian." At the same time, the Fed became much more fixated on low inflation, fiscal deficit cuts, and other neoliberal policies, and thus began to support a broader political-economic regime that can legitimately be labelled neoliberal. At that point, the Fed's "Keynesian" and "neoliberal" roles did not yet appear obviously contradictory. Only if we consider these roles together are we able to make sense of the multidimensional politics of money out of which technocratic neoliberalism emerged.

5

The Waxing of Technocratic Neoliberalism in the European Union

In the early 1980s, central bankers in Europe were confronted with inflation, like the Volcker Fed, yet in a radically different institutional context. In the absence of a federal structure at the European level, they worked in national central banks, most of which remained legally subordinate to their governments, and oversaw national currencies, whose exchange rates were for the most part pegged within a European Monetary System (EMS). By the late 1980s, a major shift toward a new monetary regime at the European level was in the works. Europe's central bankers came up with a basic blueprint for an Economic and Monetary Union around a single currency managed by an independent ECB, and for binding rules limiting member governments' budget deficits. Only a few years later, that Economic and Monetary Union (EMU) became a reality. On January 1, 2002, a new currency, the euro, began to circulate within and across twelve member countries. As euro coins and bills entered the daily lives of millions of people, the European Union suddenly became a much more tangible reality than ever before. The newly established ECB, a supranational body based in Frankfurt, was tasked with monetary policy geared toward the maintenance of price stability. While European member states of the Eurozone retained their national fiscal prerogatives, they now exercised the power of taxing and spending within the Stability and Growth Pact, a legally binding framework of multilateral fiscal surveillance.

This chapter investigates the role of central bankers in the birth of the euro, itself a fundamentally new monetary regime, and in the new neoliberal political-economic regime that this entailed at the European level. As I argue, we need to reconsider a conventional image of Europe's central bankers as an intellectually unified community that prepared a blueprint for a technocratic, depoliticized monetary union. To be sure, central bankers had network ties with a strand of neoliberal thinking that had been developing for decades in

European economic policy circles around the Mont Pélerin Society.¹ They generally favored tight money and fiscal prudence, and they had little trouble agreeing on the future ECB's independence and on its primary objective of monetary stability. In this generic sense, they were a unified community. At the same time, central bankers formed an arena traversed by important and distinctive cleavages. In addition to worrying about inflation like the Fed, Europe's central bankers in the 1980s faced another issue that the Fed did not have – namely, the presence of different sovereign currencies with recurrently unstable exchange rates. They hoped that monetary union would establish monetary stability, not only in the sense of fighting inflation but also in the sense of ending exchange rate instability. Yet they were fully aware that such a radical change as the creation of a new European money would also raise thorny issues of sovereign authority and political-economic regime.² Only later did they and other public officials paper over their differences as the euro came into existence, and as the ECB closed ranks to become the keystone of Europe's technocratic neoliberalism.

5.1 THE CONTESTED ARENA OF EUROPE'S CENTRAL BANKERS

It has long been known that Europe's central bankers were central characters in the genesis of the euro. The progressive opening, after thirty years, of ECB archives affords a direct examination of their deliberations.³ Until recently, those archives were not open, and scholarly works on the making of the Economic and Monetary Union from the 1980s through the early 1990s (including my own) relied by necessity on publicly available documents and interviews.⁴ In what follows, I focus on the transcripts of the most important and wide-ranging discussions that central bankers held on the future architecture of the Economic and Monetary Union, within the framework of the Delors Committee (July 1988–April 1989). As in the case of the Volcker Fed, I observe the politics of money among and around Europe's different national central bankers. I discuss the main lines of cleavage among central bankers, how these related to outside cleavages in professional and public arenas, and their role in Europe's adoption of a new monetary regime and a European version of technocratic neoliberalism. Unlike the Fed, these central bankers at the time did not yet make a single monetary policy within a unified and independent

---

[1] Foucault 2008; Burgin 2012; Mirowski and Plewhe 2015.
[2] As Christine Desan (2023: 79–80) puts it from the perspective of constitutional theory, "making money also makes the market" and "our market, including its operation, character, and material consequences, depends on the money that makes it." See also Desan 2014.
[3] The archives can be found on the ECB website: www.ecb.europa.eu/ecb/access_to_documents/archives/delors/html/index.en.html.
[4] An exception is the first study by economic historian Harold James of the work of the committee of central bank governors, which was commissioned by the ECB and for which it waived the 30-year embargo on its archives (James 2012: x).

ECB. Although they did not alone decide what the new monetary and political-economic regime would look like, the input they provided in the late 1980s in the form of the Delors Report was, as it turned out, crucial.

Scholars have primarily addressed the decision-making process that led to the creation of the euro from two perspectives. A first group of scholars have focused on converging economic interests in accordance with the "Mundell–Fleming" model in economics. In a world of increasingly mobile capital, markets placed pressures on national policymakers to forego their autonomy if they wanted to preserve fixed exchange rates.[5] National economic interests thus converged on an Economic and Monetary Union that entrenched market-friendly policies.[6] As Nils Thygesen, an economics professor who was also a member of the Delors Committee in 1988–1989, summarized it in hindsight: "[T]here was both a strong economic case for moving towards a single currency [...] no matter how desirable such a move might have seemed on political grounds."[7] A second group of scholars, by contrast, have foregrounded the broader political context – Germany's reunification and the end of the Cold War, but also and especially the ideational convergence among Europe's economic policymakers. From this political economy perspective, the euro institutionalized what Kathleen McNamara has called a "neo-liberal policy consensus" around Germany's "monetarist" model.[8] In the end, the euro marked "the triumph of technocratic elitism over the idea of political democracy."[9]

This chapter builds on existing work about the widely acknowledged role of central bankers, but it underscores the fact that they formed a much more conflicted arena than previously thought. From his study of committee of governors' archives, economic historian Harold James concluded that "there was an economic as well as a political logic behind the creation of the single currency."[10] Those two logics, however, did not foreclose the emergence of distinctive cleavages among central bankers about what the Economic and Monetary Union should look like.

To be sure, central bankers formed a community – many were veterans of the EMS negotiations of the late 1970s, and they met regularly in Basel, Switzerland as a committee of governors to coordinate their policies. Although Europe's national central bank governors undeniably looked like a close-knit "epistemic community," the archives that are now open do not suggest that they collectively promoted a "German model."[11] My archival analysis of central bankers' cleavages thus parallels and prolongs recent archive-based scholarly efforts that have challenged conventional accounts of the "monetarist" or "neoliberal" intents of central bankers in the run-up to the Economic and Monetary Union.[12] Contrary

---

[5] Frieden 1991; Eichengreen and Frieden 1998.   [6] Moravcsik 1998; Boix 2000.
[7] Thygesen 2016: 12. See also Gros and Thygesen 1998.
[8] McNamara 1998. See also Verdun 1999.   [9] Dyson and Featherstone 1999: 801.
[10] James 2012: 1.   [11] Verdun 1999.
[12] Bateman and Van't Klooster 2024; Mourlon-Druol 2025.

5.1 The Contested Arena of Europe's Central Bankers

to their consensual image, central bankers' dislike of inflation and preference for fiscal discipline did not prevent important disagreements that resonated with contests in the professional arena of economists and in the broader public arena of Europe's international and domestic politics.

Just as within the US Federal Reserve, some central bankers were clearly more "hawkish" or more "dovish" than others. But in Europe, a deeper and more apparent cleavage existed among central bankers who oversaw "weak" or "strong" currencies, in terms of their vulnerability to exchange rate crises within the EMS.[13] That cleavage manifested both the hierarchy and the instability of the EMS. The deutschmark was at the top of an informal currency hierarchy within the EMS, due to Germany's tendency to generate trade surpluses and to see its currency periodically revalued. If market actors believed that a realignment of exchange rates was imminent, they would try to profit from arbitrage opportunities, by selling or buying the various national currencies. This could result in large deviations between effective exchange rates and official EMS rates, also known as exchange rate crises. National central banks could then defend the official value of their currencies, but that required them to purchase their own currencies with foreign exchange reserves – if their currencies became objects of massive sell-offs – or, conversely, to flood the markets with their own currencies – if market actors flocked toward their currencies. Since foreign exchange reserves are, by definition, limited, currency speculation was most threatening to countries whose currencies were prone to being attacked and devalued, *alias* "weak currency" countries. Unless "weak currency" countries enlisted the help of "strong currency" countries, they could run out of reserves and find themselves forced to devalue their currencies within the EMS.

Reflecting this basic cleavage, the Committee of Governors that organized exchange rate coordination within the EMS in the 1980s was an arena traversed by latent and sometimes overt contests. As evident in Figure 5.1, disagreements peaked in times of currency crises in 1980–1983 and then again in 1986–1988, with a relative lull in 1984–1985 (both in terms of the absolute number and of the proportion of contentious statements per meeting). Some of the most contentious meetings took place before and after the Basel-Nyborg agreement of September 1987, which redefined the pegs between the different EMS currencies in an attempt to make the EMS more crisis-proof.

To understand this basic cleavage, we have to put ourselves in the shoes of central bankers of "weak" and "strong" currency countries. The central bankers who oversaw more vulnerable currencies dreaded the prospect of seeing their currencies attacked on financial markets, for two main reasons. First, maintaining the official EMS value of the currency in currency crises overshadowed all other goals of monetary policy. If their currency became

---

[13] For an analysis of EMS instability in an environment of "globalizing capital," see especially Eichengreen 1996: 136–187.

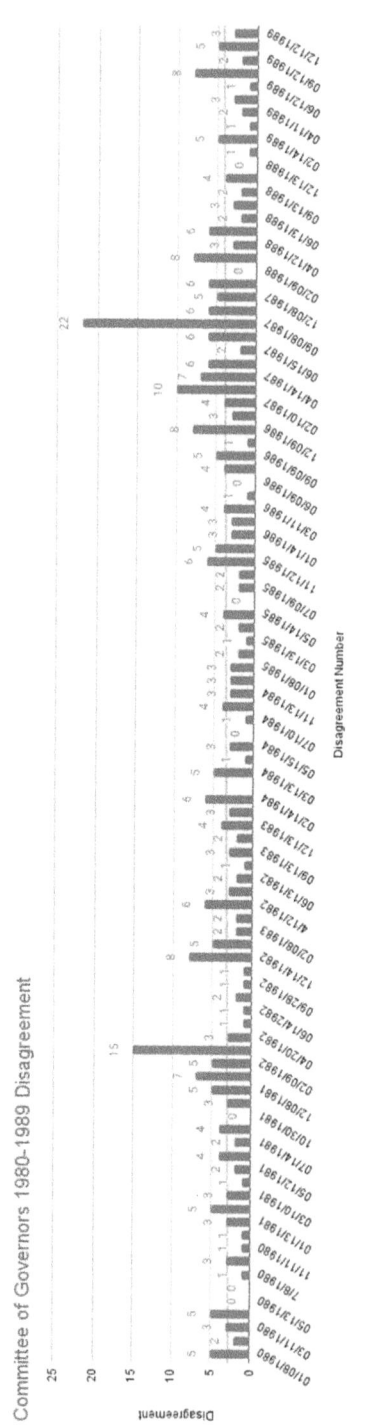
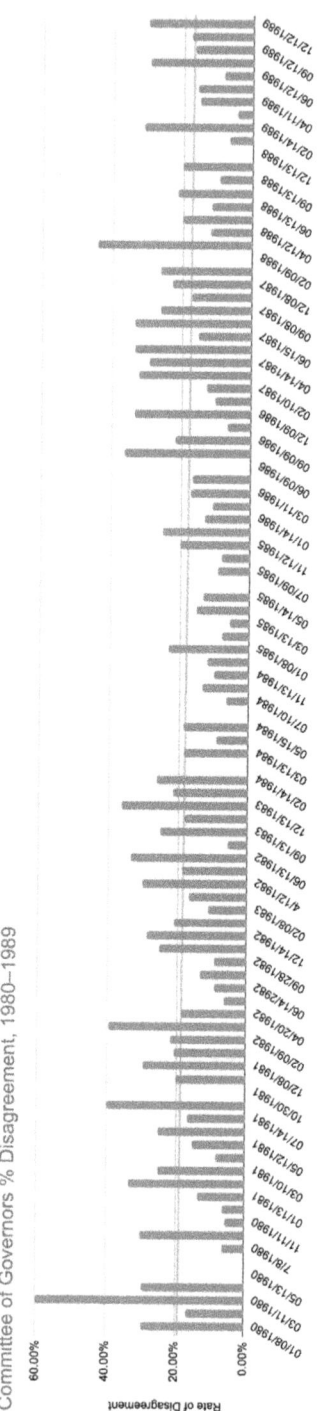

FIGURE 5.1 Disagreement on the Committee of Governors, 1980–1989.

the object of speculative attacks, central bankers had to considerably raise interest rates in the hope of attracting foreign capital into their currency, thus depressing domestic spending and growth. Second, central bankers found themselves in a hot seat when the national currency was attacked, because a devaluation was perceived as a politically fraught loss in national prestige. A devaluation also had material consequences, in the form of more expensive imported goods and foreign travel, and it had to be negotiated with other member states. Countries with stronger currency, by contrast, faced the threat of cheaper imports and decreased exports. They therefore demanded concessions in exchange for accepting the devaluation of vulnerable currencies, usually in the form of budget cuts and market liberalization to ensure greater "market discipline." In sum, central bankers of "weak" currency countries wanted to strengthen the EMS against the threat of market speculation, whereas central bankers of strong-currency countries mostly feared "imported inflation" from their "undisciplined" neighbors.

By the summer of 1988, two main camps within the central bankers' arena had emerged and became most vocal at meetings of the Delors Committee. The first camp, comprising mostly central bankers from strong-currency countries, was generally satisfied with the *status quo*. They used monetary policy to stabilize their own domestic economic cycles, and they wanted to minimize their own contribution to the preservation of the EMS. Bundesbank President Karl Otto Pöhl was clearly its leader on the Delors Committee, seconded by Dutch central bank president Wim Duisenberg. The second camp's primary goal was to strengthen the EMS due to the economic costs of interest rate hikes in currency crises, when central bankers from vulnerable currencies had to stem capital flight. The leadership of this second camp was more diffuse, but three men stood out: Delors himself, the chair of the committee, and the only committee member aside from Thygesen who was not a central banker; Alexandre Lamfalussy, the managing director of the Banque of International Settlements; and Banque de France Governor Jacques de Larosière, who knew that the French national currency remained vulnerable to speculation, despite France's policy of *franc fort* ("strong franc").[14] Ultimately, the Delors Report charted a compromise between the first camp's effort to preserve the status quo and the second camp's bid to end currency crises through monetary unification.

Latent discord sometimes became more acutely visible on the Delors Committee, especially – as Figure 5.2 suggests – in late 1988 and in the first semester of 1989, as the June 1989 deadline for the committee's report got closer. That conflict among central bankers was not simply an extension of the conflict between different national interests, however. First, Delors and Lamfalussy were inclined to favor greater EMS cooperation by virtue of their

---

[14] To be complete, there was also a third camp, reduced to Bank of England Governor Robin Leigh-Pemberton. But that camp mattered much less, since the United Kingdom was not yet fully in the EMS and had no plans to join the future monetary union.

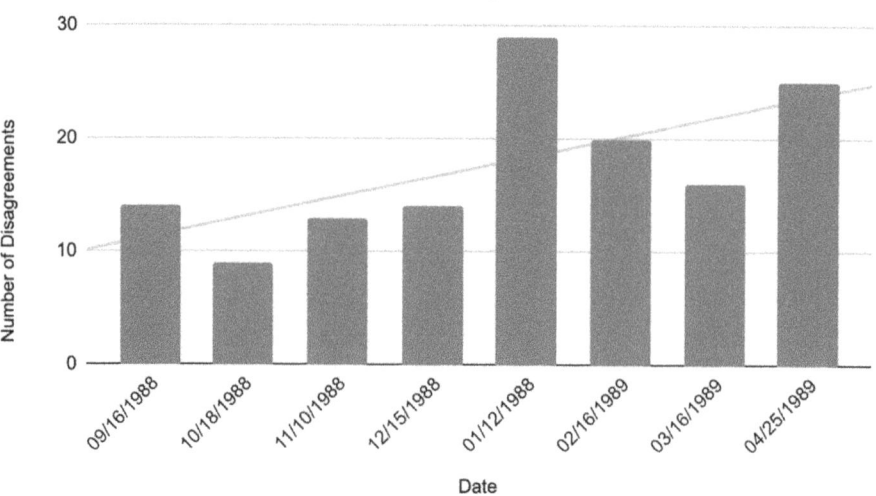

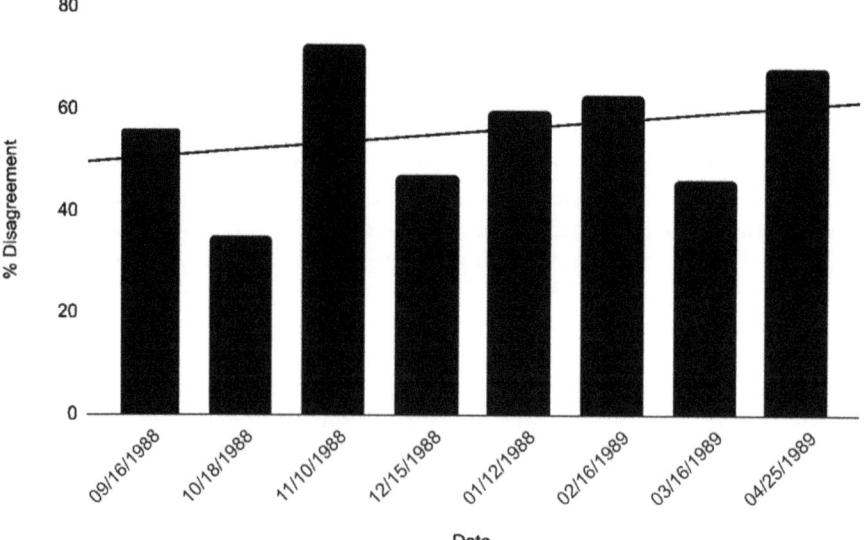

FIGURE 5.2 Disagreement on the Delors Committee, 1988–1989.

institutional roles as heads of the European Commission and the Bank of International Settlements. Second, national central bank governors were in an unusual situation, since they were appointed to the committee as "personal representatives" of their governments but, unlike diplomats, they did not receive negotiating instructions from their governments. For example, France's Jacques de Larosière accepted the principle of central bank independence, even though that position was beyond the pale in French government circles.[15] Perhaps even more remarkable, Germany's Karl Otto Pöhl found himself not only proposing a radical move toward a single currency, but also reluctantly accepting the logic of moving "irreversibly" toward it. Germany had long resisted that scenario, for fear that it would jeopardize German policy preferences. In hindsight, the fact that central bankers did not have precise bargaining instructions therefore enabled compromises between radically different positions that had eluded governments since the 1970s.

In the end, the Delors Committee paved the way for a monetary regime shift to the euro that would also trigger a broader political-economic regime change – namely, the emergence of a European version of technocratic neoliberalism. As we will see, Europe's central bankers painfully reached a compromise that involved what the Delors Committee discussed as "parallelism." On the one hand, progress toward an Economic and Monetary Union would liberate weak-currency countries from the threat of currency crises. On the other hand, progress toward free capital movements would reassure strong-currency countries that the future currency would be built on economic convergence and "market discipline." In this sense, monetary union and market reforms were the product of a *political* linkage, rather than a convergence of economic interests or ideas. It is impossible to understand the European progress toward the liberalization of capital movements without seeing the attraction of an Economic and Monetary Union for weak-currency countries. Conversely, it is impossible to understand the institutional design of the euro without considering the need to reassure strong-currency countries – especially Germany – that Economic and Monetary Union was not just a hostile takeover of their cherished currency by reckless partners. The main internal driver of the Delors Committee was therefore its recognition of this political linkage – even though that recognition was mostly papered over in public. The need to keep Economic and Monetary Union on track during a decade of difficult negotiations then powered a move toward a broader neoliberal political-economic regime, with technocrats at its helm.

5.2 THE "PARALLELISM" BETWEEN ECONOMIC AND MONETARY UNION

On the surface, the Delors Committee looked like another round of recurring discussions of monetary unification that had taken place since the dawn of the

---

[15] As Harold James (2012: 276) points out, the French governor got into trouble with the then-director of the French Treasury, Jean-Claude Trichet, who accused him of betraying French interests.

European integration process in the 1950s. It occurred in the context of the EMS, itself the product of a 1979 agreement to stabilize exchange rates between different European currencies.[16] The EMS was essentially a regional substitute for the defunct global Bretton Woods regime. It symbolized both a step toward the further political integration of Europe and a shared resolve between French President Valery Giscard d'Estaing and German Chancellor Helmut Schmidt to re-establish regional monetary stability and to fight inflation. In May 1981, however, Giscard was defeated by François Mitterrand, a socialist running on an anti-austerity platform. In the global disinflationary context of the Volcker Shock, Mitterrand's reflationary policies quickly prompted market speculation against the French franc.[17] In March 1983, Mitterrand decided against the option of leaving the EMS, choosing instead to devalue the French franc.[18] In exchange, the French government assured Germany and other EMS partners that France would adopt *rigueur* – a euphemism for fiscal retrenchment. After 1983, this reorientation was de facto institutionalized as a permanent feature of French economic policymaking. This evolution is best epitomized by the personal trajectory of Pierre Bérégovoy, originally an advocate of EMS exit who later became, as finance minister and then prime minister, the staunchest advocate of a "*franc fort*" policy. As they adopted various neoliberal policies to defend the value of the French franc on financial markets, French policymakers repeated that there was "no alternative."[19] The return to floating exchange rates, in particular, was equated with the foreclosed option of France peeling away from its European partners.

This episode was still fresh in the minds of Europe's central bankers when they sat down in the summer of 1988 in Basel for the first meeting of the Committee for the Study of Economic and Monetary Union – better known as the Delors Committee. Members of the Delors Committee had front-row seats to the divisive exchange rate crises within the EMS. In the early 1980s, the Banque de France had, in compliance with the EMS, spent foreign exchange reserves to defend the franc's parity with the deutschmark, and had lobbied within the French state in favor of fiscal discipline.[20] Although Jacques de Larosière had only been governor of the Banque de France since 1987, he had been the managing director of the IMF and director of the French treasury under Giscard before that. Likewise, Karl Otto Pöhl had been finance minister under Schmidt, who later appointed him as president of the Bundesbank; he had witnessed the recurrent exchange rate crises within the EMS since its inception. Delors, the chair of the committee, had successfully advocated the turn to *rigueur* as Mitterrand's finance minister during the March 1983 EMS crisis, before becoming president of the European Commission in 1985. A fervent advocate of European integration, Delors had convinced European leaders in June 1988 to appoint him as committee chair, and to mandate the

---

[16] James 2012: 146–180; Mourlon-Druol 2012.
[17] Dyson and Featherston 1999: 317–318; Warlouzet 2018. [18] Parsons 2003.
[19] Fourcade-Gourinchas and Babb 2002: 569. [20] James 2012: 192.

committee "to study and propose concrete stages leading towards economic and monetary union."

5.2.1 The Delors Committee and the Issue of Capital Liberalization

The Committee's recommendations, published in April 1989, are well known. The Delors Report, as it was called, articulated a sequence for the Economic and Monetary Union, with three "stages," and the recommendation that "the decision to enter upon the first stage should be a decision to embark on the entire process."[21] The timing of that sequence, in turn, was left to the discretion of European leaders, but the Report recommended that the first stage "should start no later than 1 July 1990 when the Directive for the full liberalization of capital movements come into force."[22] This may have seemed like an innocuous step when the Delors Report came out, since European finance ministers had already unanimously adopted in June 1988 a directive that legally committed the member states to fully liberalize capital movements. Yet that directive itself was a radical move. To this day, scholars often find it puzzling that Europe's political leaders took such a radical decision with apparently little concern for its ramifications.[23] Capital controls had been central to the Bretton Woods era and remained in place in most of Europe until the late 1980s, thanks to an escape clause to the 1957 European Treaty that mandated freedom of capital movements "to the extent necessary for the proper functioning of the Common Market."[24] Among European member states, only Germany, the Netherlands, and the United Kingdom had fully lifted their capital controls before June 1988. In other words, it was a reality only in the country whose currency was the "anchor" of the EMS, in its closest partner, and in a large country outside the EMS. This was not a coincidence. Within the EMS, capital controls enabled central bankers in charge of vulnerable currencies to better weather the tide of market speculation in case of currency crisis. Of course, they knew that the various forms of capital controls were becoming increasingly porous and ineffective at curbing cross-border capital flows in times of currency crisis.[25] Yet the rationale for retaining capital controls had not disappeared, since they still represented a guarantee for exchange rate stability within the EMS.[26]

Capital liberalization in Europe can only be understood if we consider its linkage to the process of monetary unification. European leaders formed the Delors Committee at exactly the same time as they decided to move forward with capital liberalization. From Delors' perspective, but also for other committee members who wanted to strengthen the EMS, the task was to establish what he kept referring to as the "parallelism" between economic and monetary union – a principle taken from the 1970 Werner Report, which was tabled for

---

[21] Delors Report, p. 27. [22] Delors Report, pp. 30–33. [23] Piketty 2020: 553.
[24] Rome Treaty, article 67. [25] Goodman and Pauly 1993.
[26] Giavazzi and Pagano 1988; Gros and Thygesen 1988.

discussion at the first meeting of the Delors Committee. At the second meeting, Delors highlighted the objective of achieving a "sort of magical square" between free trade, free capital movements fixed exchange rates, and a common monetary policy.[27] At the same time, he dramatized the stakes of the committee's work:

> Deep inside, do you believe that there will really be a full liberalization of capital movements for eight countries on July 1, 1990, and that there will be an internal market in early 1993 – do you believe it? [...] If some of you believe that without any more other changes there will be on July 1, 1990, a full liberalization of capital movements and in early 1993 a large market without borders, I believe you are mistaken.[28]

The method of "parallelism" was an old European recipe for engineering integrationist "spillovers," closely related to the well-known method of "linkage" in international negotiations (or "log-rolling" in parliamentary negotiations).[29] Policymakers would identify several individual issues where there was an apparent deadlock, and then they would break that deadlock by negotiating a compromise package on several issues at the same time. Since the early 1980s, German and Dutch monetary officials had refused to consider other countries' requests to strengthen the EMS before these countries liberalized capital movements and submitted their economic policies to the test of "market discipline."[30] Banque de France's governor de Larosière noted that the freedom of capital movement would make economic union "much further advanced than at Werner's time," but he called parallelism a "very powerful idea" because capital liberalization could be linked with a strengthening of the EMS. He thus expressed a widespread perception among French public servants that international capital liberalization must be "governed."[31]

The linkage between capital liberalization and monetary union made sense because the different camps held radically different views on these two topics. Dutch central banker Wim Duisenberg deplored an "insufficient convergence of government finance" and called for a broad "transfer of sovereignty." Pöhl expressed support for "something close to a European Central Bank," while at the same time relegating it into an indefinite future: "[N]obody I think is seriously expecting that the European governments or parliaments would be ready today to pass, to transfer substantial sovereignty rights."[32] At the second meeting, Pöhl tabled an ambitious proposal of a full-fledged federal union around a single currency. Over subsequent meetings, however, it became clear that Pöhl himself was ambivalent about the realism of his own maximalist proposal: "[I]n my country I could easily describe what would come close to a

---

[27] Delors Committee, Meeting on October 10, 1988, p. 16 (my translation).
[28] Delors Committee, Meeting on October 10, 1988, p. 17 (my translation).
[29] Haas 1958; Coombes 1970; Haas 1980.   [30] Bakker 2012.   [31] Abdelal 2007.
[32] Delors Committee, Meeting on September 13, 1988 (transcript), pp. 6, 10; Meeting on November 11, 1988, p. 13.

5.2 The "Parallelism" between Economic and Monetary Union

revolution if (...) the right to decide on interests rates (...) should be transferred to an institution in Basel, Strasbourg, Brussels, or wherever, it would create a lot of problems. The same would happen in countries where the finance ministers have that competence which they wouldn't like to transfer to this committee."[33] In response to Pöhl's skepticism, France's de Larosière unexpectedly replied that he was open to the idea of independent central banks across Europe: "I am going to tell you something which is a little bit the reverse of what you have in your view: (...) what I am suggesting in my paper implies (...) a profound modification of the relationship between the governing body of the Banque de France and the Ministry of Finance. (...) Don't you think Europe would be stronger with central banks that would be more independent (...)?"[34]

The back-and-forth between committee members over the next few meetings is remarkable because the positions voiced at the end of 1988 changed relatively little after that. Most of the meetings were devoted to deliberations in which individual members formulated their respective positions and tried to build alliances with others. Pöhl claimed to be defending the "realistic" or "median" view, and tried to paint opposing views as "extreme" or "futuristic," while de Larosière worked hard to reject that label and to lean on other committee members.[35] The main action from January through April 1989 was about the way in which the Delors Report would be drafted. In the end, Pöhl suggested, with Duisenberg's support, the possibility that the Delors Report elaborate two alternative scenarios, "A" and "B." In the name of "realism," Pöhl and Duisenberg favored a scenario that may go all the way to full-fledged federal union in the future, but with few if any steps along the way. The possibility of a full-fledged monetary union could then be revisited at a later stage, after national economic policies had converged. By contrast, France's de Larosière proposed to adopt institutional steps upfront, including a pooling of foreign exchange reserves within a "European Reserve Fund" to protect weak currencies from speculative attacks – an idea that Banca d'Italia Governor Carlo Ciampi supported. Pöhl adamantly opposed it: "I don't think we need major institutional changes, for instance, in order to avoid a crisis in the EMS if it would happen."[36]

Yet Pöhl was constantly pressed by other committee members on the risk of an increased instability of the EMS, due to increasing capital mobility. Ciampi underscored, with Delors' and Lamfalussy's strong support, his preference for a unique scenario in order to give more weight to the Delors Report and its plea in favor of strengthening the EMS.[37] As head of the Bank of International Settlements, Lamfalussy also spoke out in favor of moving quickly toward

---

[33] Delors Committee, Meeting on November 8, 1988, p. 14.
[34] Delors Committee, Meeting on November 8, 1988, p. 19.
[35] Delors Committee, Meeting on April 12, 1989, pp. 1–4.
[36] Delors Committee, Meeting on January 10, 1989, p. 18.
[37] Delors Committee, Meeting on January 10, 1989, p. 16.

greater coordination between national central banks within the EMS. In his view, central bankers should be able to engage in "an ex ante coordination effort of monetary policies."[38] Pöhl's adamant disagreement to such a scheme brought him in opposition with de Larosière and Ciampi, in addition to Lamfalussy and Delors: "I am not sure, Alexandre, that we have really agreed an ex ante coordination of monetary policies, this is not in the text and I would not be able to deliver, because this would not be consistent with the existing laws in the Fed[eral] Rep[ublic] of Germany which I have to obey."[39] In the end, Pöhl did not insist that the Report should put forward two distinct scenarios, and he endorsed the linkage that the Delors Report established between capital liberalization and monetary union through its advocacy of an "irreversible" commitment to its three-stage sequence. Meanwhile, the Delors Report mentioned de Larosière's pet idea of a European Reserve Fund, but only as a possible option for the first stage – an option that would be quietly shelved in subsequent treaty negotiations.

5.2.2 The Delors Committee and the Thorny Issue of Sovereignty

For central bankers, a thorny issue that came up repeatedly was the need to remain technical, rather than infringe on the "sovereign" or "political" prerogatives of governments and elected officials. To the extent that the Delors Committee agreed on broad epistemic principles, these certainly had to do with their institutional identity as technocrats. Early on, Delors had cautioned against "a mechanism that would abstract from economic history, from the traditions of our countries, and the reluctance to concede sovereignty transfers."[40] All central bankers and Delors were also keenly aware of the boundaries within which they had to remain if they wanted politicians to take their advice seriously. Yet the border between what is technical and what is political was hotly contested.

This issue came to a head during the March 1989 meeting. Although an automated count yields only a moderately high number of disagreements (sixteen), a manual reading of the transcript reveals their *intensity*. Committee members who were present remember that the discussion "almost derailed."[41] At that meeting, Pöhl pointed out that the German government has issued "a warning against premature institutional changes." As he put it: "I don't know about France, I don't know whether governments in Europe are prepared at this stage to negotiate a Treaty which would imply far reaching transfers of sovereignty rights."[42] De Larosière fired back: "I think we have to count ourselves, you cannot speak for everybody. I could accept the proposal

---

[38] Delors Committee, Meeting on March 14, 1989, p. 2; Delors Committee, Meeting on March 14, 1989, p. 14.
[39] Delors Committee, Meeting on April 12, 1989, p. 20.
[40] Delors Committee, Meeting on September 13, 1988, p. 22.   [41] James 2012: 253.
[42] Delors Committee, March 14, 1989, transcript, pp. 4–5.

5.2 The "Parallelism" between Economic and Monetary Union

that we embark on a Treaty, I could accept that."[43] A little later, an especially tense exchange occurred between Delors and Pöhl on the appropriateness for central bankers to adopt what Delors saw as a "political" rather than a "technical" stance on EMU membership:

THE CHAIRMAN: (...) As for participation, membership, there is disagreement. (...) Anyway if you say that one will be able to go in for EMU only if everybody is part of the EMS then you are taking up a political and not only a technical position.
HERRN K.O. PÖHL: I haven't said that, Mr Chairman, that is really unfair. That is a misinterpretation of what I have said. (...)
THE CHAIRMAN: That is not unfair (...)[44]

One area where the Delors Committee foresaw a complicated division of labor between central bankers and politicians was the coordination between monetary and fiscal policy. Central bankers did not seem to have too much difficulty with Pöhl's definition of the ultimate stage of monetary union as the achievement of a single currency. They were able to imagine an independent ECB that would make monetary policy for the future shared currency. They figured that balance of payment deficits in a single monetary area would be less problematic than between countries with different currencies. The Irish central bank governor, Maurice Doyle, worried that in an Economic and Monetary Union, Ireland could "turn into the national park of Europe" if nobody invested there and its people migrated.[45] Yet Delors pointed out – and others agreed – that uneven development existed within the member states and did not jeopardize their monetary integrity. As long as Europe adopted policies that extended investment opportunities in less economically developed regions, the different member states could move together, led by the dynamism of core regions. To finance such "structural" policies, the Delors Committee envisioned a somewhat larger European budget, amounting to 3–5 percent of Europe's GDP up from 1 percent at the time. Central bankers were therefore optimistic on the prospect of a sizable common budget and, in hindsight, did not anticipate future tensions between the "core" and the "periphery" of the eurozone.

While many committee members welcomed fiscal federalism, they clearly worried about fiscal deficits and debts. They had trouble imagining "sovereign" governments agreeing on something like a common fiscal policy stance as a counterpart to the single monetary policy. As Wim Duisenberg put it as early as the first meeting of the Delors Committee: "[I]t cannot be denied we have deep differences of opinion on the nature and the measure wherein there has to be a transfer of sovereignty to a centralised institution, whether it be in a federal form or completely centralised."[46] Even with a somewhat expanded central

---

[43] Delors Committee, March 14, 1989, transcript, pp. 4–5.
[44] Delors Committee, March 14, 1989, transcript, pp. 7–8.
[45] Delors Committee, October 10, 1988, transcript, p. 12.
[46] Delors Committee, September 9, 1988, transcript, p. 5.

budget, many believed that most of Europe's fiscal powers would remain sovereign national prerogatives. By December 1988, however, they started discussing the coordination of national fiscal policies. As Delors summarized it, it was "very difficult to have an economic union if the differences are too great between our various countries," so there was a need for "not a uniform system – but a framework and the Community budget would play the role of an instrument which could encourage or control."[47] This is how the Delors Committee came to discuss rules that would keep the member governments in line with a fiscal position that they would define in common.

Although the design of the Economic and Monetary Union was later often described as "technocratic" or "ordoliberal," central bankers on the Delors Committee actually went out of their way to respect the space for "sovereign" decision-making on fiscal matters. Delors liked the idea of a new institution: A "centre for economic policy would fix the fiscal constraints, would implement joint policies based on the Community budget and would define the policy mix" of Europe's monetary and fiscal policies.[48] In his mind, the common rules were not rigid straightjackets, but safeguards against the temptation of conducting reckless fiscal policy: "We cannot forecast with absolute accuracy what is likely to happen during the next 50 years, but the committee clearly wishes to combine the two ideas: binding rules together with a comprehensive attitude towards the situation in each country and the domestic mechanism which will enable these deficits to be financed and which will lead towards greater convergence."[49] He also recognized that a central fiscal institution was a sensitive issue beyond the committee's strict mandate: "Suddenly one finds that one goes beyond the mandate that was given us and starts thinking about the future of the Community institutions in the long term. Do we really wish to open that Pandora's box?"[50] In the end, the Delors Committee decided to leave this question to the member governments:

THE CHAIRMAN: (...) if we propose a new institution on the economic side, that means a revolution in the institutional framework of the Community. This is my problem.
M. J. DE LAROSIÈRE: Yes, I know, we mustn't provoke them. We must say that it is a question.[51]

The question of sovereignty also came back in the controversial March 1989 meeting. The word "sovereignty" (or "sovereign") was explicitly mentioned four times in that meeting. Lamfalussy pointed out the problem that overshadowed the whole meeting, namely the absence of a single fiscal counterpart to the future ECB: "[Y]ou know perfectly well that there is no budgetary

---

[47] Delors Committee, December 15, 1988, transcript, p. 8.
[48] Delors Committee, December 15, 1988, transcript, p. 15.
[49] Delors Committee, February 14, 1989, transcript, p. 10.
[50] Delors Committee, December 15, 1988, transcript, p. 15.
[51] Delors Committee, February 14, 1989, transcript, p. 20.

committee comparable to the Governors and with independent sovereign states that doesn't mean much."[52] In the end, the Delors Report remained relatively vague on economic union, but asserted the principle of "subsidiarity," that is, the notion that decisions must be taken at the most appropriate level – a tacit acknowledgment that fiscal sovereignty was not going to go away.

5.3 THE MOMENTUM BEHIND MONETARY UNIFICATION IN THE PUBLIC ARENA

If we now zoom further out from the central bankers' arena to consider the issue of sovereignty from the perspective of politicians, the political momentum of EMU in the public arena also becomes easier to understand. As we saw, Delors highlighted a "magical square" to central bankers, which was reminiscent of what economists call the Mundell–Fleming "inconsistent trinity" between fixed exchange rates, free capital movement, and national policy autonomy. This inconsistent trinity can be intuitively understood as a conflict between financial markets and sovereign nations in a world of capital mobility.[53] If market actors are free to move their money across borders and think that a particular country's interest rates are too low or government deficits too high, there is nothing to prevent capital flight toward a currency that offers higher returns on capital. If they want to avoid an exchange rate crisis and a devaluation, central bankers lose policy autonomy since they are forced to raise interest rates.

In strictly economic terms, prioritizing an exchange rate objective was perfectly possible. Foregoing national monetary policy autonomy and "tying one's hands" to the German currency "anchor" was a viable option within the EMS.[54] That is basically how the gold standard had historically operated. The French, in particular, had remained attached to it well into the 1960s and 1970s.[55] Thus, many prominent economists remained skeptical at the time whether the balance between the costs and benefits of monetary union was clearly positive.[56] Within the Delors Committee, Belgian central banker Jean Godeaux quite candidly explained to his colleagues that, after a devaluation in 1982, the Banque Nationale de Belgique's "policy" consisted in accepting "that our currency would remain in a mediocre position within the European Monetary System so as to avoid having politicians tell us: 'now we don't have problems any longer, so we can stop our efforts.' In fact, efforts must still be made on the fiscal side."[57] Of course, targeting an exchange rate to the deutschmark could be costly, since the alignment of Belgium's monetary policy

---

[52] Delors Committee, March 14, 1989, transcript, p. 2.   [53] Mundell 2002.
[54] Giavazzi and Pagano 1988.   [55] Jabko and Schmidt 2022: 641–642, 649.
[56] Eichengreen 1992. For a more positive assessment (albeit commissioned by the EU), see Emerson, Gros, Italianer, Pisani-Ferry, and Reichenbach 1992.
[57] Delors Committee, Meeting on October 10, 1988, p. 14.

with Germany's could be inadequate for the Belgian economy. But as Godeaux explained, it also presented the benefit of keeping pressure on "politicians" to keep making fiscal "efforts" rather than expand Belgium's fiscal deficit and potentially fuel inflation. On balance, the fact that the deutschmark became the dominant currency of the EMS was not necessarily an economic problem. To ensure monetary stability, the EMS did not require that its constituent currencies have equal status.

Yet from a *political* standpoint, the renunciation of monetary autonomy could be difficult to swallow. A subordination to the yellow metal is easier to accept than a subordination to your next-door neighbor – especially if we are talking about France's subordination to Germany. For historical and electoral reasons, the preservation of national monetary autonomy remained a potent symbol as well as a policy objective. Ever since the creation of the EMS, successive French governments consistently but vainly tried to prevent its evolution into a de facto "deutsche mark zone"[58] – just like de Gaulle's France had previously resisted the evolution of the Bretton Woods system into a dollar standard unmoored from gold in the 1960s. Meanwhile, the Bundesbank had successfully thwarted the project of a European Monetary Fund that could dilute its monetary leadership.[59] While small countries like Belgium and even the Netherlands could accept living in a deutschmark zone, and even turn it to their advantage, the bigger states like France – and also Italy, which remained partly outside the system – increasingly perceived it as an unacceptable subordination to German power.[60] This was not what the EMS – and more generally the integration of Europe – was supposed to be about when French and German leaders had created it in the 1970s.

In 1987, French politicians therefore started to intensify their pressure for a reform of the EMS. In January of that year, a currency crisis within the EMS forced France to devalue and to raise interest rates, despite its unflinching commitment to the "franc fort" policy. French finance minister Edouard Balladur authored a *Financial Times* article titled "EMS: Advance or Face Retreat."[61] At that point, Balladur was pleading for "strengthening the EMS" and reducing its "asymmetry" to a relatively narrow audience of European policy elites.[62] By 1988, monetary reform was one of the issues at stake in France's election campaign.[63] France's Prime Minister Jacques Chirac – the leader of the Gaullist party – declared that unless the EMS were strengthened, "it would be better to abolish it."[64] In the 1970s, the Gaullist opposition to

---

[58] Mourlon-Druol 2012.   [59] James 2012: 181, 388.
[60] Author interviews with Belgian and Dutch central bankers.
[61] "EMS: Advance or Face Retreat," *Financial Times*, June 17, 1987.
[62] James 2012: 220, 227–228.
[63] "Barre, Balladur, Bérégovoy: Les projets des '3 B,'" *La Tribune de l'Expansion*, April 22, 1988.
[64] "M. Chirac annonce qu'il prendra des initiatives dans le domaine monétaire," *Le Monde*, January 9, 1988.

monetary union in the name of "sovereignty" – including from Chirac himself – had been an important obstacle to monetary unification. Back then, French politicians "were torn between the objective of having a common external monetary policy and their fear of loss of national sovereignty."[65] By the 1980s, however, the EMS had become institutionally entrenched, so the political rhetoric of "sovereignty" played in favor of monetary union. French politicians saw a reform of the EMS as a way to reinvigorate, rather than dilute, French "sovereignty."

There was therefore a political logic, well beyond the walls of the Delors Committee, to presenting monetary union as the logical next step toward European integration. In 1988, Europe's Internal Market was not yet a firmly entrenched reality and may have never seen the light of day, which (as we saw) Delors forcefully pointed out at the second meeting of the committee. The Internal Market required market reforms that would be politically difficult to introduce and to implement. In addition, the decision to move to a single European currency still required a leap of faith out of national currencies, clearly distinct from the decision to move toward an Internal Market without borders. When the euro was launched many years later, Robert Mundell himself expressed retrospective surprise with the European Union's "colossal gamble" and its "sudden death" approach to "hallmarks of sovereignty that have existed for thousands of years."[66] A durable bone of contention between the French and the Germans was the French reluctance to forego the dirigiste financial policies, traditionally used in industrial policy and for rewarding various interest groups. German monetary officials saw these policies as deeply flawed because of their inflationary potential. In this respect, Pöhl and Duisenberg's positions on the Delors Committee were in line with the long-standing positions of the German and Dutch governments. While Delors, Lamfalussy, and de Larosière accepted the German–Dutch demand to liberalize capital movements, they also supported France's demand for a stronger EMS that would protect its currency from speculative attacks. In so doing, they were trying to undercut both the dirigiste nostalgia of French politicians and the German apprehensions regarding their partners' commitment to low inflation.

On the French side, it remained possible for politicians to argue against monetary union in the name of preserving sovereignty, but this argument rang increasingly hollow. The objective subordination of the Banque de France to the Bundesbank, perceived at the time as the "bank that ruled Europe," was an important change from the 1970s.[67] There is little evidence, conversely, that French policymakers were converted to the German model of monetary stability for its own sake. For French Treasury officials, the main attraction of what they called "competitive disinflation" is that lower inflationary pressures made French goods and services cheaper if trade partners experienced greater

---

[65] Tsoukalis 1977: 80.   [66] Mundell 2002: 124, 141.   [67] Marsh 1992.

inflation in wage costs and other inputs.[68] In other words, low inflation was desirable less for its own sake – as monetarist economists would argue – than because of the growth resulting from real exchange rate depreciation.[69] On the German side, the removal of controls made it increasingly hard for Germany to resist the pressure of its neighbors and of Delors' European Commission in favor of EMS reform. German government officials saw the EMS as a haven of relative stability in a highly volatile international monetary environment.[70] Although German politicians did not have an obvious interest in revamping the EMS, even those most skeptical of monetary union were attached to the EMS as an instrument of exchange rate stability vis-à-vis Germany's main trade partners.[71] Since they knew that other member states could eventually defect from the EMS, they were also concerned that the EMS was perceived as an instrument of German hegemony.

The Delors Report was signed by all its members and then endorsed by Europe's political leaders in June 1989. Although it was only the beginning of the push toward Europe's Economic and Monetary Union, that report retrospectively appears as the blueprint for the Economic and Monetary Union that was born a decade later. Bundesbank President Karl Otto Pöhl clearly hoped to influence the terms of whatever compromise was achieved on EMU – and he did. The other members of the Delors Committee, including Delors himself, quickly understood that EMU would have to proceed on terms that were roughly agreeable to the German central bank.

At the time and until the archives were recently opened, the exact tenor of committee deliberations was deliberately shrouded in a protocol of strict secrecy.[72] Although most committee members remained tight-lipped, some apparently felt that Pöhl dominated the discussion: "One committee member said the document contained 'a lot of German thinking.' Another said Mr Pöhl 'had good reason to look happy.'"[73] One committee member was reported as saying that "Karl Otto got everything he wanted."[74] Most evidently, Pöhl's single currency proposal had the effect of shooting down de Larosière's typically French idea of promoting the role of the European Monetary System's ECU as a composite "common currency." De Larosière kept coming back again and again to his idea that a single currency was not a panacea: "I have a little difficulty with this one-money concept."[75] Yet he was clearly aware that his proposal, without Pöhl's support, was stillborn. The transcripts indicate that everybody on the committee realized that Pöhl's signature was necessary for the Delors Report to carry any weight and for monetary union to see the light of day sometime in the future.

---

[68] Trichet 1992. [69] De Boissieu and Pisanni-Ferry 1998: 49–90.
[70] Henning 1994: 203–209. [71] Stoltenberg 1997: 327–329.
[72] Meeting on September 13, 1988, pp. 1–3.
[73] "Bankers Agree on EC Route to Unity," *Financial Times*, April 13, 1989.
[74] *Institutional Investor*, May 1989.
[75] Delors Committee, Meeting on December 13, 1988, p. 3.

5.3 The Momentum behind Monetary Unification in the Public Arena

At the same time, the Delors Report triggered a political process that largely escaped the control of the Bundesbank. Pöhl was aware that the committee's mandate was to delineate the modalities of an economic and monetary union, despite the doubts he frequently expressed about the realism of that plan in the foreseeable future.[76] Yet he appears to have miscalculated the extent to which there was a desire outside Germany to move beyond the EMS. He repeatedly doubted the will of Germany's partners, especially France, to truly move toward financial liberalization and to make their central bank independent – despite de Larosière's repeated assurances that this was a distinct possibility. He apparently was not aware that a unanimous vote among member governments was not required to start an intergovernmental treaty negotiation.[77] Most importantly, he misjudged the extent to which European political leaders were ready to move toward an Economic and Monetary Union – which became obvious when the Berlin Wall fell a few months later. The magnitude of Pöhl's miscalculations and misjudgments can be better understood, however, once we consider the pressures that were exerted on him to reach an agreement. In a later interview, Pöhl expressed regrets about his decision to participate in a committee where he "couldn't defend German interests."[78] Once the Report was published, the best that Pöhl could do was to control the damage and to try and shape the future Economic and Monetary Union in accordance with the Bundesbank's vision.

The Delors Report was formally approved by the European Council in Madrid as early as June 1989 – well before German unity was remotely in sight. Retrospective accounts have sometimes downplayed the importance of the Delors Report.[79] Of course, monetary union was not sealed as a political deal until the Maastricht Treaty was signed, in the context of German reunification. The fall of the Berlin Wall certainly precipitated discussions between Germany and France on how to achieve a more united Europe. Yet it also almost derailed Europe's monetary unification process, after Kohl decided to convert the East German currency into deutschmark at a one-to-one exchange rate. To offset the inflationary risks of East Germany's consumer boom, the Bundesbank began a policy of high interest rates that other countries were forced to emulate if they wanted to remain in the EMS. Germany's reunification thus drove a wedge between the economic policy cycles of Germany and the rest of Europe, which triggered a series of EMS exchange rate crises.[80] A counterfactual claim that EMU would have occurred even in the absence of German reunification is inherently impossible to prove. But complaints about the lack of "symmetry" within the EMS already fueled the growing demand for

---

[76] On Pöhl, see also James 2016. [77] Delors Committee, Meeting on April 12, 1989, pp. 7, 13.
[78] Grant 1994: 121. [79] James 2012: 210–211.
[80] In September 1992, the most serious EMS crisis forced the British currency out of the EMS – and established George Soros' fame as a savvy financier for shorting sterling. See "Currency Chaos: The Inside Story," *Institutional Investor*, October 1992.

monetary union in the context of capital liberalization, as clearly transpired in the Delors Committee deliberations.

In the end, the central bankers' imprimatur gave momentum to the dynamic of monetary regime change that ultimately gave birth to the euro. A new political-economic regime came into existence, centered on a new currency, a new ECB, and a new multilateral framework for public finances and fiscal policies. In this sense, the European Union that was born in the 1990s qualitatively departed from the prior regime of international monetary and economic cooperation that had existed among the member states of the European Community. Because the stakes of this monetary and economic integration were evidently high, the Delors Committee more often felt like an arena of contest between "strong" and "weak" currency countries than like an "epistemic community" of central bankers with shared ideological preferences. What emerged from this contested committee was the basic design of a new monetary governance regime around a single currency managed by an independent central bank tasked with the maintenance of price stability in an environment of free capital movements. In the following decade, however, a monetary union largely motivated by a collective desire to "strengthen" the EMS and to end Germany's dominance within it began to appear, paradoxically, as the ultimate triumph of the Bundesbank.

5.4 HOW TECHNOCRATIC NEOLIBERALISM CARRIED THE DAY

Alliances that cut across different arenas loomed large in Europe's adoption of technocratic neoliberalism. After political leaders firmly decided to move toward monetary union by signing the Maastricht Treaty, Europe's central bankers increasingly moved toward neoliberal positions on issues of broad economic governance. From their perspective, the emerging neoliberal political-economic regime served to ring-fence the future monetary regime. To achieve the promise of Economic and Monetary Union, its advocates found it necessary to consolidate a core political constituency and to defuse potential political opposition. The Delors Report's argument in favor of making "price stability" the cardinal priority of the future ECB appeared as an unavoidable step to keep the Bundesbank on board. Although the decision to engage in monetary union was formally a prerogative of the German government, the Bundesbank played an important role in German public debates.[81] Thus, the Bundesbank was informally able to shape the official German position regarding the modalities of that transition process.

Since Germany was in a position to refuse a monetary union that other EU leaders wanted, the politics of money across Europe was increasingly tilted toward German priorities and the "German model." French Prime Minister

---

[81] Goodman 1992; Henning 1994.

5.4 How Technocratic Neoliberalism Carried the Day

Pierre Bérégovoy clearly articulated the French government's reasoning at the time: "If I came over to the idea of central bank independence, which Germany considered a sine qua non [for EMU], it is because it appeared to me that the central bank would be counterbalanced by a strong and democratic economic authority (...)."[82] The fact that many countries had anti-inflationary policies resulted in large part from prior political choices to stick with the EMS and to accept the logic of capital liberalization, rather than from a Europe-wide ideational shift toward German-style neoliberalism.

Central bankers, for their part, were willing to recognize "sovereign" prerogatives of governments in fiscal policy, but they identified "exchange rate policy" – and increasingly the French idea of *"gouvernement économique"* – as a bone of contention. Members of the Delors Committee had studiously avoided taking a stance on fiscal policy, which was considered a "sovereign" prerogative. Yet many central bankers suspected politicians, and especially the French, of wanting to claw back monetary policy powers. During the committee deliberations, Pöhl had introduced the idea of establishing a budget deficit ceiling ("let us say below 3 percent of GDP") to ensure steady progress toward the cautious fiscal management of monetary union. This was the first time this figure was aired in a policy discussion, but it was later duly inserted into the Maastricht Treaty.[83] Central bankers also insisted that monetary stability should be the overriding goal of the future monetary union. Delors had summarized the committee's stance in favor of rules but also in favor of "a comprehensive attitude towards the situation in each country."[84] The Delors Report's assertion of "subsidiarity" as a principle of economic policymaking had therefore been balanced by the observation that "uncoordinated and divergent national budgetary policies would undermine monetary stability and generate imbalances in the real and financial sectors of the community."

In the final text of the Maastricht Treaty, however, the quantitative approach prevailed. In order to qualify for EMU membership, governments had to reach numerical targets for inflation, budget deficits, public debts, exchange rate fluctuation margins, and long-term interest rates. Qualifying clauses were also nonetheless inserted in the Treaty, ensuring flexibility to assess fulfillment of the convergence criteria. The Treaty also went further than the Delors Committee toward the prohibition of "monetary financing" of public deficits by the ECB, but it kept a door open for the indirect support of national treasuries through bond purchases on sovereign debt markets.[85]

In retrospect, the turn toward monetary and fiscal retrenchment in the early 1990s remains remarkable. It also went further than central bankers' intentions as reflected in Delors Committee deliberations. In addition to Germany's strong

---

[82] Pierre Bérégovoy, address to the French Assemblée Nationale during the debate on the constitutional revision required by the Maastricht Treaty, May 9, 1992 (author translation).
[83] James 2012: 251. [84] Delors Committee, February 14, 1989, transcript, p. 10.
[85] Bateman and Van't Klooster 2024: 427–428.

bargaining position, changing economic circumstances played an important role. As EMS member states were forced to adjust to the Bundesbank's post-reunification interest rate hike by adopting similarly restrictive monetary policies, the convergence criteria increasingly appeared as quantitative straitjackets on economic growth. Independent (Keynesian) economists often became vocal critics of the criteria.[86] The European unity of the previous decade around the fight against inflation began to crumble in the face of a serious economic recession. To fulfill the criteria, many governments had little choice but to cut public expenditures and forego some economic growth. In Germany, the dilemma was less stark because of the monetary reflation taking place in the East, but Kohl's government was under heavy pressure from the Bundesbank and Bundestag to insist on other member states' fulfilling the convergence criteria before adopting the euro.[87] The credibility of governmental commitment to respect the convergence criteria and to achieve EMU was increasingly in doubt, which repeatedly triggered exchange rate crises in the EMS in 1992–1993.

From then on, the transition to Europe's Economic and Monetary Union occurred under increasingly conservative auspices – for several interrelated reasons. First, the advocates of EMU increasingly invoked neoliberal ideas to effectively insulate the EMU process from outside interference. After the "convergence criteria" were enshrined in a European treaty, they acquired legal force. Even though these criteria were not and had never been the object of an unambiguous policy consensus, they became the cement of a cross-cutting alliance that promoted monetary union for a variety of reasons. EU officials were committed to implement the new Maastricht Treaty and attempted to capitalize on the success of the 1992 program. The Commission had opened the public relations campaign under Delors, by presenting the single currency as the "logical" next step after the single market.[88] By the mid-1990s, as the European Union was still barely coming out of a recession, Commission officials berated member states that "lagged" on implementing the convergence criteria, claimed the "necessity" of stabilizing public deficits, and pronounced "dead" the "Keynesian model" of countercyclical economic policy.[89] After 1994, the newly created European Monetary Institute (precursor to the ECB) joined the Commission in lobbying for monetary union. Although the euro remained an abstract goal without a clear constituency, there surely existed a constituency for the "convergence criteria" – politicians who favored fiscally conservative policies, central bankers and finance ministry officials, business and especially

---

[86] De Grauwe 1993.   [87] Schönfelder and Thiel 1996: 157.
[88] Emerson, Gros, Italianer, Pisani-Ferry, and Reichenbach 1992.
[89] See, for example, "Brussels Points Finger at Fiscal Policy Laggards," *Financial Times*, May 26, 1994; interview of Commissioner de Silguy by *Le Monde*, December 12, 1995; "Santer Makes Plea on Public Spending Cuts," *Financial Times*, June 27, 1995; Yves-Thibault de Silguy, "Vers la monnaie unique," *Commentaire*, no. 74 (Summer 1996).

financial actors, and, more generally, all actors or social groups that identified a political, bureaucratic, or economic interest in the provision of fiscally conservative policies. As unemployment rates reached all-time highs and the recession increased pressure on public budgets, these actors and groups were searching for ways to entrench their policy preferences.

Second, the movement toward a neoliberal political-economic regime conveniently enabled advocates of monetary union to fudge their disagreements until the euro came into existence. For some actors, especially in France, the painful economic prescription of respecting the Maastricht Treaty was a necessary evil for the Economic and Monetary Union to become a reality.[90] There clearly were some moments of uneasiness in the French government and serious frictions with the Bundesbank and the German government. On September 3, 1992, President Mitterrand appeared to renege on central bank independence by saying that monetary policy was part of economic policy and therefore in the hands of the Council of Ministers. This immediately provoked a series of articles, "Paris Calls ECB Independence into Question," in the Bundesbank's weekly publication, *Auszüge aus Presseartikeln*. As late as November 1996, Prime Minister Alain Juppé blundered by declaring that the "economic government" favored by the French government would "control interest rates." Meanwhile, the official Bundesbank position in favor of strictly respecting the criteria to preserve and diffuse the German model of monetary policy was also dubious. When the Bundesbank raised interest rates in 1992, many speculated that this move was aimed at forcing a realignment within the EMS or even an indefinite postponement of EMU.[91] Commission officials consistently tried to prevent or defuse potential conflicts about the political meanings and purposes of EMU. For example, when prominent French politicians started to demand a "weak" euro at a time when the German government was trying to convince the German public that the euro would be "as strong as the mark," Commission officials tried to deflate this controversy by saying that it was "completely beside the point" since the value of the euro would be decided primarily by the market.[92]

Third, the bargaining situation of the 1990s over the contours of the future Economic and Monetary Union also served the transition to a broadly neoliberal political-economic regime. After the Maastricht Treaty was signed, it became ipso facto a negotiating baseline as well as an instruction manual for the member states that aspired to EMU. Any deviation from its specific terms

---

[90] In an author interview in 1997, this choice was presented to me by a member of the French negotiating team at Maastricht: "Assuming that we sacrificed one percentage point of growth [in the early 1990s] and in the end we obtain EMU, then the balance sheet will be positive."
[91] Henning 1994: 36–37.
[92] "Bonn et Paris se mobilisent pour dégripper le moteur européen," *Le Monde*, December 10, 1996.

weakened not only a country's chances of reaching the promised land of Eurozone membership, but also its bargaining position for deciding the details of EMU. Having a strong bargaining position was important because the Treaty had left many points open for negotiation – including the possibility of anticipating deadlines, the membership of the future Eurozone, the degree of monetary policy coordination during the long first and second stages of EMU, the character of economic policy coordination in the third stage, the location of the ECB, and the external representation of the euro. Countries that appeared to cut corners in the EU-wide competition for fiscal consolidation therefore found themselves in a weaker bargaining position. Even Germany's negotiating position could be weakened for that reason, as happened in the spring of 1997 when the German government announced its intention to reevaluate the Bundesbank's gold reserves to better meet the convergence criteria. That announcement immediately boosted the chances of member states that German officials sometimes called derisively the "Club Med" countries – especially Italy – to enter the euro club.

Fourth, and not least important, technocratic neoliberalism also carried the day because of pressures from politicians and voters in national public arenas. In several member states, opposition or challenger politicians often seized on the difficulties of their government to abide by the convergence criteria. In the German parliamentary ratification debate, the government had to commit to defend the convergence criteria as a prerequisite for German consent to EMU.[93] By the mid-1990s the *Dreikommanull* coalition (named after the 3 percent convergence criterion on public deficits) led by Bavarian premier Edmund Stoiber also put pressure on the German government to remain inflexible. Public criticism of the government reached a peak in 1996, when the German finance ministry was trying to tamper with the rigor of the convergence criteria. The German government responded by demanding a "stability pact" that would extend the convergence criteria beyond completion of EMU.[94] In the end, the member states adopted the pact alongside the Amsterdam Treaty in the spring of 1997.[95] Despite the objections of France's newly elected socialist prime minister, the French government did not go to war against the pact, mostly for fear of alienating its German counterpart. At the same time, it was able to forestall the main German demand for automatic penalties in case of deviations from the pact.[96] The other main change that France obtained was changing the name of the "stability pact" to "Stability and Growth Pact." Meanwhile, the official line of central bankers in the European Monetary Institute was quite restrictive and supported German demands

---

[93] Schönfelder and Thiel 1996: 157.   [94] Heipertz and Verdun 2010.
[95] The pact mandated member state budgets "close to balance or in surplus" and mandated financial sanctions if a member state's deficit exceeded 3 percent of national GDP.
[96] Segers and van Esch 2007.

for an "automaticity" of sanctions.[97] European Commission officials did not go as far, and stayed officially neutral in the debate between the member states – mostly France and Germany – on fiscal policy coordination or the exchange rate policy of the euro – even though they were often "German" in insisting on macroeconomic convergence and stability-oriented policies.

5.5 EU TECHNOCRATIC NEOLIBERALISM CIRCA 2000

Although Delors Committee members who wanted to rebalance the EMS had put the German Bundesbank on the defensive, the new political-economic regime that emerged at the end of the twentieth century went further and also looked more German than they had envisioned. The main proponents of monetary unification rarely dwelled on their differences, however. The fact that the often-touted convergence of views between German and French leaders remained superficial was not immediately apparent. There were good political reasons for central bankers and European Commission officials, as well as French and German political leaders, to downplay their differences. In the face of increasing economic hardship and political turbulence, the priority was to reassure market actors that the euro would indeed be implemented according to plan. The advocates of Economic and Monetary Union therefore increasingly closed ranks. It would have been impolitic to highlight their mutual differences. To stay the course, European and national political elites were willing to pay the price of a prolonged recession.

In the eyes of many observers, Europe's Economic and Monetary Union thus came to be seen as the embodiment of German-style neoliberalism – alias "ordoliberalism" – run by ECB technocrats insulated from political pressures. Like the Fed under Volcker, the new independent ECB presided over a version of technocratic neoliberalism with the fight against inflation at its core. Under the terms of the treaty, the ECB could pursue other policy objectives, but only "without prejudice" to its primary objective of price stability. The ECB's independence was very extensive and constitutionalized in the EU Treaty. The ECB determined its own targets and its policies independently. The EU member states who abided by the Maastricht convergence criteria acceded to the Economic and Monetary Union only to find themselves caught in the strictures of the 1997 Stability and Growth Pact. The Stability and Growth Pact was later reformed in 2005, but it remained marked by its origin as a set of rules and sanction mechanisms against fiscally deviant states. Meanwhile, the Eurogroup did not develop into the kind of *gouvernement économique* that successive French governments called for during and beyond the Maastricht Treaty

---

[97] See "Stark Home Truths of a Stability Pact," *Financial Times*, December 4, 1996; "EMI Chief Takes Hard Maastricht Line," *Financial Times*, November 20, 1996.

negotiations. Until the 2010s, it was caught in ambiguities and silences which, as we saw, the Delors Committee had discussed and openly recognized as problematic – namely, the persistence of national fiscal sovereignty and the difficulty of collectively defining a fiscal stance shared among member governments.

At the turn of the twenty-first century, however, the politics of money had decidedly changed – both within and beyond the ECB. Led by a Dutch and later by a French citizen and in charge of a currency that instantly became the most tangible symbol of European unity, the ECB had replaced the Bundesbank as Europe's central bank. In addition, Eurozone member states were no longer at the mercy of currency crises that had been the bane of the European Monetary System. Although the crisis of the 2010s later overshadowed this legacy by showing that the Eurozone did not shield member states against all kinds of crisis, the Eurozone-wide decline of interest rates and easier access to foreign capital carried benefits for state autonomy, especially for the Eurozone's periphery.[98] Compared with the era of the EMS, in which national interest rates were jacked up by the ever-present risk of currency crises, this was a much more comfortable situation – one that also secured considerable space for the central bank's discretionary policies. Yet from a central banker's perspective, this carried the risk that governments might become too comfortable with destabilizing deficits. As the Fed in the United States, the ECB therefore became a key institutional advocate for fiscal conservatism as well as other neoliberal policies.

Although the record of internal ECB deliberations is not open for the early 2000s, central bankers' interactions with the public arena – especially their testimonies to the European Parliament – are revealing. From the outset, the young ECB insisted on a division of labor between "technical" monetary and financial matters and "political" matters[99] – a way of thinking reminiscent of the Delors Committee's effort to stay out of but also to act as a guardrail against "sovereign" decisions. Its first president, Wim Duisenberg, asserted the ECB's role as a neutral advisor of governments: "I am talking to governments when I talk about budget deficits ... I do not think in any way that my advice is lopsided to any part of society."[100] Judging from reactions at the European Parliament, however, such "hawkish" encouragements to fiscal conservatism satisfied the Right more often than the Left. In a strong assertion of its independence in fleshing out its own Treaty-defined mandate of "price stability," the ECB announced in 2002 an inflation "reference value" of "close to but below 2%" by way of a simple press conference. The ECB also publicly refused to contemplate the fact that there might be a trade-off, at least in the short term, between price stability and growth. When questioned over this issue, ECB

---

[98] Jones 2003.   [99] Jabko 2003.
[100] Hearing of W. F. Duisenberg, president of the ECB, European Parliament, March 5, 2001, questions, p. 14.

5.5 Europe's Technocratic Neoliberalism circa 2000

officials typically repeated their favorite mantra *ad nauseam*: "[T]he best contribution that monetary policy can make to promote growth is to ensure price stability."

The ECB also played a role in ring-fencing its monetary regime of low inflation with a broader political-economic regime of technocratic neoliberalism that overlapped with the agenda of conservatives in the public arena. Like Volcker and Greenspan when they spoke of US government deficits, Europe's central bankers typically threw the ball of growth promotion back onto the politicians' court, by reminding them that they should keep their fiscal house in order. In addition, the ECB consistently advised governments to undertake "structural reforms" to increase growth.[101] In the context of monetary unification in the 1990s, "structural reform" had increasingly become a code word for liberalization, especially of national labor markets.[102] As Duisenberg put it, "There exists today a broad consensus, also at the level of governments, on the fact that the currently favourable growth prospects in the euro area would be further improved by deeper structural reforms in the euro zone."[103] The recurrent invocation of "consensus" served to stonewall disagreements in arenas external to the ECB – among politicians on the Left, but also among many Keynesian economists who favored national "social pacts" rather than neoliberal policies that were clearly beyond strict ECB prerogatives.

A particularly telling episode was the reform of the Stability and Growth Pact in 2005. In 2003, the German and French governments both breached the 3 percent public deficit-to-GDP ceiling set in the Pact. While Germany faced continuing costs in its transition to a reunified economy, France's government was reluctant to cut the fiscal deficit after the strong showing of the far right in 2002. At that point, France was resigned to paying the (relatively symbolic) fine mandated by the Pact's sanction mechanism; but German Chancellor Gerhard Schröder feared that this would weaken his SPD majority's position vis-à-vis the conservative CDU and FDP opposition, who in the 1990s had negotiated the Pact.[104] Reversing Germany's earlier position, Schröder complained that the implementation of the Stability and Growth Pact should not only be focused on stability: "it is not just a stability pact, but also a growth pact."[105] Consistent with their positions in the 1990s, Europe's central bankers – like the European Commission – came out against a "weakening" of the Pact and in favor of "automatic" sanctions. Governments decided against that view, and the Stability Pact was effectively made less stringent. Yet this apparently strengthened central bankers' resolve that they had to hold the line against

---

[101] Braun, Di Carlo, Diessner, and Düsterhöft 2024.   [102] Baccaro and Howell 2017: ch. 9.
[103] Hearing of W. F. Duisenberg, president of the ECB, European Parliament, March 20, 2000, questions, p. 4.
[104] Author interview, French President's office, November 3, 2010.
[105] "Schröder tells EU to back off on deficits," *Euractiv*, January 17, 2005.

government deficits[106] – even by taking the partisan side of conservative politicians against Social Democrats if necessary.[107] At that point, Delors' position in favor of "a comprehensive attitude" in applying the rules was essentially out of the window. The ECB not only toed a "hawkish" line but officially supported a technocratic form of neoliberal governance that bolstered conservative circles of economists and politicians.

5.6 CONCLUSION: THE ECB'S MOVE TOWARD NEOLIBERALISM

In sum, the 1980s politics of money in Europe resulted in a political-economic regime that was broadly similar to that of the United States. Central bankers increasingly asserted their independence by prioritizing the fight against inflation and by favoring neoliberal policies over other economic policy goals. Yet there were also important transatlantic nuances in the cross-cutting alliances to which central bankers participated and in their monetary and political-economic regime results. The arena of European central bankers was initially traversed by important disagreements due to differences in the relative vulnerability of national currencies, which often overshadowed debates about desirable monetary and economic policies. Central bankers overcame their mutual disagreements by publicly advocating the adoption of a single currency in parallel with capital liberalization. The public arena was likewise divided by a cleavage that echoed the main cleavage among central bankers, but that was more squarely focused on what politicians regarded as the sphere of national sovereignty. As I argued, policymakers progressively finessed their differences by painfully delivering an Economic and Monetary Union managed by an independent ECB focused on price stability and – unlike the United States – a legally binding system of fiscal consolidation rules. While the 1990s were already a heyday for US technocratic neoliberalism in the United States, Europe's version of technocratic neoliberalism was fully consolidated only after the European Union graduated to a new monetary regime around the euro at the turn of the twenty-first century.

Conventional narratives focused on economics and political economy both provide insights about the economic and ideational factors that facilitated the birth of Europe's Economic and Monetary Union. Yet they hardly explain the advent of an Economic and Monetary Union in its specific neoliberal form, despite important disagreements among member states about economic governance. In fact, the waxing of technocratic neoliberalism in the European Union was a product of cross-cutting alliances in different but related arenas. To uncover this politics of money, I have focused on contests over monetary governance among and around Europe's central bankers during a period of

---

[106] Van't Klooster 2022.   [107] Matthijs and Blyth 2017: 114.

5.6 Conclusion: The ECB's Move toward Neoliberalism

turmoil, which were later papered over to smooth out the transition to the euro in the late 1990s and early 2000s.

Ultimately, the advent of EU technocratic neoliberalism and of the ECB also altered the politics of money. Within the new organizational arena of the ECB, a new cleavage – familiar to observers of the Fed – emerged between hawks and doves. Within the professional arena of economists, debates about monetary governance were less oriented by national concerns than before. With its growing in-house staff of economists, the young ECB cultivated its links with a pan-European economics profession that moved closer to the US neo-Keynesian mainstream. And in the broader public arena, the main new cleavage was now between member governments and politicians that were satisfied or dissatisfied with the ECB's single monetary policy. Countries where economic growth was slower than the Eurozone average would have benefited from more accommodating policy – as was the case for Germany in the early 2000s – whereas those with more rapid growth faced inflationary pressures – such as Ireland. In addition, the European parliament's formal role in overseeing the ECB added a new cross-national partisan dimension to public cleavages about monetary policy.

Circa 2000, Europe's version of technocratic neoliberalism, centered on the fight against inflation and the advocacy of fiscal consolidation and market reforms, was nonetheless firmly in place. Central bankers knew that the distinction between "political" and "technical" issues could be tenuous, but it had become their official line of defense against political encroachments. To delineate internal cleavages within the ECB, we can only rely on indirect sources – such as reporters' accounts, central bankers' speeches, and confidential interviews – since the records of central bank deliberations are not open for the early 2000s. In private, ECB officials as well as national central bankers sometimes conceded that growth was their ultimate concern, and that the fight against inflation was not the only objective of monetary policy – as was going to become much more obvious in the 2010s. Yet the official ECB line mattered, since the ECB was the most powerful voice on macro-economic policy and thus able to set the tone of economic policy debates at the EU level. Although the Stability and Growth Pact's sanctions were difficult to implement, their mere legal existence was a source of political capital for member states that abided by the rules and a scarlet letter for those that did not. The young ECB of the early 2000s downplayed its internal disagreements and broadly supported neoliberal policies – until the global financial crisis of 2008 erupted.

6

The Waning of Technocratic Neoliberalism in the United States

A housing price collapse followed by a global financial crisis in 2007–2008 destroyed massive amounts of wealth, and then the "Great Recession" that started in 2009 brought double-digit unemployment. In the face of the worst economic downturn since the Great Depression, central bankers in the 2010s fretted that they were "the only game in town"[1] – a phrase that Paul Volcker had already used in January 1981.[2] Later reflecting on his experience as Fed chair in the early 2010s, Ben Bernanke spoke of the birth of a "new monetary regime" around "unorthodox" monetary policies.[3] That shift had far-reaching implications. As in the 1980s, the Federal Reserve's new monetary regime also signaled a broader change of political-economic regime. Decisively moving away from tight money, the Bernanke Fed not only extended a massive monetary stimulus but also increasingly tried to discourage fiscal austerity. The neoliberal advocacy of conservative fiscal and monetary policies did not cease, but it no longer came from Fed leaders. In this sense, the broadly neoliberal regime that had governed the US economy for decades lost crucial technocratic support. In turn, that political-economic regime's long-standing Republican supporters became strident critics of the Fed. As the Tea Party movement and later Donald Trump went to war with the Fed, neoliberalism became a markedly more populist project.

Building on meeting transcripts of the Federal Open Market Committee (FOMC), this chapter traces the complex politics of money behind the Fed's cautious adoption of innovative ("unorthodox") policies. Fed leaders had to simultaneously navigate several contested arenas – the Fed itself as an

---

[1] El-Erian 2016.
[2] Silber 2012: 201. Volcker said this in a conversation about inflation with newly elected President Reagan.
[3] Bernanke 2022: 135–167.

organization, the economics profession, and the public arena of administration officials, politicians, and American politics at large. As we will see, the Fed deliberations led to the consolidation of monetary regime change, with new Fed policies that echoed these contests but also significantly reshaped them. The changing politics of money thus also had a remarkable impact on America's broader political-economic regime. Since the 1980s, free-market conservatives had seen central banks as bulwarks against fiscal redistribution and other exertions of governmental authority to manage the economy. After 2008, the Fed's incorporation of unorthodox tools into its policy toolbox set the stage for a growing mutual disaffection between central bankers and conservative supporters of all-out neoliberal policies among the Tea Party. As we will see, right-wing populism contributed to the survival of the neoliberal project, whereas technocrats retreated from it.

6.1 FROM "UNORTHODOX" POLICIES TO AN EXTENDED POLICY PANOPLY

A lot of scholarly ink has been spilled about the mistakes that the Fed as well as other US policymakers made in responding to the 2008 global financial crisis and to the long economic slump that followed. From the perspective of economics, some scholars attribute the depth and duration of the downturn to policymakers who bent to political pressure and thus failed to adopt policies that the economic situation demanded. In his influential *New York Times* column, Paul Krugman regularly derided "austerians" who stood against deficit spending, but also criticized Fed chair Ben Bernanke for being out of touch.[4] Prominent economists thus faulted the Fed first for letting Lehman Brothers default in 2008, and later for providing insufficient stimulus due to what Barry Eichengreen called a "hard right turn toward austerity."[5] From a political economy perspective, scholars have often highlighted the deeper roots of the crisis and the inadequacy of a market- and finance-friendly regime of political economy. As Lawrence Jacobs and Desmond King put it, Fed policymakers ensured that "finance wins" in all circumstances.[6] Many have analyzed central bankers' pro-finance orientations in terms of continuity with the past, resulting in increasing inequality.[7] In this vein, some have also shown that the Fed systematically underestimated the extent of the crisis, especially at the outset.[8] Such claims also dovetail a large scholarship about the "Wall

---

[4] Krugman 2020: 157–160; Paul Krugman, "Earth to Bernanke," *New York Times*, April 29, 2012.
[5] Eichengreen 2012, 2015: 7, 281–311. See also Blinder 2022: 294–311; DeLong 2022: 447.
[6] Jacobs and King 2021. See also Pontusson 2018; Adolph 2018: 737; Cooper 2024: 84.
[7] Blyth 2013; Tooze 2018; Moschella 2024; Cooper 2024.
[8] Fligstein, Brundage, and Schultz 2017; Abolafia 2020: 11–29.

Street-Washington corridor," "financialization," and the "structural power" of finance.⁹

Both these economics and political economy perspectives thus largely blame the firemen, including the Fed, for being also the arsonists, and attribute the severity of the crash on policymakers. Although I sympathize with some of these criticisms, the goal of this chapter is not to add my own. Rather, it aims to cast light on important blind spots in many accounts of the predicament in which the Fed found itself. For Bernanke's "new monetary regime" of "unorthodox" easy-money policies to take hold beyond the immediate moment of the 2008 crisis, central bankers needed to durably incorporate them into their policy panoply – and that was no easy task. Since the Volcker Shock, conservative actors had formed the political bedrock of a long-standing neoliberal political-economic regime that was largely organized around the cardinal value of low inflation and defended by an assertive Fed. Conservative attacks on the Fed's monetary stimulus therefore ran much deeper than a partisan reaction against the Obama administration. Despite the Fed's legal independence, the Fed could therefore not simply ignore these attacks and implement what most economists identified as the correct policies. While scholars who adopt a political economy perspective are more attentive to the long-standing neoliberal nature of economic governance, they often conversely gloss over the fact that the Fed's new monetary regime change counteracted austerity. In this sense, the Fed broke with the political past at least as much as it defended the status quo. Insofar as conservative critics of the Bernanke Fed often invoked the free market to attack the Fed, they do not fit the generic image of a popular backlash against the neoliberal regime of political economy.

To better make sense of the Fed's actions, I will argue that changing alliances across the FOMC, the economics profession, and the public arena caused durable monetary regime change at the Fed and, ultimately, the waning of technocratic neoliberalism. At the outset, these three arenas were all characterized by cleavages that made the consolidation of monetary and political-economic regime change inherently difficult. Even though neo-Keynesian ideas were dominant among economists in the 2010s, conservative avatars of monetarism remained a powerful force within and outside the Fed.¹⁰ In addition, there was considerable political resistance to altering the broader regime of political economy that had been built over the preceding decades. As a normative project, neoliberalism remained alive in the 2010s, even as it was undergoing "mutations."¹¹ As the Fed turned to monetary stimulus and thus veered away from its long-standing anti-inflationary stance, it had to consider and navigate these deep cleavages to be able to sustain its new policies. Even though

---

⁹ Johnson and Kwak 2010; Krippner 2011; Culpepper and Reinke 2014; Brown 2022; Dafe, Hager, Naqvi, and Wansleben 2022.
¹⁰ Blinder 2022: 307–311.
¹¹ Callison and Manfredi 2019; Plehwe, Slobodian, and Mirowski 2020.

6.1 From "Unorthodox" Policies to an Extended Policy Panoply

the Fed retreated from the neoliberal political-economic regime that it had contributed to build, the conservative forces that supported that regime did not suddenly vanish. Yet the central bankers' shift to a new monetary regime meant that those forces lost their technocratic mooring. As a result, the neoliberal regime that they supported became distinctly less technocratic and more populist than before 2008.

The Fed responded to the crisis and the economic downturn by adopting "unconventional" policies that progressively became part of the Fed's panoply. This incorporation involved considerable innovation at the Fed. The Fed's unorthodox policies were initially dictated by the urgency of the financial crisis in the fall of 2008. When it adopted these policies, the Fed just wanted to "exit" from them as soon as possible. Unlike the monetarist experiment of the 1980s, however, Fed leaders ultimately deemed this experiment successful. Far from exiting unconventional measures quickly, the Fed ultimately ceased to see "asset purchases" and "forward guidance" as outlandish tools. In addition, the Bernanke Fed also dialed down its former advocacy of deficit reduction and quietly counteracted the fiscal austerity of the early 2010s. None of these actions went uncontested, however. Within the Fed itself, Bernanke's and then Yellen's "dovish" inclination to prioritize the fight against unemployment did not please the "hawks," who were concerned about potential inflationary pressures and the need to keep monetary clearly separate from fiscal policy. But the changing politics of money at the Fed, in the economics profession, and in the public arena was such that the hawks became a dwindling minority. Within the economics profession, the Fed's new unconventional approach was supported by a majority of "neo-Keynesians." Last but not least, the Fed had to contend with a strident opposition among Republicans in Congress and their supporters in the public. The Republican Party resented not only the Democrats' fiscal stimulus, but also the Fed's easy-money policies, which ran not only against their partisan interest but also against the subjective inclinations of many voters.

These organizational, professional, and public arenas interacted, each with its own cleavages. As will become apparent, the most salient cleavage between "hawks" and "doves" within the Fed, as experienced by Fed officials themselves, mattered enormously. FOMC officials tended to choose camps and to then defend the position of their camp. This cleavage can be articulated in terms of the Fed's "dual" mandate to pursue "maximum employment" and "stable prices."[12] As Bernanke, for example, sums it up: "Through the decades, borrowing from the language of diplomacy, Fed policymakers putting greater weight on the employment mandate have been called *doves* and policymakers more focused on inflation have been called *hawks*."[13] While FOMC officials

---

[12] United States Congress, *Federal Reserve Reform Act*, November 16, 1977.
[13] Bernanke 2022: 28.

are not card-carrying members of these two camps in the same way that elected officials are Republicans or Democrats, this cleavage is nonetheless quite established and understood as such by Fed officials. At the same time, as Bernanke hastens to add: "Of course the definitions are fluid, with policymakers sometimes shifting from hawk to dove and back again, depending on economic conditions." Deliberation takes place and FOMC members sometimes are drawn to the other side in view of the economic situation. Such a collegial dynamic was obvious in the fall of 2008, but the persistent cleavage between hawks and doves contributed to the slow incorporation of unconventional policies into the Fed's policy panoply.

Despite many interactions between the Fed, the economics profession, and the public arena, the cleavage between hawks and doves in the internal arena of the FOMC cannot be simply reduced to cleavages at play in the Fed's external environment. On the one hand, Christopher Adolph's statistical study of central bankers' career backgrounds makes the case that "economists are reliable partisans."[14] Republican appointees and FOMC members with a finance background are more likely to adopt hawkish positions. In a similar vein, Mitchell Abolafia remarks that "those with the strongest faith in market restoration and the deepest concern about inflation tend to be found among regional bank presidents, especially those from the South and the Midwest, where the state is more likely to be mistrusted and free market ideology is the strongest."[15] On the other hand, the cleavage between hawks and doves overlaps imperfectly with political affiliation and social origins – in part because of the "fluidity" between the two camps that Bernanke mentions. While hawks often identify as Republicans and doves are more often Democrats, there are important counterexamples. For example, Ben Bernanke was (initially) a Republican and an admirer of Milton Friedman, but he was also a self-professed "new Keynesian" who became the leader of the doves during his tenure as Fed chair.[16] Likewise, presidents of the Fed's regional district banks are not all as reliably "hawkish" or "dovish" as their backgrounds or geographical districts may indicate. A case of full-blown conversion is that of St. Louis Fed President James Bullard, a hawk who became a dove as he worried about deflation in 2010.[17] Some hawks were from urban or

---

[14] Adolph 2013: 135.   [15] Abolafia 2020: 192.

[16] As we saw in Chapter 4, the opposite was true of Paul Volcker, a Democrat who led the Fed toward hawkish policies. The Greenspan years were more complicated. "Maestro" Alan Greenspan was a Republican and was generally an inflation hawk. Yet Greenspan's most admired feat as Fed chair was his dovish resistance to interest rate hikes even in the face of rapid job growth in the mid-1990s – against the (temporarily) hawkish sentiment of Clinton appointees Janet Yellen and Alan Blinder, even though they usually leaned more on the dovish side. Greenspan had not permanently turned into a dove, but he had diagnosed – as it turned out, correctly – large productivity gains across the US economy, which allowed considerably lower unemployment without fueling inflation. See Woodward 2000: 176–177.

[17] Sewell Chan, "Within the Fed, Worries of Deflation," *New York Times*, July 29, 2010.

"purple" districts – for example, Philadelphia (Charles Plosser). At first glance, this anomaly might be explained by the fact that Plosser was a University of Chicago-trained economist.[18] Yet Minnesota Fed President Narayanna Kocherlakota's personal evolution – another hawk who "became a dove" – suggests that even Chicago-trained hawks are amenable to conversion.[19]

Above all – and unlike political controversies between Democrats and Republicans – discussions between hawks and doves within the FOMC arena manifest sociological boundaries for what is or is not considered appropriate in the context of FOMC discussions. The debate at the FOMC remains strictly focused on economic issues, and governed by the ever-present norm that it must take place in a collegial, deliberative, and ostensibly nonpolitical fashion. As we will see in the rest of this chapter, the transcripts reveal both that the hawks were often entrenched in their opposition, and that their opposition was increasingly marginalized. Yet the automatically generated graphs of disagreements within the FOMC in the 2008–2017 decade (Figure 6.1) show consistent and relatively low levels of contention – fewer than fifty of participants' utterances express disagreements, which typically correspond to 5–15 percent of all utterances.

To figure out the politics of money, it becomes necessary to zoom in on specific detected disagreements in FOMC transcripts, and to zoom out of the FOMC arena by looking at its professional and public environment. In many cases, the disagreements are minor, and do not closely correspond to the divide between hawks and doves. Yet the hawks continued to be present in FOMC debates and sometimes expressed fundamental disagreements. In such cases, FOMC members listen politely to the hawks during the "go-round," and never call them out in political terms. The near-absolute absence of partisan politics from the transcripts reveals the power of this sociological norm. Hawkish views often hewed close to Republican talking points – for example, that QE was a covert form of fiscal policy, or that monetary as well as fiscal stimulus carried a high risk of inflation. But even when they cast vocal dissents from majority decisions, FOMC members always articulated them in terms of economics or general principles – never in overtly partisan terms. As we will see now by analyzing the changing politics of money in the 2010s, the new monetary

---

[18] Adolph 2013: 140. In a similar vein, other scholars have argued that economics training within the Chicago School or within the Keynesian tradition shapes the hawkish or dovish identities of FOMC members (Lepers 2018; Bordo and Istrefi 2023). Plosser seems to illustrate this importance of economics training, since he was a prominent figure of "real business cycle" theory, a body of neoclassical scholarship that viewed money as a veil and that tried to remedy the Keynesian models' "lack of sound theoretical foundations" (Plosser 1989: 51).

[19] After signing in 2009 a petition promoted by the conservative-leaning Cato Institute against the Obama administration's fiscal stimulus, Kocherlakota – in his own words – "became a dove" as the Great Recession unfolded and inflation remained subdued. See Michael S. Derby, "Dr. Kocherlakota, or How I Learned to Stop Worrying and Love Quantitative Easing," *Wall Street Journal*, March 14, 2013.

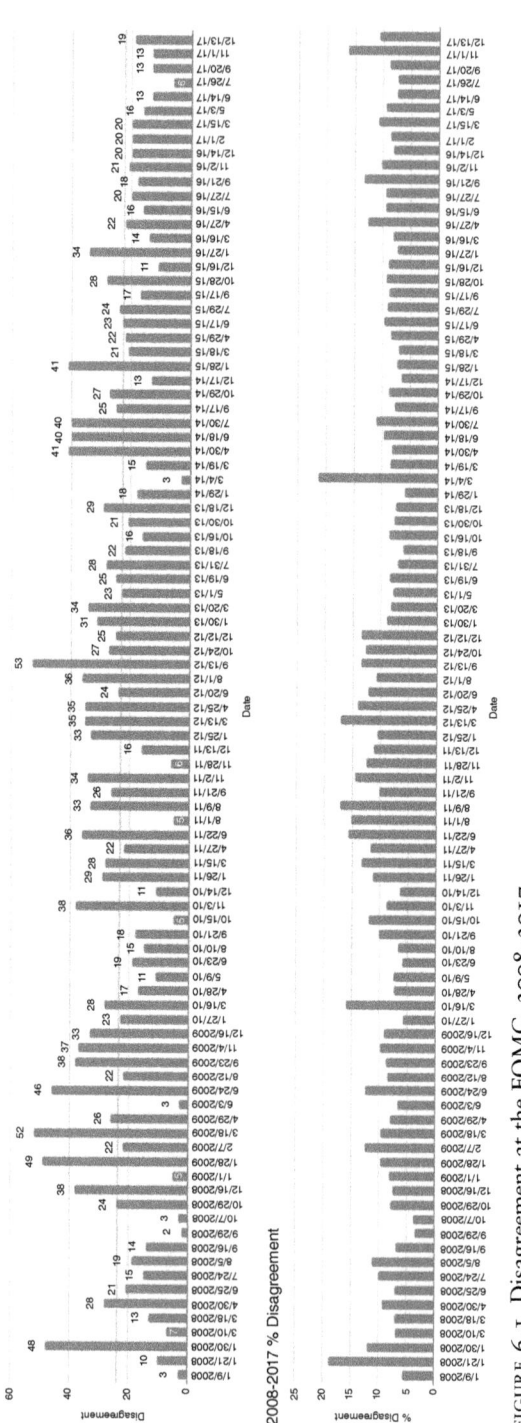

FIGURE 6.1 Disagreement at the FOMC, 2008–2017.

6.2 "Unorthodox" Policy Experimentation in the FOMC Arena

regime was quickly operative and became accepted by a majority of the FOMC. As the FOMC majority turned dovish, tensions increased between the Fed's new and Keynesian-inspired regime of easy money and the broader neoliberal political-economic regime that still characterized US economic governance.

6.2 "UNORTHODOX" POLICY EXPERIMENTATION IN THE FOMC ARENA

The Fed was notoriously slow in realizing the buildup and then the gravity of the financial crisis from the mid-2000s to the fall of 2008. Retrospectively, Ben Bernanke himself has offered a kind of *mea culpa* for the Fed's many "mistakes" in the run-up to the most acute phase of the crisis in the fall of 2008 – largely under his watch as Fed governor and then chair. As early as 2005, "most policymakers (...) downplayed the risks" of a housing bubble, and Bernanke honestly admits: "I doubt I would have been more foresighted than those who were there. Today the transcript of that meeting makes for painful reading."[20] Even a cursory reading of the minutes – let alone the transcripts – confirms the slowness of the Fed's evolution until remarkably late in the game. What it affords, however, is a first appreciation of the cleavage between hawks and doves – how deep it was, but also how dramatically it receded in the fall of 2008 as the FOMC shifted gears toward "unorthodox" policies.

The FOMC's long-standing (hawkish) concern with inflation was progressively overwhelmed by an increasing (dovish) consensus among FOMC members that the priority was to prevent a catastrophe on the employment front. Although the Fed eventually shifted toward unprecedented monetary easing, that new consensus was anything but immediate. Even shortly before Lehman's bankruptcy filing on September 15, 2008, there was still some cautious optimism in Fed quarters that a full-blown recession could be averted – and some hawkish FOMC members still worried above all about inflation. In August 2008, the Fed decided to keep its policy rate at 2 percent, but there was a dissenting voice: "Mr. Fisher dissented because he favored an increase in the target federal funds rate to help restrain inflation and inflation expectations, which were at risk of drifting higher."[21] Even at the following meeting, held on the day *after* Lehman's bankruptcy: "Participants agreed that economic growth was likely to be sluggish in the second half of 2008. Several participants had marked down their near-term outlook for economic activity and some judged that downside risks had increased, but most continued to expect a gradual

---

[20] Bernanke 2015: 88. Bernanke (2022: 107, 110) also recalls an equally embarrassing March 2007 Congressional testimony, in which he declared that the subprime problems were "likely to be contained," and he further explains that "in the summer of 2007 [when interbank lending suddenly froze], financial panics seemed like ancient history, at least in the United States."

[21] Minutes of the Federal Open Market Committee, August 5, 2008.

recovery in 2009."²² This time there was no dissent, and the FOMC unanimously decided to keep its policy rate unchanged at 2 percent.

Through the summer of 2008, the relative optimism of Fed officials – especially that of Fisher and Plosser, who favored rate hikes – is surprising in hindsight. Scholarly analyses of transcripts have shown that most FOMC members, not just the hawks, underestimated the systemic nature and extent of the financial crisis.²³ But FOMC decisions must also be considered alongside those of other central banks' monetary policies and the opinions of outside economists at the time. From this perspective, the FOMC's optimism appears as tempered. In response to rising commodity prices, the ECB announced a 25-basis point rate hike in July 2008. The Fed was also less optimistic than Alan Greenspan, who had stepped down as chair in January 2006 but remained influential.²⁴ In September 2008, Greenspan still expressed confidence in the "flexibility and resilience of markets" despite the ongoing "credit crunch," worried about "pervasive inflationary pressures," and predicted a need for "higher long-term interest rates in the decade ahead."²⁵ Perhaps most surprising in hindsight was the failure to prevent the fall 2008 collapse of Lehman Brothers on the part of the Bernanke Fed and President Bush's Treasury Secretary Henry Paulson. From an economics perspective, scholars have questioned whether Ben Bernanke was an appropriate Fed leader for times of crisis.²⁶ They have suggested that a financial crisis could have been averted if the Fed chair had been less "consensus-oriented" or if he had overlooked "legal niceties" and used the Fed's authority to prevent Lehman's failure. Bernanke himself claims in his memoir that he had renounced seeking consensus at the FOMC in 2008, but that he lacked the legal power to prevent Lehman's bankruptcy.²⁷

6.2.1 The Fed's Contested Shift to "Unorthodox" Policies

The controversy about the Fed's responsibility in the Lehman fiasco serves to underscore the fact that the Fed as well as the Treasury were under enormous pressure. Bernanke's observation that "popular, political and media views were hardening" against a Lehman bailout is difficult to deny.²⁸ Despite the Fed's statutory independence, Ben Bernanke – and *a fortiori* Henry Paulson – could not totally ignore this adverse external environment. Central bankers act not

---

[22] Minutes of the Federal Open Market Committee, September 16, 2008.
[23] Fligstein, Brundage, and Schultz 2017; Abolafia 2020: 11–29.
[24] Although his star as the former "Maestro" had faded since the housing market crisis, Greenspan was still widely listened to, including by Paulson in July 2008 (Mallaby 2016: 658).
[25] Greenspan 2008: 479, 523, 531–532. These are excerpts from an epilogue to the paperback edition of Greenspan's memoirs, published on September 8, 2008.
[26] Eichengreen 2015: 189, 287, 290; Ball 2016, 2018.   [27] Bernanke 2015: 135, 248–269.
[28] Bernanke 2015: 260–261.

6.2 "Unorthodox" Policy Experimentation in the FOMC Arena

only according to economic cost-benefit reasoning as familiar to economists, but also in response to pressures from different arenas. First, the independent Fed must rally support within and justify its actions to the professional arena of economists. The many economists who criticized the Fed's actions included Anna Schwartz, the influential author with Milton Friedman of *A Monetary History of the United States* – to this day a classic interpretation of the Great Depression as a product of Fed mistakes among economic historians, and a formative intellectual influence on Bernanke in particular.[29] Second, the Fed was under pressure from the public arena, and especially from Congress. Bernanke judged, after Lehman's default, that he could not continue the Fed's discretionary ("rogue") actions without Congressional input and support.[30] The economic case for bailing out Lehman may seem overwhelmingly compelling in hindsight, but the public case was extremely difficult to make *before* Lehman failed – and barely a few weeks before election day. The fact that Congress initially rejected outright any bank rescue package illustrates that political predicament. Although the financial storm unleashed by Lehman's bankruptcy increased public pressures on Bernanke, it also opened new possibilities for the Fed to dramatize the crisis and engage in radically new action.

After September 2008, the FOMC quickly shed any remaining optimism and the FOMC then started to operate in crisis mode. The FOMC deliberated over different frames that enabled its members to "make sense" of the crisis.[31] They puzzled over a global financial panic and a systemic crisis that they had never experienced firsthand before. As usual, central bankers questioned whether they should prioritize inflation or unemployment, but they also invented ad hoc new frames in a "seat-of-the-pants operation."[32] The Fed's decision to trigger what became known as the first phase of quantitative easing (QE1) thus avoided the kind of strident controversy between hawks and doves that marked the early phase of the crisis. The three FOMC meetings (including two unscheduled conference calls) in late September and October were crisis meetings, during which inflation fears were set aside. Despite coming closer to the "zero lower bound" of the federal funds rate, "the Committee agreed that it would take whatever steps were necessary to support the recovery of the economy"[33] and to "focus on other tools [than the Fed's policy rates] to impart additional monetary stimulus (...)."[34] From September through December 2008, there

---

[29] Bernanke therefore did not fail to notice Schwartz's criticism: "[P]olitical tolerance for what Milton Friedman's former coauthor Anna Schwartz called the Fed's 'rogue' operations had reached its limits." (Bernanke 2016: 30, 33).

[30] Bernanke 2015: 290.

[31] Abolafia 2020. "Sense-making" analysis can be understood from the perspective of pragmatist organization theory, and also in terms of what Kahneman (2011) and other cognitive psychologists call "fast thinking."

[32] Abolafia 2020: 3.

[33] Minutes of the Federal Open Market Committee, October 28–29, 2008.

[34] Minutes of the Federal Open Market Committee, December 15–16, 2008.

were no dissents from the inflation hawks at any of the FOMC meetings. The "whatever steps were necessary" formulation of the October minutes underscores the FOMC's determination to expand its panoply of tools to conduct expansionary monetary policy.

While this sudden consensus arose in exceptionally dire circumstances, it nonetheless marked a remarkable truce in the usual contest between hawks and doves at the FOMC. In December 2008, the FOMC unanimously endorsed measures that Bernanke had adopted "unilaterally" in his role as chair of the Federal Reserve Board in late November 2008.[35] Bernanke had apparently backed out from his initial resolve to be a consensus-building Fed chair already in early 2008, when he told New York Fed President Tim Geithner that he "wouldn't meet 'the hawks' halfway anymore."[36] On January 21, 2008, the dovish FOMC majority had decided to carry out the "biggest rate cut since 1982."[37] That was the beginning of a long series of cuts that took the federal funds rate from 4.25 percent in January 2008 to zero in December 2008. Until August 2008, these rate cuts were resisted by the hawks, who regularly cast dissenting votes at FOMC meetings. As the global financial crisis unfolded in the fall of 2008, however, the hawks' camp fell silent.[38] The Fed started quantitative easing with purchases of $600 billion of debt and mortgage-backed securities from Fannie and Freddie Mac: "[T]he Committee stands ready to expand purchases of agency debt and agency mortgage-backed securities, and (...) it is evaluating the potential benefits of purchasing longer-term Treasury securities."[39] December 2008 thus marked the beginning of a new phase of particularly massive monetary easing – and a fundamentally new monetary regime that would last several years. Casting aside the traditional Fed concern with inflation, the FOMC would prioritize what its majority saw as the economic need for a steady supply of easy money from the Fed.

6.3 "HEADWINDS" FOR MONETARY POLICY IN THE PUBLIC ARENA

Meanwhile, things were unfolding quite differently in the public arena – not only at the White House and on Capitol Hill, but also outside the Washington beltway. Anger against bankers and the financial "elite" had started to develop

---

[35] Bernanke recalls that this "unilateral" move went against his personal preference for a "deliberative, consensus-building style." Yet these measures were considered so exceptional at the time that Bernanke did not immediately see them as part of monetary policy, and therefore subject to normal FOMC deliberation. See Bernanke 2022: 135–138.
[36] Geithner 2015: 143; see also Bernanke 2022: 135.   [37] Bernanke 2015: 195.
[38] Bernanke's renewed concern with FOMC collegiality may have also played a role. In Bernanke's recollection, "After hearing from unhappy Reserve Bank presidents, I realized that their concern was not about the substance of the purchase program – most were comfortable with it – (...) but about process and legitimacy." Bernanke 2022: 137.
[39] Minutes of the Federal Open Market Committee, December 15–16, 2008.

6.3 "Headwinds" for Monetary Policy in the Public Arena

early on. In March 2008, the first major bailout of a financial firm, Bear Stearns, triggered a broad controversy that would only become more strident as the financial crisis worsened. The Fed's response to controversy was, perhaps inevitably, awkward. According to their memoirs, Ben Bernanke and Tim Geithner were acutely aware of "populist" opposition to the bailouts, and both expressed sympathy for the moral outrage that these bailouts provoked. Bernanke acknowledged criticisms about the "unfairness of bailing out Wall Street (a sentiment with which I agreed)" and said in a television interview that "it makes me angry" – even though his main concern at the time was "what would have happened had we not acted."[40] In a similar vein, Geithner called the "moral argument about justice" a "valid" concern – but added that "the truly moral thing to do during a financial inferno is to put it out."[41] Both identified an "Old Testament" desire to attribute blame and exact punishment for the crisis – and both also recognized their inability to convince the public that "pouring hundreds of billions of taxpayer dollars was the solution" to the crisis.[42] As Geithner recalled, "I never found an effective way to explain to the public what we were doing and why. We did save the economy, but we lost the country doing it."[43]

In the last few months of the Bush administration in late 2008, the Treasury and the Fed faced a risk of complete financial meltdown. To avoid that, Treasury Secretary Henry Paulson sought authorization from Congress for a financial package of 700 billion dollars that would rescue imperiled Wall Street firms via the purchase of "toxic assets" – the Troubled Assets Relief Program (TARP). Congress angrily rejected Paulson's first TARP package proposal. Americans increasingly perceived the bailouts as presents to Wall Street at the expense of Main Street, and blamed policymakers in the administration and the Federal Reserve for catering to financial interests. Paulson was also evidently concerned about his own reputation as a supporter of free markets and small government.[44] Geithner's account underlines the "populist fury of the moment" and Bernanke's the "sweeping populist indictments of bankers."[45] These "populist" critiques initially came both from the Left and the Right. The controversy over Wall Street bailouts fueled the rise of both the Occupy Wall Street and the Tea Party movements. Among elected officials, Bernanke singles out both Bernie Sanders and Rand Paul as politicians who "shared a strong populist streak."[46] In late 2008 and early 2009, patience was therefore already wearing thin among politicians and the American public – even before any discussion of stimulus, and before the Republicans' victory in the 2010 midterm elections.

The question of whether the February 2009 Economic Recovery Act could have realistically provided more fiscal stimulus has been hotly debated.

---

[40] Bernanke 2015: 222, 261, 286.   [41] Geithner 2015: 9.
[42] Bernanke 2015: 319, 334; Geithner 2015: 9.   [43] Geithner 2015: 18.   [44] Paulson 2013.
[45] Geithner 2015: 9; Bernanke 2015: 320.   [46] Bernanke 2015: 449.

Obama's memoirs suggests that he understood Keynes' broad message about the need for government to act as a "spender of last resort" to avert depression.[47] Yet the Obama administration's stimulus package of 787 million dollars appears relatively modest and, in retrospect, was insufficient to boost spending and prevent a major recession. In January 2009, Paul Krugman's *New York Times* column called the Obama fiscal stimulus "well short of what's needed."[48] Obama administration economists were aware of that problem, if we are to believe Geithner's and Obama's memoirs. The whole economic team – Geithner, but also Larry Summers, and especially Christina Romer and Jared Bernstein – wanted to increase the size of the stimulus.[49] But "unfortunately, 'stimulus' had become a dirty word in American politics," and Obama's political advisor Rahm Emanuel later "made it clear there was no appetite for 'more stimulus' on the Hill."[50] The media was filled with reports and opinion pieces about the immorality of asking taxpayers to foot the bill for Wall Street's recklessness and for irresponsible borrowers' debts. Obama reports in colorful terms a discussion that took place in December 2008, during which Christina Romer recommended that the size of the stimulus reach a trillion dollars: "'There is no fucking way,' Rahm said.[...] I turned to Joe [Biden], who nodded in assent."[51]

Observers have often questioned the Obama administration's commitment to Keynesian policies.[52] The Obama administration's archives are not yet fully accessible so it is hard to settle this debate. Still, it may be that asking whether Obama or even his economic team were "really" Keynesian is beside the point. When it comes to fiscal policy choices, economic logic alone cannot matter as much as political considerations. The relatively modest size of the stimulus may have been a mistake, but the post-bailout political environment was impossible to ignore.[53] The fact is that Obama decided not to make a case to the American public for more stimulus and even appeared to concede that fiscal deficits were

---

[47] Obama 2020: 236–237. According to Geithner (2015: 376), Obama "was a Keynesian, but he didn't see the point of belaboring Keynesian arguments that the public wasn't buying."
[48] Krugman 2020: 115. [49] Geithner 2015: 372. [50] Geithner 2015: 375.
[51] Obama 2020: 237.
[52] Based on interview evidence, *Wall Street Journal* reporter Ron Suskind (2011) told a (controversial) story of an inexperienced Obama, torn between his economic advisors' advice to go for a big stimulus and his political advisors' opposition to it, ultimately resulting in policies that preserved the status quo. Historian Adam Tooze (2018: 280) concluded that there was a "self-censorship of the economics team in the name of politics." Economists Brad DeLong (2022: 510–511) and Stephanie Kelton (2020: 37) noted the anti-Keynesian flavor of Obama's January 2010 state of the Union speech, in which Obama encourages the federal government to "tighten its belt," and of a May 2009 C-Span interview in which he declared that "we're out of money now" and that he wanted to "get control of the deficit."
[53] As Alan Blinder puts it, Obama's fiscal stimulus "may have been too little economically even though it was nearly too much politically." Blinder 2022: 297.

6.3 "Headwinds" for Monetary Policy in the Public Arena

the problem. To convince Americans that more public money should be spent was an especially tall order for the country's first Black president, however. As the administration put forward its relatively modest fiscal stimulus, the Republicans and *Fox News* immediately started pouncing on it as an illegitimate government payout.[54] The rise of the Tea Party movement must be understood in the context of resentment against the stimulus and against perceived freeloaders who defaulted on their mortgages.[55] Obama's declaration that the government should "tighten its belt" corresponded to a widespread and seemingly intuitive sentiment, itself the result of decades of neoliberal policies. After the Republican Party and its new Tea Party wing captured the US House of Representatives in the November 2010 election, the political situation became even worse for the Obama administration.

The following years were a period of acrimonious debate between the Republican-controlled House and the Democrat-controlled Senate. In December 2010, just before the newly elected representatives were seated, Congress negotiated a two-year extension of the Bush tax cuts of the early 2000s (until the next election) alongside a cut in payroll taxes.[56] As it turned out, these so-called Obama tax cuts were the extent of fiscal stimulus that the Republicans were prepared to contemplate. As the Obama fiscal stimulus of 2009–2010 faded away, America entered a period of fiscal retrenchment. In the summer of 2011, Republicans in Congress only agreed to authorize a raise in the US federal debt ceiling after securing spending cuts. The crisis took the federal government to the verge of default and led Standard & Poor to downgrade the United States' credit rating. At the end of 2012, the looming end of many of the Bush and Obama tax cuts threatened to take the country onto the edge of a "fiscal cliff" and back into a slump.[57] To avoid falling off that cliff, Congress signed a last-minute deal into law in January 2013 that essentially made the Bush tax cuts permanent, except for high-income earners. In the spring of 2013, the spending cuts agreed in the summer of 2011 went into effect, in the form of budget sequestrations that forced various government departments to shut down for two weeks. At that point and again in 2015 and 2016, shutdowns or threats of shutdowns constantly dragged the US economy down.[58]

---

[54] "It's Not a 'Stimulus' Plan – It's a 'Porkulus' Plan," *Fox News*, February 2, 2009. www.foxnews.com/opinion/its-not-a-stimulus-plan-its-a-porkulus-plan.

[55] Williamson, Skocpol, and Coggin 2011: 26.

[56] *The Washington Post* called it "the most significant tax bill in nearly a decade." See "Congress Votes to Extend Bush-era Tax Cuts," *The Washington Post*, December 17, 2010.

[57] As the Congressional Budget Office puts it: "Under current law, the federal budget deficit will fall dramatically between 2012 and 2013 owing to scheduled increases in taxes and, to a lesser extent, scheduled reductions in spending – a development that some observers have referred to as a 'fiscal cliff.'" Congressional Budget Office, *Economic Effects of Reducing the Fiscal Restraint That Is Scheduled to Occur in 2013*, CBO Report, Washington, DC, May 2012, p. 1.

[58] According to the CBO at the time: "In the absence of sequestration, CBO estimates, GDP growth would be about 0.6 percentage points faster during this calendar year, and the equivalent of

Despite its legally established independence and its Republican-appointed chair Ben Bernanke, the Federal Reserve was in an awkward position in the face of such political as well as economic turmoil. Rather than being caught in partisan crossfire, central bankers studiously tried to avoid political controversy. Within their internal FOMC arena, they talked about US fiscal policy as a "headwind" – as if it were a completely external phenomenon, like the weather. When politics inevitably came into the economic picture – for example, when they discussed the fiscal stimulus, the debt ceiling, or the government shutdown – the transcripts reveal conversations that were primarily about the economic consequences of government policies, and whether these policies were helping or hindering the economy. Unlike Greenspan (and unlike Volcker before that) Bernanke decided to talk about fiscal policy in the public arena as little as possible, because this was "outside the Fed's jurisdiction" – even though "speaking publicly about the fiscal headwind was a particular challenge."[59] The Fed chair nonetheless signaled to Congress that fiscal retrenchment, be it in the form of tax increases or spending cuts, was inappropriate in an economic slump.[60] After an emergency meeting convened to discuss the risk of government default if the debt ceiling was not raised, the FOMC's official statement did not mince words: "Participants agreed that while the Federal Reserve should take whatever steps it could, the risks posed to the financial system and to the broader economy by a delay in payments on Treasury securities would be potentially catastrophic, and thus such a situation should be avoided at all costs."[61] Yet there was ultimately little that the Fed could do to prevent such powerful "headwinds."

6.4 THE CONSOLIDATION OF MONETARY REGIME CHANGE

Although the Fed was not immune to political "headwinds," its independence provided some insulation for the conduct of monetary policy – in contrast to fiscal policy. In this sense, the Fed's easy-money policies did become the "only game in town." The December 2008 FOMC meeting marked what Bernanke has called the advent of a "new monetary regime" characterized by "the end of orthodoxy" and the beginning of "a new era of policy activism."[62] Accordingly, the transcript of that meeting has attracted scholarly attention

---

about 750,000 more full-time jobs would be created or retained by the fourth quarter." CBO, "Automatic Reductions in Government Spending – aka Sequestration," CBO Blog, February 28, 2013: www.cbo.gov/publication/43961.

[59] Bernanke 2015: 504.

[60] As his memoirs elaborate, Bernanke (2015: 504) settled on a two-pronged posture – first, that "the economy needed help from Congress" and, second, that the deficit "while a serious matter, was primarily a longer-run concern" that should therefore not be addressed by raising current taxes or cutting current spending. See also Bernanke 2015: 120, 191–192.

[61] Minutes of the FOMC, October 29–30, 2013.   [62] Bernanke 2015: 135–167, 418, 421.

6.4 The Consolidation of Monetary Regime Change

as the start of a "new regime."[63] In March 2009, the Fed would initiate its policy of purchasing large quantities of Treasury bonds and mortgage-backed securities in order to decrease long-term interest rates, *alias* quantitative easing. This moment of monetary regime change and the Fed's immediate crisis response in 2008–2009 did not put an end to America's economic troubles, however.[64] The post-crisis slump continued well into the 2010 decade, and the recovery was quite slow, especially on the employment front. While the Fed did not jumpstart the economy as effectively as a more important fiscal stimulus might have done, it did provide massive monetary stimulus and thus placed a floor under the United States' descent into economic slump.

The central bankers' retreat from the kind of neoliberal policies that they had supported since the 1980s is particularly noteworthy. While the initial reaction of the Fed is understandable as a largely improvised reaction to the financial crisis in the fall of 2008, we cannot understand why the new "monetary regime" was consolidated so slowly if we do not consider the politics of the Fed's incorporation of unorthodox policies into its policy panoply. To some extent, Fed officials' changing patterns of thinking and intraorganizational debate can be understood in terms of cognitive and organizational psychology.[65] As we will now see, an important factor in the slow pace of monetary regime consolidation at the Fed is the fact that this consolidation also required political work. The fact that this consolidation did occur, however slowly, creates difficulties both for the conventional economic story about political-ideological mistakes and for political economy accounts in terms of the Fed's entrenched "austerian" or "pro-finance" logic. Scholars often gloss over a new reality, namely the chasm between the Fed and political conservatives that became increasingly evident throughout the 2010s.

Despite deep misgivings from the Fed's "hawks," monetary policy did become increasingly expansionary – and, in this process, counteracted an increasingly restrictive fiscal policy. In 2008–2009, monetary and fiscal policy were moving in stride, but that did not last long. The effects of the 2009 stimulus package dissipated over time, and states and local governments started to cut spending as the slump continued and as their tax revenues decreased. As spending cuts became the name of the fiscal game, the Fed increasingly set aside the hawks' concerns and provided renewed monetary stimulus, thus quietly bucking fiscal policy trends. The majority of the FOMC, starting with Bernanke, held a positive view of fiscal as well as monetary stimulus as a response to the global financial crisis and the incipient recession. "Participants generally thought that fiscal stimulus was a necessary and important

---

[63] Abolafia 2020: 141–152.   [64] Eichengreen 2012, 2015.
[65] Scholars of psychology and organization show how difficult innovation can be in social and organizational settings. Actors typically turn to "satisficing" and "muddling through" rather than comprehensive revisions of their assumptions, and alternate between "fast" (intuitive) and "slow" (deliberative) thinking. See Simon 1947; Lindblom 1959; Kahneman 2011.

complement to the steps the Federal Reserve and other agencies were taking."[66] In the early days of the Obama administration – before stimulus became a "dirty word," as Geithner put it – the Committee expressed satisfaction that fiscal and monetary policies appear to be working in stride: "Fiscal and monetary policies were likely to contribute significantly to aggregate demand in coming quarters."[67] As the Fed had done when it had bailed out Bear Stearns and other endangered financial firms under the Bush administration, the FOMC went out of its way to help the Obama administration and provide monetary accommodation early on.

This was controversial among FOMC members, however, especially among hawks. In particular, Richmond Fed President Jeffrey Lacker consistently expressed dissent as early as QE1 started. In his eyes, monetary policy should not intervene directly on markets by extending credit to one category of creditors, such as consumers or homeowners: "Mr. Lacker dissented because he preferred to expand the monetary base by purchasing U.S. Treasury securities rather than through targeted credit programs. [...] he was concerned that such programs channel credit away from other worthy borrowers, amount to fiscal policy, would exacerbate moral hazard, and might be hard to unwind."[68] The transcript of that January 2009 FOMC meeting further reveals a tense debate about the stimulus between the majority and Jeffrey Lacker who worried about the Fed doing something that the Treasury and Congress should be doing:

MR LACKER. [...] my view is that, no matter how you feel about our credit programs – whether you are for them or 'agin' them – it would be better for the Treasury to finance them. I don't see any operational impediment to transferring our credit programs to the Treasury. [...]

CHAIRMAN BERNANKE. Thank you. I think, in principle, that we agree that it would be better to have all of this done by the Treasury. I think we have to accept political realities [...]

In other words, Jeffrey Lacker and Ben Bernanke agreed that the Treasury and Congress, rather than the Fed, should ideally decide to roll out the Fed's "targeted credit programs," but disagreed on whether it was appropriate for the Fed to take the initiative if political stalemate prevented such programs. Lacker was not explicitly against QE as such, but against targeted credit programs not going through the banking system, which in his mind amounted to "fiscal policy" because they helped particular segments of the population. The Fed's purchases of mortgage-backed securities, in this view, provided fiscal-like subsidies to homeowners, as opposed to purchases of Treasury securities that subsidized the government's debt issuances and that the government could therefore decide to allocate as it saw fit through normal budgetary procedures.

---

[66] Minutes of the Federal Open Market Committee, January 27–28, 2009.
[67] Minutes of the Federal Open Market Committee, March 17–18, 2009.
[68] Minutes of the Federal Open Market Committee, January 27–28, 2009.

6.4 The Consolidation of Monetary Regime Change

Bernanke, by contrast, thought that monetary policy should be cognizant of "political realities" and compensate for the incapacity of fiscal policy, in the likely event of a deadlock in Congress, to avert a credit crunch.

The return of the cleavage between hawks and doves in the FOMC arena – along with the hawks' concern about "worthy" borrowers and "moral hazard" – resonated with the remarkably quick rise of the Tea Party movement in the broader public arena. In February 2009, CNBC reporter Rick Santelli burst into a "rant" in front of a floor of financiers, which would mark the birth of the Tea Party movement.[69] Santelli called for "capitalists" to rally against "losers" who "can't pay their bills." The racial innuendos of Santelli's accusation were clear to his audience, who knew that the unfolding housing crisis had been triggered by a crisis in subprime loans.

Ironically, however, just as American politics was on the way to becoming ever more polarized, the effective rollout of the fiscal and monetary stimulus made subsequent FOMC debates somewhat less tense. Since the economic situation seemed to be improving in the spring of 2009 and through the end of the year, the conflict between the hawks and the doves at the Fed became less acute. Aggregate spending boosted growth, even though the situation did not improve quickly on the unemployment front. There were therefore more unanimous FOMC votes in 2009 than the year before. The FOMC even envisioned the eventuality to "gradually slow the pace" of its $300 billion Treasury security purchases.[70] In September, the FOMC expressed a cautiously optimistic outlook: "[E]conomic activity had picked up following its severe downturn; most thought an economic recovery was under way."[71] In late 2009, however, unemployment reached its most worrisome level during the Great Recession: "The employment-to-population ratio had fallen to a 25-year low, and aggregate hours of production workers had dropped more than during the 1981-82 recession."[72] QE therefore remained in place for now and the FOMC kept its policy rates near zero.

In 2010, it became increasingly clear that growth remained sluggish, that inflation was uncomfortably low, and that unemployment remained much too high. A debate then took place at the FOMC on whether the Fed should do more monetary accommodation. As the doves led by Ben Bernanke greatly outnumbered the hawks, they consistently outvoted them and decided to undertake more policy accommodation. The FOMC then engaged in a second round of quantitative easing (QE2) in November 2010 – again for a total amount of $600 billion, but this time mostly in the form of purchases of treasury securities rather than mortgage-backed securities: "[M]ost members judged it appropriate to take action to promote a stronger pace of economic

---

[69] Williamson, Skocpol, and Coggin 2011: 25.
[70] Minutes of the Federal Open Market Committee, June 23–24, 2009.
[71] Minutes of the Federal Open Market Committee, September 22–23, 2009.
[72] Minutes of the Federal Open Market Committee, December 15–16, 2009.

recovery and to help ensure that inflation, over time, is at levels consistent with the Committee's mandate. In their discussion of monetary policy for the period immediately ahead, nearly all Committee members agreed to keep the federal funds rate at its effective [zero] lower bound [...] the Committee decided to continue its existing policy of reinvesting principal payments from its securities holdings into longer-term Treasury securities and intended to purchase a further $600 billion of longer-term Treasury securities."[73] Importantly, in this context of renewed monetary stimulus, the majority of the FOMC unambiguously welcomed the fiscal stimulus: "The new fiscal package was generally expected to support the pace of recovery next year."[74]

The hawks' marginalization occurred over time and never became complete, however. As the financial crisis seemed to be over, hawkish central bankers began to question the continuation of the Fed's easy-money policies. The following is a typical summary of the FOMC debate: "Several participants noted that a continuation of lower-than-expected inflation and high unemployment could eventually lead to a downward movement in inflation expectations that would reinforce disinflationary pressures. By contrast, a few participants noted the possibility that a potentially unsustainable fiscal position and the size of the Federal Reserve's balance sheet could boost inflation expectations and actual inflation over time."[75] The transcript of the December 2009 FOMC meeting reveals that Minneapolis Fed President Kocherlakota was, among the inflation hawks (before he "became a dove"), especially nervous: "I am concerned about a tail risk of a low-probability but high-inflation outcome. The size of the government debt held in the private sector has increased by more than 30 percent in the past two years. This rise in the debt can only be funded by future tax increases, spending cuts, or higher inflation. Any uncertainty about the Congress's will to exercise the required fiscal restraint translates directly into uncertainty about current or future inflation."[76]

In 2010, Kansas City Fed President Thomas Hoenig became a voting member on the FOMC and took up the role of the most vocal hawkish dissenter that year – with eight dissents in all eight meetings. Hoenig would be the first of a succession of Fed district presidents who would consistently dissent in the 2010s. When we look at the pattern of dissenting FOMC votes over two decades (2000–2019), we note that it is anything but random (see Figure 6.2). Dissenting votes markedly increased after the 2008 crisis, with above eight dissenting votes per year – one per meeting. In addition, dissenting votes were overwhelmingly cast by a handful of district Fed presidents: Jeffrey Lacker (Richmond, fifteen dissents), Esther George (Kansas City, fifteen dissents),

---

[73] Minutes of the Federal Open Market Committee November 2–3, 2010.
[74] Minutes of the Federal Open Market Committee, December 14, 2010.
[75] Minutes of the Federal Open Market Committee, June 22–23, 2010.
[76] Meeting of the Federal Open Market Committee, December 15–16, 2009, transcript, p. 75.

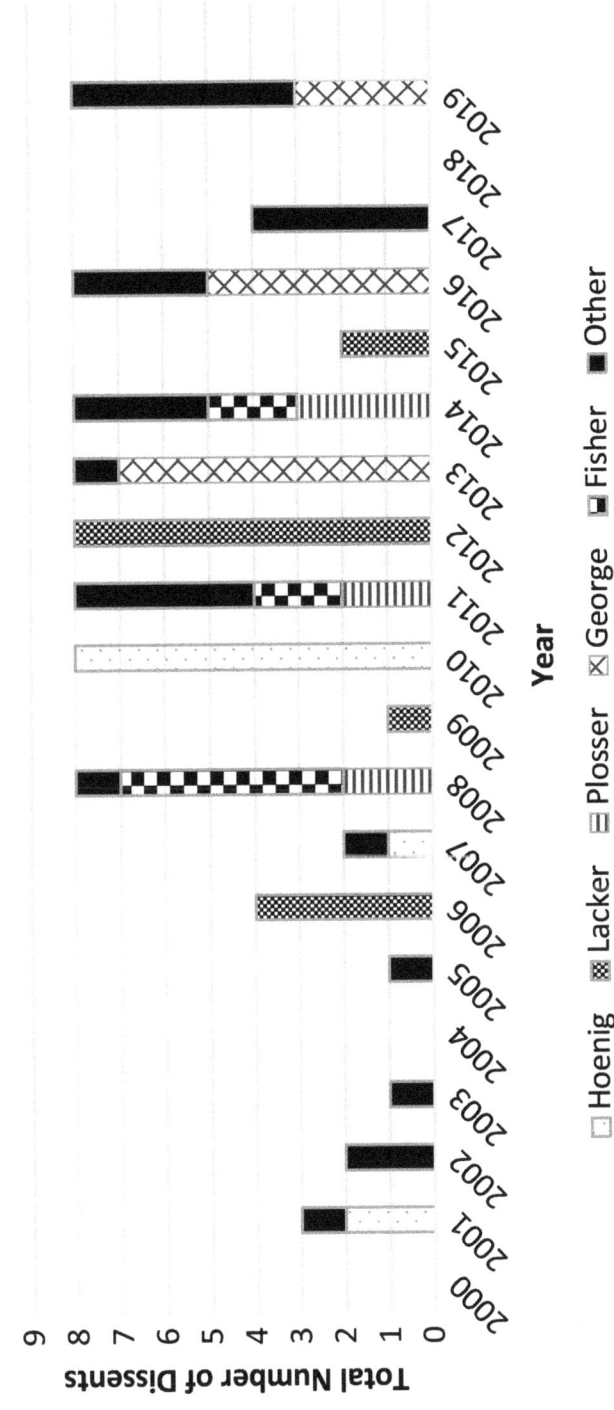

FIGURE 6.2 FOMC dissents, 2000–2019.

Thomas Hoenig (Kansas City, twelve dissents), Richard Fisher (Dallas, nine dissents), Charles Plosser (Philadelphia, seven dissents).[77]

As summarized by the Fed minutes of the January 2010 meeting, Hoenig was "concerned that, under these improving conditions, maintaining short-term interest rates near zero for an extended period of time would lay the groundwork for future financial imbalances and risk an increase in inflation expectations."[78] In his memoirs, Ben Bernanke expressed his displeasure about Hoenig's "increasingly public campaign" and "provocative rhetoric."[79] In this case, the power of the Fed's norm of collegiality clearly manifested itself in the breach. After Hoenig stepped down, he confided his frustration with Bernanke to a journalist and claimed that he was primarily concerned not with inflation but with the "allocative" effects of QE, namely the fact that it worsened economic inequality.[80] On the surface, this perspective seems to confirm the frequent critiques of QE from a political economy perspective, and their suggestions that the Fed should instead have distributed "helicopter money" directly to citizens.[81] Critics of QE on the FOMC in the early 2010s were quite far from that position, however. Instead, they made the case that QE was a threat to "fiscal discipline" and that it was hurting senior citizens and "savers" while favoring the rich:

MR. FISHER – (…) here, we suffer, just to stay with my diaper analogy, from fiscal incontinence. If this were to change, then I would make a case for accommodation, but that is not yet happening. And by providing monetary accommodation, I would suggest we are reducing the odds of fiscal discipline being brought to bear. (…)

(…) I find no delight in it, and I see considerable risk in conducting policy with the consequence of transferring income from the poor, those most dependent on fixed income and the saver, to the rich. Senior citizens and others who saved and played by the rules are earning nothing on their savings, while big debtors and too-big-to-fail oligopoly banks benefit from their subsidy.[82]

There is little doubt that large-scale asset purchases (QE) were the Fed's attempt to discourage saving behavior and boost consumer demand through what economists call a "wealth effect." QE had the effect of inflating the price of financial assets and making credit less costly which, by definition, disproportionately benefited people who had financial wealth. From this perspective, QE

---

[77] Thornton and Wheelock 2014. See also: www.stlouisfed.org/on-the-economy/2014/september/a-history-of-fomc-dissents.
[78] Minutes of the Federal Open Market Committee, January 26–27, 2010.
[79] Bernanke writes that Thomas Hoenig's dissents "risked undermining public confidence in the Fed and disrupting the Committee's deliberative process by staking out inflexible positions before hearing other Committee members' views." Bernanke 2015: 488.
[80] Leonard 2022.
[81] Blyth and Lonergan 2014; Fontan, Claveau, and Dietsch 2016; Adolph 2018: 738; Cooper 2024: 84.
[82] Meeting of the Federal Open Market Committee, November 2–3, 2010, transcript, pp. 152, 154.

6.4 The Consolidation of Monetary Regime Change

was indeed increasing inequality. Yet if we consider the politics of money within the FOMC arena – not to even mention the broader public arena – the realistic alternative to QE, if we consider FOMC dissents in the early 2010s, was clearly not "helicopter money."[83] Rather, FOMC dissenters wanted to stop monetary accommodation and to come out on the side of "fiscal discipline" by returning to a more orthodox monetary policy.

The Fed's unorthodox policies have been the subject of two broad scholarly criticisms. From a political economy perspective, as we saw, many have criticized the Fed for worsening rather than reducing inequality. The Fed's policies certainly did not place money directly into people's pockets, which might have been the quickest way to boost consumer demand and mitigate inequality. This helps explain the popularity of the cry "where's my bailout?"[84] Instead, they pumped money into financial markets, by driving interest rates down to zero and then by buying large quantities of government bonds and asset-backed debt securities. Although these Fed actions did not help the people most in need, they did favor a large middle class of homeowners, many of whom were able to take out cheaper mortgages or refinance at lower rates. That corresponded to more than 60 percent of the US population – not only "the rich." By pumping money into the economy, the Fed also aimed to prevent a worse recession that would have disproportionately hurt the less affluent. From this perspective, its actions can be seen as a continuation of the kind of "mortgage Keynesianism" and other forms of credit subsidization that scholars have argued was a long-standing American substitute for welfare payments to the poor.[85] Despite deep contests within the FOMC and in the public arena, the Fed managed to increase median household wealth.

Second, the Fed has been criticized from an economics perspective for doing too little, too slowly. In the late 2000s and the early 2010s, the US economy was caught in what Keynesian economists called a "liquidity trap" – that is, a situation in which uncertainty was so high that money was typically hoarded or invested in safe assets (e.g., US government paper, gold, etc.) rather than spent in the real economy. Therefore, standard monetary accommodation was like "pushing on a string" – as Krugman wrote in his blog in 2008.[86] Instead, a more effective policy would have been to boost demand through fiscal deficit spending. But, as we saw, the appetite for fiscal stimulus in Congress quickly waned. Although the Fed could have conducted more heavy-handed

---

[83] Bernanke himself had toyed with this idea of "helicopter money" – inspired by Milton Friedman – before becoming Fed chair, thus earning the nickname "helicopter Ben." Yet he later saw firsthand the obstacles to a central bank acting in this way, and he never seriously pushed this idea in the 2010s. For a sympathetic but skeptical discussion, see Bernanke 2022: 359–363.
[84] Obama (2020: 522) himself commented on it in his memoirs.
[85] Hyman 2011; Prasad 2012; Reisenbichler 2020.
[86] Paul Krugman, "Pushing on a String," February 15, 2008, and November 21, 2008.

unconventional policies early on, this would have invited more attacks from the Right in the public arena; it would also have further compromised the FOMC's internal unity as an organizational arena. These political constraints were real, since Fed leaders needed to justify their actions to Congress and a vocal FOMC minority was dead set against QE. Insofar as it boosted consumer demand through a wealth effect, the Fed's response was therefore more effective than any other politically realistic alternatives at the time – both in the public arena and within the FOMC arena.

6.5 THE FED'S RELIANCE ON NEO-KEYNESIANS IN THE ECONOMICS PROFESSION

Starting in 2011, Fed officials came to realize that they would no longer be able to count on fiscal policy to support the recovery. FOMC participants then worried about "the continuing fiscal adjustments by U.S. state and local governments" and "the possibility of larger-than-anticipated near-term cuts in federal government spending."[87] In turn, this reactivated the long-standing cleavage between hawks and doves about the proper stance of monetary policy. The doves on the FOMC wanted more accommodation to boost growth and to lower unemployment, whereas the hawks focused on the danger of rising commodity and energy prices:

MR DUDLEY. (…) We don't have much experience sitting at the zero lower bound for years, and I hope we won't repeat this in the future. That's why I think we must be open-minded and challenge our assumptions that the current stance of monetary policy is as stimulative as we think it is. […]

MR. PLOSSER. (…) Given the inflation developments and the economic outlook, I am increasingly uncomfortable with the funds rate sitting at zero.[88]

In August 2011, the FOMC decided to shift toward a more accommodative "forward guidance" – that is, to commit to a longer period of near-zero interest rates. This led three FOMC members to cast dissenting votes: Fisher, Kocherlakota, and Plosser.[89] At its November and December meetings, however, the FOMC decided not to make any more changes, which led to a (rare) dissent by a dove who wanted the Fed to adopt more rather than less dovish policies.[90] The question for the Fed leadership was what to do about fiscal "headwinds," both to maintain the FOMC's internal coherence and to chart a course for the future that would be communicable to the outside.

---

[87] Minutes of the Federal Open Market Committee, March 15, 2011.
[88] Transcript of FOMC meeting on June 21–22, 2011, pp. 133, 176. The same three would dissent again on further accommodative actions at the meeting of September 20–21, 2011.
[89] Minutes of the Federal Open Market Committee, August 9, 2011.
[90] Minutes of the Federal Open Market Committee, November 1–2, 2011.

6.5 The Fed's Reliance on Neo-Keynesians in the Economics Profession

The "headwinds" of American politics also showed little sign of abating. As Bush-appointed governors vacated their seats on the Federal Reserve Board, the administration faced hurdles even to appoint a bipartisan slate of nominees – Jerome Powell, a former Wall Street executive and a Republican, and Jeremy Stein, a Harvard economist who had served in the Treasury Department as senior advisor to the secretary under Obama.[91] After Obama's reelection in November 2012, the House remained majority Republican and opposed the administration's budget. Although the Democrats had a comfortable majority of fifty-three in the Senate, it was not a supermajority. To maintain unity at the FOMC would therefore remain an important concern for Fed leaders.

In part to resolve such difficulties, Bernanke and later Yellen moved to commit themselves to a new framework of rules, while at the same time maintaining considerable policy discretion. By so doing, they hewed close to the "neo-Keynesian" mainstream within the economics profession. Bernanke essentially struck a balance between neoclassical and Keynesian economics, by advocating "constrained discretion."[92] On the one hand, the preference for monetary "rules" over "discretion" originally derived from Milton Friedman's distrust of central bankers' discretionary actions. It had later become a hallmark of the classical critique of Keynesian economics in the name of "time consistency."[93] A vocal minority at the FOMC remained in that neoclassical tradition – and generally leaned on the hawkish side.[94] On the other hand, Bernanke and Yellen built on work by neo-Keynesian economists on monetary rules – such as Columbia University economist Michael Woodford's concept of "forward guidance." Bernanke's reflections about Japan's deflationary experience had led him to champion a "flexible" but explicit inflation target of 2 percent.[95] For neo-Keynesian economists, a low but positive inflation target would steer the economy away from deflation as well as from inflation. While his proposed 2 percent target thus addressed Keynesian concerns, Bernanke also tried to reassure the FOMC hawks that their concerns were being heard:

At the same time that we are using every power we have to try to fight this incredible crisis, there are concerns on the other side that, by expanding our balance sheet and the like, we risk inflation increasing in the medium term. It is important for us to communicate that we will be effective and timely in removing that stimulus, so that we will not have an inflation problem during the exit from our current policies.[96]

---

[91] Mark Felsenthal and David Lawder, "Old Feud Appears to Sink Obama's Fed Nominees," *Reuters*, May 7, 2012.
[92] Bernanke 2022: 178.   [93] Friedman 1962: 62; Kydland and Prescott 1977.
[94] Alan Blinder (2022: 307) suggests that the 2010s may have been "monetarism's last gasp."
[95] Bernanke 2015: 40.
[96] Conference call of the FOMC on January 16, 2009, transcript, pp. 14–15. See also Bernanke 2015: 470.

While there surely was a strictly economic rationale for increasing the "transparency" and "predictability" of monetary policies through rules, this effort also served the political purpose of reducing contestation – within the arena of the FOMC, in the professional arena of economics, and among politicians concerned with "accountability" in the public arena. Since the Greenspan years, the Fed had worked with an inflation target that remained "informal," because Greenspan was reluctant to forgo the Fed's discretion. When the issue of inflation targeting first surfaced in the 1990s in the United States, it was often associated with a rigid rule of zero inflation. Connie Mack and Jim Saxton, two Republican members of Congress, started to champion bills that would make disinflation the primary or even the sole mandate of the Fed.[97] Within the Fed, inflation targeting imposed by Congress was controversial because it could be interpreted as a downgrade of the Fed's employment mandate or as an infringement on the Fed's independence.[98] Although Greenspan initially seemed comfortable with a zero percent target, he had eventually agreed with Janet Yellen's proposal at a July 1996 FOMC meeting that an inflation target should be around 2 percent.[99]

After the mid-1990s, the advocacy of inflation targeting became more and more distant from its classical origins. According to his biographer, Greenspan identified early on as "un-Keynesian."[100] Yet the Fed under Greenspan increasingly went in the direction of what was emerging as the "neo-Keynesian" mainstream in the macroeconomic profession. In a paper assessing the "Greenspan standard" presented in Greenspan's presence at the Jackson Hole conference, former Fed Governor Alan Blinder underscored that Greenspan's insistence on "discretion" could be interpreted as Keynesian.[101] Blinder himself, but also Bernanke, Yellen, and most other prominent economists who were appointed to the Federal Reserve Board since the 1990s identified as "neo-Keynesians." For them, inflation targeting was as much a way of avoiding deflation and therefore maximizing employment as it was a way of fighting inflation. But as the January 2009 FOMC conference call made clear, inflation targeting was also popular among FOMC hawks. As Bernanke said, it addressed "concerns on the other side that, by expanding our balance sheet and the like, we risk inflation increasing in the medium term." Bernanke concluded the discussion by saying that it was "interesting" and that he would confer with Congress before making a move in that direction.[102]

---

[97] Author interviews, US Congress, March 20, 22, 24, 2006.
[98] Author interviews, Federal Reserve officials, March 16, 20, 2006; Princeton economics department March 27, 2006.
[99] Mallaby 2016: 487–491. [100] Mallaby 2016: 26–38.
[101] Blinder and Reis 2005. In his more recent book, Blinder makes the case that Greenspan conducted a "policy of fine-tuning in deed though not in word." (Blinder 2022: 244).
[102] Conference call of the Federal Open Market Committee on January 16, 2009, transcript, p. 57.

6.5 The Fed's Reliance on Neo-Keynesians in the Economics Profession 129

In the same vein, the FOMC issued "exit strategy principles" in June 2011 "as part of prudent planning," with a view toward "normalizing" the Fed's monetary policy at some indeterminate point in the future.[103] According to his memoirs, Bernanke was wary of tightening monetary policy too early, with the risk of adding to the fiscal policy "headwinds." Yet he agreed to discuss the "mechanics of normalizing policy" at the FOMC "in the interest of good planning," and also to assuage the hawks' discomfort with the prospect of indefinitely long monetary accommodation.[104] The FOMC formed a committee led by San Francisco Fed President Janet Yellen, and in 2012 endorsed its guidelines on "policy normalization" around the "long-term goals of monetary policy strategy."[105] As part of this drive for an exit strategy, the Bernanke Fed also formally announced an inflation target of 2 percent. Continuing with Fed leaders' concern to balance the respective concerns of hawks and doves, that statement announced its commitment to a "balanced approach" in pursuit of the Fed's inflation and employment objectives.

The Fed's adopting of an explicit inflation target did not appear to mollify the inflation hawks on the FOMC, however, since they continued to oppose the Fed's unconventional policies. But it stole much of their fire and contributed to further marginalize their dissent. Richmond Fed President Jeffrey Lacker became the hawks' flagbearer in 2012, dissenting eight times in eight meetings, as he "expected that a preemptive tightening of monetary policy would be necessary to prevent an increase in inflation projections or inflation expectations."[106] The transcripts also reveal that Lacker was not only always outvoted, but also evidently isolated at FOMC meetings. He was often at great pains to make the case that he was deliberating in good faith, rather than dogmatically defending his position. As one interviewee put it, the fact that he always dissented "discounted" the value of his dissenting votes.[107] Some FOMC members often implied that they did not believe any rational argument would change him, which in turn diminished his standing in a committee with a strong norm of collegiality.

While a few remaining hawks on the FOMC continued to worry primarily about inflation, most FOMC members judged that weak government spending and the possibility of further fiscal tightening meant that "fiscal policy would continue to be a drag on economic growth over coming quarters."[108] The minutes and transcripts of the FOMC meetings of the early 2010s increasingly

---

[103] Minutes of the Federal Open Market Committee, June 21–22, 2011.
[104] Bernanke 2015: 470.
[105] FOMC, "Statement on Longer-Run Goals and Monetary Policy Strategy," January 24, 2012.
[106] Minutes of the Federal Open Market Committee, January 24–25, 2012.
[107] Interview, former FOMC member, Cambridge, MA, May 8, 2023.
[108] Minutes of the FOMC, June 19–20, 2012. See also, Minutes of the FOMC, September 12–13, 2012.

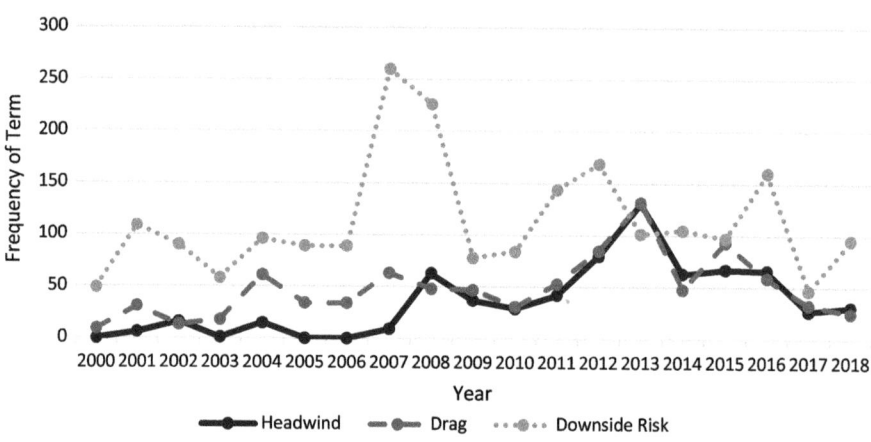

FIGURE 6.3 Frequency of terms "headwind," "drag," and "downside risk" from 2000 to 2018.

mention the "headwind," "drag," and "downside risk" of fiscal retrenchment (see Figure 6.3).

As fiscal austerity worsened in 2012, the FOMC decided on a third round of quantitative easing (QE3). The Fed would implement $85b of monthly asset purchases – both treasury security and mortgage-backed security purchases – without a clear ceiling or end date.[109] Jeffrey Lacker dissented again, both because he thought QE was unnecessary and risky and "because he viewed it as inappropriate for the Committee to choose a particular sector of the economy to support."[110]

In December 2012, the Fed even decided to continue its asset purchases under QE3 beyond the end of the year – and, in fact, indefinitely. Again, Jeffrey Lacker dissented – his last dissent of 2012 before his FOMC voting seat was rotated to another Fed district bank president, as per Federal Reserve rules. The FOMC's dovish majority realized the costs of massive asset purchases, but they saw them as worth incurring in order to get the country on the path to employment recovery. Newly appointed Governor Janet Yellen put it in stark terms:

While I do worry about the costs and risks associated with our asset purchase program, I think it is essential to recognize that we do not have any riskless policy options. We face a profound risk that slow progress in moving the economy back toward full employment will not only impose immense costs on American families and the economy at large, but may also do permanent damage to the labor market. We also face the serious risk that inflation (...) could decline further over time, (...) making it yet more difficult for monetary policy to provide meaningful stimulus.[111]

---

[109] Minutes of the FOMC, September 12–13, 2012.
[110] Minutes of the FOMC, September 12–13, 2012.
[111] Meeting of the FOMC, December 11–12, 2012, transcript, pp. 184–185.

6.5 The Fed's Reliance on Neo-Keynesians in the Economics Profession

The Fed's decision to continue its monetary accommodation indefinitely drew persistent dissent, but from a dwindling number of hawks. Along with others, Minneapolis Fed Governor Kocherlakota "became a dove."[112] As Hoenig recognized in September 2012, "I think everybody agrees at the table that inflation is not an immediate or presently foreseeable threat. Our desired port, given our mandate, is increased employment."[113] After Lacker stepped down from his role of most consistent dissenter of 2012, Kansas City Fed President Esther George took up that role in 2013 and cast her first dissenting vote out of concern about "inflation expectations."[114]

There is also evidence that the FOMC's decisions to provide more monetary stimulus were partly prompted by concerns about the Fed's standing vis-à-vis the economics profession and in the public arena. In 2013, Christina and David Romer, two prominent economists (including Obama's former CEA chair), praised the FOMC's renewed activism as an indication that its members "now think they had been underestimating the effectiveness of the tools, or overestimating the costs" of monetary accommodation.[115] Yet the transcripts – which were not public at the time – suggest that the FOMC members were not motivated only by their own changing views of the economic situation. FOMC members often discussed the economics profession's views about what they should do – including Christina Romer's own calls for Fed action on unemployment.[116] In this sense, the prominent economists who commented on the Fed's actions were more than just external observers of FOMC debates. In addition, FOMC members were motivated to act in anticipation of fiscal "headwinds" in 2013, and to defend the Fed's independence:

MR. ROSENGREN (...) While there are political risks with our balance sheet activities, there are political risks from very high unemployment, below-target inflation, and stopping our actions. Japanese central bank independence is endangered because they did too little, not because they did too much.[117]

The FOMC held a special meeting by videoconference on October 16, 2013, due to the risk of government default on its debt if the debt ceiling was not raised. Again, the FOMC did not mince words in expressing its displeasure: "Participants agreed that while the Federal Reserve should take whatever steps it could, the risks posed to the financial system and to the broader economy by a

---

[112] Michael S. Derby, "Dr. Kocherlakota, or How I Learned to Stop Worrying and Love Quantitative Easing," *Wall Street Journal*, March 14, 2013. See also, Sewell Chan, "Within the Fed, Worries of Deflation," *New York Times*, January 29, 2010.
[113] Meeting of the Federal Open Market Committee, September 12–13, 2012, transcript, p. 69.
[114] Minutes of the Federal Open Market Committee, January 29–30, 2013.
[115] Romer and Romer 2013: 159.
[116] Meeting of the Federal Open Market Committee, November 1–2, 2011, transcript, pp. 25, 27, 73, 74, 92. That FOMC discussion referred to: Christina Romer, "Dear Ben: It's Time for your Volcker Moment," *New York Times*, October 29, 2011.
[117] Meeting of the Federal Open Market Committee, March 19–20, 2013, transcript, p. 156.

delay in payments on Treasury securities would be potentially catastrophic, and thus such a situation should be avoided at all costs."[118]

Only in the mid-2010s, after Ben Bernanke stepped down in January 2014 and Janet Yellen took over as Fed Chair, did the economic situation begin to markedly improve.[119] District Fed presidents Charles Plosser and Richard Fisher – the main dissenters in 2014 – then wanted to withdraw monetary accommodation as soon as possible. In December 2014, Kocherlakota joined them as a – rare – third dissenter.[120] But unlike Plosser and Fisher, Kocherlakota – as a newly converted dove – actually favored "a more accommodative stance."[121] The majority still judged unemployment too high through 2015, however. The Yellen Fed's hopes of quick economic recovery and complete withdrawal of QE were met with disappointment in 2016. The economic situation during most of Yellen's tenure as chair kept improving, but slowly, so the Fed kept interest rates low and withdrew QE cautiously. Through the end of 2015, the majority still judged unemployment too high to quickly withdraw monetary support.[122] In December 2015, the FOMC decided to raise the federal funds rate above zero for the first time since 2008, but the rate still remained low at .25–.50 percent through December 2016, the Fed kept its balance sheet steady at about 4.4 trillion dollars of assets through 2018.

In that context, the "Taylor rule," which suggested that the Fed's monetary policy was too accommodative, became a recurrent topic of FOMC conversation. John Taylor was a Stanford economist known both as a neo-Keynesian and as a prominent critic of the Fed. Within the FOMC arena, many also doubted that the Taylor rule was a panacea:

VICE CHAIRMAN DUDLEY. (...) I've had a headache about the Taylor rule for a long time, as you all know – in large part because of the slavish adherence to a constant real equilibrium rate of 2 percent, which I think has been contradicted by the actual performance of the economy over the past few years.[123]

Like Bernanke before her, Janet Yellen also relied on the neo-Keynesian mainstream in the professional arena of economics, which is why John Taylor's criticisms posed a special difficulty. Taylor was respected in the professional arena of economics, but he also fared well among Republicans in the public arena. He had advised Republican presidential candidate Mitt Romney in 2012 and had criticized the Obama fiscal stimulus and the Fed's

---

[118] Minutes of the Federal Open Market Committee, October 29–30, 2013.
[119] Minutes of the Federal Open Market Committee, June 17–18, 2014.
[120] Blinder (2022: 324) calls this relatively high number of dissenting votes a situation "akin to a mass mutiny" at the FOMC.
[121] Minutes of the Federal Open Market Committee, December 16–17, 2014.
[122] Minutes of the Federal Open Market Committee, July 28–29, 2015.
[123] Meeting of the FOMC, March 17–18, 2015, transcript, p. 189. See also Kocherlakota's retrospective "self-criticism" of his former role as hawk after 2008: meeting of the FOMC September 16–17, 2015, transcript, p. 168.

6.5 The Fed's Reliance on Neo-Keynesians in the Economics Profession

easy-money policies as completely "off track."[124] Like Milton Friedman – and later in Friedman's footsteps as president of the Mont-Pelerin Society (2018–2020) – Taylor believed that fiscal policy should be used rarely if ever, and that monetary policy should be strictly rule-based. These positions estranged him from the neo-Keynesian mainstream within the professional arena of economics.[125] Yet John Taylor's political connections, especially to Republican Congressman Jeb Hensarling, created trouble for the Fed.[126] In 2014, House Republicans introduced a bill that would have strictly bound the Fed to a rule-based policy mandate. In response, Yellen testified that "it would be a grave mistake for the Fed to commit to conduct monetary policy according to a mathematical rule."[127]

The House Republicans' bid to force the Fed to adopt the Taylor rule was a serious threat for the Fed. Although the bill did not become law, the challenge came from the economics profession and from Congress – the two arenas, other than the FOMC itself, where contestation can be most problematic for central bankers. In the 2016 presidential campaign, Donald Trump berated Yellen for helping Democrats with low Fed interest rates.[128] As Trump considered replacing Yellen, Congressman Hensarling and Phil Gramm recommended John Taylor to President Trump as Fed chair.[129] Although Taylor was one of the top-three finalists for the job, Trump reportedly "found Taylor too rigid and old."[130] Now led by Trump, the Republican Party had changed, and John Taylor was apparently not destined to be a rule-oriented tight-money chair of the Federal Reserve. Instead, Trump appointed Fed board member Jerome Powell as chair, reportedly because he liked Powell's views on deregulation.

President Trump then soon soured on his own pick for Fed chair, as the Powell Fed did not immediately deliver the easy-money policies that Trump wanted. Instead, the FOMC gradually increased its federal funds rate from zero to 2–2.50 percent, partly in response to higher growth fueled by "expansionary fiscal policies enacted over the past year" – in other words, by Trump's unfinanced 2017 tax cut.[131] Although Powell also worried about the effects of Trump's trade policy, he favored a wait-and-see approach on that front. As he told the FOMC: "A trade war has the potential to slow down growth," but

---

[124] Taylor 2013.
[125] In Alan Blinder's words, "Lord Keynes would have been shocked" (Blinder 2022: 303).
[126] Bernanke 2022: 225
[127] Binyamin Appelbaum, "Yellen Says Restraining the Fed's Oversight Would Be a 'Grave Mistake'," *New York Times*, July 16, 2014.
[128] Harriet Torry, "Donald Trump Attacks Federal Reserve, Yellen During Debate," *Wall Street Journal*, September 26, 2016.
[129] Dorn, Hensarling, Gramm, and Taylor 2020.   [130] Ullmann 2022: 317.
[131] Minutes of the Federal Open Market Committee, November 7–8, 2018.

the outcomes of trade disputes were "uncertain."[132] The FOMC never discussed Trump's increasingly disparaging comments on Powell, however. During his first administration, Trump considered "firing" the Fed chair, but did not test his legally questionable authority to do so.[133] He also tried, unsuccessfully, to get the Senate to appoint Judy Shelton to the Federal Reserve Board. Shelton was a Trump loyalist and advocate of a return to the gold standard.[134] At that point, however, even a president as disruptive as Donald Trump was patently unable to turn the independent Fed into a tool for his partisan agenda.

In his memoirs published in 2015, a year after he stepped down as Fed chair, Ben Bernanke expressed his discomfort with a "radicalized" Republican Party that "saw inflation where it did not exist [...] invoked conspiracy theories [and] advocated discredited monetary systems, like the gold standard."[135] He was irked by their attacks on the Fed and on him personally, despite the fact that he had worked with and been appointed as Fed Chair by President George W. Bush. As Bernanke recalls it, "I still considered myself a conservative. (...) I didn't leave the Republican Party. I felt that the party left me." Bernanke was not the only economist close to the Republican Party to be unhappy about its evolution. Harvard economist Greg Mankiw, the former chair of Bush's Council of Economic Advisors, also announced that he was leaving the party.[136] Although that was arguably less surprising coming from a Democratic appointee, former Fed chair Janet Yellen expressed similar dismay about President Trump's "lack of grasp" of macroeconomic policy.[137] Both Bernanke and Yellen expressed a widespread sentiment among economists. In their eyes, Trump and the Republicans were disrespecting the Fed's independence and pursuing dangerous policy and personnel options.

In sum, Fed leaders found themselves increasingly estranged from Republican elected officials in the 2010s. Tight monetary and fiscal policies that the Fed had supported under Volcker were irrelevant to address the problem of collapsed spending and low growth that they confronted. In reaction to the deepest recession since World War II and to the continuing slump of the early 2010s, the Federal Reserve turned to unprecedented monetary stimulus. Comforted by their independence and technocratic ethos, Fed officials tried to do what they thought was best for the American economy, at a time when

---

[132] Meeting of the Federal Open Market Committee, July 31, August 1, 2018, transcript, p. 135.
[133] Peter Conti-Brown, "What happens if Trump tries to fire Fed chair Jerome Powell?" Brookings Blog, Monday, September 9, 2019.
[134] Jeanna Smialek and Emily Cochrane, "Judy Shelton, Trump Fed Nominee, Fails to Advance to Final Vote," *New York Times*, November 17, 2020.
[135] Bernanke 2015: 432-433, see also p. 521.
[136] N. Gregory Mankiw, "Why a 'Republican Economist' Plans to Vote in the Democratic Primary," *New York Times*, November 14, 2019.
[137] Matthew Choi, "Yellen says Trump doesn't have a grasp on macroeconomic policy," *Politico*, February 25, 2019.

the main problem diagnosed by most mainstream economists was high unemployment rather than inflation. Meanwhile, the Republicans fanned a distinctly new and more populist kind of neoliberal agenda. Key Republican figures still advocated free markets, but they also favored fiscal and monetary restraint in the midst of a recession – with their strong stance against the Obama fiscal stimulus, their charge against the Fed's monetary stimulus, and their frequent calls to "end the Fed."[138] Such neoliberal advocacy was populist in the sense that it claimed to speak for the American people and Main Street, but that it was unburdened by concerns of intellectual coherence. In addition to his pet pursuit of tariffs that reversed decades of trade liberalization, Trump later turned up the volume of these populist attacks against Democrats, Wall Street, the Fed, and other corrupt "elites."

6.6 CONCLUSION: THE FED'S RETREAT FROM NEOLIBERALISM

In retrospect, the post-2008 crisis consolidation of an unorthodox monetary regime of easy money was a remarkable development. It is easy to underestimate the Fed's political predicament and its broader consequences for America's political-economic regime. From an economics perspective, Fed policymakers have often been criticized for their mistakes and their hesitation to stand up against political pressures. From a political economy perspective, the Fed has been blamed for its neoliberal, pro-finance orientation. Yet neither perspective does justice to the political difficulty for the Fed to break away from a low-inflation monetary regime, itself lodged at the core of America's political-economic regime. When the Fed moved toward easy-money policies, it faced a rebellion of conservatives on many fronts – at the FOMC, in the economics profession, and in the public arena.

Because they saw themselves as technocratic guardians of the US economy, Fed leaders worked to offset the "headwind" of fiscal austerity through "activist" policies of monetary stimulus and abandoned an anti-inflationary stance that they deemed inappropriate to the situation. Faced with political as well as economic turmoil, Fed leaders consolidated the new monetary regime of easy money by marginalizing inflation hawks within the FOMC, by relying on mainstream neo-Keynesian economists, and by toning down the Fed's advocacy of fiscal consolidation and other neoliberal economic policies.

By changing their alliances, American central bankers retreated from technocratic neoliberalism and thus changed the character of America's political-economic regime. Their retreat from technocratic neoliberalism was not the stuff of news headlines – in part because it was neither complete nor fully recognized. It was incomplete in the sense that the Fed historically supported

---

[138] Paul 2009.

and continued to support many pro-market economic policies – especially by relying on financial markets and resisting what they saw as overly stringent regulation. It was not recognized because, in principle, the Fed remained in favor of long-term fiscal consolidation. This may explain why the Fed's conservative role in supporting America's neoliberal and finance-friendly regime often remains taken for granted. Yet in a deep slump without any inflation, the Fed clearly opposed austerity and supported reflationary policies. Many conservative actors duly took note and saw the Fed's policies as a betrayal of market purity and sound money. The Tea Party of the early 2010s coalesced as a movement against "losers" who were being "bailed out" by the government. Such concerns later also fueled the rise of the MAGA movement, led by Donald Trump who regularly fumed against Democrats, Wall Street, the Fed, the "deep state," and "elites" intent on "destroying America."

Ultimately, the Fed's retreat from technocratic neoliberalism pushed conservative actors' neoliberal project in a decidedly more populist direction. As they grew apart from conservatives, Fed leaders reconnected with a concern about "populism" that was familiar to their forebears. In the early twentieth century, the framers of the Federal Reserve wanted to bring modern central banking to America, but also to undercut the populist case in favor of cheap credit and against the gold standard.[139] After gold receded from the historical stage in the 1970s, the Volcker Fed had asserted itself as the new bulwark of sound money. By the early 2010s, however, the Fed confronted a radically different populist challenge. While the traditional left-wing populist critique of the Fed still existed, the Tea Party of the early 2010s espoused a right-wing form of populism. After his 2016 electoral victory, President Trump pushed for policies that favored moneyed interests, such as tax cuts or deregulation, but he also drove the budget deficit higher and pressured the Fed to pump money into the economy. Such orientations illustrated Trump's anti-elite rhetoric – a hallmark of populist politics – but they further undermined the technocratic version of neoliberalism that the Fed had supported since the 1980s.

---

[139] On the Fed's founding, see Lowenstein 2015. For the origins of anti-debt populism, see Zackin and Thurston 2024.

7

The Waning of Technocratic Neoliberalism in the European Union

Like the US Federal Reserve, the ECB had an outsized role in responding to the global financial crisis and to the economic downturn of the late 2000s and 2010s – which also involved, in Europe, a crisis of the Eurozone. Perhaps even more than the Fed, however, the ECB considerably evolved during that period. Around 2000, the ECB was viewed as a copycat of the German central bank, rigidly bent on its anti-inflationary mandate. It was the nemesis of the Left, as it was regularly accused of not doing enough to support growth and employment. In the early 2010s, its French president, Jean-Claude Trichet, widely appeared as the main backer of a "Brussels-Frankfurt consensus" in favor of price stability, fiscal retrenchment, and neoliberal reforms. When Italian central banker Mario Draghi was chosen to succeed Trichet, the German best-selling tabloid *Bild* endorsed him as an honorary German with a spiked helmet.[1] Yet over the 2010s, the ECB turned into a rather different organization. After Trichet's successor Mario Draghi promised to do "whatever it takes" to save the euro, the ECB broadened its recession-fighting panoply and adopted easy-money policies. The ECB was also increasingly attacked by conservatives. *Bild* even caricatured its president as a "Count Draghila" sucking on the blood of German savers and retirees.[2] Under Christine Lagarde, the ECB moved further into unchartered territory, away from a strictly defined inflation-fighting focus, for example, by embracing "green central banking."

The widespread notion that the ECB somehow became more enlightened under Mario Draghi is too simple, however. Like the Fed, the ECB struggled to squeeze various emergency actions into its policy panoply. Although the ECB

---

[1] "So Deutsch ist der neue EZB-Chef," *Bild*, April 29, 2011.
[2] "So Saugt Graf Draghila unsere Konten leer," *Bild*, September 13, 2019.

initially supported fiscal contraction and enlisted governments and other EU bodies behind its cause, austerity policies soon turned into monstrous politics that the ECB no longer controlled. To stabilize the situation, ECB officials had to consolidate a new monetary regime and, for that purpose, work on reshaping the European Union's political-economic regime. The euro is managed independently by the ECB, but the ECB must still relate with other EU bodies, EU member governments, politicians, and the public. In addition, the ECB steers the European economy and, increasingly, supervises banks and financial markets. As was the case for the Fed, the ECB's status as an independent central bank facilitated its retreat from the neoliberal regime that had originally justified its independence. After a long hiatus, the ECB pushed back against fiscally conservative policies that had become popular with large sections of the public in Germany and beyond. ECB leaders thus slowly moved away from tight-money policies and its advocacy of fiscal retrenchment as well as other neoliberal policies. In so doing, they considerably distanced themselves from the ECB's long-standing conservative allies.

7.1 THE ECB'S SLOW ESCAPE FROM THE "FRANKFURT CONSENSUS"

The tale of the ECB's belated enlightenment after 2008 comes in two distinct flavors. From an economics perspective, many stress the Trichet ECB's policy mistakes and the counterproductive influence of politics and ideology. Thus, Jean-Claude Trichet is often indicted for his misguided "Teutonic" outlook and for encouraging "a hard right turn toward austerity" by turning into an "enforcer of fiscal consolidation and structural reform."[3] By preaching austerity and refusing to backstop the sovereign bond markets, the ECB of the early 2010s did not play the role of "lender of last resort."[4] By wielding its collateral framework as a "disciplinary device," it failed to exercise "self-restraint" – until all that finally changed under Draghi.[5] From a political economy perspective, scholars tend to highlight the importance of financial interests and neoliberal (or "ordoliberal") ideas and institutions in the pursuit of unpopular policies and in the defense of Germany and other creditor states' interests.[6] To the extent that the ECB later modified its policies, this is often interpreted as a result of ideational change toward a more "systemic" understanding of the crisis, or a

---

[3] Eichengreen 2015: 4, 7–8, 39.
[4] De Grauwe 2011; De Grauwe and Ji 2012; Buiter and Rahbari 2012.
[5] Micossi 2015; Orphanides 2017; Tucker 2018.
[6] Hall 2012; Blyth 2013; Schmidt and Thatcher 2013; Schäfer and Streeck 2013; Schimmelfennig 2015; Matthijs and McNamara 2015; Helgadottir 2016; Farrell and Quiggin 2017; Matthijs and Blyth 2017.

process of "reinterpreting rules 'by stealth.'"[7] Some scholars also stress the "infrastructural power" and "de-politicized" logic of financial markets, which first led the ECB to an "obsession with liquidity," "pro-cyclical" policies, and a concern with its "reputation" as inflation fighter.[8] After the "collapse of the Brussels-Frankfurt consensus," ECB policymakers evolved when both financial markets' expectations and EU institutions evolved, resulting in a "paradigm shift" toward "technocratic Keynesianism" and a "revolution without revolutionaries" or with "unexpected revolutionaries."[9]

Altogether, scholars of various stripes have thus abundantly highlighted the ECB's economic mistakes or political-economic biases in responding to the challenges that it faced after 2008. Yet the economics and political economy perspectives each begs questions about the puzzling separation between ECB leaders and the ECB's longtime conservative supporters – within the ECB Governing Council, within the economics profession, among governments and the public. The ECB surely made mistakes, as economic historian Barry Eichengreen has abundantly pointed out.[10] But it could not easily ignore the fact that many conservative politicians and large segments of the European public on whom they relied for support demanded austerity. Likewise, explanations in terms of neoliberal or structural bias only go so far. As political scientist Vivien Schmidt points out, the ECB's practice of "governing by rules" led to a "crisis of legitimacy," that was "exponentially greater" in countries that received EU assistance.[11] Yet it remains to be explained why the independent ECB would be willing to alienate its most faithful conservative supporters to repair its legitimacy in countries that largely resented ECB actions.

Rather than minimizing the ECB's mistakes or biases, my intent in this chapter is to highlight the ECB's initial political predicament and its agency in progressively escaping it. As I will demonstrate, ECB leaders actively worked to reshape the different arenas in which they operated to address the problems that they confronted. As most observers recognize, the ECB's and more generally the EU's response to the crises and downturn of the late 2000s and 2010s was anything but linear. After massive liquidity injections, bank bailouts, and fiscal deficit spending in the late 2000s, the EU moved to policies of fiscal austerity after 2010, while the ECB progressively stepped up its monetary response. The fiscal and monetary components of these responses are reflected in the evolution of Eurozone public deficits and public debts in proportion to GDP (Figures 7.1 and 7.2), the ECB overnight facility interest rate (Figure 7.3), and ECB assets in proportion of GDP (Figure 7.4).

---

[7] Brunnermeier, James, and Landau 2016: 2–4; Ferrara 2020; Schmidt 2016; Schmidt 2020: 150–175; Braun, Di Carlo, Diessner, and Düsterhöft 2024.
[8] Gabor and Ban 2016: 627, 628; Fontan 2018; Braun 2020; Birk and Thieman 2020; Braun and Gabor 2021; Wansleben 2023; Moschella 2024.
[9] Jones 2013; Van't Klooster 2021; Gabor 2021; Van't Klooster 2022; Moschella 2024.
[10] Eichengreen 2015.   [11] Schmidt 2020: 14–15. See also Moschella 2024: 113–114.

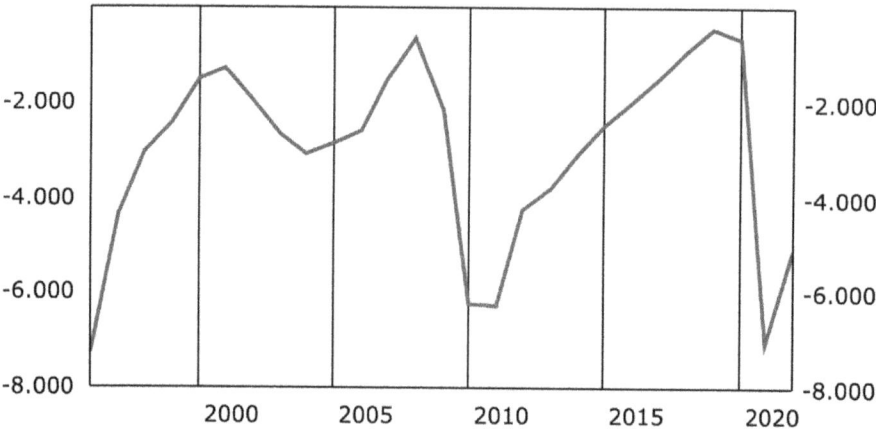

FIGURE 7.1 Eurozone public deficit as percentage of GDP (source: ECB Statistical Data Warehouse).

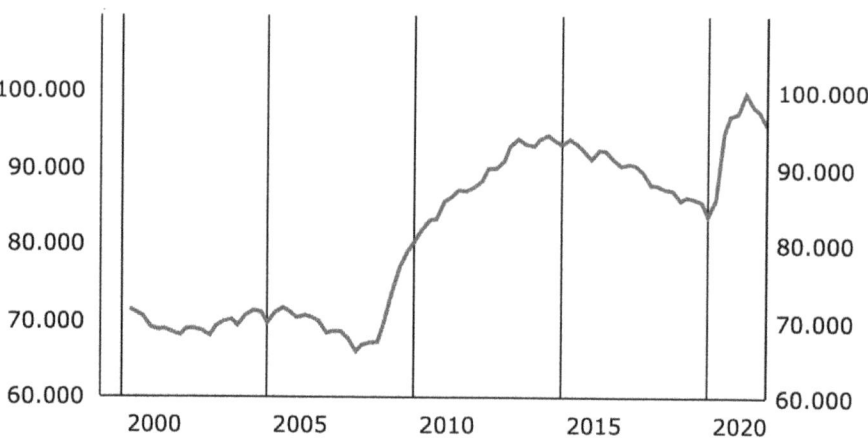

FIGURE 7.2 Eurozone public debt as percentage of GDP (source: ECB Statistical Data Warehouse).

Two important questions emerge from a cursory examination of these figures. First, why did the ECB shift to easy-money policy so late? In comparison to the Federal Reserve, the Bank of Japan, or the Bank of England, the ECB was slow to expand its balance sheet. It even tried to raise interest rates early in the downturn, and it implemented massive asset purchases (*alias* QE) only in 2014 – unlike, for example, its swift later reaction to the pandemic. Second, why did the ECB not encourage greater recourse to deficit financing in response to continued downturn at the beginning of the 2010s decade? This question concerns not only the Eurozone, since many countries stopped fiscal stimulus and turned to austerity after the global financial crisis

7.1 The ECB's Slow Escape from the "Frankfurt Consensus"

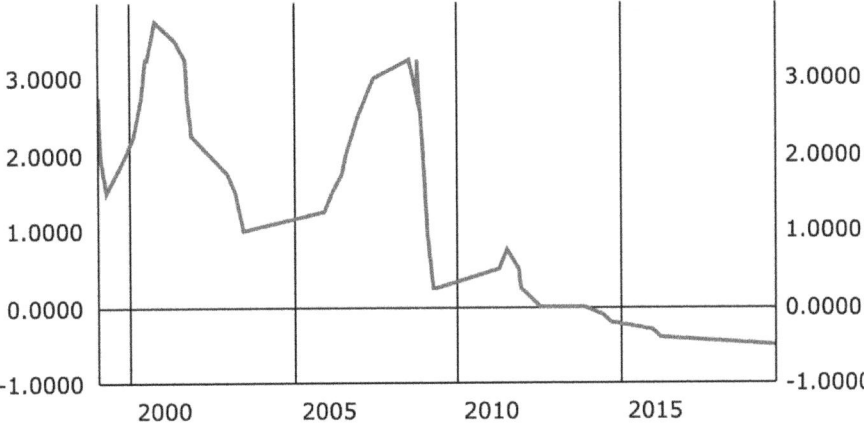

FIGURE 7.3 ECB overnight deposit interest rate (source: ECB Statistical Data Warehouse).

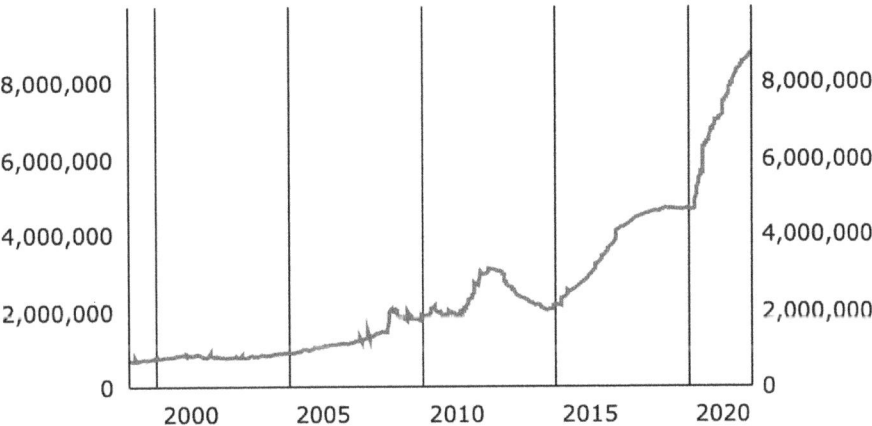

FIGURE 7.4 Eurosystem assets, in millions of euros (source: ECB Statistical Data Warehouse).

and the deep recession of the late 2000s.[12] It is especially relevant to the Eurozone, however, since there was increasing evidence that Eurozone growth remained weak and that fiscal austerity was a counterproductive strategy for addressing what quickly turned into a crisis of the Eurozone. In comparison to the United States or Japan, aggregate Eurozone public debt long remained at relatively low levels (well below 100 percent of GDP).

As we will see, the ECB's initially cautious response and its much-delayed activism manifested a politics of money that was both similar to and different

[12] Blyth 2013.

from its US counterpart. Like the Fed, the ECB adopted "unconventional" policies, and later squeezed them back into its policy panoply, thus making them de facto conventional. As in the United States, conservative actors outside the central bank resisted at almost every step a departure from the tight-money regime that they had supported since the late twentieth century. Yet the situation in Europe also differed in some important respects, insofar as the ECB did not initially backstop sovereign debts.[13] Sovereign debt ratings by private rating agencies and the soaring costs of access to capital markets that governments faced resulted in dramatically higher costs of credit in the Eurozone's periphery. The ECB, financial markets, and politicians mutually adjusted to each other's actions, however. Rather than being bound by a stable "Frankfurt consensus," the ECB's actions were remarkably syncretic. Changes that initially seemed relatively small and exceptional turned out, in fact, to be momentous and permanent. No other change was more important in triggering conservative resistance than successive ECB decisions to purchase government bonds. In sum, the EU's political-economic regime evolved considerably over time.

It is difficult to trace precisely the internal ECB's decision-making process that led to the evolution of its policy framework, since there is no public access to voting records, let alone to "proceedings" (transcripts) of the ECB Governing Council's monetary policy meetings. Under the Treaty-defined Statute of the ECB, these proceedings are strictly confidential. In 2015, the ECB decided to publish its "monetary policy accounts."[14] These anonymized minutes, without voting records, provide a useful window into the ECB's monetary policy decisions in light of recurrent cleavages among central bankers. The ECB did not make its minutes from the period before 2015 available retroactively, however – unlike the Federal Reserve's transcripts and minutes after 1993. My repeated requests for such documents, even in edited form, have been unsuccessful (see Appendix B). I therefore chose to reconstruct the internal ECB decision-making process of the early 2010s with the help of ECB releases, central bankers' speeches and memoirs, as well as reporters' accounts based on their interviews with central bankers.[15] I have also occasionally relied on other scholars' reconstructions of this process from central bankers' speeches as a "battle of ideas."[16] Most of my analysis,

---

[13] De Grauwe 2011; Gabor and Ban 2016; Van't Klooster 2022.

[14] The "monetary policy accounts" (minutes) are all on the ECB's website: www.ecb.europa.eu/press/accounts/html/index.en.html.

[15] In the genre of interview-based books, Neil Irwin (2013) and Carlo Bastasin (2015) are especially informative. For a central banker's testimony, see Bini Smaghi 2013. I also myself conducted confidential interviews with central bankers over many years of research.

[16] Ferrara 2020. See also Brunnermeier, James, and Landau 2016; Schmidt 2020; Braun, Di Carlo, Diessner, and Düsterhöft 2024. The drawback of speech analysis, however, is that it may lead scholars to attribute too much weight to ideas and not enough to political factors in causing ECB policy changes. For a theoretical critique of ideational analyses of the Eurozone crisis, see Jabko 2019.

however, focuses on available evidence of central bankers' interactions within the ECB's internal arena and with the external professional and public arenas in which they navigated.

While an account of the internal ECB arena after 2008 cannot be as steeped in ECB archives as for the Fed, European central bankers' agency can nonetheless be demonstrated in a complex and specifically European politics of money. Europe's central bankers tried to "muddle through" extraordinary circumstances based on their institutionalized habits, as organization theory and social psychology would predict. They implemented emergency measures, including "non-standard" policies, but they were often held back by standard ECB habits. To maneuver more effectively, ECB leaders therefore also participated in contests about money in various arenas. Within the ECB's internal arena, they neutralized their most conservative critics by advocating fiscal discipline even while buying distressed government bonds. After unleashing austerity, however, the ECB soon lost control of its creature. In the public arena, conservatives stridently resisted bailouts in the name of national sovereignty. Accompanying other EU actors, the ECB then cautiously retreated from an absolute refusal of bailouts and started consolidating monetary regime change in the public arena. In the professional arena of economics, central bankers increasingly leaned on mainstream Keynesian economists – like the Fed, even though scholars suggest that ECB economists had a distinctive European profile.[17] By asserting the importance of fiscal policy, they relegated German central bankers increasingly to the rear guard of the ECB – like some district Fed presidents vis-à-vis the Fed in the United States.

7.2 "EXTRAORDINARY" CIRCUMSTANCES AND ECB HABITS

With the global financial crisis of the late 2000s, the ECB was thrust into a new and uncomfortable world. Its president, Jean-Claude Trichet, had long been committed to sound money. As a French treasury chief before becoming head of the Banque de France and later of the ECB, he had spearheaded the 1980s *franc fort* policy of trying to emulate German anti-inflationary policies, and then he had participated in the drafting of the Maastricht Treaty, including the provisions that defined the ECB as an independent central bank primarily committed to price stability. Under the pressure of economic circumstances, however, Trichet and his ECB colleagues had to modify their policy framework and address challenges other than inflation. From an organizational standpoint, this was a difficult task for the young ECB because its anti-inflationary mandate was deeply institutionalized in its statute and procedures.[18] The tension

---

[17] Mudge and Vauchez 2016; Ban and Patenaude 2019.
[18] Salines, Glöckner, and Truchlewski 2012.

between practical considerations and ingrained habits produced a remarkably disjointed pattern of policymaking, as the Trichet ECB constantly tried to reconcile its "non-standard" actions with its institutional identity as a guardian of sound money.

7.2.1 The ECB's Changing Habits in the Face of "Exceptional" Circumstances

The ECB's evolution was much less linear than suggested by the frequent assessment of Draghi's ascent to the presidency of the ECB as a moment of radical change. On the one hand, the ECB evolved considerably under Trichet. It all started in August 2007, when Trichet started implementing what he called "exceptional" or "non-standard measures" in response to "extraordinary" or "exceptional" circumstances.[19] To compensate for the freezing of inter-bank lending, the ECB was especially active, pumping €95b of emergency liquidity assistance on the single day of August 9, 2007. This quick ECB reaction was widely praised and earned its president Jean-Claude Trichet the title of *Financial Times* "Person of the Year" for 2007.[20] Since commercial banks were no longer able to borrow short-term from each other in order to manage their cash flows and balance their books, they were invited to refinance themselves directly, against collateral, at the ECB's prevailing base interest rates on overnight deposits. Central banks across the world, including the Fed, quickly followed the ECB's example. Coming on the heels of the US subprime mortgage crisis, this episode was in fact the first early manifestation of the global financial crisis. The ECB's action was in line with Milton Friedman's admonition that central banks should address liquidity crises in the economy through increases in money supply. Although this remedy could be presented as part and parcel of a long-standing economic orthodoxy, it also prepared the way for bolder and much less orthodox actions.

The real vortex of the global financial crisis, leading to more "extraordinary" central bank actions, started in 2008 when several major US financial firms went bankrupt – first Bear Stearns, then Lehman Brothers, and AIG. This started an era of highly accommodative monetary policy in Europe as well as in the United States, with policy rates moving toward and later below the "zero lower bound" below which central banks' conventional tools of monetary policy are no longer sufficient (Figure 7.3). On October 8, 2008, the world's leading central banks engaged in a coordinated rate reduction move. Central bankers committed to provide European banks virtually unlimited liquidity at low cost and against a broad range of collateral, thus making central bank money more cheaply available to borrowers and investors. In the fall of

---

[19] Trichet 2010. [20] *Financial Times*, December 24, 2007.

2008 and in 2009, individual EU member governments rescued their national commercial banks by providing loans or even by recapitalizing them.[21] These financial flows prompted popular resentment that paralleled the US anger against taxpayer-funded bailouts. Unlike the Fed, however, the ECB did not overtly take part in the member states' bank rescues, in the absence of a common banking supervision, resolution, and deposit insurance scheme at the time. It only supported the banking sector indirectly, mostly through its decision to purchase about €60b of "covered" bank bonds.[22] Trichet also advised governments behind the scenes to "save their banks" – most controversially the Irish government, even wielding a controversial threat of withdrawing liquidity support to banks that did not have government support.[23] Thus, the ECB avoided many of the controversies about bank bailouts that engulfed governments at the time.

To address the most serious recession since the end of the Second World War, Eurozone member governments engaged in massive deficit spending. Aggregate fiscal deficits in 2009 and 2010 shot up to over 6 percent of Eurozone GDP, resulting in increasing public debts (Figures 7.1 and 7.2). Along with the European Commission, member states agreed to suspend the rules of the Stability and Growth Pact. In April 2009, the ECB reportedly struck a "hidden grand bargain" with struggling banks – the ECB provided them with liquidity as a quid pro quo for their purchases of government bonds.[24] After the revelation of Greece's double-digit public deficit figures in late 2009, the governments of the Eurozone faced increasingly diverging financing conditions ("spreads") as bond market investors started to get nervous. At that point, the ECB also started taking a more active role in supporting Eurozone government bond markets – despite a "no-bailout" clause that had been "enshrined" in the 1992 EU Treaty to ensure that there would be no monetary financing of states' fiscal deficits.[25] In May 2010, the ECB started its Securities Market Program (SMP), under which it purchased limited quantities of sovereign debt on secondary markets. A few days later, Trichet called for a "quantum leap in the governance of the euro area" and declared that Greece shared a "common destiny" with other member states.[26] Shedding old ECB suspicions about the French idea of *gouvernement économique*, Trichet effectively endorsed a new debate about governance that quickly became an EU policy mantra[27] (see Figure 7.5). From May 2010 to September 2012, the SMP also purchased a total of €218 billon of battered Greek, Irish, and Portuguese and later

---

[21] Woll 2014; for the example of France, see Jabko and Massoc 2012. [22] Trichet 2010: 13.
[23] Whelan 2014: 438; Tooze 2018: 362–363. [24] Bastasin 2015: 114–117.
[25] Dyson and Featherstone 1999: 783.
[26] Interview of Jean-Claude Trichet, *Der Spiegel*, May 15, 2010. [27] Jabko 2019.

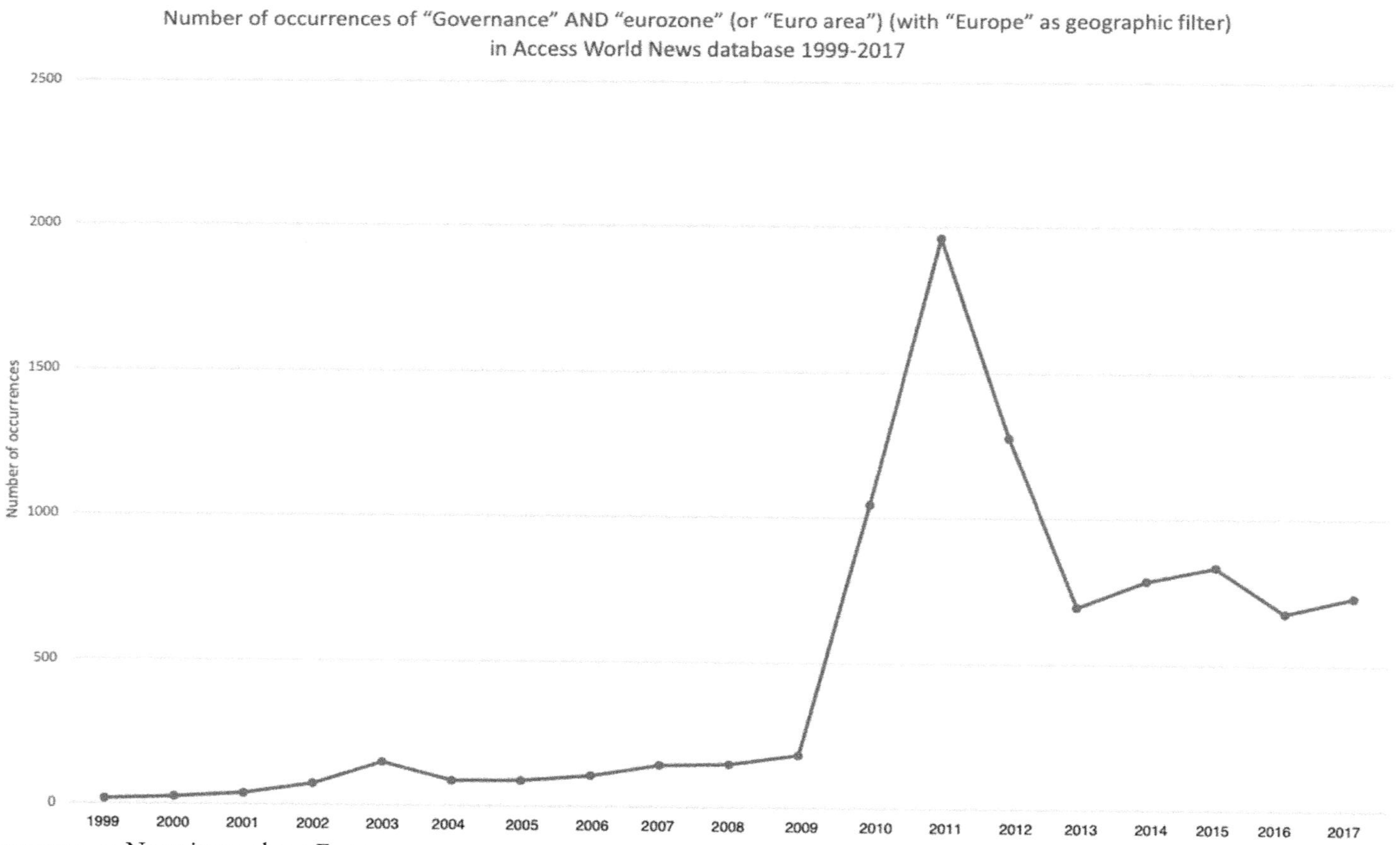

Number of occurrences of "Governance" AND "eurozone" (or "Euro area") (with "Europe" as geographic filter) in Access World News database 1999-2017
Number of occurrences
2500
2000
1500
1000
500
0
1999
2000
2001
2002
2003
2004
2005
2006
2007
2008
2009
2010
2011
2012
2013
2014
2015
2016
2017

FIGURE 7.5 News items about Eurozone governance.

Italian and Spanish government bonds, effectively supporting these countries' sovereign debt issuances and contributing to lower their interest rates.

The radical nature of the Securities Market Program is obviously debatable. On the one hand, it was not at all on the same scale as the Federal Reserve's large-scale purchases of US government bonds (or "quantitative easing") after November 2008. The ECB's interventions on secondary debt markets were limited and also "sterilized" – that is, compensated by ECB withdrawals of monetary liquidity to offset the program's effect on the money supply.[28] On the other hand, the ECB's intervention signaled to bond market investors that the ECB was endorsing and assisting the member states' direct commitment of loans to peripheral countries. Officially, the ECB wanted to avoid a contagious upward spiral in the long-term interest rates on peripheral countries' public debts, which would have threatened the "monetary policy transmission mechanism" since these interest rates had a direct impact on the cost of credit in the Eurozone's periphery. In addition, the ECB's purchases of peripheral governments' debts were financially risky, since these purchases were not protected against default risks. Even though these bonds were, on paper, high-yield investments that the ECB bought significantly under their nominal values, the possibility of sovereign debt "haircuts" leading to net losses for the ECB balance sheet was not merely theoretical[29] – especially in the case of Greece. In view of these risks and of the EU Treaty's "no-bailout" principle, the Trichet ECB had come a long way.

7.2.2 The ECB's Habitual Defense of the Frankfurt Consensus

At the same time as it was engaging in such "non-standard" actions, the ECB encouraged fiscal austerity and defended the political-economic status quo that became known – and decried – as the "Frankfurt consensus." Even though the ECB worked early on to contain the global financial crisis, it did much less than its American counterpart to help fiscal authorities address the Great Recession. At that early stage of the Eurozone crisis, many ECB officials considered that they should remain focused on their price stability mandate.[30] There is little doubt that the ECB interpreted its own role in a conservative manner, especially in its rigid defense of its own collateral rules and of the Eurozone's fiscal deficit rules, which both contributed to an unprecedented crisis of the Eurozone.[31] After 2008 and until the Eurozone was in full-blown crisis, the leaders of the ECB – unlike their American counterparts at the Bernanke Fed – called for fiscal retrenchment rather than continued deficit spending.

---

[28] ECB Monthly Bulletin, June 2010, pp. 24–26.   [29] Bini Smaghi 2013: 8
[30] Salines, Glöckner, and Truchlewski 2012.
[31] On the ECB's collateral rules, see Van't Klooster 2022; on Eurozone austerity, see Blyth 2013.

Even though ECB archives are not open, plenty of publicly available evidence points to central bankers' excessive optimism about growth and a premature push for austerity. Trichet's May 2010 call for a "quantum leap" in Eurozone governance primarily focused on the need to "prevent bad behavior," rather than any kind of fiscal stimulus capacity. In July 2010, Trichet wrote in the *Financial Times* that Eurozone governments should "stimulate no more – it is now time for all to tighten."[32] Trichet also came out in favor of a hawkish program of "expansionary fiscal contraction."[33] In September 2010, Trichet reminded a press conference audience that the ECB's decision to keep its interest rates unchanged had been "unanimous," and declared to the attention of Eurozone governments that they needed to restore "credibility" by adhering strictly to the EU fiscal rules and the ECB's "structural reform" gospel: "Fiscal consolidation and structural reforms must go hand in hand to strengthen confidence, growth prospects and job creation."[34] In August 2011, Trichet co-signed a secret (later leaked) letter with the then-Italian central bank governor – and appointed Trichet successor – Mario Draghi, asking Italian Prime Minister Silvio Berlusconi to "restore the confidence of investors" through cuts in government expenditures and privatizations as an implicit condition for SMP purchases of Italian bonds.[35]

More than the EU's early turn to austerity in 2010–2011 in response to bond market pressures, it is perhaps the continuation of austerity and the delayed debt restructuring that are most puzzling. In the face of anemic growth, high unemployment, and falling wages and prices, the evidence accumulated that the crisis threatened to engulf more Eurozone states. The IMF's chief economist recognized that the Fund had been previously too optimistic in its assessment of fiscal retrenchment as a remedy for Greece's problems.[36] As senior European Commission officials admitted, "fiscal profligacy is neither the sole nor the main origin of Europe's fiscal crisis."[37] Still, ECB officials, in their "Troika" with the European Commission and the IMF, continued to act as enforcers of the Eurozone's fiscal rules in countries that received financial assistance.[38] In 2012, European Commissioner for economic and monetary affairs Oli

---

[32] Jean-Claude Trichet, "Stimulate No More – It Is Now Time for All to Tighten," *Financial Times*, July 22, 2010.
[33] Blyth 2013: 136–142; Bastasin 2015: 153–156.
[34] ECB monetary policy press conference, September 2, 2010.
[35] Michel Rose, "Trichet's Letter to Rome Published, Urged Cuts," *Reuters*, September 29, 2011. After dramatic spikes of interest rates on Italian bonds caused by reduced ECB bond purchases, and with a bit of assistance from German and French political leaders, Berlusconi was practically forced to resign. A similar letter was sent to the Spanish prime minister at the same time, but did not have the same dramatic political effect. See Bastasin 2015: 319–321; Henning 2016: 182–186.
[36] Blanchard and Leigh 2013.   [37] Buti and Carnot 2012: 903.
[38] Eichengreen 2015: 39; Henning 2017: 201–232; Schmidt 2020: 171–173.

Rehn declared that "Europe must stay the austerity course."[39] As the Eurozone crisis worsened, highly indebted governments scrambled to convince bond markets that they were serious borrowers. They feared the prospect of sovereign debt downgrades by rating agencies, which further increased their financing costs. Governments cut spending partly for these reasons, but also because of persistent EU austerity policies and the absence of explicit ECB backstop of bond markets.

7.3 CRACKS IN THE "CONSENSUS" OF THE ECB'S INTERNAL ARENA

In assessing the ECB's actions, most scholars have come to the reasonable judgment that the ECB's actions fell well short of what was needed in the face of the Eurozone's dire descent into crisis. From an economic perspective, it is difficult to understand why Trichet adopted such a "Teutonic" outlook and why the ECB made so many mistakes, thus "making things as difficult as possible."[40] From a political economy perspective, the ECB's oscillation between creative and dogmatic actions turned it into both a "hero" and an "ogre" of the Eurozone crisis.[41] Yet the rationales for the ECB's actions remain rather opaque. Depending on what aspect of the ECB's actions we observe, the glass can appear as either half-full or half-empty. To make sense of the ECB's underwhelming and apparently schizophrenic actions, we must first consider its contested organizational arena.

Since the turn of the twenty-first century, the young ECB had asserted its independence as a technical actor above the political fray.[42] It staunchly supported EU fiscal rules – while often relying on conservative economists and politicians for political cover. This rule orientation, in turn, enabled the ECB Governing Council to make most decisions by consensus. If we only consider EU rules, there was nothing surprising in the EU's early turn to austerity in 2010. After a new Greek government revealed a double-digit public deficit in October 2009, Greece looked like a textbook violation of the EU's fiscal rules. Even Keynesian economists who were critical of the EU's response opined that "a major dose of austerity was clearly required."[43] By March 2010, member governments pledged to work toward "better budgetary discipline" that would enable "the exit from the exceptional support measures (...) once recovery is

---

[39] Oli Rehn, "Europe Must Stay the Austerity Course," *Financial Times*, December 10, 2012.
[40] Eichengreen 2015: 4, 337.   [41] Blyth 2013; Schmidt 2020: 150–175.
[42] Jabko 2003; see also Chapter 5.
[43] Eichengreen 2015: 7. According to a retrospective econometric assessment by Gourinchas, Philippon, and Vayanos 2017: "given the size of the fiscal imbalances, a substantial fiscal correction was inevitable" (p. 4, see also p. 60).

fully secured."[44] They conceived the Greek assistance package of May 2010 as just another "exceptional" measure adopted at the tail end of the global financial crisis – much like the ECB's "non-standard" measures. By agreeing to undertake purchases of Greece's as well as other Eurozone governments' bonds threatened by spiraling debt financing costs, the ECB had gone as far as it could go to support the member governments. From Trichet's perspective as well as many other central bankers, the onus was now on politicians to "stimulate no more" and to consolidate national budgets. This is obviously not what happened, however. Premature calls for fiscal retrenchment epitomized what quickly appeared to prominent economists as policymakers' exaggerated optimism.[45] Like the ECB's restrictive monetary policies, fiscal consolidation in economies that had not fully recovered from the effects of the global financial crisis fueled market concerns about the sustainability of sovereign debts – but all that became clear above all in hindsight, and it does not fully explain why the ECB, unlike the Fed, persisted in its increasingly apparent mistakes.

However modest, the ECB's bond market purchase program (SMP) was intensely controversial in the internal arena of the central bank.[46] The ECB launched that program at a time when the ECB was still staunchly defending a strict interpretation of the EU Treaty's no-bailout rule and did not play a role of "lender of last resort" comparable to that of other central banks.[47] Trichet clashed with the German members of the Governing Council, who wanted to maintain that status quo and were outvoted on the decision to create the SMP. German Bundesbank President Axel Weber – who was then Trichet's heir apparent – also publicly criticized the program.[48] First, its critics accused the SMP to be outside the primary mandate of the ECB as defined by the EU Treaty, which is to maintain price stability. ECB leaders justified the SMP by invoking their responsibility to ensure homogenous borrowing conditions and to protect the entire euro area from contagious debt crises, but their critics argued that it could jeopardize price stability. Second, and most importantly, critics of the bond purchase program accused it of circumventing the Treaty's "no-bailout" clause. In their view, the ECB could not just backstop member states' sovereign debts by purchasing government bonds or even by accepting banks' government bonds as high-quality collateral without making itself vulnerable to the charge of bailing out profligate member states.

---

[44] European Council, Conclusions. Brussels, March 26, 2010, pp. 1, 2. [45] Eichengreen 2012.
[46] Irwin 2013: 229–232; Bini Smaghi 2013: 125; Bastasin 2015: 218–219; Verdun 2017: 216.
[47] De Grauwe and Ji 2012. About the evolution of central banks' role from "lender of last resort" to "dealer of last resort" on money markets, see Mehrling 2011.
[48] "Kaufprogramm birgt erhebliche Risiken" Interview with Weber, *Börsen Zeitung*, May 11, 2010.

7.3 Cracks in the "Consensus" of the ECB's Internal Arena

In light of the ECB Governing Council's internal divisions, two especially puzzling aspects of the Trichet ECB's decisions in comparison to the Bernanke Fed's decisions at the same time begin to make a lot more sense – the ECB's delayed monetary policy accommodation and Trichet's persistent calls for fiscal retrenchment, as well as the limits the ECB placed on the SMP. First, there was an internal political logic to Trichet's hawkish fiscal and monetary stance. Although Trichet himself was certainly not a dove, he was trying to assert his leadership as the spokesperson for an "overwhelming majority" of central bankers against an extremely vocal opposition to the SMP.[49] One way to rebuild ECB unity was to keep the conduct of monetary policy separate from the SMP bond-buying program and other "non-standard" policies. Trichet made an explicit distinction between "standard" monetary policy, that is, the need to set interest rates to maintain price stability, and the "non-standard" policies designed to deliver sufficiently low borrowing conditions in the struggling periphery.[50] Eurozone-wide inflation numbers repeatedly overshot the ECB's target of 2 percent, prompting Trichet's hawkish calls to "stimulate no more" but also the ECB's "unanimous" decisions to raise its policy rates in July 2008, April 2011, and July 2011.[51] By siding with the hawks on the ECB's monetary as well as fiscal policy stance, Trichet was preempting a possible hawkish rebellion against "non-standard" policies among central bankers who feared their potentially inflationary consequences.

Second, the SMP program was certainly not a full-fledged backstop of Eurozone bond markets – let alone an open-ended commitment to stimulate the economy below the "zero lower bound" like the Bernanke Fed's quantitative easing program. Like Ben Bernanke at the FOMC, Trichet leaned on the majority of the ECB Governing Council to adopt unconventional policies, and he also made a step in the direction of hawkish central bankers by recognizing the need to "exit" these policies as soon as possible. Trichet's step toward the hawks was much greater than Bernanke's, however. On this count, institutional differences between the European Union and the United States mattered – not just Trichet's "Teutonic" outlook. Unlike Fed leaders, ECB leaders needed to defend their pursuit of the Securities Market Program against their dissenting colleagues' charge – propagated well beyond the walls of the ECB – that they were violating the "no bail-out" clause of the Treaty.

---

[49] James Mackenzie, "ECB Trichet Rejects Weber View on Bond Buying," *Reuters*, October 17, 2010.
[50] Jean Claude Trichet, "Central Banking in Uncertain Times," speech at the Jackson Hole central bankers' symposium, August 27, 2010.
[51] ECB monetary policy press conferences on July 3, 2008; April 7, 2011; July 7, 2011. The ECB reversed its July 2008 rate hike in the fall of that year – after Lehman's bankruptcy – and its 2011 rate hikes in December 2011 – after Draghi took over as ECB president.

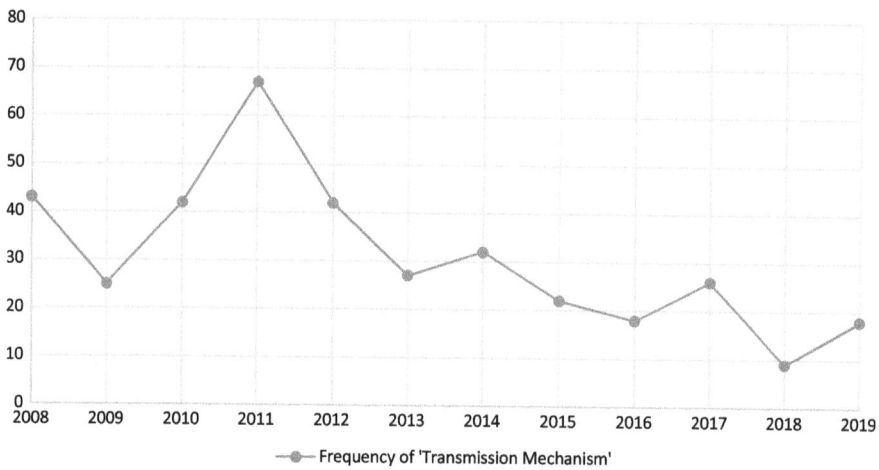

FIGURE 7.6 References to "transmission mechanism" in ECB speeches, 2008–2019.

In response to ECB dissenters, ECB leaders highlighted punitively high interest rates in the Eurozone periphery. In their public speeches in 2010–2011, central bankers increasingly evoked the need to preserve the "transmission mechanism" of monetary policy – in other words, the integrity of the Eurozone (see Figure 7.6.).

In sum, Trichet chose to present the SMP strictly as a tool to ensure the transmission of monetary policy, while also doubling down on his calls for fiscal retrenchment. By adopting a narrow rationale for the SMP, Trichet sought to rally as many central bankers as possible behind it. That also served to reassure bond market investors about the strength of the ECB's commitment to intervene on peripheral member states' bond markets through the SMP. The fact that the Eurozone was a relatively recent monetary union between different member states, each with its own fiscal policy, was a key difference with the United States that contributes to explain many central bankers' reluctance toward quantitative easing. Insofar as the SMP aimed to reduce "spreads" between the long-term interest rates on Eurozone government bonds, it also contributed to lower the costs of access to bond markets for states that faced debt downgrades. The ECB's adoption of the SMP was therefore already a move away from its long-standing endorsement of a strictly market-based treatment of government debt.[52] Trichet could not simply admit that the ECB was helping governments, since that could have easily appeared as Treaty-prohibited monetary financing. To explain the huge political echo of internal ECB opposition to the SMP program, however, we must zoom out of the ECB's

---

[52] Van't Klooster 2022.

internal arena and consider the resonance of that opposition in arenas external to the ECB.

7.4 THE CONSERVATIVE RESISTANCE TO BAILOUTS OUTSIDE THE ECB

As the Eurozone went into full-blown crisis mode, the EU Treaty's "no-bailout" clause quickly became a focus of attention – not only among central bankers, but also in the public arena. In combination with the small size of the EU budget, that clause sharply limited reciprocal fiscal obligations among member states. The Stability and Growth Pact codified sanctions against rule violators, and yet the imposition of sanctions by unelected EU bodies against democratically elected governments was inherently tricky – as illustrated by the notorious lack of enforcement against Germany and France in 2003.[53] Rather than open this Pandora's box, the ECB counted mostly on financial markets to impose their discipline and prevent excessive indebtedness. After the 2003 crisis of the Stability and Growth Pact, it had adopted minimum credit rating requirements for assessing the quality of government bonds that it accepted as collateral for its refinancing operation.[54] As the global financial crisis and then the Eurozone crisis revealed, however, "market discipline" was more procyclical and lumpy than policymakers had hoped – and the ECB's collateral framework only exacerbated that problem. After a decade of benefiting from borrowing conditions only slightly less favorable than Germany, the governments of Greece, Ireland, Portugal, and Spain suddenly faced soaring debt financing costs that raised the specter of partial default on these countries' debts (or "haircuts"). The idea that there would be no bailout of any kind was therefore no longer credible.

7.4.1 The ECB and the "No-Bailout" Rule

After the bank bailouts of 2008, however, the political prospects for an easy bailout of struggling debtor states were dim – a situation that scholars often understate. From an economics perspective, scholars often note that the ECB was very secure in its Treaty-guaranteed independence – even more than the Fed – and therefore could and should have prevented a crippling spiral of austerity, instead of turning into its "enforcer."[55] From a political economy perspective, scholars fault the ECB's focus on rescuing banks rather than preserving citizens' welfare. Because German and French banks held large amounts of debt from Greece and other states in the European periphery, many scholars concluded that a French–German push for austerity by Chancellor

---

[53] See Chapter 5. [54] Gabor and Ban 2016, Van't Klooster 2022.
[55] Eichengreen 2015: 7, 39.

Angela Merkel and President Nicolas Sarkozy was in fact a rescue of their respective banks' interests, with the ECB's helping hand.[56] Thus, Trichet's demand that member governments "save their banks" is often held as a sign of the ECB's "willfully simplistic and conservative interpretation" of its own role.[57]

Yet if we consider the intergovernmental arenas as well as the ECB arena, the situation appears more complex than a hidden rescue of French and German banks. Rather than simply bailing out French and German banks on the back of Greek taxpayers, Merkel and Sarkozy initially wanted to organize "private sector involvement," *alias* haircuts on Greek debt. Both the French and the German governments actually asked their respective banks to retain plummeting Greek bonds on their books.[58] As for the interpretation of Trichet's actions as "conservative," it is useful to remember that he had to contend with Axel Weber's even more conservative opposition on the ECB Governing Council.[59] Weber rejected purchases of government bonds as a violation of the Treaty's "no-bailout" rule, whereas Trichet deserves some credit for pushing political leaders – especially a reluctant Merkel – to establish a permanent bailout mechanism.[60] In December 2010, member governments authorized the future European Stability Mechanism (ESM) to lend to member governments by exception to the Treaty's "no-bailout" rule – but only when the "stability of the euro area" was in jeopardy, and subject to "strict conditionality."[61] Member governments that received financial assistance under the ESM had to undertake reforms to restore their public finances. This conditionality was important for central bankers because it would give them political cover to step up purchases of distressed government bonds without facing the accusation of bailing out insolvent states.[62] As part of a "troika" with the IMF and the European Commission, the ECB monitored the implementation of loan conditions before allowing scheduled disbursements of financial assistance, thus exerting considerable pressure in favor of austerity measures.

If we zoom further out of central bankers' and intergovernmental arenas, the political backdrop was even more dicey. Across Northern Europe and especially in Germany, polls suggested that voters were increasingly suspicious of any kind of financial flows – much like the generalized suspicion of stimulus in the United States. Scholars of political economy have often

---

[56] Hall 2012; Blyth 2013; Schimmelfenig 2015. [57] Matthijs and Blyth 2017; Tooze 2018: 366.
[58] As Elsa Massoc (2020) shows, French bankers, who had closer ties with the French state, complied with this request better than German bankers.
[59] James Mackenzie, "ECB Trichet Rejects Weber View on Bond Buying."
[60] Author interview, Elysée Palace, Paris, December 22, 2010.
[61] Article 136. On the ESM, see also Gocaj and Meunier 2013; Jabko and Sheingate 2018: 316–317.
[62] Bini Smaghi (2013: 70–74, 119–120, 128–129) articulates central bankers' long-standing frustration with the "game of chicken" that the ECB had to play with governments prior to the establishment of the ESM.

focused on Europe's growing "crisis of legitimacy" due to its rigid adherence to rules.[63] To be sure, new "anti-system" forces in Greece, Spain, or Italy largely owed their rise in the early 2010s to their strident critiques of the EU and of its austerity programs.[64] Yet many citizens in creditor states resented European solidarity toward indebted states for the same reason that citizens of debtor states resented the disciplinary measures imposed by the EU – namely, because they saw it as an infringement on their sovereignty.[65] In addition, critiques of the ECB in the name of democratic legitimacy were not particularly new, and the ECB had quite successfully stonewalled them in the past.[66] At the turn of the twenty-first century, the ECB had sided with conservatives by endorsing a large range of neoliberal economic policies. What was much more threatening for the ECB was the growing revolt of its long-standing conservative base of support. Far from demanding that the ECB ditch its ordoliberal outlook, many European conservatives – especially in Northern Europe – demanded that the ECB, and the EU more generally, remain inflexible on the "no-bailout" rule.

In Germany or the Netherlands, Greece's problems revived 1990s German fears of "Club Med" countries (now called "PIIGS") using their membership in the Eurozone to take advantage of their more frugal northern neighbors. Within the parties of Merkel's conservative coalition – with her own CDU party and especially in the FDP – many favored a strict "ordoliberal" interpretation of the "no bailout" rule.[67] Although it progressively became a far-right party, Alternative für Deutschland (AfD) was initially a home for dissatisfied CDU members who rejected the euro and Merkel's policies. Like Merkel, the ECB had to maneuver in the face of a purist insistence that the EU remains true to the self-help philosophy that German political leaders had always held up as a guarantee that Germany would not become the paymaster of Europe. While the independent ECB stood above the political fray, it did not operate in a political vacuum. All central bankers had to justify their actions before parliamentary committees and to navigate a broad public arena, both at the EU and at the national levels. In particular, the appointments of central bank board members are entirely political processes. Like anybody else, German central bank president Axel Weber understood that. By hewing close to the German government's official rejection of a change to the "no-bailout" clause in the summer of 2010, Weber was, in effect, positioning himself to secure Merkel's support in his bid to succeed Trichet as the head of the ECB.[68]

---

[63] As Vivien Schmidt (2020: 14–15) put it: "The problem of democratic legitimacy for program countries have been exponentially greater than for normal non-program countries subject to EU rules."
[64] Hopkin 2020.   [65] Jabko and Luhman 2019.   [66] Jabko 2003.   [67] Jacoby 2014.
[68] Jack Ewing, "Central Banker Takes a Chance by Speaking Out," *New York Times*, November 1, 2010.

7.4.2 The ECB's Retreat from a Fundamentalist Interpretation of the "No-Bailout" Rule

In the fall of 2010, the political tide in Germany began to turn against the most conservative vision of the ECB. After the German government adopted Europe's biggest fiscal stimulus package in 2009, German officials' frequent references to ordoliberalism increasingly appeared as a self-serving "myth."[69] In agreeing to support a permanent bailout mechanism, Angela Merkel deflected a narrowly conservative conception of German sovereignty. Coming under fire from both conservatives and the Left in the German Parliament, she declared for the first time in December 2010: "Nobody in Europe will be abandoned (...) The euro is our common fate, and Europe is our common future."[70] Even before Axel Weber unexpectedly announced his resignation in February 2011 as Bundesbank president, his opposition to the Securities Market Program meant that he was no longer Trichet's obvious successor as ECB president. By siding against nationalists and ordoliberal fundamentalists in her governing coalition, Merkel increasingly became the de facto spokesperson of a more centrist "informal 'Grand Coalition'" that extended toward the Left.[71] Dramatizing the crisis, she declared to the German Parliament: "We need more Europe (...) If the euro fails, Europe fails."[72] At the same time, Merkel draped herself in the defense of German taxpayers, declaring that "Eurobonds" would not come into existence "as long as I live."[73] Running on a balanced approach between her defense of national fiscal interests and her support of Europe, Merkel's electoral victory in 2013 enabled her to ditch her FDP alliance partner and to enter into a more centrist coalition with the social-democratic party (SPD).

The tide was turning at the ECB as well, as central bankers attempted to navigate between a strictly disciplinarian view of the Eurozone and what they saw as necessary to preserve the integrity of the Eurozone. In August 2011, Trichet and his successor Mario Draghi attempted to influence the Italian government's fiscal policy in exchange for ECB purchases of Italian bonds, which led to a scandal in Italy – as well as to the Italian prime minister's resignation. In the face of German opposition on the ECB Governing

---

[69] Vail 2014; Young 2014.
[70] Quentin Peel, "German MPs clash on Future of Eurozone," *Financial Times*, December 15, 2010.
[71] Zimmermann 2014; Kriesi and Grande 2016: 270.
[72] "Regierungserklärung von Kanzlerin Merkel zum Europäischen Rat und zum Eurogipfel, Berlin," October 26, 2011: www.bundesregierung.de/ContentArchiv/DE/Archiv17/Regierungserklaerung/2011/2011-10-27-merkel-eu-gipfel.html.
[73] "Merkel Vows 'No Euro Bonds as Long as I Live,'" *Spiegel International*, June 27, 2012. In a country still bruised by the recent memory of a costly reunification process, Merkel's stance proved to be an effective campaign strategy and she won a landslide victory in the 2013 election. See Newman 2015: 117, 125.

7.5 Consolidating Monetary Regime Change

Council, Trichet needed as much cover as he could muster.[74] In the end the ECB majority led by Trichet and Draghi outvoted German dissenters.[75] Like his predecessor Axel Weber before him, Bundesbank President Jens Weidmann – who was also Merkel's former economic advisor – publicly criticized the ECB's bond purchase program. Voicing a sentiment shared by other central bankers, former ECB Board member Lorenzo Bini Smaghi expressed his irritation about these public criticisms that "reflected the prevailing public opinion" in Germany: "The fact that two successive presidents of the Bundesbank, who sit on the ECB's Governing Council, have spoken publicly against the purchase of government bonds" was "undermining the ECB's independence."[76] While he refrained from such public criticisms, German ECB Executive Board member Jürgen Stark resigned in September 2011 after voting against ECB bond purchases.[77]

7.5 CONSOLIDATING MONETARY REGIME CHANGE

By the time Draghi succeeded Trichet at the end of 2011, the stage was set for a clearer break with past ECB practice. Since the Trichet days, the ECB had accompanied EU leaders in building a governance framework that veered away from a fundamentalist interpretation of the Treaty's "no-bail out" rule. Under Draghi, the ECB continued with its "non-standard" policies, but also broadened their scope. In December 2011, the ECB initiated unlimited three-year loans to Eurozone banks, known as Long-Term Refinancing Operations. The ECB was officially still just lending to private sector banks, rather than financing governments. The LTRO program immediately lowered Italy's and Spain's borrowing costs, without violating the letter of the Treaty. But that was not enough to keep interest rates low in the Eurozone periphery in the face of growing investor apprehensions about the fragility of European banks.[78] Because banks were under national rather than European supervision, their reserves were mostly in national government ("sovereign") bonds, so they risked a default if these bonds were suddenly devalued, thereby further dragging down their sovereigns. It took another large spike in Spanish and Italian "spreads" before member governments decided in June 2012 to "break the vicious circle between banks and sovereigns" – and to empower the ECB to

---

[74] Bastasin 2015: 307.
[75] As Bini Smaghi (2013: 128) put it: "The decision to intervene was made over the weekend, but it was not unanimous. Some members of the Governing Council were not convinced that the commitments would be respected."
[76] Bini Smaghi 2013: 121.
[77] "ECB Executive Board Member Juergen Stark Resigns," *Wall Street Journal*, September 9, 2011.
[78] Micossi 2015: 15; Véron 2024: 14–15.

supervise large European banks.[79] The ECB would therefore be able to work with the ESM to recapitalize insolvent European banks, thus approximating the lender-of-last-resort function to European banks that the Treaty had not originally planned for the ECB.[80]

7.5.1 "Whatever It Takes"

The ECB's backstop of Eurozone government bond markets finally became explicit after its President Mario Draghi famously declared in July 2012 that "within our mandate, the ECB is ready to do whatever it takes to preserve the euro."[81] A month later, the ECB rolled out a new program of Outright Monetary Transactions (OMTs), allowing the purchase of unlimited quantities of treasury bonds of countries that had entered an ESM program. After the European Stability Program started its operations in the fall of 2012, the ECB was able to make its debt purchases "unlimited" without violating the "no-bailout" clause. In retrospect, the "Draghi put" of 2012 – his assurance that he would do "whatever it takes" – appeared as a watershed. It did not pull the Eurozone decisively out of its economic stagnation, but it undoubtedly defused the crisis.[82] As the slump deepened and ECB interest rates came closer to the "zero lower bound" in the course of the 2010s, bond purchases by the ECB went from unconventional measures to practically the main instrument of monetary policy. A long list of "non-standard" measures were introduced in subsequent years – most importantly the Asset Purchase Program (APP), initiated in December 2014 and better known as quantitative easing – in addition to successive versions of direct loan programs (LTROs). Four years after the Federal Reserve, the ECB thus completed its move away from its initial resistance to even indirectly support member governments' spending through limited bond purchases to unlimited bond purchases when they were needed.

Central to this belated consolidation of monetary regime change at the ECB was the fact that the Bundesbank's once enormous influence within the ECB had waned. Contrary to the widespread expectation that the independent ECB would always be focused on the sole task of fighting inflation, Europe's central bankers began to assert their independence quite differently than the Bundesbank, and to forge ahead with "non-standard" policies. The Bundesbank under Jens Weidmann consistently tried to stem massive ECB

---

[79] Euro area summit statement, Brussels, June 29, 2012.
[80] The new European banking union, while imperfect, was "radical" (Véron 2015; see also Véron 2024). In the future, the ECB would be able to direct banks to diversify their reserves, so that they would no longer risk a devastating collapse if their sovereign's bonds suddenly lost value.
[81] ECB, Verbatim of the remarks made by Mario Draghi, London, July 26, 2012.
[82] Darvas, Pisani-Ferry, and Wolff 2013.

7.5 Consolidating Monetary Regime Change

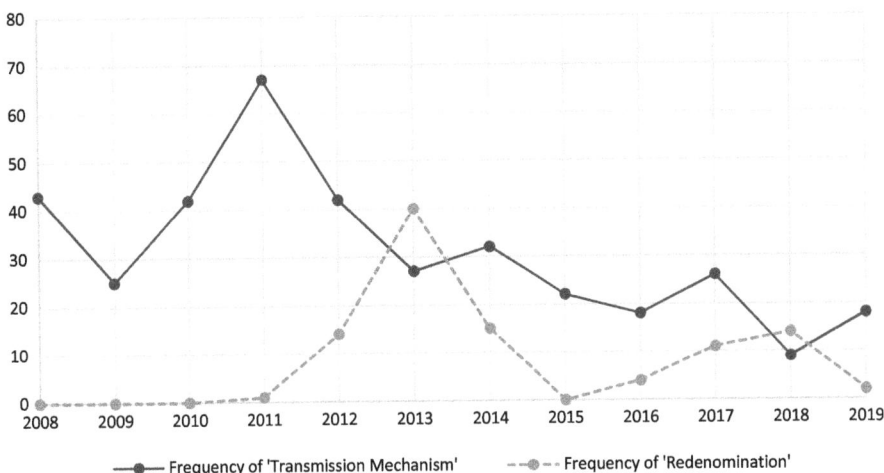

FIGURE 7.7 References to "transmission mechanism" and "redenomination" in ECB speeches, 2008–2019.

bond purchases. Weidmann was the only central banker who voted against the OMT program in 2012.[83] In internal debates among central bankers, the theme of "redenomination risk" – originally introduced by an ECB staff paper – played an increasingly important role.[84] If investors believed that a country of the Eurozone would be forced to exit the euro, then they would demand higher interest rates on its government bonds to reflect the risk of seeing that country's debt redenominated in a new currency. This argument gave a leg up to central bankers who argued that the ECB should pursue the OMT program, and later QE, to ensure the transmission of monetary policy across the Eurozone. Evidence of the growing importance of this theme can be seen in the growing number of references to "redenomination" in central bankers' speeches from 2012 on, in addition to the now established theme of the "transmission mechanism" (see Figure 7.7).

An important dimension of the turning tide at the ECB also took place in the external arena of the economics profession but also – much more so than in the United States – in the legal arena. The influence of Keynesian economists is reflected in central bankers' speeches, which increasingly talked up the risk of "systemic crisis" starting in 2012 in comparison to the "moral hazard" of bailing out fiscally undisciplined member states.[85] Belgian LSE economist Paul De Grauwe's criticisms of austerity as a factor of systemic risk and later

---

[83] Bastasin 2015: 419; Paul Carrel, Noha Barkin, and Annika Breidthardt, "Inside Mario Draghi's Rescue Plan," *Reuters*, September 25, 2012.
[84] Author interview with former ECB central banker, September 26, 2023. [85] Ferrara 2020.

his defense of Draghi's OMT program were echoed by the *Financial Times* and by other leading economists, such as Paul Krugman in his many columns about the Eurozone crisis in the *New York Times*.[86] To be sure, the "moral hazard" position was still defended by prominent German ordoliberal economists, such as Hans-Werner Sinn, who described the euro as a "trap" for Germany.[87] Yet that position's public influence diminished, even in Germany after Merkel came out strongly against a Eurozone breakup. The ECB's evolution thus reflected both a shifting public arena and the growing influence of mainstream Keynesian analysis in the economics profession, as was the case at the Fed. From 2014 on, the ECB thus implemented unconventional policies such as QE, "forward guidance," and even negative interest rates – a tool that the Fed never adopted.[88]

A difference with the Fed, however, was the importance of courts of law as arenas where different claims about ECB policies were adjudicated – and where central bankers themselves relitigated their internal debates. Perhaps because economic arrangements were steeped in law in the ordoliberal tradition, the Eurozone crisis gave rise to court cases against the ECB's OMT and quantitative easing program at the German Constitutional Court and the European Court of Justice.[89] The case before the German Constitutional Court, which had been filed by conservative activists, promised to be tricky for the ECB. The Court had defined the EU as "an association of sovereign states, and, hence, a secondary political entity" and had asserted a "German right to fiscal stability."[90] In 2013, Bundesbank President Jens Weidmann testified as a critic of the ECB's OMT program, while ECB Board member Jorg Asmussen testified in defense.[91] Asmussen was Stark's successor on the ECB Board and also German, but had voted in favor of the OMT program. Much like his predecessor's and his own prior public criticisms of ECB bond purchases, Weidmann's critical stance on the OMT program did not go down well among other central bankers.[92] At that point, however, the German government had shifted its position and Merkel's finance minister Wolfgang Schaüble declared in court that "the ECB is acting within its mandate." Rather than ruling that the ECB had overstepped its authority, the German court referred the case to the European Court. In 2015, the ECJ asserted the legality of the OMT program,

---

[86] De Grauwe 2011; De Grauwe and Ji 2012; Paul De Grauwe, "Stop this Guerilla Campaign against the ECB Policy", *Financial Times*, October 22, 2012; Krugman 2020: 175–189.
[87] Sinn 2014.
[88] For overviews of ECB policy tools, see Hartman and Smets 2018; Rostagno et al. 2019.
[89] Borger 2016; Saurugger and Fontan 2019. [90] Schorkopf 2009: 1220; Bignami 2020.
[91] Jack Ewing, "Debate on the Euro in a German Courtroom," *New York Times*, June 11, 2013.
[92] According to one central banker, many found Weidmann's decision to testify as a critic "unacceptable." Author interview with former central banker, September 26, 2023.

7.5 Consolidating Monetary Regime Change

and even Weidmann came to accept it in 2019.[93] In the meantime, however, this created legal uncertainty and likely contributed to the delayed turn to QE.

7.5.2 Asserting a "Macroeconomic" Perspective and "Fiscal Space"

From 2014 on, the ECB increasingly came out in favor of major changes in Eurozone monetary and also fiscal policies. At the Jackson Hole meeting of central bankers in August 2014, Draghi explained – like Yellen at the Fed – that "the 'risks of doing too little'" to prevent high unemployment "outweigh those of 'doing too much'" monetary stimulus and thus rekindles inflation.[94] Therefore, he called for an "accommodative monetary policy for an extended period of time." Second, Draghi dropped a bomb in the EU policy debate by calling for "a more growth-friendly overall fiscal stance for the euro area." In plain English, he was calling for fiscal policy to veer in the direction of less rather than more fiscal restraint – a remarkable deviation from the ECB's earlier avoidance of this topic and from its ritual calls to respect the rules of the Stability Pact and to reduce their deficits. Unsurprisingly, this aspect of Draghi's Jackson Hole speech opened a rift between Draghi's ECB and a German government still strongly committed to fiscal retrenchment.[95] The ECB's monetary expansion would effectively not only aim at preventing a recession, but also at countering the deflationary effects of fiscal consolidation.

From then on, Draghi himself resisted conservative appeals to focus on price stability that were coming from Germany – including from German central bankers on the ECB's Governing Council. A few weeks after Jackson Hole, Draghi clarified his thinking by declaring – without naming Germany – that "governments with fiscal space should act in an effective and timely manner."[96] In other words, countries with low public debts and deficits should increase their spending to make the Eurozone's overall fiscal policy stance more accommodative. Draghi's veiled call to Germany to use its "fiscal space" ran against the German government's long-standing support for low fiscal deficits. But it also provoked a strong reaction from Bundesbank President Jens Weidmann, who declared that "calls for a public fiscal stimulus plan in Germany to boost the Eurozone economy are amiss."[97] Meanwhile, ECB

---

[93] Mark Schieritz, "Jens Weidmann Accepts Sovereign Bond Purchases," *Die Zeit*, June 19, 2019.
[94] "Unemployment in the Euro Area," Speech by Mario Draghi, President of the ECB, Annual central bank symposium in Jackson Hole, August 22, 2014. For the economic background of Draghi's call for monetary expansion, see Micossi 2015: 19–23; Hartman and Smets 2018: 35; Rostagno et al. 2019: 237–240.
[95] "Merkel Increasingly Isolated on Austerity," *Spiegel*, September 3, 2014.
[96] Press Conference of Mario Draghi, President of the ECB, September 12, 2019.
[97] Andrea Thomas, "Bundesbank's Weidmann Rejects Calls for German Stimulus Plan," *Wall Street Journal*, November 28, 2014. Weidmann had repeatedly expressed this view over the years, for example in an interview with the *Financial Times* on November 13, 2011.

Board member Sabine Lautenschläger – Asmussen's successor on the ECB Board, and a former Bundesbank official – opposed ECB government bond purchases in the name of price stability.[98] She joined Weidmann in his early opposition to quantitative easing and later broke ranks with the ECB Board by publicly opposing QE.[99] This internal German opposition placed Draghi in a tight spot vis-à-vis the German government and public opinion. Yet that no longer seemed to matter as much as in the early 2010s, when the German government's support was sorely needed to build up an institutional framework to govern the Eurozone.

In addition to news reports and interview evidence, a close reading of the minutes ("monetary policy accounts") that the ECB has published since 2015 reveals traces of robust internal disagreements in the central bankers' arena about the stance that Draghi adopted at Jackson Hole in 2014. Central bankers evidently tried to balance their traditional support of the Stability and Growth Pact against Draghi's new theme of "growth-friendly" fiscal policy. Statements that carefully expressed this balance became a recurring theme of the minutes: "As regards fiscal policies, it was essential that all countries intensified their efforts towards achieving a more growth-friendly composition of public finances, while remaining in compliance with the EU fiscal rules."[100] Central bankers typically made a distinction between countries that had "fiscal space" and countries that needed to rebuild "fiscal buffers." Countries with "fiscal space" had budgets close to balance and relatively low public debts, and they therefore needed to contribute more to this desirable "growth-friendly" fiscal stance. Those with high public debts or deficits had less fiscal space and needed to rebuild "fiscal buffers," and therefore had to abide strictly by the Eurozone fiscal rules. Both types of countries always remained unnamed, at least in the ECB's carefully sanitized "monetary policy accounts." But everyone on the ECB Governing Council presumably understood which country had or did not have "fiscal space."

These ECB debates were reminiscent of debates that took place in the late twentieth century between European governments and central bankers – but with quite different results. Germany was once again doing better than its neighbors, and once again was refusing to be the "locomotive" of Europe's recovery by running deficits that may benefit its neighbors more than itself. The German government reduced its own fiscal deficits on the back of an

---

[98] Brian Blackstone, "ECB's Lautenschlaeger Opposes Government Bond Purchases," *Wall Street Journal*, November 29, 2014.
[99] "ECB's Lautenschlaeger Casts Doubts on QE's Effectiveness," *Reuters*, April 2, 2015.
[100] Account of the monetary policy meeting of the Governing Council of the European Central Bank, held in Frankfurt am Main on Wednesday and Thursday, March 8–9, 2017. Similar wording can be found in the minutes of the meetings of October 22, 2015, December 2–3, 2015, March 9–10, 2016, July 20–21, 2016.

7.5 Consolidating Monetary Regime Change

export-fueled domestic recovery, and it preached fiscal consolidation and structural reform to its neighbors. This conveniently ignored the fact that much of the Eurozone remained in deep trouble, and that Germany itself had conducted a large Keynesian reflation before reducing its deficit.[101]

The difference, however, was that the ECB now existed and had considerable weight in the Eurozone economic policy debate. Draghi was in a position to say that German fiscal policy should be more expansive, and to oppose Weidmann's fiscal conservatism. Draghi's often-repeated call to "governments with fiscal space" fell on deaf German ears even as the ECB undertook massive monetary accommodation. But he effectively countered the "moral hazard" framing of fiscal deficit spending that Germany – with the ECB's help – had expounded at the outset of the crisis. Thus, the ECB's new stance facilitated the Eurozone's adoption of more fiscal accommodation. In January 2015, the Commission adopted a formal communication about "flexibility within the existing rules."[102] In that document, the European Commission rejected "one size fits all" and argued for "flexibility" and "discretion" in responding to different circumstances.[103] That was a remarkable move away from its earlier support of automatic sanctions against violations of EU fiscal rules.

While the ECB's minutes still contain a litany of statements repeating the importance of the Stability Pact, they also suggest that central bankers – and certainly the ECB president – increasingly welcomed the change in the fiscal stance of the Eurozone. In March 2015, they expressed a concern that "a flexible interpretation of the Stability and Growth Pact" might have the effect of "weakening the credibility of the fiscal framework (...). At the same time, the point was made that, from a macroeconomic point of view, one should be cautious in calling for too restrictive a fiscal policy stance at the current juncture."[104] To be sure, the fiscal reforms of 2011 created a legal obligation to impose fines on member states that breached the new rules, and thus to restrict the fiscal space of all Eurozone member states.[105] Those that received ESM assistance were especially constrained by their loan conditions – and the ECB fully supported these conditions. In 2015, after the election of a Greek government staunchly opposed to austerity refused the conditions of a new

---

[101] Vail 2014.   [102] Interview, European Commission, Brussels, August 19, 2016.
[103] European Commission, *Making the Best Use of the Flexibility within the Existing Rules of the Stability and Growth Pact*. Strasbourg, January 13, 2015, p. 4.
[104] Account of the monetary policy meeting of the Governing Council of the European Central Bank held in Nicosia on Wednesday and Thursday, March 4–5, 2015. According to an author interview (September 26, 2023), this statement summarized positions typically expressed by ECB Board members Peter Praet, Benoit Coeuré, and some governors of national central banks.
[105] Matthijs and Blyth 2017.

European loan, the ECB effectively forced the Greek government back to the negotiating table. Greece's finance minister Yanis Varoufakis later reported that Draghi waged the threat of a withdrawal of central bank liquidity to Greek banks.[106] When given a choice between fiscal austerity and a de facto exit from the Eurozone, the Greek government did not cling to a maximalist vision of popular sovereignty and, ultimately, it backed down.

Greece was the exception that confirmed the rule, however. After the toxic conflicts of the early 2010s and in the new context of "growth-friendly" fiscal policies, EU bodies were quite reluctant to encroach on the sovereign economic policy prerogatives of broadly compliant member states. Even when the Commission was indeed required to recommend fines, it could circumvent that obligation. In August 2016, the EU Council endorsed a Commission recommendation of a financial sanction of zero euros against Portugal and Spain, in overt disagreement with German officials' advocacy of stricter discipline.[107] The EU Council's controversial decision drew a remarkably sanguine reaction from the ECB: "Concerns were expressed with regard to recent decisions at the European level that cast doubt on the functioning of the Pact. At the same time, it was also recalled that a more growth-friendly composition of fiscal policies could support the economic recovery, as could the use of fiscal space, where available." Draghi himself was even blunter in the press conference that he gave after that meeting. Rather than blaming Portugal and Spain, he declared: "Countries that have fiscal space should use it. Germany has fiscal space."[108] Clearly, the ECB – and the EU with it – had turned a corner and was now rejecting the neoliberal notion that fiscal austerity was always a good idea.

Even the ECB's long-standing pleas in favor of structural reforms changed considerably after 2014. Although Draghi's Jackson Hole speech still praised Germany and other countries that had introduced more "flexibility in the labour market" and thus reduced "structural unemployment," it also pointed out the need for "reforming structural policies" in the direction of active labor market policies aimed at "raising skills" through "education" and "lifelong learning."[109] In line with his plea for "growth-friendly" policies, Draghi added: "Without higher aggregate demand, we risk higher structural unemployment, and governments that introduce structural reforms could end up running just to stand still." In other words, the ECB no longer held neoliberal labor market reforms that made it easier to hire and fire as a panacea for reducing

---

[106] Varoufakis 2017. For an account that places less blame on the ECB and more on other actors, including Varoufakis himself, see Dendrinou and Varvitsioti 2019.

[107] Council of the EU, Press release, "Excessive deficit procedure: Council agrees to zero fines and new deadlines for Portugal and Spain," August 9, 2016.

[108] ECB monetary policy press conference, Frankfurt, September 8, 2016.

[109] "Unemployment in the Euro Area," Speech by Mario Draghi, August 22, 2014.

7.5 Consolidating Monetary Regime Change

unemployment – a noticeable change away from the previous ECB official line and standard EU recommendations about structural reforms. After 2015, the ECB increasingly "fell silent on the topic" of structural reform.[110] The central bankers who were most vocal about the "contractionary effects" of structural reforms in their speeches were apparently ECB Board members Benoît Coeuré and Victor Constancio.[111] Incidentally, both were close allies of Draghi against the more hawkish members of the ECB's Governing Council. Without access to ECB transcripts, it is difficult to say more, but it is not unreasonable to think that important differences among central bankers transpired in internal discussions of this topic.

As time went by, conflict became more overt in the ECB arena between the majority led by Draghi and a group of dissenters around Weidmann. The minutes of the December 2016 Governing Council meeting mention a "well-known general scepticism regarding the APP and public debt purchases" of "a few members of the governing council (...) According to this view, the latter should remain a contingency instrument to be employed only as a last resort in an adverse scenario, such as a situation of imminent deflation."[112] Although the anonymized minutes do not reveal who were the "few members," the "doctrine of last resort" came straight out of Germany's chancellery[113] – where Jens Weidmann had been Merkel's economic advisor before moving to the Bundesbank. The minutes of September 2019 mentions the same reservation (among others) when the ECB Governing Council decided to restart its Asset Purchase Program (QE). Draghi's ECB Board championed that move when inflation once again undershot the 2 percent target by a half percentage point. "A clear majority of members (of the ECB Governing Council) agreed," but "a number of members assessed the case for renewed net asset purchases as not sufficiently strong."[114] After that meeting, *Bild* published its caricature of Draghi as "Count Draghila" preying on German savings, and a few days later German ECB Board member Sabine Lautenschläger resigned, reportedly "amid unprecedented discord at the top of the ECB, where a third of policymakers (...) dissented," including Weidmann but also the French and Dutch central bank governors.[115] By then, many in Germany and beyond no longer saw the ECB as a hawkish technocratic pillar of sound money.

---

[110] Braun, Di Carlo, Diessner, and Düsterhöft 2024: 2.
[111] Braun, Di Carlo, Diessner, and Düsterhöft 2024: 13.
[112] Account of the monetary policy meeting of the Governing Council of the European Central Bank, held in Frankfurt am Main on Wednesday and Thursday, December 7–8, 2016.
[113] Sandbu 2015: 59.
[114] Account of the monetary policy meeting of the Governing Council of the European Central Bank held in Frankfurt am Main on Wednesday and Thursday, September 11–12, 2019.
[115] Thomas Escritt and Francesco Canepa, "ECB hawk Lautenschlaeger Resigns Amid Policy Backlash," *Reuters*, September 25, 2019.

7.6 CONCLUSION: THE ECB'S RETREAT FROM NEOLIBERALISM

Like the Fed, albeit later, the ECB considerably retreated during the 2010s from a European version of technocratic neoliberalism, often dubbed "Frankfurt consensus." Central bankers implemented a large monetary stimulus, stopped advocating expansionary austerity, and no longer prescribed all-out market liberalization. From an economics perspective, the ECB has been blamed for its belated implementation of monetary regime change. From a political economy perspective, the ECB has often been depicted as a prisoner of neoliberal ideas or financial structures, struggling to maintain its legitimacy. Yet neither perspective really addresses the puzzling fact that ECB leaders, over time, peeled away from long-standing conservative supporters. It required political work, in multiple arenas, for central bankers to move away from the "Frankfurt consensus." Within the ECB's Governing Council, ECB leaders increasingly outvoted the long-dominant hawks. In an increasingly internationalized economics profession, they relied on neo-Keynesians. In the public arena, they no longer systematically adopted pro-German positions.

Over time, ECB leaders consolidated a new and initially "unconventional" monetary regime of easy money. As a result, the ECB no longer appeared as a conservative temple of sound money pushing back against reckless spending and monetary instability. The turnaround was neither immediate nor obvious, however. The Trichet ECB was largely responsible for devastating austerity policies in the early 2010s. Like Dr. Frankenstein, however, the ECB lost control of its monster. After the danger of Eurozone disintegration finally receded in 2012, Europe's central bankers navigated in a new economic and political climate. In the absence of inflationary pressures and as the threats of Eurozone stagnation and deflation loomed larger, ECB leaders became less urgently concerned with public deficits and debts. In official statements, Europe's central bankers, like their Fed counterparts, continued to preach sound money and fiscal prudence – especially vis-à-vis member states that received EU assistance. Like the Fed as well, however, the ECB increasingly used its independence to fend off conservative critics and to implement "unconventional" policies that counteracted fiscal retrenchment and deflation. In the end, ECB leaders largely reframed the Eurozone's economic policy debate away from its predominantly neoliberal turn-of-the-century terms.

The flip side of the coin is that, while central bankers retreated from their erstwhile support of neoliberal policies, conservative forces did not always follow them. The ECB's retreat from technocratic neoliberalism is surprising because many citizens and scholars still perceive the European Union as the archetype of an essentially elitist, technocratic, and neoliberal construct. Notwithstanding superficial similarities, the neoliberal project after 2012 had a quite different support base than in the late twentieth century. As central bankers stepped up their unconventional policies, neoliberalism turned increasingly populist and decidedly less mainstream. As in the United States, Europe's

7.6 Conclusion: The ECB's Retreat from Neoliberalism

central bankers had to battle populist inclinations toward fiscal frugality rather than extravagance. Right-wing populists in Northern Europe, like the German Afd, now wanted to prevent their taxes from being spent to rescue financiers or foreigners. At some point, this concern became a near obsession, and the neoliberal project lost its technocratic mooring at the EU level. The conservative center of European partisan politics shrank, as it increasingly had to contend with nationalist and xenophobic rivals. That, however, is another story.

8

Beyond Neoliberalism?

This chapter considers whether the book's explanation of political-economic regimes in terms of cross-cutting alliances travels beyond the specific cases that I have analyzed so far. For that purpose, I start from a simple observation: The early 2020s witnessed an accelerated sequence, in reverse order, of the monetary regime changes of the previous forty years. The Covid-19 pandemic's economic standstill was first followed by an episode of ultra-accommodative policies. The Fed and the ECB rolled out rapid monetary accommodation in response to the pandemic, with a much quicker and more decisive return to quantitative easing than in the 2010s. Then, barely two years later, the mood changed considerably amid resurging concerns about inflation. Fed and ECB central bankers shifted to tighter monetary policies, with the most rapid hikes in interest rates since the early 1980s.

This quick evolution after 2020 therefore raises two important questions. First, does either of these two successive monetary policy responses signal the beginning of broader political-economic regime shifts? Some observers see departures from the status quo ante exemplified by the Fed and the ECB in the context of the pandemic and a growing climate emergency as harbingers of a new era of "post-neoliberalism." Others are skeptical that policymakers' responses to crisis mark a truly profound reorientation, after decades of market-oriented policies across advanced liberal democracies. Second, how much variation have we seen in the politics of money across the world, beyond the United States and the European Union? In both the 1980s and the 2010s, the Fed could not completely ignore the turning tides of US politics and the evolution of partisan cleavages between Republicans and Democrats. Domestic partisan cleavages were less central in Europe than in the United States, since European central bankers acted mostly in the context of territorial cleavages between different sovereign states. How such partisan and territorial cleavages have, to this day, prompted central bankers to take part in different alliance configurations across the ocean deserves to be examined. In addition, we must consider whether the cross-cutting alliances that formed in the United States and Europe in the 1980s and 2010s were idiosyncratic to these times and places, or whether they are more broadly representative drivers of global political-economic regime change.

Any analysis of recent and rapid turnarounds, with limited access to central bank records or other archives, is necessarily tentative. With this caveat, this chapter engages two discussions. First, I consider what happened at the Fed and the ECB in the early 2020s. Based on Fed and ECB minutes and other sources, I consider US and EU responses to the pandemic in 2020, and then to inflationary tensions in 2022, and I compare the evolution of the Fed's and the ECB's respective policy frameworks after a decade of "unconventional" policies. Second, I turn to the waxing and waning of technocratic neoliberalism in "shadow cases" that illustrate parallel trajectories in the politics of money at other technocratic organizations of the advanced capitalist world since the 1980s. Without a more detailed examination that is beyond the scope of this book, I cannot definitively prove that the book's argument is equally relevant to other times and places. But I can at least begin to extrapolate the argument in the form of research hypotheses. For this extrapolation, I will briefly focus on the IMF, the Bank of Japan, and the Bank of England.

8.1 THE EARLY 2020S AT THE FED AND AT THE ECB

It is hard to overstate the atmosphere of emergency in the early months of 2020, as the Covid pandemic spread across the world and especially in the United States and Europe. In addition to the public health emergency, the world economy literally shut down, and unemployment briefly shot up to levels not seen since the Great Depression.[1] In response, the Fed led the way for the ECB and other central banks to take the unprecedented step of increasing their asset purchases to trillions in just a few months.[2] The long hesitations of central bankers to flood the economy with money in the 2010s suddenly seemed like distant history. From our perspective, the question is: How did central bankers so swiftly overcome the divisive politics of money that had been so paralyzing in the 2010s? To begin to answer these questions, it is useful to consider how central bankers not only muted their internal conflicts, but also acted as opinion leaders in external arenas.

8.1.1 The Normalization of Unconventional Policies

In the United States, the FOMC quickly decided to respond boldly to the economic perils caused by the pandemic. On March 2, the FOMC held a

---

[1] Tooze 2022.   [2] Timiraos 2022.

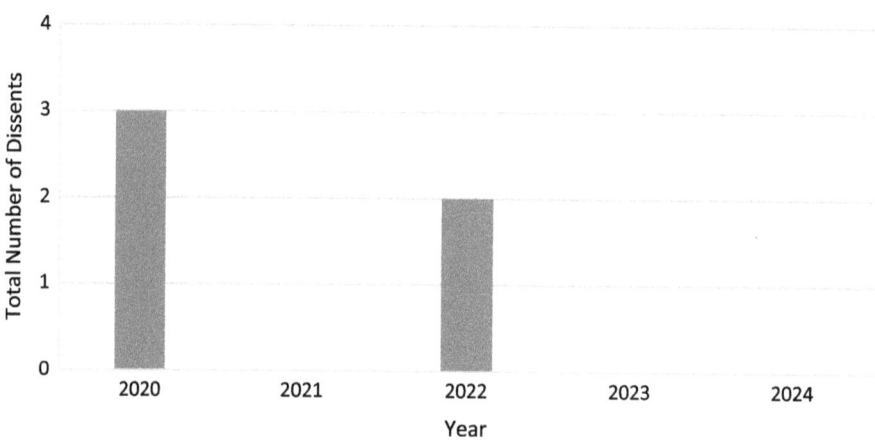

FIGURE 8.1 FOMC dissents, 2020–2024.

meeting by videoconference in which they decided unanimously to cut the federal funds rate by 50 basis points. According to the minutes of that meeting: "A forceful monetary policy action could provide a clear signal to the public that policymakers recognized the potential economic significance of the situation and were willing to move decisively (...)."[3] This was followed on March 18 by a further decision to cut rates by a full 100 basis points – with only one dissenter favoring a cut of 50–75 basis points but otherwise "fully supportive" of the FOMC's actions.[4] The Fed swiftly created new "facilities" with carefully chosen names that tried to address the criticisms leveled against the asset purchases of the early 2010s. The Main Street Lending Program and the Paycheck Protection Program Liquidity Facility, in particular, were designed to funnel money not just into financial markets, as asset purchases of the 2010s, but directly to small businesses and American workers.[5] Unlike 2011, no FOMC members expressed fundamental opposition to these programs, or indeed to the principle of major monetary policy accommodation. Although three dissenting votes were cast in 2020, the total number of dissenting votes in the 2020–2024 period was remarkably low (see Figure 8.1). In August 2020, the FOMC also came up with a revised statement of its monetary policy framework, which was also unanimously adopted. After periods of near-zero inflation, "appropriate monetary policy will likely aim to achieve inflation moderately above 2 percent for some time."[6] That formulation became a mantra for the FOMC to justify the maintenance of monetary easing in 2020 and 2021.

---

[3] Videoconference meeting of March 2, in Minutes of FOMC meeting, March 15, 2020, p. 13.
[4] Minutes of FOMC meeting, March 15, 2020, p. 12. [5] Timiraos 2022.
[6] FOMC press release, August 27, 2020.

8.1 The Early 2020s at the Fed and at the ECB

In a bid to preempt the raucous partisan conflicts of the early 2010s about deficit spending, the FOMC also warned other policymakers as early as March 15, 2020 that "growth in the U.S. economy depended on the containment measures put in place, as well as the success of those measures, and on the responses of other policies, including fiscal policy."[7] In plain English, the Fed called for fiscal stimulus. At the following meeting, the FOMC congratulated Congress on its swift passing of the CARES Act and on its willingness to backstop new Fed facilities: "Participants noted that recently enacted fiscal programs were crucial for limiting the severity of the economic downturn. In particular, the Cares Act and other legislation, which represented more than $2 trillion in federal spending in total, had provided direct help to households, businesses, and communities. (...) Participants acknowledged that even greater fiscal support may be necessary if the economic downturn persists."[8] It surely mattered for Republican support to such massive fiscal spending that Donald Trump, a right-wing populist, had succeeded Barack Obama at the White House. Despite their rhetoric about limiting the public deficit, Republicans in Congress did not seriously obstruct federal government spending until after Trump's defeat in the 2020 election. For the time being, Powell was also apparently successful in convincing President Trump that he was not such a bad Fed chair after all – despite Trump's incessant badmouthing of Powell in 2017–2019. Helped by the president's support, the Powell Fed acted as a cheerleader for a swift US fiscal response to the pandemic in the spring of 2020: "The fiscal response to economic developments had been large and timely and was providing much needed support for economic activity."[9] As in the 2010s, a Republican appointee at the helm of the Fed conducted an activist monetary policy with the support of the White House – first under Trump, and later also under Biden.

In the European Union, the ECB acted in a similar way to preempt internal and external conflicts in response to the pandemic. When the pandemic hit Europe, the ECB's policy rates were already close to zero, so the Council just decided to leave them there. Above all, the ECB Council established yet another ECB bond purchase program, the Pandemic Emergency Purchase Program: "[A] large majority of members supported the proposal" to pump €750b into the Eurozone economy by the end of the year, even though "reservations were expressed by some members."[10] In a clear reminiscence of the internal conflicts of the early 2010s, some worried that the ECB's sovereign bond purchases might "encourage irresponsible behaviour on the part of governments," whereas others "underlined that this was by no means a justification for the Governing

---

[7] Minutes of FOMC meeting, March 15, 2020, p. 6.
[8] Minutes of FOMC meeting, April 28–29, 2020, p. 9.
[9] Minutes of FOMC meeting, June 9–10, 2020, p. 10.
[10] Account of the monetary policy meeting of the Governing Council of the European Central Bank held by means of a teleconference on Wednesday, March 18, 2020, p. 5.

Council not to fulfil its price stability mandate and support monetary policy transmission" including "addressing self-fulfilling redenomination risk and fragmentation (...)."[11] Despite that recurring internal debate, the ECB came this time to a much swifter conclusion in favor of massive monetary easing, and later even increased its Pandemic Emergency Purchase Program to €1,350 billion.[12] Ratifying this remarkable shift, the July 2021 revision of the ECB's official "monetary policy strategy" normalized the recourse to "forward guidance, asset purchases and longer-term refinancing operations, as appropriate."[13] As ECB Board member Isabel Schnabel put it, "the range of policy instruments used over the last few years will remain part of our toolkit in the future too, meaning they should no longer be regarded as 'unconventional.'"[14]

The ECB's new "monetary policy strategy" is especially instructive not only in comparison to the old strategy that it had adopted shortly after its birth, but also because it can be compared to the Fed's own policy framework after several revisions that were formalized in the 2010s. For the first time, the ECB highlighted the importance of an "inflation buffer" above zero percent – like the Fed, but quite unlike the ECB's original "monetary policy strategy." The ECB's internal debate in the early 2000s on inflation targeting had led to the adoption of a "reference value" for inflation that was "below but close to 2%"[15] – with German central bankers defending the view that a 2 percent target was too high. At the time, the Federal Reserve did not yet have a formal inflation target, but it was widely understood that the Fed's informal 2 percent inflation target, adopted in the 1990s under Greenspan, was a "symmetric" target. Unlike the ECB, the Fed did not consider 2 percent to be a ceiling, but a positively desirable goal that would prevent deflation as much as inflation. The ECB's July 2021 revision was therefore a way of quickly catching up with the Fed, whose formalization of a symmetric inflation target had taken place more incrementally in the 2010s.[16] After years of hesitations and internal contests, the ECB left its monetarist past behind and moved closer to the economics profession's neo-Keynesian mainstream in favor of "flexible" inflation targeting. The ECB now declared a positive and "symmetric" target of 2 percent that committed central bankers to act more forcefully if the inflation rate was too low. Significantly, this shift was shepherded by Isabel Schnabel,

---

[11] Account of the monetary policy meeting of the Governing Council of the European Central Bank held in Frankfurt am Main on Wednesday and Thursday, April 29–30, 2020, p. 12.

[12] Account of the monetary policy meeting of the Governing Council of the European Central Bank, June 3–4, 2020, p 18.

[13] European Central Bank, "The ECB's monetary policy strategy statement" (2021). (Available on ECB website.)

[14] Speech by Isabel Schnabel, Member of the Executive Board of the ECB, at the virtual Financial Statements series hosted by the Peterson Institute for International Economics, Frankfurt am Main, July 14, 2021.

[15] Press conference given by W. F. Duisenberg, Frankfurt, October 13, 1998.   [16] See chapter 6.

a German central banker who, unlike most of her predecessors, fully supported the consolidation of the ECB's new monetary regime.

In addition, the ECB immediately encouraged a bold common fiscal response to the pandemic from the European Union and its member governments. Far from resigning itself to being the only game in town, the ECB warned as early as March 11–12, 2020, that there were "limits to what monetary policy could do to address the immediate consequences of the coronavirus pandemic," and asserted the "need for a more supportive and targeted fiscal stance."[17] From then on, the ECB minutes repeatedly called even more pressingly for "an ambitious and coordinated fiscal stance" to "complement" the ECB's measures of monetary expansion.[18] In June 2020, the ECB unambiguously endorsed an EU-level fiscal spending proposal. Its Governing Council "strongly welcomed the European Commission's proposal for a recovery plan dedicated to supporting the regions and sectors most severely hit by the pandemic (...)."[19] The EU governments' unanimous adoption in July 2020 of Next Generation EU, a €750b recovery fund partly financed for the first time by bonds issued by the EU rather than by its member states, was, however, not a foregone conclusion.[20] Populist neoliberalism had been riding high for a decade in Northern Europe, just as it had among Republicans in the United States. Until the last minute, a group of "frugal" member states led by the Netherlands lobbied against the EU pandemic recovery fund.[21] Ultimately, German Chancellor Angela Merkel broke ranks with these states and supported the deal, thus putting pressure on "frugal" governments and paving the way for EU member governments' swift adoption of the Next Generation EU package.

Merkel's acceptance of EU fiscal solidarity, in marked contrast with her attitude during the 2010s Eurozone crisis, was and remains puzzling to this day.[22] Until government archives are open, it is difficult to precisely assess the different factors that contributed to the German chancellor's turnaround and to a stance that contrasted sharply with Germany's pro-austerity position in the early 2010s.[23] Yet one factor that was visibly different than in the early 2010s was the advice that she was hearing from the ECB. Instead of pushing member states in the direction of austerity, the ECB in 2020 now pushed them strongly

---

[17] Account of the monetary policy meeting of the Governing Council of the European Central Bank held in Frankfurt am Main on Wednesday and Thursday, March 11–12, 2020, p. 14.
[18] Account of the monetary policy meeting of the Governing Council of the European Central Bank, March 11–12, 2020; March 18, 2020; April 29–30, 2020; June 3–4, 2020; July 15–16, 2020; September 9–10, 2020; October 28–29, 2020; December 9–10, 2020; January 20–21, 2021.
[19] Account of the monetary policy meeting of the Governing Council of the European Central Bank, June 3–4, 2020, p. 18.
[20] Truchlewski, Schelkle, and Ganderson 2021.   [21] Buti and Fabbrini 2023.
[22] Was and Rittberger 2024. See also Smeets and Beach 2023.
[23] For an analysis of Germany's break with its "budgetary taboo," however, see Crespy and Schramm 2024.

in the direction of a strong fiscal stimulus. That surely played a role in steering other EU policymakers toward fiscal solidarity. After the Next Generation EU deal was announced, the ECB asserted that "fiscal support was critical, should arrive as early as possible and should not be withdrawn too soon."[24] The ECB was not at all talking about the need to rein in or to "exit" fiscal spending. This may be because central bankers had "learned" a lesson from the ECB's failures during the Eurozone crisis of the early 2010s.[25] The ECB's dramatically different internal politics may have been at least as important, however, in prompting this change. This time, the ECB president and other central bankers apparently paid much less attention to the most hawkish views expressed within the ECB Council. Unlike the early 2010s, German central bankers on the ECB Governing Council were no longer in a position to strenuously resist monetary stimulus. Shedding its fixation on the EU Treaty's "no-bailout clause" during the Eurozone crisis, the ECB had turned an important corner.

8.1.2 The Return of Technocratic Neoliberalism?

The renewal of inflationary pressures led US and EU central bankers to refocus on the fight against inflation and to engage in interest rates hikes not seen since the early 1980s. The Fed's and the ECB's acceptance of "transitory" inflation or an "inflation buffer" would soon come back to haunt them as inflation picked up. At a Senate hearing in November 2021, Powell acknowledged *sotto voce* that the Fed was behind the curve and that it was "probably a good time to retire" the adjective "transitory" when the Fed spoke of inflation.[26] The question now, in the face of renewed inflationary pressures, was whether central bankers would turn once again into anti-inflation crusaders. From early 2022 to mid-2023, the Fed progressively raised its main policy rate from zero to above 5 percent, while the ECB raised its own rate from -0.5 percent to 4 percent (see Figures 8.2 and 8.3). By mid-2024, inflation in the United States and the European Union had fallen close to the 2 percent inflation rate that both the Fed and the ECB targeted. Therefore, both central banks cautiously signaled that they were ready to cut rates in the near future – unless of course inflation picked up again.

In the face of persistent inflation, central bankers could of course be expected to raise interest rates. Unless inflation spiraled out of control, however, drastic monetary tightening was not the most likely scenario. In the 2010s and early 2020s, both the Fed and the ECB moved away from staunchly hawkish monetary policy. During the pandemic, both implemented massive asset purchases

---

[24] Account of the monetary policy meeting of the Governing Council of the European Central Bank held in Frankfurt am Main on Wednesday and Thursday, September 9–10, 2020.
[25] Quaglia and Verdun 2023.   [26] www.youtube.com/watch?v=MhAeUHLJoKk.

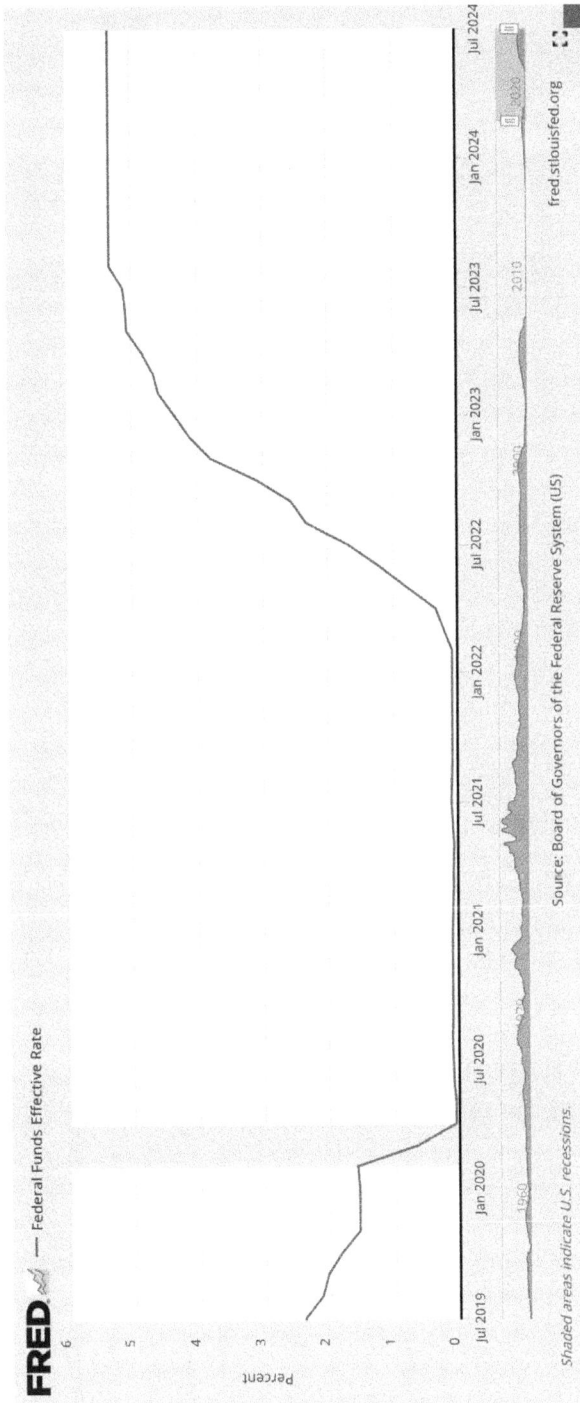

FIGURE 8.2 Federal Reserve's federal funds rate, July 2019–July 2024 (source: St. Louis Fed).

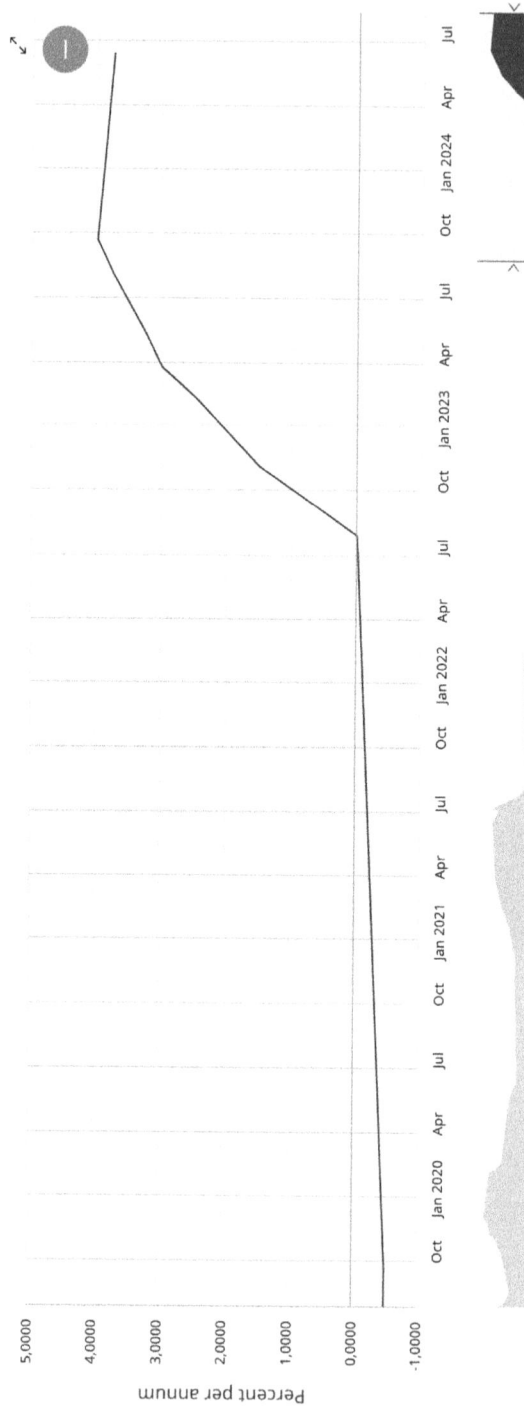

FIGURE 8.3 ECB deposit facility rate, August 2019–July 2024 (source: ECB data portal).

8.1 The Early 2020s at the Fed and at the ECB

and supported fiscal expansion. Thus, a full-fledged reversion to the tight-money policies of the 1980s – let alone a shift to a 1980s-style politics of money – was unlikely. Among mainstream economists, strict monetarists became a rear guard after the 1980s. While central bankers still sometimes invoked Milton Friedman, their global community had moved toward a "neo-Keynesian" position. In the 2010s, the politics of money had shifted across monetary policy committees, the economics profession, and the broader public arena.

In comparison with the 2010s, the Fed's recourse to unconventional measures during the pandemic was increasingly accepted. The Fed under Bernanke and Yellen had repeatedly tried to "exit" its unconventional measures – partly as a way to reassure the most hawkish central bankers and thus to avoid recurrent conflict – and had adopted its formal 2 percent inflation target as part of its 2012 strategic review, complete with "policy normalization" guidelines.[27] Judging from its new strategic review of 2021, the Fed became apparently more willing to accept "uncomfortable knowledge" and to give itself more flexibility in pursuing its monetary policy.[28] In the face of rising inflation, Powell repeatedly stressed that the Fed's 2 percent inflation target was a "medium-term" goal. In effect, this initially enabled the Fed to accommodate large deviations above that target, by taking the position that inflation was only "transitory" – until Powell declared that it was "time to retire that word."[29]

Some scholars have interpreted the Powell Fed's subsequent rate hikes as evidence that the Volcker "playbook" of tight money and high interest rates may be coming back.[30] Yet an analysis of the politics of money's different arenas raises some doubts about this diagnosis. First, the Fed took a much longer time to tighten its monetary policy than some FOMC members and prominent mainstream economists recommended – including some Democrats such as Larry Summers. Second, there was little appetite for drastic interest rate hikes in the public arena. Despite Americans' persistent frustrations about rising prices, the Biden administration did not encourage the Fed's use of a Volcker-style tight-money shock therapy to kill nascent inflation – and the Trump administration even less so. As long as this remained the case, a new waxing of technocratic neoliberalism appeared as a distant prospect in the early 2020s.

---

[27] See Chapter 6. [28] Best 2022.
[29] Rich Miller, "Powell Ditches 'Transitory' Tag, Paves the Way for Rate Hike," *Bloomberg News*, November 30, 2021.
[30] Blyth and Fraccaroli 2025. In a similar vein, Arbogast et al. (2024: 825) analyze the 2021 strategic review as well as FOMC members' speeches and conclude on a "comeback" to a "traditional NAIRU interpretation" that raised concerns about de-anchored inflation expectations. See also Leah Downey, "The Fight against Inflation Is Becoming a Class War," *Foreign Policy*, February 16, 2022.

The situation was broadly similar in Europe. Like the Fed under Jerome Powell, the ECB under Christine Lagarde delayed a tightening of its monetary policy, and then started raising its policy rates in 2022 in response to rising inflation. But perhaps the most politically revealing aspect of ECB policymaking under Lagarde was her signature endorsement of a transition toward a "green" economy.[31] Scholars have sometimes highlighted ideational change as the main factor that pushed the ECB toward "green central banking."[32] Yet there were many skeptics among central bankers, including Jens Weidmann, the Bundesbank's president, who argued against green central banking in the name of "market neutrality."[33] In response, ECB Board member Isabel Schnabel explained that an "inefficient" allocation of resources by the market could lead to dangerous systemic risks.[34] This debate between "market neutrality" and "market efficiency" was framed in economic terms, as is usually the case among central bankers. But the debate was also taking place in the public arena of the European Parliament, where Lagarde's green agenda generally fared better.[35] Pressures also mounted from ecological activists, who organized demonstrations outside ECB headquarters and even landed gliders on its rooftop. All this enabled Lagarde and her allies to overcome internal ECB critics of green central banking – not because these critics were convinced by their colleagues' ideas, but because they lacked external support.[36] Contrary to its long-standing image as an orthodox institution, the ECB thus moved even further away than the Fed from a narrow focus on price stability.

In an inverted mirror image of the European Union, the US public arena was much less permissive for green central banking in the United States, so the Fed did not cross that Rubicon. Unlike the ECB's strategic review, the Fed said nothing on the topic. This is a priori surprising, since one might have expected the Fed to embrace green central banking earlier than the ECB. The Fed's "dual mandate" was more open-ended than the ECB's "primary mandate" of price stability, and the influence of neo-Keynesian and systemic risk ideas had been greater and more long-standing within the Fed than within the ECB. In 2019, the Federal Reserve of San Francisco had published reports and had even hosted economists and policymakers for an event on "the economics of climate

---

[31] For a fully detailed account, see Jabko and Kupzok 2024.
[32] Van't Klooster 2022; Deyris 2023; Siderius 2023; Quorning 2024.
[33] "*Climate change and central banks,*" Welcome address by Dr. Jens Weidmann, President of the Deutsche Bundesbank and Chairman of the Board of Directors of the Bank for International Settlements, at the Deutsche Bundesbank's second financial market conference, Frankfurt am Main, October 29, 2019.
[34] "*From market neutrality to market efficiency,*" Welcome address by Isabel Schnabel, Member of the Executive Board of the ECB, at the ECB DG-Research Symposium "Climate change, financial markets and green growth" Frankfurt, June 14, 2021.
[35] Massoc 2025.   [36] Author interviews with central bankers and central bank officials.

change."[37] Some policy advocates – including former Fed Governor Sarah Bloom Raskin – called for a greener Federal Reserve.[38] Yet in the public arena, the Republican Party had increasingly turned toward climate change denialism. When President Biden nominated Bloom Raskin to the Federal Reserve Board, the fossil fuel industry and Republican senators went to war against her appointment. Senator Joe Manchin, a Democrat but also the senator of coal-heavy West Virginia, ultimately killed it.[39] From then on, senior Fed officials and policymakers concluded that they could not venture on the terrain of climate change without being caught in a political crossfire.[40] The Fed's freedom to innovate was apparently limited by its inability to successfully peddle green policies in America's polarized partisan environment.

8.2 THE IMF, THE BANK OF JAPAN, AND THE BANK OF ENGLAND

This book has focused on the Fed and the ECB, the world's two leading independent central banks. I have engaged in what comparative politics scholars call a "similar-case comparison" of the two most watched and globally important central banks. In the late twentieth and early twenty-first centuries, the United States and the European Union saw the formation of a relatively similar – albeit not identical – alliance between central bankers, economists, and politicians. The transatlantic political-economic regime that resulted from this cross-cutting alliance, in turn, had enormous repercussions on other countries. Technocratic neoliberalism became the prevailing regime of political economy across advanced liberal democracies well beyond the United States and the European Union – in part because of the US' and EU's economic and political weight in the world. In this section, I therefore mobilize various primary sources as well as existing scholarship to briefly ask whether the Bank of England, the Bank of Japan, and also the IMF are also subject to similar politics of money as the Fed and the ECB, and whether the effects – namely, the waxing and waning of technocratic neoliberalism – are comparable.

Once we move beyond the cases of the Fed and the ECB, more variation is to be expected, and more caveats are therefore in order. One important difference is that the Fed, and to a lesser extent the ECB, had a much greater degree of freedom than other central banks because these two central banks oversaw the

---

[37] Federal Reserve Bank of San Francisco, *The Economics of Climate Change*: www.frbsf.org/economic-research/events/2019/november/economics-of-climate-change/.
[38] Sarah Bloom Raskin "Why Is the Fed Spending So Much Money on a Dying Industry?" *New York Times*, May 28, 2020.
[39] Emily Cochrane and Jeanna Smialek, "Manchin Won't Support Raskin for the Fed, Imperiling Her Nomination," *New York Times*, March 14, 2022.
[40] Author interviews, September 27, 2023 and October 18, 2023.

world's leading international currencies. Since the 1970s and Nixon's decision to stop abiding by the rules of the Bretton Woods regime, the United States has often been accused of "benign neglect" of its partners when it comes to international monetary governance. As the steward of the world's leading reserve currency, the Fed could afford to focus primarily on domestic concerns. The US dollar has been sitting at the apex of a "hierarchy of money," and that hierarchy has only recently started to be challenged by other currencies, including the euro.[41] As this book has argued, changing US and EU contests over monetary governance across interacting organizational, professional, and public arenas led to the waxing and waning of new monetary and political-economic regimes. In the face of both economic stagnation and rising inflation in the 1970s, the Fed first chose to prioritize employment rather than price stability – until that changed after 1979 when the Fed implemented the "Volcker Shock."

The United States' preeminent position in the international monetary hierarchy, in turn, largely contributed to the global trend toward central bank independence and hawkish monetary policies. Neoliberal practices – including central bank independence – have typically spread from the top of the monetary hierarchy down, via a complex mix of coercion, competition, and imitation.[42] Once the country with the most important international reserve currency adopted tight-money policies, no other central bank could easily afford expansionary monetary policies in a situation of international capital mobility – unless they were willing to face exchange rate depreciation, a loss of foreign investments, and capital flight. That was true even in prosperous European nations – where currencies' exchange rates were pegged within the European Monetary system – and *a fortiori* in other places that experienced financial crises in the 1980s, such as Latin America. The politics of money beyond the United States has therefore featured many more concerns about sovereignty and financial instability than was the case in the United States. Even after the advent of the euro, the European Union remained more exposed to these concerns than the United States.

8.2.1 The Slow Waning of Technocratic Neoliberalism after the 1980s

The International Monetary Fund (IMF) is not a central bank, but it is an international financial institution that has in many ways come to define what it means for countries to conduct sound macroeconomic policies. Not coincidentally, the IMF is also one of the largest employers of economics PhDs in the world – second only to the Fed and the ECB – with a permanent staff of about 170 economics PhDs.[43] Like central banks, it is an important locus of interaction between the economics profession and the public arena. Finally, the IMF

---

[41] Eichengreen 2011; Cohen 2015; Pistor 2017.
[42] Dobbin, Simmons, and Garrett 2007; Johnson 2016.
[43] Author's calculation based on IMF website.

8.2 The IMF, the Bank of Japan, and the Bank of England

is a Washington-based hub where central bankers interact with each other and with American financial officials. For example, Jacques de Larosière – whom we encountered as governor of the Banque de France and member of the Delors Committee in 1988–1989 – had previously been the head of the IMF, while Paul Volcker chaired the Fed. In sum, the IMF is an organization with its own internal contests, tightly networked with the economics profession, with the IMF's member governments, and with Washington DC policy circles.

This is not the place for a detailed study of the politics of money in which the IMF participated, but it appears strikingly similar to the politics of money within and around the Fed or the ECB. During the 1980s, the IMF became the main global proponent of structural adjustment programs under the banner of the "Washington consensus"[44] – a moniker that soon became virtually synonymous with neoliberalism. The IMF and its economists were key actors in global financial liberalization in the 1980s and 1990s.[45] They were also active in spreading the gospel of liberalization among economic technocrats in the developing world.[46] Like central banks and the economics profession, however, the IMF underwent considerable change after the 1990s. Even before the global financial crisis of 2008, the Asian financial crisis of 1997 prompted important revisions of the IMF's conventional neoliberal policy advice about international capital mobility and about macroeconomic management.[47] The IMF did not suddenly renounce sound fiscal and monetary policy, but it no longer insisted on a fully open capital account and on harsh austerity policies as standard financial crisis remedies. The IMF has also moved in the direction of the rising neo-Keynesian mainstream, especially under the leadership of Dominique Strauss-Kahn – himself a French socialist – who recruited MIT economist Olivier Blanchard as chief economist of the IMF. In the 2010s, IMF officials started wondering during the Eurozone crisis whether fiscal retrenchment was a good remedy to excessive indebtedness in the Eurozone but also, more generally, whether "neoliberalism" had been "oversold."[48]

One aspect of the IMF's evolution was its heavy involvement in European debt negotiations in the 2010s.[49] The IMF did not hesitate to advocate debt write-downs for Greece, even though these were initially ruled out by EU officials at the ECB and the European Commission who favored policies of fiscal austerity instead. This happened in the context of the IMF's increased attention to the presence or absence of "fiscal space" in its analysis of different countries' fiscal policies and public debts.[50] Some scholars see this trend as the

---

[44] Williamson 1990. [45] Abdelal 2007; Chwieroth 2010. [46] Chwieroth 2007.
[47] Abdelal 2007; Clift 2018; Babb and Kentikelenis 2018.
[48] Chapter 7. See also Blanchard and Leigh 2013; Ostry, Loundgani, and Furceri 2016.
[49] Lütz and Kranke 2014; Henning 2017.
[50] A widely cited 2005 IMF paper defined fiscal space as the "availability of budgetary room that allows a government to provide resources for a desired purpose without any prejudice to the sustainability of a government's financial position." (Heller 2005: 3)

IMF's implicit admission that fiscal consolidation is not a panacea everywhere and, therefore, as a sign of its departure from neoliberal orthodoxy.⁵¹ Whether the IMF's recourse to this concept of fiscal space was a profound change or a mere inflection, it was certainly influential in international economic policy circles. As we saw, ECB President Mario Draghi referred to "fiscal space" after 2014 as a way to turn the table against advocates of fiscal austerity in the Eurozone.⁵² It is also worth noting that Christine Lagarde had served as IMF director-general before she was appointed as ECB president – where she deviated from strictly neoliberal policy precepts.

Among the world's most important independent central banks, the Bank of Japan was perhaps the first to experiment with policies that significantly departed from the neoliberal fight against inflation. Like the United States and Europe, Japan experienced inflation in the late 1970s and early 1980s, which the Bank of Japan addressed through tight-money policies. But among advanced capitalist democracies, Japan alone suffered a major financial crisis in 1989, followed by a long period of economic stagnation with nagging deflationary tendencies in the 1990s and 2000s. In response to that crisis, the Bank of Japan was made independent from the Ministry of Finance in 1997, and Japan then became the first country to experiment with quantitative easing as early as 2001 – long before the global financial crisis of 2008.⁵³ To say that Japan decisively led the global community of central bankers away from technocratic neoliberalism would be an overstatement, however. In the 2000s, many observers – including Princeton economist and later Fed Governor Ben Bernanke – considered that the Bank of Japan's policy of quantitative easing was not nearly as bold as it should have been in view of Japan's deep recession.⁵⁴ Until the global financial crisis, the Bank of Japan implemented quantitative easing quite reluctantly. It repeatedly tried to exit that policy, only to be forced back into it by the return of deflation. This placed the Bank of Japan in a situation of quasi-permanent conflict with successive Japanese governments and with the Ministry of Finance, which de facto jeopardized its recently acquired independence.

According to many observers, Japanese central bankers were not as tightly integrated with the global economics profession. Partly for that reason, it may have been in a weaker position to defend its independence vis-à-vis the Japanese government. But there was also a specifically Japanese politics of money – within the Bank of Japan's monetary committee; within the economics profession, even if prominent Japanese economists had tighter links with the Japanese state; and surely within Japan's public arena. One research question is whether

---

⁵¹ Clift 2018.   ⁵² See Chapter 7.   ⁵³ Amyx 2006; Park, Katada, Chiozza, and Kojo 2018.
⁵⁴ Bernanke 2000. In author interviews conducted in the spring of 2007 in Washington and Tokyo, many Fed officials as well as American and Japanese academic economists routinely expressed the view that the Bank of Japan was staffed by old-school central bankers obsessed about inflation and insufficiently trained in modern macro-economics.

patterns of interactions between the Japanese prime minister's office, the bureaucracy, Parliament, and political parties imparted distinctive national characteristics to Japan's politics of money, and whether those characteristics mattered for the evolution of Japan's political-economic regimes. According to author interviews, the rather chaotic shift to quantitative easing after 2001 effectively cost the Bank of Japan some of the independence that it had gained in 1997 – even though it remained legally independent. One question is therefore whether the Bank was able to reassert its independence over time. Another one concerns the degree to which cross-cutting alliances between central bankers, economists, and politicians as well as other public organizations shaped the evolution of Japan's political-economic regime.

8.2.2 The Accelerated Waning of Technocratic Neoliberalism after 2008

After 2008, the Bank of Japan finally embraced QE more fully – but this occurred under major political pressure. Japan is therefore also a case in which technocratic neoliberalism waned after 2008. Yet the politics that spurred that political-economic regime change differed considerably from the politics that we observed in the United States and Europe. Instead of pushing back against the government's conservative fiscal policies, the Bank of Japan shed its monetary conservatism mostly *after* the government moved away from fiscal conservatism. By the time the pandemic struck in early 2020, both the government and the Bank of Japan conducted reflationary policies. As everywhere else, the return of global inflation opened the question of whether Japan would return to conservative monetary and fiscal policies under the auspices of Japanese-style technocratic neoliberalism. After going through the painful experience of several decades of economic stagnation and quasi-deflation, however, it seemed unlikely that Japan would revert to the political-economic regime of the 1990s or even to the half-hearted monetary orthodoxy of the 2000s.

The trajectory of UK monetary policy and the UK political economy more closely resembled that of its partners in continental Europe and the United States. A period of technocratic neoliberalism that lasted from the 1980s until the global financial crisis was followed by a period in which the Bank of England pursued an easy-money policy. In our examination of Europe's shift toward technocratic neoliberalism in the 1980s, we already briefly encountered the Bank of England and its Governor Robin Leigh-Pemberton.[55] Ultimately, UK Prime Minister Margaret Thatcher chose to preserve the pound sterling and to keep her country out of Europe's Economic and Monetary Union. Yet Thatcher was also one of the most outspoken defenders of neoliberal policies. To quash inflation, she had accepted her Chancellor of the Exchequer Nigel Lawson's plea in favor of joining the European Monetary System (EMS) of

---

[55] See Chapter 5.

pegged exchange rates. Although the United Kingdom dropped out of the EMS in 1992, the Bank of England continued to pursue an anti-inflationary policy that complemented the conservative orientation of successive UK governments from the 1980s to the 2020s. In 1997, one of the first acts of the newly elected Labour government headed by Tony Blair was to make the Bank of England legally independent.[56] Blair and his successor Gordon Brown wanted to tie themselves and future British governments to the mast of orthodox monetary policy. Only in the 2010s was this policy reversed, when the Bank of England decided to implement quantitative easing in response to the financial crisis.

During that 2010 decade, successive UK conservative governments pursued policies of fiscal austerity that were often criticized as "self-defeating" since they worsened the economic downturn.[57] As in the United States and the European Union, the UK movement toward fiscal austerity was at odds with the Bank of England's monetary policy. Unlike both the United States and the European Union, however, these different fiscal and monetary policy orientations were the object of an increasingly explicit coordination between the UK government and the Bank of England. The government basically counted on the Bank to pursue easy-money policies as a way to keep the UK macroeconomic orientation sufficiently accommodative, while at the same time pursuing fiscal retrenchment. The mechanism of this coordination was the annual letter sent by the Treasury to define the Bank of England's "remit." As early as January 2009, the Chancellor authorized the Bank to create an Asset Purchase Facility to conduct quantitative easing.[58] As explained by the 2013 remit letter: "Monetary activism has a vital role to play in the Government's economic strategy as the Government delivers on its commitment to fiscal consolidation."[59] In plain words, "fiscal 'austerity' was meant to be coupled with adventurous monetary easing."[60] The government's austerity policies may have also been a form of Tory political "statecraft" to ultimately supplant the Liberal Democrats, their junior coalition partners.[61] Whatever the case may be, a cursory examination of the United Kingdom suggests a waning of technocratic neoliberalism along similar lines as in the United States and the European Union. Technocrats pursued an accommodative (Keynesian) economic policy, while conservative politicians veered toward a more populist advocacy of fiscal austerity. Even though the alliance between the central bank and conservative forces did not unravel as acrimoniously as in the United States and the European Union, the Bank of England's easy-money policy became remarkably detached from successive UK governments' policies of fiscal austerity.

In the early 2020s, the UK regime of political economy continued to evolve on a trajectory that was parallel to that of the United States and the European

---

[56] King 2001; Quaglia 2005.   [57] Blyth 2013.
[58] www.bankofengland.co.uk/-/media/boe/files/letter/2009/chancellor-letter-290109.pdf.
[59] www.bankofengland.co.uk/-/media/boe/files/letter/2013/chancellor-letter-200313.pdf.
[60] Author's exchange with former Bank of England senior official.   [61] Gamble 2015.

Union. When the United Kingdom was struck by the global pandemic in 2020, the orientations of UK fiscal and monetary policies became more aligned than in the 2010s. Not only did the Bank of England step up its easy-money policies, but the UK government this time gave up on the objective of fiscal consolidation. As stated by UK Chancellor of the Exchequer Rishi Sunak in his June 2020 letter directing the Bank to conduct further quantitiative easing: "My priority is to support the economy through the immediate crisis and into the recovery" by way of "unprecedented support for public services, jobs and businesses."[62] When the pandemic subsided and inflation returned, the Bank belatedly tightened its monetary policy, like its US and EU counterparts. It remains to be seen whether this monetary tightening is the harbinger of a new waxing of technocratic neoliberalism.

8.3 CONCLUSION: TIME FOR AN OBITUARY OF NEOLIBERALISM?

After the global financial crisis of 2008, many were puzzled by the "strange non-death of neoliberalism."[63] Given the global rush to boost consumer demand in response to the pandemic and the brevity of central bankers' subsequent return to anti-inflationary policies, it is tempting to declare neoliberalism finally dead. Some observers have even adopted the term "post-neoliberalism" as a label for the new political economy of the 2020s. In progressive academic and policy circles, there was considerable buzz around the emergence of a "paradigm" that would finally go "beyond neoliberalism."[64] To be sure, neoliberal ideas were no longer as widespread among central bankers and economists as was the case in the 1980s, and many politicians had veered toward populism. Policy change was visible in areas that had been primary venues for neoliberal ideas, such as trade or antitrust.[65] In many ways, the "neoliberal order" that existed until the financial crisis of 2008 seemed "broken."[66] An obituary of neoliberalism may be premature, however. While there is little doubt that technocratic neoliberalism has waned, financialization has continued to proceed and to foster avatars of the neoliberal project.[67] Whether circumstances will lead to the consolidation of a more populist version of the neoliberal political-economic regime, relegating technocrats and economists to a more secondary role, remains to be seen. It is safe to say that the politics of money, however reconfigured, will still matter for the future of political-economic regimes.

---

[62] www.bankofengland.co.uk/-/media/boe/files/letter/2020/chancellor-apf-letter-june-2020.pdf.
[63] Crouch 2011.
[64] The Hewlett Foundation, in particular, has been at the forefront of funding new research on "post-neoliberalism" in political economy: https://hewlett.org/library/beyond-neoliberalism-rethinking-political-economy/. See also Davies and Gane 2021.
[65] On antitrust, see for example Berk 2026.   [66] Gerstle 2022: 293.   [67] Slobodian 2025.

9

Technocrats, Neoliberalism, Keynesianism, and Democracy

Central bankers are cautious yet powerful people. They sometimes clash with politicians who support what they see as destabilizing policies. This book has addressed a puzzling reversal of roles over a few decades. In the 1980s, American and European central bankers sharply turned toward tight-money policies to fight inflation. They forcefully asserted their independence and turned into folk heroes for many conservatives. Then, in the 2010s, the Fed, the ECB, and other central banks themselves veered toward easy-money policies to help economic recovery. Despite some misgivings, central bankers antagonized large segments of the political class and of the public that suddenly appeared more conservative than central bankers. Central bankers stood accused of betraying conservative principles of sound money and economic responsibility.

As I have argued, cross-cutting alliances between central bankers, economists, and politicians enabled the consolidation of both these monetary regimes. Because monetary governance is central to broader political-economic governance, these monetary regime changes also led to to the waxing and waning of technocratic neoliberalism – a broad regime centered on the prioritization of the fight against inflation over other concerns. Although central bankers quietly abandoned monetarism in the 1980s, they continued to support fiscally conservative policies as well as market liberalization – until they conducted monetary stimulus and began to encourage a more active use of fiscal policy in the 2010s. At that point, the populist dimension of neoliberalism supplanted its technocratic dimension.

9.1 NEOLIBERALISM AND KEYNESIANISM

Scholars of economics and political economy often have trouble making sense of this waxing and waning of technocratic neoliberalism. Many mainstream economists – as well as many central bankers themselves – see the monetary regime change of the 2010s as a new kind of Keynesian response to the economic slump that followed the global financial crisis. But they often downplay the neoliberal logic of the broader political-economic regime, to which central bankers largely contributed at the end of the twentieth century. By contrast, many scholars of political economy focus on central bankers' active role in the push for neoliberalism and financialization before and after the global financial crisis. What they often miss, however, is the depth of monetary regime change since the global financial crisis. They often diagnose this reorientation as another step in the process of financialization, rather than as a Keynesian response.[1] In highlighting a broad structural logic of change, however, they often sidestep the economics debate.

To be sure, some scholars of political economy have sought to build bridges with economists – either by spelling out the "micro-foundations" of their theories and models, like "neo-Keynesian" economists;[2] or by advocating a more heterodox, "post-Keynesian" approach to political economy.[3] This debate within political economy thus echoes the continuing debate, within economics, between different mainstream and heterodox Keynesians. Yet we must remember that disciplinary debates are not only debates about who is "right." Mainstream economists are at the top of a professional hierarchy. They tend to consider the broader political context as extraneous to economic debates. This apolitical stance also helps them to buttress their expert legitimacy among policymakers. Whether scholars of political economy should simply replicate the debate between mainstream and heterodox economists therefore raises uncomfortable questions about truth and power. Such replication would likely reproduce the same hierarchy that exists within the economics profession – irrespective of who is right.

This book has adopted a different, more horizontal approach to political economy. Unlike many scholars of economics or political economy, I have not declared a fundamental analytical commitment to particular assumptions – for example, by siding with mainstream ("new") Keynesian or monetarist economists, or with heterodox ("post-Keynesian") economists, or by subscribing to a structural explanatory logic such as financialization. Instead, I have treated mainstream economics as an authoritative yet contested repertoire that central bankers and economists use to discuss various policy options. Then, I have analyzed changes in monetary regimes with methods and concepts drawn not only from comparative politics, but also from economic sociology, science

---

[1] Many recent accounts thus built on Greta Krippner's stark distinction between the post-1980s "era of financialization" and the preceding "Keynesian era" (Krippner 2011: ch. 6).

[2] For example, the microeconomic calculations of firms are at the center of different "varieties of capitalism" (Hall and Soskice 2001).

[3] For example, macroeconomic preferences and demand management are central to the study of "the politics of growth and stagnation" (Baccaro, Blyth, and Pontusson 2022).

studies, and pragmatist theory. I have refrained from making heroic assumptions and instead endeavored to approach monetary regimes agnostically, as elements of larger and more complex political-economic regimes. In an era of increasing central bank transparency and access to digitalized archives, a rigorous comparative historical analysis of the contests that lead to monetary regime change has become easier.

What I have found is that contests among central bankers and economists are distinct from, but interact with, political contests in the public arena. The fact that central bankers' positions may or may not be aligned with their professional or partisan identities (or, in Europe, national identities) could be seen as a logical result of their legally guaranteed independence. Yet central bankers also enter alliances that cut across organizational, professional, and public arenas. We have encountered hawkish central bankers aligned with conservatives or with center-left politicians; hawks who became doves, and conversely; Keynesian economists who allied with conservatives, or who moved away from them; French or Italian or German central bankers who allied with monetarist or ordoliberal economists, or who peeled away from them; and so on. Although these changing alliances are not straightforward manifestations of central bankers' independence, they are not predictable results of fixed organizational, professional, or political allegiances either. That is why archival analysis is a powerful tool to chart out the politics of money and its impact on the evolution of political-economic regimes.

From this standpoint, labels such as "Keynesianism" or "monetarism" are meaningful shorthand, insofar as they capture some guiding principles of monetary and economic policymaking. At the same time, these can easily turn into reductionist categories that prevent us from understanding the messiness of the real world. Mainstream economics is a remarkably syncretic repertoire. What mainstream economists call the "new Keynesian" or "new neoclassical synthesis" in macroeconomics has been incorporated into a broader and constantly evolving toolbox of permissible central bank actions and policies. That repertoire enables central bankers to hedge their bets between the best-identified sources of instability in today's capitalist economies – until new instabilities are revealed.

The question, therefore, is not merely whether central bankers act in a "Keynesian" or in a "monetarist" fashion – or whether "New Keynesian" macroeconomics is a form of neoliberalism in the broad context of "financialization." In times of turmoil, central bankers typically step out of their usual scripts. As our examination of decades of central banking in the United States and Europe repeatedly demonstrated, central bankers took into account political "realities" and "headwinds"; affirmed the importance of "rules" that they later disregarded or modified; swerved between their different responsibilities; and constantly oscillated between "sound money" principles in the face of inflationary pressures, "Keynesian" policies when demand was too weak, and "backstops" when a financial crisis reared its ugly head. Only after the fact can these ad hoc policies be labeled neoliberal, or monetarist, or Keynesian.

9.2 TECHNOCRATS IN A DEMOCRACY

When we zoomed out of central banks, we also saw that the most important monetary regime changes that central bankers implemented after the 1970s occurred against the background of profound turmoil. In the United States, in Europe, and beyond, the widespread perception of crisis supplanted the business-as-usual perception of money as a neutral reality. Central bankers' outsized role in these critical moments raises the question of whether independent central banks' policies truly conform to the public interest – in other words, whether they are sufficiently democratic.

Independent central bankers operate in relative insulation from electoral politics. Central bankers cherish and defend their independence, but they obviously live in a political world. Typically, they seek allies in the public arena as well as in the economics profession. In their interactions with politicians since the nineteenth century, central bankers have often been concerned about the "populist" risk of fiscal recklessness and runaway inflation. This concern goes a long way toward explaining their alliance with conservative forces in the late twentieth century. Yet in the face of persistently dismal growth after the global financial crisis, they discovered that populist calls for austerity among conservatives could be equally if not more worrisome. A new breed of neoliberal conservatives now claimed to speak for the people against a corrupt elite.[4] In the 2010s, monetary as well as fiscal stimulus was equated with "bailouts" for the "elite" and for undeserving outsiders – often minorities or foreigners stigmatized as "reckless debtors," as opposed to the self-discipline of redblooded Americans or the Swabian housewife. Needless to add, racial animus – especially in the United States – and nationalism – especially in Europe – also played a role.

From the perspective of central bankers, populism was once again an adversary – but for reasons opposite to those of the past. Although criticisms of monetary orthodoxy were still heard on the Left, many populist critics of central bankers were no longer opposed to sound money. On the contrary, many new critics now demanded a restoration of strictly orthodox policies. In the United States, some called for a return to the gold standard; in Germany, to the deutschmark. Central bankers came under heavy political fire from advocates of monetary as well as fiscal retrenchment. At that point, central bankers discovered that their interest was to disassociate themselves from supporters of such neoliberal policies. As technocratic neoliberalism waned, neoliberalism turned increasingly populist.

---

[4] See also Slobodian 2025.

One possible conclusion – often drawn by economists – from the experience of the 1970s and the 2010s is that politics tends to produce destructive attempts to manipulate the money supply. Therefore, central banking is best left to technocrats, if we want to avoid inflation or deflation.[5] Central bankers themselves often see themselves as nonpolitical experts whose job is, in part, to counteract the irrational tide of partisan politics. Things are not so simple, however. As we saw, American and European central bankers in the 1980s relied on their reputation of expert neutrality to pursue orthodox inflation-fighting strategies, in relative insulation from political critics. They also endorsed neoliberal policies of fiscal conservatism and economic liberalization, based on purely economic rationales. By lending authority to conservative aspirations, however, they greatly contributed to the ascent of neoliberalism as a widespread form of popular subjectivity. By the 2010s, this neoliberalism gave birth to austerity politics, and central bankers' turn toward easy-money policies was blamed as a betrayal of sound money.

A diametrically opposite conclusion – sometimes drawn by scholars of political economy – is that putting monetary policy powers in the hands of elected officials would make the governance of money more democratic.[6] Yet the problem, here, is that the genie is now out of the bottle. Central bank independence was supposed to make money more neutral; instead, the action of independent central bankers has become more contested. Left-leaning critics of central bankers in the name of democracy often portray them as a technocratic elite aligned with finance and conservative interests. Yet it is far from evident that a more democratic governance of money would necessarily result in more progressive central banking. If central bankers had not been firmly in charge of monetary policy in the 2010s, for example, conservative attacks on monetary stimulus might have further compromised the excruciatingly slow recovery from the global financial crisis. In a context of growing distrust of economic technocrats on the Right, the independence of central banks can therefore appear as a guardrail against authoritarian politics.

---

[5] Such a conclusion would draw implicit or explicit support from many economists. See, for example, Blinder 2022.

[6] See, for example, Downey 2024.

Appendix A

Natural Language Processing (NLP) Methodology and Results

This appendix presents a methodology that was developed to assess the level of conflict or disagreement in transcripts of central banks' monetary policy committees. Central bankers usually meet to discuss monetary policy on a monthly schedule. The book covers two decades of meetings – the 1980s and the 2010s – in two central banks – the US Federal Reserve and the European Central Bank (and, for the 1980s, its predecessor the European Community's Committee of Central Bank Governors). Committee transcripts are generally well over 100 pages. This results in tens of thousands of pages of transcribed discussions in natural language. With this volume of data, it would have required a prohibitively large amount of human effort to identify individual moments of disagreement. The objective of our methodology was to automatically detect moments and patterns of contention in transcripts of committee meetings by using natural language processing (NLP) techniques.

A core problem is that disagreements between central bankers are pervasive and, at the same time, not always obvious. In any given monetary policy meeting, there is usually more disagreement than suggested by the always relatively small number of dissents acknowledged in the voting record. Observers usually highlight an underlying cleavage between "hawks," who prioritize the fight against inflation, and "doves," who are primarily concerned about unemployment. But those are not fixed identities, unlike say Democrats or Republicans in the US Congress. In addition, central bankers are usually trained in economics, so they share a professional ethos and agree on many parameters of analysis. Fundamental value-laden disagreements may be couched in highly technical terms that make them seem innocuous, especially to non-economists – again, unlike the often-obvious disagreements between Democrats and Republicans. Finally, committee meeting transcripts reflect strong norms of collegiality and of rational deliberation on data and policy options. Committee members typically try to avoid overt conflict among themselves. To preserve their standing among their peers, they are each under pressure to show that they keep an open mind – even when they fundamentally disagree.

To mitigate this problem, NLP technology is useful because it relies on algorithmically normalized understandings of contention, identified in terms of their linguistic or conversational patterns. These patterns may not be always immediately visible in a cursory reading, but they can be considered weak signals that will be automatically detected by the algorithm. The detected disagreements in the meetings (or parts of meetings) can then be counted and built into statistical charts within and across meetings. Human intuition and judgment are still required to analyze the exact nature and depth of committee disagreements in the transcripts, but the NLP technology helps us focus on the times and areas of most intense contention in the transcripts. In essence, it builds a humanly manageable corpus of text data in which disagreements stand out. Once that corpus has been automatically built and charted out, it becomes possible to delve into central bankers' disagreements through a manual reading of the relevant parts of the transcripts.

A.1 NATURAL LANGUAGE PROCESSING AND CENTRAL BANK TRANSCRIPTS

Current State of Natural Language Processing: NLP refers to the branch of computer science (more specifically, the branch of artificial intelligence) concerned with giving computers the ability to understand text and spoken words in much the same way human beings can. NLP combines computational linguistics – rule-based modeling of human language – with statistical methods, machine learning, and deep learning models. NLP has recently gained attention for representing and analyzing human language computationally, through large language models such as ChatGPT. Currently, NLP has the capacity to perform tasks in various fields such as machine translation, email spam detection, information extraction, summarization, medical records, and question answering.

What is Semantic Analysis? The relevant problem in our application of NLP falls under the umbrella term semantic analysis. Three classification subproblems are especially relevant: *topic classification, sentiment analysis,* and *stance detection*. These subproblems have been explored in the context of central bank committee data. Semantic analysis is the overarching task of drawing meaning from human language. *Topic classification* is the task of sorting text into predefined categories based on its content. For example, in the paper "Central Bank Communication about Climate Change,"[1] the authors attempt

---

[1] Arseneau, Drexler, and Osada 2022.

to classify what speeches are "climate-related" from the set of all central bank speeches available from the Bank of International Settlements from January 1997 to December 2021. *Sentiment analysis* is the process of analyzing text to determine the emotional tone of a speaker or text. For example, the paper "FOMC minutes sentiment and their impact on financial markets" classified the text in FOMC documents based on optimistic sentiment, which the author correlates to "hawkish" intent, versus negative sentiment, which the author correlates to "dovish" intent.[2] *Stance detection* is the identification of a speaker's opinions and judgment toward a given proposition. Our problem is a combination of all three of these tasks.

In general, the automatic detection of controversy by NLP models is anything but a trivial problem. As one recent comprehensive review of different NLP methods for stance detection put it: "Achieving stance detection is challenging due to the fact that determining stance is subjective. In addition, concepts and opinions are formed through a variety of expressions and linguistic compositions, making it more difficult to detect."[3] The most common application of existing NLP models involve sentiment analysis and stance detection analyses on social media. Even though controversy can be notoriously loud on social media, NLP experts have found it difficult to elaborate models capable of detecting controversy in these applications. Controversy detection has therefore become an important and rapidly evolving area of NLP research.

As illustrated by the above examples, there is an existing literature that uses NLP to analyze central bank communications. Yet these efforts are mostly focused on topic classification and sentiment analysis rather than stance detection, and thus do not directly address our problem. The closest attempt to use NLP to map out central bankers' agreements and disagreements can be found in a book by Cheryl Schonhardt-Bailey about the making of the Fed's monetary policy under Paul Volcker and Alan Greenspan.[4] A recent survey of text-as-data methodologies for social scientists calls that book "a brilliant example" of inquiry into the role of deliberation and actors' strategies in the policy process.[5] Schonhardt-Bailey focuses on the reason-giving requirement of deliberation – that is, on how members of the FOMC provide reasons for their claims and positions, and respond to others' reasons and counter arguments. For that purpose, the author uses Alceste, a software that helps her identify "exactly the form of argumentation [and] how that evolved over time."[6]

The Alceste software analyzes the prevalence of themes in the transcripts by finding "lexical worlds" in the speakers' discourse, and it classifies text segments on that basis. It analyzes the distribution of words in the corpus, sorting

---

[2] Tadle 2022. [3] Alturayeif, Luqman, and Ahmed 2023. [4] Schonhardt-Bailey 2013.
[5] Grimmer, Roberts, Stewart 2022: 44. [6] Schonhardt-Bailey 2013: 6.

Elementary Context Units (ECUs) into various classes. The main semantic aspects that are built in the software are grammatical dictionaries that reduce verbal forms to a single root, and that classify words into various grammatical classes. It is then up to the researcher to formulate an interpretation, including defining, naming, and qualifying the classes.[7] While the Alceste software may be able to track the particular themes raised in FOMC meetings, its focus on changing themes may overstate the extent of consensus around new themes. Since it does not perform any sentiment analysis, it also cannot detect subtle disagreements or mood changes.

A.2 HOW WE DEVELOPED OUR METHODOLOGY

A.2.1 Initial Approaches

We decided to test different software tools to detect controversy. The first tool we tested was speakai.co, a sentiment analysis software. We tested the software on a few Fed transcripts and the output was a line-by-line sentiment breakdown, scored on a scale from -1 (most negative sentiment) to 1 (most positive sentiment). The software was able to detect the central bankers' positive or negative sentiments, but these sentiments reflected their assessments of the economy rather than agreement or conflict among themselves. Although the software did not reveal its reasoning, its scores apparently focused on the negative or positive valence of certain words. For example, the presence of words with negative valence, such as "inflation," "unemployment," or "recession," would lead the software to score a particular sentence or paragraph as reflecting negative sentiment. Conversely, the presence of words such as "growth" or "confidence" would lead to positive scores. Like other sentiment analysis tools, we saw that speakai could be useful to detect central bankers' general sentiment about the economy – which is the main way in which sentiment analysis has been used to analyze central bankers' speeches and transcripts. But the software did not score the level of conflict among central bankers, which was not necessarily correlated with the state of the economy. Therefore, it was not useful for our purposes, since it was clearly not very good at detecting disagreements among central bankers.

We then tested the service MeaningCloud[8] in the hope of detecting disagreement, not just negative or positive sentiment about the economy. MeaningCloud's sentiment analysis model determines what sentiment

---

[7] The software produces statistical data on the strength of a given content word's association to each of the classes. This output is in the form of two tables: one showing "significant presences" and another showing "significant absences" for each class. The interpretation cannot be formulated in absolute terms, but rather with expressions such as "more frequently" or "less frequently."
[8] www.meaningcloud.com/.

Appendix A

(positive, negative, or neutral) a text section expresses, as well as a total sentiment value for the entire text (i.e., whether the whole text is positive, negative, or neutral). This tool gave similar results as the one we observed with the speakai.co model, however. Then we also tested the topic extraction model of the MeaningCloud platform. We hoped this model would provide us topic changes that would correspond to moments of disagreement. Although the model was able to detect some topic changes, it was not fine-grained enough for our purposes. More importantly, its results did not give us any insight into disagreement between speakers, even though the model was able to detect some of the changes in the speakers' positions about certain metrics, such as projected inflation rates.

A.2.2 Our Approach

Given the inconclusive results of our previous approaches, we turned to working with OpenAI's GPT models. A Generative Pre-trained Transformer, commonly known as a GPT model, is a type of neural network model that uses a mechanism called "attention." This mechanism allows the neural network to give more attention to the most important parts of a text passage, and to give less attention to the least important parts of a text passage. Most computer scientists view these models as the latest generation and best-performing NLP models today. The GPT models can be queried using prompts (a text input) and a text output is returned. Specifically, we used the GPT3.5-Turbo model family which can analyze 4,000 tokens (words) at a time. We also tested the GPT4 model but the performance was the same when we checked manually, whereas the cost of using GPT4 at scale on our data was (at the time) about thirty times more than GPT3.5.

To gather the Fed transcripts we wanted to analyze, we used a simple Python web crawler to collect all relevant documents. We processed the text documents to remove unnecessary content, and we split the documents into different speakers' interventions. For each speaker's intervention at the meeting, we input the text into GPT3.5-Turbo and queried if there was disagreement. We followed a similar method for the European data, with the additional step of translating into English any intervention that was not already in English. (There were a few interventions in French in the course of the Delors Committee meetings of 1988–1989).

We found that this method was more conclusive than other methods we tested to identify disagreements among speakers. Our queries about disagreements not only led the model to detect the most important disagreements in the transcripts, but the model was also able to explain briefly what the disagreements were about. We therefore were able to obtain a manageable corpus of disagreements for each transcript (always fewer than 100 per transcript), and an automated analysis of the substance of the disagreements. This automatically detected and pre-analyzed corpus of disagreements then opens the way for a systematic manual reading and analysis that can quickly focus on all automatically detected disagreements.

A cursory comparison of GPT3.5-Turbo's results in specific transcripts where disagreements are known to historians and easily identifiable by readers (e.g., in the Fed's fall 1979 discussions of monetary targets, or in the Delors Committee's spring 1989 discussion of monetary union membership criteria) suggests GPT3.5-Turbo is a relatively reliable tool for detecting disagreements. There are a few false positives, namely instances in which the software detects disagreements that are so minor as to be almost insignificant. But since the number of disagreements that the software detects is relatively limited, the reader can quickly decide that this is the case. Above all, there are very few false negatives. In other words, the software is good at detecting important disagreements, even though these disagreements are relatively rare and often buried in the text. This is reassuring, since false negatives would have been an important concern for a systematic analysis of transcripts that can be hundreds of pages long.

We were also able to perform a statistical treatment of the relevant transcripts and transcript sections where disagreements are most visible. Our graphs (Figure A.1 and Figure A.2) plotted the sheer number of occurrences of disagreements, both within transcripts and over time, in the United States and Europe in the two critical decades under study (the 1980s and the 2010s). One issue is that the duration of meetings and therefore the length of transcripts vary considerably. Long meetings can be a sign that there is a lot of contention, but they can also simply reflect the fact that there is a lot on that meeting's agenda, including largely technical (rather than contentious) discussion. To normalize our results for transcripts of different lengths, we therefore also plotted the percentage of disagreeing statements per transcript.

A.2.3 Main results for the Fed Data

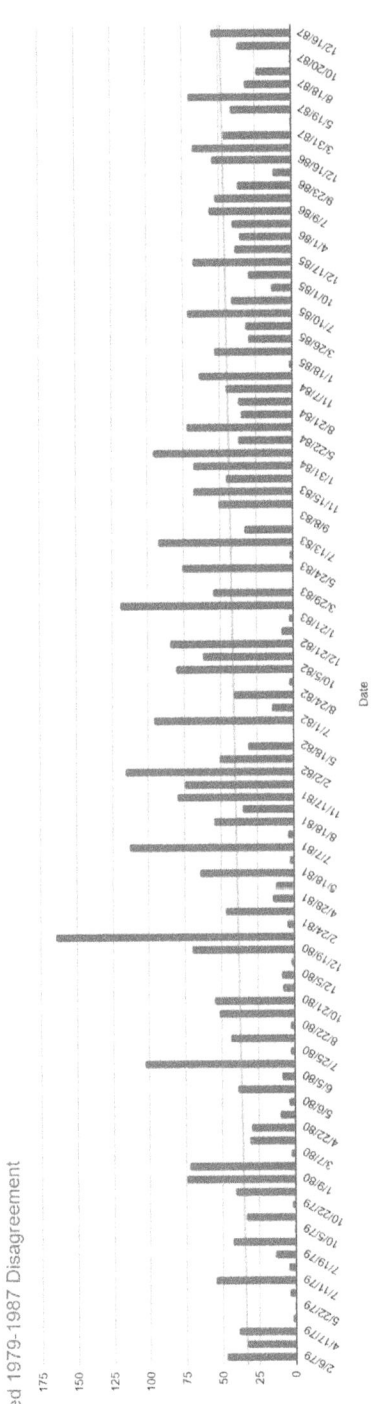

FIGURE A.1 Disagreement at the FOMC, 1979–1987.

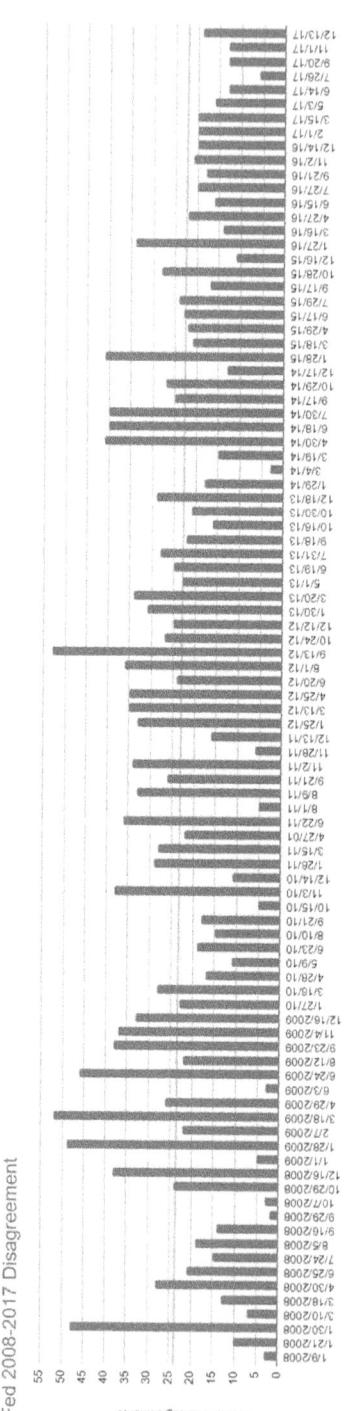

FIGURE A.2 Disagreement at the FOMC, 2008–2017.

Appendix A

A.2.4 Extension of Our Approach to Data from the European Central Bank of the 1980s

After analyzing the Fed Data, we extended our approach to data from the European Central Bank – meetings transcripts from the Delors Committee (1988–1989), and the detailed minutes of Committee of Governors meetings (1980–1989). Although we wanted to apply the same treatment as for the Fed, we had to make changes in extracting the data. The format and style of the Delors Committee meetings differed, with fewer utterances that are much longer. As a result, we are able to pinpoint disagreements more easily in the Fed Data due to shorter utterances. In the Delors Committee data, we can detect disagreements, but we cannot easily pinpoint them. In fact, many of the utterances were too long for the GPT model to process. So we had to preprocess the data differently from the Fed data, and to split the utterances for analysis by the GPT model. The fact that Delors Committee transcripts were not always in English was not a problem, however. While many of the meetings of the Delors Committee were in French, the GPT model was still able to answer the English-language prompt when given French text. The graph on Figure A.3 showcases the main results for the Delors Committee.

We followed the same procedure as that of the Delors Committee for the data from the Committee of Governors, with some slight changes to account for stylistic differences. As in the data for the Delors Committee, many documents are in French – except in the latter half of the 1980s, at which point some of the documents were translated into English. As discussed in the section of the Delors Committee, however, the GPT model has no issue with processing data in the French language. The graph on Figure A.4 represents the results for the data from the Committee of Governors.

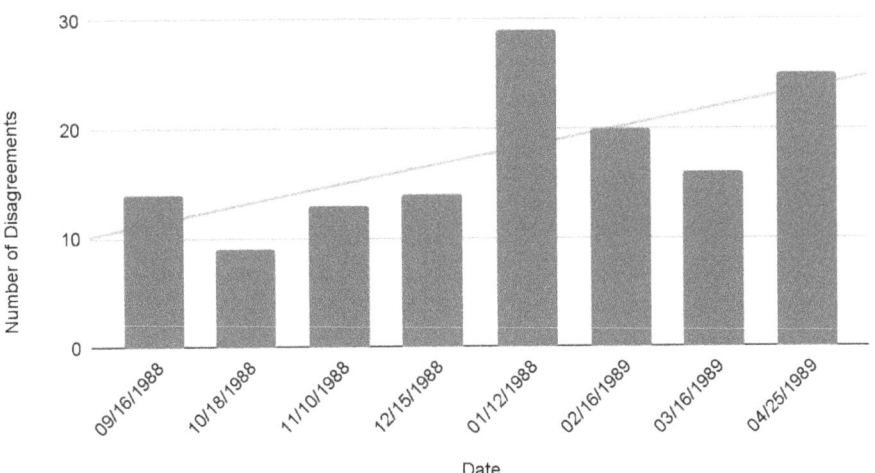

FIGURE A.3 Disagreement on the Delors Committee.

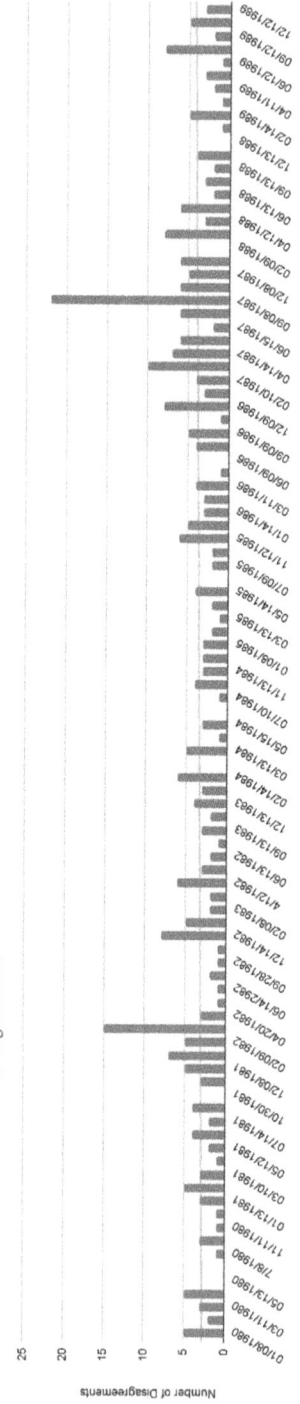

FIGURE A.4 Disagreement on the Committee of Governors.

Appendix A

All GPT-analyzed data and the resulting graphs are available at the following location:

https://drive.google.com/drive/folders/1H7HeNo5jFy2S7FTMC-kE2sxDeR1wuOsu?usp=sharing

Appendix B

Correspondence with the ECB Executive Board

On July 26, 2022, following the ECB's denial of an official "request for documents" made through the ECB's website, I wrote the ECB Executive Board a letter (Figure B.1) to appeal the ECB's denial of my request. In response, the ECB Executive Board rejected my appeal in a letter (Figure B.2) dated September 8, 2022.

JOHNS HOPKINS UNIVERSITY
DEPARTMENT OF POLITICAL SCIENCE
Baltimore, MD 21218-2686
USA

Executive Board
European Central Bank
60640 Frankfurt am Main, Germany

July 26, 2022

Dear Members of the Executive Board:

In accordance with the ECB's procedure for access to documents, I am writing you today to respectfully ask you to reconsider the ECB's refusal in response to my request of June 1, 2022.

I am a political scientist doing historical research on ECB policies during the 2010s, as part of a broader comparison with the policies of the US Federal Reserve. In my original request, I asked for access to excerpts of ECB Governing Council meetings minutes regarding discussions of the Securities Market Program (meeting of May 9, 2010), Outright Monetary Transactions (meetings of August 2, 2012, and September 6, 2012), and the European Commission's "flexible" interpretation of fiscal rules (meeting of March 4-5, 2015).

In a telephone conversation and an email exchange about my request for access, Ms. Petra Senkovic greatly clarified the ECB's position from a legal perspective. Ms. Senkovic distinguished the *deliberations* of the Governing Council, which are absolutely confidential under the Treaty, and the *outcomes* of Governing Council meetings, which can legally be made public by a decision of the ECB.

Accordingly, the ECB has decided since 2015 to publish "monetary policy accounts" – which are, in effect, anonymized minutes of the Governing Council meetings, without voting records. These accounts are very similar to the published minutes of the US Federal Reserve, minus the voting records. They are extremely valuable to scholars like me who try to understand the rationales of historical ECB decisions at a much deeper level than can be inferred from other ECB communications (press conferences, press releases, published summaries of decisions of the Governing Council). Unfortunately, these anonymized minutes without voting records were not made available retroactively before 2015.

I do understand that it would be burdensome for the ECB General Secretariat to retroactively edit the minutes for all Governing Council meetings all the way back to 1999. However, I am asking the ECB Executive Board to authorize access to anonymized accounts of ECB Governing Council minutes for *only three meetings* – May 9, 2010; August 2, 2012; September 6, 2012. (I hereby drop my request for excerpts of meeting minutes for March 4-5, 2015, since there is a monetary policy account for that date.)

Let me also add that my intent is in no way to question the Treaty's confidentiality requirement regarding ECB proceedings. I fully understand that, due to the multinational nature of the ECB, its proceedings are more sensitive than the transcripts of the US Federal Reserve – which are published after five years, including retroactively, since 1995.

Yet there is an overriding public interest in better understanding ECB Governing Council decisions that are of major historical importance, such as the authorization of the Securities Market Program and Outright Monetary Transactions in 2010-2012. In this regard, the release of anonymized minutes (minus voting records) of only three key meetings would serve both the public interest and the ECB's own commitment to transparency, without any prejudice to the Treaty's confidentiality requirement.

TEL: 410-516-7540 ❖ FAX: 410-516-5515 ❖ E-MAIL: political.science@jhu.edu

FIGURE B.1 Author's letter to ECB.

Appendix B

Sincerely,

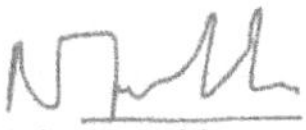

Nicolas Jabko
Associate Professor of Political Science, Johns Hopkins University
For 2022-23: Visiting Scholar at the Warren Center for Studies in American History, Harvard University

Email: nicolas.jabko@jhu.edu

FIGURE B.1 (*cont.*)

Appendix B

EUROPEAN CENTRAL BANK

EUROSYSTEM

Christine LAGARDE
President

ECB-UNRESTRICTED

Prof. Nicolas Jabko
Associate Professor of Political Science
Johns Hopkins University
Visiting Scholar
Charles Warren Center for Studies in American History
Harvard University

8 September 2022
Reference: LS/CL/2022/212

RE: Confirmatory application for public access to ECB documents

Dear Professor Jabko,

I refer to your confirmatory application of 26 July 2022, requesting the Executive Board of the European Central Bank (ECB) to review the ECB's decision of 29 June 2022 (reference: LS/PS/2022/34) refusing access to excerpts of ECB Governing Council meetings minutes of discussions of:

(i) the Securities Market Program, at the meeting on 9 May 2010;

(ii) outright monetary transactions, at the meetings on 2 August 2012 and 6 September 2012; and

(iii) the European Commission's "flexible" interpretation of fiscal rules, at the meetings on 4 and 5 March 2015.

On 23 August 2022, in line with Article 8(2) of Decision ECB/2004/3, as amended, of the European Central Bank[1], the ECB extended the time limit set for reply by 20 working days owing to its increased workload as a result of a high number of simultaneous requests.

1. Introductory remarks

In your confirmatory application, the request for access was limited to "anonymized accounts of ECB Governing Council minutes" of the meetings on 9 May 2010, 2 August 2012 and 6 September 2012.

---

[1] Decision of the European Central Bank of 4 March 2004 on public access to European Central Bank documents (ECB/2004/3) (OJ L 80, 18.3.2004, p. 42).

Address
European Central Bank
Sonnemannstrasse 20
60314 Frankfurt am Main
Germany

Postal address
European Central Bank
60640 Frankfurt am Main
Germany

Tel.: +49 69 1344 0
E-mail: info@ecb.europa.eu
www.ecb.europa.eu

FIGURE B.2 ECB's letter to author.

Appendix B

ECB-UNRESTRICTED

We would point out, however, that the ECB's monetary policy "accounts" differ from anonymized versions of its Governing Council meeting minutes in that they are separate documents. The accounts are prepared for publication and provide an overview of financial market, economic and monetary developments, as well as a fair and balanced summary of the Governing Council discussions, in a contextualised, clear and unattributed form. As explained previously, the Governing Council did not decide to publish "monetary policy accounts" until 16 December 2014, and then only starting from its meeting on 22 January 2015, without retroactive effect. Consequently, no "monetary policy accounts" exist, as such, for the three meetings you refer to in your application, and no obligation is imposed on any EU institution to create a document for which it has been asked to grant access but which does not exist[2].

In the light of this, the Executive Board has therefore assumed that your confirmatory application is limited to the "certified ECB excerpts of final minutes regarding discussions that took place at meetings of the ECB Governing Council" that were referred to in your initial application.

The Executive Board wishes to underline that the ECB's decision of 29 June 2022 provided you with comprehensive background information and explained in detail the reasons why the documents identified in your initial application could not be disclosed and, as you acknowledge, the Director General Secretariat has already provided you with further helpful clarifications, both over the telephone and by email.

Following its review, the Executive Board upholds the ECB decision of 29 June 2022 not to grant access to the documents concerned given their protection under the first indent of Article 4(1)(a) and Article 4(1)(c) of Decision ECB/2004/3, taken in conjunction with Article 10.4 of the Statute of the ESCB, as well as the second indent of Article 4(1)(a) of Decision ECB/2004/3 (financial, monetary or economic policy of the Union).

This letter further elaborates on the reasons for non-disclosure.

2. Protection of the public interest as regards the confidentiality of information that is protected as such under European Union law

The Executive Board would like to emphasise that the right of access to documents of the European Union's institutions, bodies, offices and agencies that is conferred on EU citizens under Article 15(3) of the Treaty on the Functioning of the European Union, is not unfettered and must be exercised in accordance with, and subject to, the limits set by the principles and rules laid down in the applicable legislation.

More specifically, as already clarified in the reply to your initial application, the confidentiality of Governing Council proceedings is enshrined in Article 10.4 of the Protocol on the Statute of the European System of Central Banks and of the ECB[3] and the same principles are also reflected in Article 23.1 of the ECB's Rules

---

[2] See Guido Strack v European Commission, Case C-127/13 P, ECLI:EU:C:2014:2250, paras. 39-47.
[3] Article 10.4 of the Protocol on the Statute of the European System of Central Banks and of the ECB states that the "proceedings of the meetings shall be confidential".

FIGURE B.2 (*cont.*)

ECB-UNRESTRICTED

of Procedure[4]. Consequently, the disclosure of Governing Council proceedings reflecting "discussions that took place at meetings of the ECB Governing Council" must be refused based on first indent of Article 4(1)(a) (the confidentiality of the proceedings of the ECB's decision-making bodies, the Supervisory Board or other bodies established pursuant to Regulation (EU) No 1024/2013), and Article 4(1)(c) (confidentiality of information that is protected as such under European Union law) of Decision ECB/2004/3, taken in conjunction with Article 10.4 of the Statute of the European System of Central Banks.

In your confirmatory application you note that "there is an overriding public interest in better understanding ECB Governing Council decisions that are of major historical importance, such as the authorization of the Securities Market Program and of the Outright Monetary Transactions in 2010-2012". In this regard, the Executive Board wishes to underline that the confidentiality of the Governing Council proceedings is absolute and that the proceedings themselves cannot be made public. This means that the ECB has no discretion to consider the possible existence of an overriding public interest.

Concerning the outcome of its deliberations, the Governing Council has the discretion to decide whether, and to what extent, it will be made public.[5] As already explained, the outcome of certain discussions of interest to you were duly recorded in the decisions taken by the Governing Council of the ECB (in addition to decisions setting interest rates) and were made public[6]. The ECB also published press releases providing detailed information on the decisions of 9 May 2012 and 6 September 2012[7]. Consequently, the Governing Council had already decided on the extent to which the outcome of its deliberations at the meetings at issue should be made public, and the rationale behind that decision remains unchanged.

The Executive Board thus confirms the ECB decision of 29 June 2022 not to grant access to the documents identified in your confirmatory application given that Governing Council discussions must be protected and their disclosure refused based on the first indent of Article 4(1)(a) and Article 4(1)(c) of Decision ECB/2004/3, taken in conjunction with Article 10.4 of the Statute of the ESCB.

3. Remedies

I would like to inform you that, under Article 8(1) of Decision ECB/2004/3, in the event of total or partial refusal, the applicant may have recourse to the remedies open under Articles 263 and 228 of the Treaty on the Functioning of the European Union.

---

[4] Article 23.1 of the ECB's Rules of Procedure (Decision ECB/2004/2 of 19 February 2004 adopting the Rules of Procedure of the European Central Bank (OJ L 80, 18.3.2004, p. 33), as last amended by Decision ECB/2016/27 (OJ L 258, 24.9.2016, p. 17)) states that the "proceedings of the decision-making bodies of the ECB, or any committee or group established by them, [...] shall be confidential unless the Governing Council authorises the President to make the outcome of their deliberations public".

[5] European Central Bank v Espírito Santo Financial (Portugal), Case C-442/18, ECLI:EU:C:2019:1117, paras 43-46.

[6] See Decisions taken by the Governing Council of the ECB (in addition to decisions setting interest rates) May 2010, Decisions taken by the Governing Council of the ECB (in addition to decisions setting interest rates) August 2012 and Decisions taken by the Governing Council of the ECB (in addition to decisions setting interest rates) September 2012.

[7] See the press release "ECB decides on measures to address severe tensions in financial markets" of 10 May 2010, and the press release on the "Technical features of outright monetary transactions" of 6 September 2012.

FIGURE B.2 *(cont.)*

Appendix B

ECB-UNRESTRICTED

I hope that this response has been helpful in clarifying the ECB's decision.

Yours sincerely,

[signature]

FIGURE B.2 (*cont.*)

References

Abdelal, Rawi. 2007. *Capital Rules: The Construction of Global Finance.* Cambridge: Harvard University Press.
Abolafia, Mitchel Y. 2005. "Making sense of recession: Toward an interpretive theory of economic action," in Victor Nee and Richard Swedberg, eds., *The Economic Sociology of Capitalism.* Princeton: Princeton University Press: 204–226.
  2012. "Central banking and the triumph of technical rationality," in Karin Knorr Cetina and Alex Preda, eds., *The Oxford Handbook of the Sociology of Finance.* Oxford: Oxford University Press: 94–112.
  2020. *Stewards of the Market: How the Federal Reserve Made Sense of the Financial Crisis.* Cambridge: Harvard University Press.
Adolph, Christopher. 2013. *Bankers, Bureaucrats, and Central Bank Politics: The Myth of Neutrality.* Cambridge: Cambridge University Press.
  2018. "The missing politics of central banks." *PS: Political Science & Politics* 51, no. 4: 737–742.
Ahmed, Amel. 2025. *The Regime Question: Foundations of Democratic Governance in Europe and the United States.* Princeton: Princeton University Press.
Algan, Yann, Marion Fourcade, and Etienne Ollion. 2015. "The superiority of economics." *Journal of Economics Perspectives* 29, no. 1: 89–114.
Alturayeif, Nora, Hamzah Luqman, and Moataz Ahmed. 2023. "A systematic review of machine learning techniques for stance detection and its applications." *Neural Computing and Applications* 35, no. 7: 5113–5144.
Amyx, Jennifer M. 2006. *Japan's Financial Crisis: Institutional Rigidity and Reluctant Change.* Princeton: Princeton University Press.
Ansell, Chris, and Arjen Boin. 2019. "Taming deep uncertainty: The potential of pragmatist principles for understanding and improving strategic crisis management." *Administration & Society* 51, no. 7: 1079–1112.
Arbogast, Tobias, Hielke Van Doorslaer, and Mattias Vermeiren. 2024. "Another strange non-death: The NAIRU and the ideational foundations of the Federal Reserve's new monetary policy framework." *Review of International Political Economy* 31, no. 3: 805–830.

Arseneau, David M., Alejandro Drexler, and Mitsuhiro Osada. 2022. "Central bank communication about climate change," *Finance and Economics Discussion Series 2022-031*. Washington: Board of Governors of the Federal Reserve System.

Ayoub, Phillip. 2015. "Contested norms in new-adopter states: International determinants of LGBT rights legislation." *European Journal of International Relations* 21, no. 2: 293–322.

Babb, Sarah L., and Alexander E. Kentikelenis. 2018. "International financial institutions as agents of neoliberalism," in Damien Cahill, Melinda Cooper, Martijn Konings, and David Primrose, eds., *The SAGE Handbook of Neoliberalism*. New York: Sage: 16–27.

Baccaro, Lucio, Mark Blyth, and Jonas Pontusson. 2022. *Diminishing Returns: The New Politics of Growth and Stagnation*. Oxford: Oxford University Press.

Baccaro, Lucio, and Chris Howell. 2017. *Trajectories of Neoliberal Transformation: European Industrial Relations since the 1970s*. Cambridge: Cambridge University Press.

Baccaro, Lucio, and Jonas Pontusson. 2016. "Rethinking comparative political economy: The growth model perspective." *Politics & Society* 44, no. 2: 175–207.

Bakker, Age FP. 2012. *The Liberalization of Capital Movements in Europe: The Monetary Committee and Financial Integration 1958–1994*. Dordrecht: Springer Science & Business Media.

Ball, Laurence. 2016. "Ben Bernanke and the zero bound." *Contemporary Economic Policy* 34, no. 1: 7–20.

2018. *The Fed and Lehman Brothers: Setting the Record Straight on a Financial Disaster*. Cambridge: Cambridge University Press.

Ball, Laurence, and N. Gregory Mankiw. 2002. "The NAIRU in theory and practice." *Journal of Economic Perspectives* 16, no. 4: 115–136.

Ball, Laurence, N. Gregory Mankiw, David Romer, George A. Akerlof, Andrew Rose, Janet Yellen, and Christopher A. Sims. 1988. "The new Keynesian economics and the output-inflation trade-off." *Brookings Papers on Economic Activity* 1988, no. 1: 1–82.

Ban, Cornel, and Bryan Patenaude. 2019. "The professional politics of the austerity debate: A comparative field analysis of the European Central Bank and the International Monetary Fund." *Public Administration* 97, no. 3: 530–545.

Bastasin, Carlo. 2015. *Saving Europe: Anatomy of a Dream*. Washington: Brookings.

Bateman, Will, and Jens Van't Klooster. 2024. "The dysfunctional taboo: Monetary financing at the Bank of England, the Federal Reserve, and the European Central Bank." *Review of International Political Economy* 31, no. 2: 413–437.

Beckert, Jens. 2016. *Imagined Futures: Fictional Expectations and Capitalist Dynamics*. Cambridge: Harvard University Press.

Bennett, Jane. 2010. *Vibrant Matter: A Political Ecology of Things*. Durham: Duke University Press.

Berk, Gerald. 2026. "Antitrust after neoliberalism." *Perspectives on Politics* (forthcoming).

Berk, Gerald, and Dennis Galvan. 2009. "How people experience and change institutions: A field guide to creative syncretism." *Theory and Society* 38, no. 6: 543.

Berk, Gerald, Dennis Galvan, and Victoria Hattam, eds. 2013. *Political Creativity: Reconfiguring Institutional Order and Change*. Philadelphia: University of Pennsylvania Press.

Bernanke, Ben S. 2000. "Japan's slump: A case of self-induced paralysis?," in Adam Posen and Ryoichi Mikitani, eds., *Japan's Financial Crisis and Its Parallels to US Experience*. Washington, DC: Institute for International Economics: 149–166.

2004. "The Great Moderation," Remarks at the meetings of the Eastern Economic Association, Washington, DC, February 20.
2015. *The Courage to Act: A Memoir of a Crisis and Its Aftermath*. New York: WW Norton & Company.
2022. *21st Century Monetary Policy: The Federal Reserve from the Great Inflation to COVID-19*. New York: WW Norton & Company.

Best, Jacqueline. 2005. *The Limits of Transparency: Ambiguity and the History of International Finance*. Ithaca: Cornell University Press.
2020. "The quiet failures of early neoliberalism: From rational expectations to Keynesianism in reverse." *Review of International Studies* 46, no. 5: 594–612.
2022. "Uncomfortable knowledge in central banking: Economic expertise confronts the visibility dilemma." *Economy and Society* 51, no. 4: 559–583.
2025. "Central banks' knowledge controversies," *New Political Economy* 29, no. 6: 857–871.

Bignami, Francesca. 2020. "The German Right to Fiscal Stability and the Counter-Majoritarian Difficulty: The PSPP Judgment of 5 May 2020." *GWU Law School Public Law Research Paper* No. 2021-07.

Binder, Sarah, and Mark Spindel. 2017. *The Myth of Independence: How Congress Governs the Federal Reserve*. Princeton: Princeton University Press.

Bini Smaghi, Lorenzo. 2013. *Austerity: European Democracies against the Wall*. Brussels: Centre for European Policy Studies.

Birk, Marius, and Matthias Thiemann. 2020. "Open for business: Entrepreneurial central banks and the cultivation of market liquidity." *New Political Economy* 25, no. 2: 267–283.

Blanchard, Olivier. 2009. "The state of macro." *Annual Review of Economics* 1, no. 1: 209–228.

Blanchard, Olivier, and Daniel Leigh. 2013. "Growth forecast errors and fiscal multipliers." *American Economic Review* 103, no. 3: 117–120.

Blinder, Alan S. 2004. *The Quiet Revolution: Central Banking Goes Modern*. New Haven: Yale University Press.
2022. *A Monetary and Fiscal History of the United States, 1961–2021*. Princeton: Princeton University Press.

Blinder, Alan S., and Ricardo Reis. 2005. "Understanding the Greenspan Standard," Federal Reserve Bank of Kansas City symposium, *The Greenspan Era: Lessons for the Future*, Jackson Hole, Wyoming, August 25–27.

Blyth, Mark. 2002. *Great Transformations: Economic Ideas and Institutional Change in the Twentieth Century*. New York: Cambridge University Press.
2013. *Austerity: The History of a Dangerous Idea*. Oxford: Oxford University Press.

Blyth, Mark, and Nicolo Fraccaroli. 2025. *Inflation*. New York: WW Norton & Company.

Blyth, Mark, and Eric Lonergan. 2014. "Print less but transfer more: Why central banks should give money directly to the people." *Foreign Affairs* 93, no. 5: 98-109.

Boix, Carles. 2000. "Partisan governments, the international economy, and macroeconomic policies in advanced nations, 1960–93." *World Politics* 53, no. 1: 38–73.

Bordo, Michael, and Klodiana Istrefi. 2023. "Perceived FOMC: The making of hawks, doves and swingers." *Journal of Monetary Economics* 136: 125–143.

Borger, Vestert. 2016. "Outright monetary transactions and the stability mandate of the ECB: Gauweiler." *Common Market Law Review* 53, no. 1: 139.

Brandes, Sören. 2019. "The market's people: Milton Friedman and the making of neoliberal populism," in William Callison and Zachary Manfredi, eds., *Mutant Neoliberalism*. New York: Fordham University Press: 61–88.

Braun, Benjamin. 2020. "Central banking and the infrastructural power of finance: The case of ECB support for repo and securitization markets." *Socio-Economic Review* 18, no. 2: 395–418.

2022. "Exit, control, and politics: Structural power and corporate governance under asset manager capitalism." *Politics & Society* 50, no. 4: 630–654.

Braun, Benjamin, and Daniela Gabor. 2020. "Central banking, shadow banking, and infrastructural power," in Philip Mader, Daniel Mertens, and Natascha van der Zwan, eds., *The Routledge International Handbook of Financialization*. New York: Routledge: 241–252.

Braun, Benjamin, Donato Di Carlo, Sebastian Diessner, and Maximilian Düsterhöft. 2024. "Structure, agency, and structural reform: The case of the European Central Bank." *Perspectives on Politics*: 1–20. doi:10.1017/S1537592723002992.

Brown, Wendy. 2015. *Undoing the Demos: Neoliberalism's Stealth Revolution*. New York: Zone.

Brubaker, Rogers. 2017. "Why populism?" *Theory and Society* 46, no. 5: 357–385.

Brunnermeier, Markus K., Harold James, and Jean-Pierre Landau. 2016. *The Euro and the Battle of Ideas*. Princeton: Princeton University Press.

Buiter, Willem, and Ebrahim Rahbari. 2012. "The European Central Bank as lender of last resort for sovereigns in the eurozone." *Journal of Common Market Studies* 50, no. 6: 6–35.

Burgin, Angus. 2012. *The Great Persuasion: Reinventing Free Markets since the Depression*. Cambridge: Harvard University Press.

Buti, Marco, and Nicolas Carnot. 2012. "The EMU debt crisis: Early lessons and reforms." *Journal of Common Market Studies* 50, no. 6: 899–911.

Buti, Marco, and Sergio Fabbrini. 2023. "Next generation EU and the future of economic governance: Towards a paradigm change or just a big one-off?" *Journal of European Public Policy* 30, no. 4: 676–695.

Çalışkan, Koray, and Michel Callon. 2009. "Economization, Part 1: Shifting attention from the economy towards processes of economization." *Economy and Society* 38, no. 3: 369–398.

Callison, William, and Zachary Manfredi, eds. 2019. *Mutant Neoliberalism*. New York: Fordham University Press.

Capoccia, Giovanni, and Daniel Ziblatt. 2010. "The historical turn in democratization studies: A new research agenda for Europe and beyond." *Comparative Political Studies* 43, no. 8-9: 931–968.

Carruthers, Bruce. 2022. *An Economy of Promises*. Princeton: Princeton University Press.

Carstensen, Martin B. 2011. "Paradigm man vs. the bricoleur: Bricolage as an alternative vision of agency in ideational change." *European Political Science Review* 3, no. 1: 147–167.

Cavaillé, Charlotte. 2023. *Fair enough? Support for Redistribution in the Age of Inequality*. Cambridge: Cambridge University Press.

Chwieroth, Jeffrey. 2007. "Neoliberal economists and capital account liberalization in emerging markets." *International Organization* 61, no. 2: 443–463.
  2010. *Capital Ideas: The IMF and the Rise of Financial Liberalization.* Princeton: Princeton University Press.
Clarida, Richard, Jordi Gali, and Mark Gertler. 1999. "The science of monetary policy: A new Keynesian perspective." *Journal of Economic Literature* 37, no. 4: 1661–1707.
Claveau, François, and Jérémie Dion. 2018. "Quantifying central banks' scientization: Why and how to do a quantified organizational history of economics." *Journal of Economic Methodology* 25, no. 4: 349–366.
Clemens, Elizabeth S. 1993. "Organizational repertoires and institutional change: Women's groups and the transformation of U.S. politics, 1890–1920." *American Journal of Sociology* 98, no. 4: 755–798.
Clift, Ben. 2018. *The IMF and the Politics of Austerity in the Wake of the Global Financial Crisis.* Oxford: Oxford University Press.
Cohen, Benjamin J. 2015. *Currency Power: Understanding Monetary Rivalry.* Princeton: Princeton University Press.
Colander, David, Richard Holt, and Barkley Rosser Jr. 2004. "The changing face of mainstream economics." *Review of Political Economy* 16, no. 4: 485–499.
Connolly, William E. 2013. "The 'new materialism' and the fragility of things." *Millennium* 41, no. 3: 399–412.
  2013. *The Fragility of Things: Self-Organizing Processes, Neoliberal Fantasies, and Democratic Activism.* Durham: Duke University Press.
Conti-Brown, Peter. 2016. *The Power and Independence of the Federal Reserve.* Princeton: Princeton University Press.
Coombes, David. 1970. *Politics and Bureaucracy in the European Community: A Portrait of the Commission of the EEC.* London: George Allen and Unwin.
Coombs, Nathan, and Matthias Thiemann. 2022. "Recentering central banks: Theorizing state-economy boundaries as central bank effects." *Economy and Society* 51, no. 4: 535–558.
Cooper, Melinda. 2017. *Family Values: Between Neoliberalism and the New Social Conservatism.* Cambridge: MIT Press.
  2024. *Counterrevolution: Extravagance and Austerity in Public Finance.* New York: Zone Books.
Crespy, Amandine, and Lucas Schramm. 2024. "Breaking the budgetary taboo: German preference formation in the EU's response to the Covid-19 crisis." *German Politics* 33, no. 1: 46–67.
Crouch, Colin. 2011. *The Strange Non-Death of Neo-Liberalism.* Cambridge: Polity.
Crowe, Christopher, and Ellen E. Meade. 2007. "The evolution of central bank governance around the world." *Journal of Economic Perspectives* 21, no. 4: 69–90.
Culpepper, Pepper D., and Raphael Reinke. 2014. "Structural power and bank bailouts in the United Kingdom and the United States." *Politics & Society* 42, no. 4: 427–454.
Dafe, Florence, Sandy Brian Hager, Natalya Naqvi, and Leon Wansleben. 2022. "Introduction: The structural power of finance meets financialization." *Politics & Society* 50, no. 4: 523–542.
Darvas, Zsolt, Jean Pisani-Ferry, and Guntram Wolff. 2013. "Europe's growth problem (and what to do about it)," *Bruegel Policy Brief.* Issue 2013/03 (April).

Davet, Gérard, and France Lhomme. 2016. *"Un Président ne devrait pas dire ça…": Les Secrets d'un Quinquennat.* Paris: Stock.

Davies, William, and Nicholas Gane. 2021. "Post-neoliberalism? An introduction." *Theory, Culture & Society* 38, no. 6: 3–28.

De Boissieu, Christian, and Jean Pisani-Ferry. 1998. "The political economy of French economic policy in the perspective of EMU," in Barry Eichengreen and Jeffry Frieden, eds., *Forging an Integrated Europe.* Ann Harbor: Michigan University Press: 49–90.

De Grauwe, Paul. 1993. "The political economy of monetary union in Europe." *World Economy* 16, no. 6: 653–661.

———. 2011. "The governance of a fragile Eurozone," *CEPS Working Documents* no. 346 (May).

De Grauwe, Paul, and Yumei Ji. 2012. "Mispricing of sovereign risk and multiple equilibria in the Eurozone," *CEPS Working Documents* no. 361 (January).

DeLanda, Manuel. 2016. *Assemblage Theory.* Edinburgh: Edinburgh University Press.

DeLong, J. Bradford. 2022. *Slouching towards Utopia: An Economic History of the Twentieth Century.* New York: Basic Books.

———. 2000. "The triumph of monetarism?" *Journal of Economic Perspectives* 14, no. 1: 83–94.

Dendrinou, Viktoria, and Eleni Varvitsioti. 2019. *The Last Bluff: How Greece Came Face-to-Face with Financial Catastrophe and the Secret Plan for Its Euro Exit.* Athens: Papadopoulos Publishing.

Desan, Christine. 2023. "The monetary structure of economic activity: A constitutional analysis." *Law and Contemporary Problems* 86, no. 4: 77–110.

———. 2014. *Making Money: Coin, Currency, and the Coming of Capitalism.* Oxford: Oxford University Press.

Dewey, John. 1922. *Human Nature and Conduct: An Introduction to Social Psychology.* New York: Random House.

Deyris, Jérôme. 2023. "Too green to be true? Forging a climate consensus at the European Central Bank." *New Political Economy* 28, no. 5: 713–730.

Dietsch, Peter, François Claveau, and Clément Fontan. 2018. *Do Central Banks Serve the People?* Hoboken: John Wiley & Sons.

Dobbin, Frank, Beth Simmons, and Geoffrey Garrett. 2007. "The global diffusion of public policies: Social construction, coercion, competition, or learning?" *Annual Review of Sociology* 33, no. 1: 449–472.

Dorn, James A., Jeb Hensarling, Phil Gramm, and John B. Taylor. 2020. 38th Annual Monetary Conference: Welcoming Remarks and Conversation. Cato Institute, November 19.

Downey, Leah. 2024. *Our Money: Monetary Policy as if Democracy Matters.* Princeton: Princeton University Press.

Dyson, Kenneth, and Kevin Featherstone. 1999. *The Road to Maastricht: Negotiating Economic and Monetary Union.* Oxford: Oxford University Press.

Eich, Stefan. 2022. *The Currency of Politics: The Political Theory of Money from Aristotle to Keynes.* Princeton: Princeton University Press.

Eichengreen, Barry. 1992. Should the Maastricht Treaty be saved? *Princeton Studies in International Finance*, no. 74 (December).

———. 1996. *Globalizing Capital: A History of the International Monetary System.* Princeton: Princeton University Press.

2011. *Exorbitant Privilege: The Rise and Fall of the Dollar*. Oxford: Oxford University Press.

2012. "Economic history and economic policy." *The Journal of Economic History* 72, no. 2: 289–307.

2015. *Hall of Mirrors: The Great Depression, the Great Recession, and the Uses – and Misuses – of History*. Oxford: Oxford University Press.

Eichengreen, Barry, and Jeffry A. Frieden, eds. 1998. *Forging an Integrated Europe*. Ann Arbor: University of Michigan Press.

El-Erian, Mohamed A. 2016. *The Only Game in Town: Central Banks, Instability, and Avoiding the Next Collapse*. New York: Random House.

Emerson, Michael, Daniel Gros, Alexander Italianer, Jean Pisani-Ferry, and Horst Reichenbach. 1992. *One Market, One Money: An Evaluation of the Potential Benefits and Costs of Forming an Economic and Monetary Union*. Oxford: Oxford University Press.

Eyal, Gil. 2019. *The Crisis of Expertise*. Medford: Polity Press.

Eyal, Gil, and Larissa Buchholz. 2010. "From the sociology of intellectuals to the sociology of interventions." *Annual Review of Sociology* 36, no. 1: 117–137.

Farrell, Henry, and John Quiggin. 2017. "Consensus, dissensus, and economic ideas: Economic crisis and the rise and fall of Keynesianism." *International Studies Quarterly* 61, no. 2: 269–283.

Fernández-Albertos, J. 2015. "The politics of central bank independence." *Annual Review of Political Science* 18, no. 1: 217–237.

Ferrara, Federico Maria. 2020. "The battle of ideas on the euro crisis: Evidence from ECB inter-meeting speeches." *Journal of European Public Policy* 27, no. 10: 1463–1486.

Fligstein, Neil, Jonah Stuart Brundage, and Michael Schultz. 2017. "Seeing like the Fed: Culture, cognition, and framing in the failure to anticipate the financial crisis of 2008." *American Sociological Review* 82, no. 5: 879–909.

Fligstein, Neil, and Doug McAdam. 2015. "Toward a general theory of strategic action fields." *Sociological Theory* 29, no. 1: 1–26.

Fontan, Clément. 2018. "Frankfurt's double standard. The politics of the European Central Bank during the eurozone crisis." *Cambridge Review of International Affairs* 31, no. 2: 162–182.

Fontan, Clément, François Claveau, and Peter Dietsch. 2016. "Central banking and inequalities: Taking off the blinders." *Politics, Philosophy & Economics* 15, no. 4: 319–357.

Foucault, Michel. 2008. *The Birth of Biopolitics: Lectures at the Collège de France, 1978-1979*. New York: Palgrave Macmillan.

Fourcade, Marion. 2009. *Economists and Societies: Discipline and Profession in the United States, Britain, and France, 1890s to 1990s*. Princeton: Princeton University Press.

Fourcade-Gourinchas, Marion, and Sarah L. Babb. 2002. "The rebirth of the liberal creed: Paths to neoliberalism in four countries." *American Journal of Sociology* 108, no. 3: 533–579.

Frieden, Jeffry A. 1991. "Invested interests: The politics of national economic policies in a world of global finance." *International Organization* 45, no. 4: 425–451.

Friedman, Milton. 1962. *Capitalism and Freedom*. Chicago: University of Chicago Press.

1968. "The role of monetary policy," *American Economic Review* 58, no. 1: 1–17.

Gabor, Daniela. 2021. *Revolution without Revolutionaries: Interrogating the Return of Monetary Financing. Transformative Responses to the Crisis.* Berlin: Finanzwende and Heinrich Böll Stiftung. http://tankona.free.fr/gabor121.pdf.

Gabor, Daniela, and Cornel Ban. 2016. "Banking on bonds: The new links between states and markets." *JCMS: Journal of Common Market Studies* 54, no. 3: 617–635.

Galbraith, James K. 1997. "Time to ditch the NAIRU." *Journal of Economic Perspectives* 11, no. 1: 93–108.

Gamble, Andrew. 2015. "Austerity as statecraft." *Parliamentary Affairs* 68, no. 1: 42–57.

Geithner, Timothy F. 2015. *Stress Test: Reflections on Financial Crises.* New York: Crown.

Gerstle, Gary. 2022. *The Rise and Fall of the Neoliberal Order: America and the World in the Free Market Era.* Oxford: Oxford University Press.

Giavazzi, Francesco, and Marco Pagano. 1988. "The advantage of tying one's hands: EMS discipline and central bank credibility." *European Economic Review* 32, no. 5: 1055–1075.

Gocaj, Ledina, and Sophie Meunier. 2013. "Time will tell: The EFSF, the ESM, and the euro crisis." *European Integration* 35, no. 3: 239–253.

Goodfriend, Marvin. 1986. "Monetary mystique: Secrecy and central banking." *Journal of Monetary Economics* 17, no. 1: 63–92.

2007. "How the world achieved consensus on monetary policy." *Journal of Economic Perspectives* 21, no. 4: 47–68.

Goodfriend, Marvin, and Robert G. King. 1997. "The new neoclassical synthesis and the role of monetary policy." *NBER Macroeconomics Annual* 12: 231–283.

2005. "The incredible Volcker disinflation." *Journal of Monetary Economics* 52, no. 5: 981–1015.

Goodman, John B. 1992. *Monetary Sovereignty: The Politics of Central Banking in Western Europe.* Ithaca: Cornell University Press.

Goodman, John B., and Louis W. Pauly. 1993. "The obsolescence of capital controls?: Economic management in an age of global markets." *World Politics* 46, no. 1: 50–82.

Gourinchas, Pierre-Olivier, Thomas Philippon, and Dimitri Vayanos. 2017. "The analytics of the Greek crisis." *NBER Macroeconomics Annual* 31, no. 1: 1–81.

Grant, Charles. 1994. *Delors: Inside the House that Jacques Built.* London: Nicholas Brealey.

Greider, William. 1987. *Secrets of the Temple: How the Federal Reserve Runs the Country.* New York: Simon and Schuster.

Greenspan, Alan. 2008. *The Age of Turbulence: Adventures in a New World.* New York: Penguin.

Grimmer, Justin, Margaret E. Roberts, and Brandon M. Stewart. 2022. *Text as Data: A New Framework for Machine Learning and the Social Sciences.* Princeton: Princeton University Press.

Gros, Daniel, and Niels Thygesen. 1988. *The EMS: Achievements, Current Issues and Directions for the Future.* Brussels: Centre for European Policy Studies.

1998. *European Monetary Integration.* London: Longman Publishing Group.

Gross, Neil L., Isaac Ariail Reed, and Christopher Winship, eds. 2022. *The New Pragmatist Sociology: Inquiry, Agency, and Democracy*. New York: Columbia University Press.

Haas, Ernst B. 1958. *The Uniting of Europe: Political, Social, and Economic Forces, 1950-1957*. Stanford: Stanford University Press.

   1980. Why collaborate? Issue-linkage and international regimes. *World Politics* 32, no. 3: 357–405.

Hacker, Jacob S., and Paul Pierson. 2010. *Winner-Take-All Politics: How Washington Made the Rich Richer–and Turned Its Back on the Middle Class*. New York: Simon and Schuster.

   2014. "After the 'master theory': Downs, Schattschneider, and the rebirth of policy-focused analysis." *Perspectives on Politics* 12, no. 3: 643–662.

Hacker, Jacob S., Alexander Hertel-Fernandez, Paul Pierson, and Kathleen Thelen, eds. 2021. *The American Political Economy: Politics, Markets, and Power*. Cambridge: Cambridge University Press.

Hall, Peter A., ed. 1989. *The Political Power of Economic Ideas: Keynesianism across Nations*. Princeton: Princeton University Press.

   1993. "Policy paradigms, social learning, and the state: The case of economic policy-making in Britain." *Comparative Politics* 25, no. 3: 275–296.

   2012. "The economics and politics of the euro crisis." *German Politics* 21, no. 4: 355–371.

   2013. "The political origins of our economic discontents," in Miles Kahler and David Lake, eds., *Politics in the New Hard Times: The Great Recession in Comparative Perspective*. Ithaca: Cornell University Press: 129–149.

   2020. "The electoral politics of growth regimes." *Perspectives on Politics* 18, no. 1: 185–199.

   2024. "Growth regimes." *Business History Review* 98, no. 1: 259–283.

Hall, Peter A., and Robert J. Franzese. 1998. "Mixed signals: Central bank independence, coordinated wage bargaining, and European Monetary Union." *International Organization* 52, no. 3: 505–535.

Hall, Peter A., and David Soskice, eds. 2001. *Varieties of Capitalism: The Institutional Foundations of Comparative Advantage*. Oxford: Oxford University Press.

Hall, Robert E. 1976. Notes on the Current State of Empirical Macroeconomics. Unpublished working paper, Stanford University.

Hardie, Iain, and Donald MacKenzie. 2007. "Assembling an economic actor: The *agencement* of a hedge fund." *The Sociological Review* 55, no. 1: 57–80.

Hartmann, Philipp, and Frank Smets. 2018. The First Twenty Years of the European Central Bank: Monetary Policy, No. 2219, ECB Working Paper.

Harvey, David. 2007. *A Brief History of Neoliberalism*. New York: Oxford University Press.

Heipertz, Martin, and Amy Verdun. 2010. *Ruling Europe: The Politics of the Stability and Growth Pact*. Cambridge: Cambridge University Press.

Helgadóttir, Oddný. 2016. "The Bocconi boys go to Brussels: Italian economic ideas, professional networks and European austerity." *Journal of European Public Policy* 23, no. 3: 392–409.

Helleiner, Eric. 1996. *States and the Reemergence of Global Finance: From Bretton Woods to the 1990s*. Ithaca: Cornell University Press.

Helleiner, Eric. 2014. *The Status Quo Crisis: Global Financial Governance After the 2008 Meltdown.* Oxford: Oxford University Press.
Heller, Peter S. 2005. "Understanding fiscal space". *IMF Policy Discussion Paper* (March).
Henning, C. Randall. 1994. *Currencies and Politics in the United States, Germany, and Japan.* Washington: Peterson Institute.
  2016. "The ECB as a strategic actor: Central banking in a politically fragmented monetary union," in James A. Caporaso and Martin Rhodes, eds., *Europe's Crises: Economic and Political Challenges of the Monetary Union.* New York: Oxford University Press: 167–199.
  2017. *Tangled Governance: International Regime Complexity, the Troika, and the Euro Crisis.* Oxford: Oxford University Press.
Herrigel, Gary. 2010. *Manufacturing Possibilities: Creative Action and Industrial Recomposition in the United States, Germany, and Japan.* New York: Oxford.
Hetzel, Robert L. 2022. *The Federal Reserve: A New History.* Chicago: University of Chicago Press.
Holmes, Douglas R. 2014. *Economy of Words: Communicative Imperatives in Central Banks.* Chicago: University of Chicago Press.
Hopkin, Jonathan. 2020. *Anti-system Politics: The Crisis of Market Liberalism in Rich Democracies.* Oxford: Oxford University Press.
Hopkin, Jonathan, and Mark Blyth. 2019. "The global economics of European populism: Growth regimes and party system change in Europe (The Government and Opposition/Leonard Schapiro Lecture 2017)." *Government and Opposition* 54, no. 2: 193–225.
Hyman, Louis. 2011. *Debtor Nation: A History of America in Red Ink.* Princeton: Princeton University Press.
Irwin, Neil. 2013. *The Alchemists: Three Central Bankers and a World on Fire.* New York: Penguin Press.
Jabko, Nicolas. 2003. "Democracy in the age of the euro." *Journal of European Public Policy* 10, no. 5: 713–742.
  2006. *Playing the Market: A Political Strategy for Uniting Europe, 1985–2005.* Ithaca: Cornell University Press.
  2019. "Contested governance: The new repertoire of the eurozone crisis." *Governance* 32, no. 3: 493–509.
Jabko, Nicolas, and Nils Kupzok. 2024. "Indirect responsiveness and green central banking." *Journal of European Public Policy* 31, no. 4: 1–25.
Jabko, Nicolas, and Elsa Massoc. 2012. "French capitalism under stress: How Nicolas Sarkozy rescued the banks." *Review of International Political Economy* 19, no. 4: 562–585.
Jabko, Nicolas, and Sebastian Schmidt. 2021. "Paradigms and practice." *International Studies Quarterly* 65, no. 3: 565–572.
  2022. "The long twilight of gold: How a pivotal practice persisted in the assemblage of money." *International Organization* 76, no. 3: 625–655.
Jabko, Nicolas, and Adam Sheingate. 2018. "Practices of dynamic order." *Perspectives on Politics* 16, no. 2: 312–327.
Jacobs, Lawrence, and Desmond King. 2021. *Fed Power: How Finance Wins.* New York: Oxford University Press.
Jacobs, Meg. 2016. *Panic at the Pump: The Energy Crisis and the Transformation of American Politics in the 1970s.* New York: Hill and Wang.

Jacoby, Wade. 2014. "The politics of the eurozone crisis: Two puzzles behind the German consensus." *German Politics and Society* 32, no. 2: 70–85.
James, Harold. 2012. *Making the European Monetary Union*. Cambridge: Harvard University Press.
    2016. "Karl-Otto Pöhl," in Kenneth Dyson and Ivo Maes, eds., *Architects of the Euro: Intellectuals in the Making of European Monetary Union*. Oxford: Oxford University Press: 170–192.
James, William. 1890. *The Principles of Psychology*. New York: Henry Holt & Co.
Jasanoff, Sheila. 2015. "Future imperfect: Science, technology, and the imaginations of modernity," in Sheila Jasanoff and Sang-Hyun Kim, eds., *Dreamscapes of Modernity: Sociotechnical Imaginaries and the Fabrication of Power*. Chicago: University of Chicago Press: 1–33.
Joas, Hans, and Jens Beckert. 2002. "Action theory," in Jonathan H. Turner, ed., *Handbook of Sociological Theory*. New York: Plenum Publishers: 269–285.
Johnson, Juliet. 2016. *Priests of Prosperity: How Central Bankers Transformed the Postcommunist World*. Ithaca: Cornell University Press.
Johnson, Simon, and James Kwak. 2010. *13 Bankers: The Wall Street Takeover and the Next Financial Meltdown*. New York: Pantheon.
Jones, Erik. 2003. "Liberalized capital markets, state autonomy, and European monetary union." *European Journal of Political Research* 42, no. 2: 197–222.
    2013. "The collapse of the Brussels-Frankfurt consensus and the future of the Euro," in Vivien A. Schmidt and Mark Thatcher, eds., *Resilient Liberalism in Europe's Political Economy*. Cambridge: Cambridge University Press: 145–170.
Kahneman, Daniel. 2011. *Thinking, Fast and Slow*. New York: Farrar, Straus and Giroux.
Kelton, Stephanie. 2020. *The Deficit Myth*. New York: Public Affairs.
Keynes, John Maynard. 1964. *The General Theory of Employment, Interest, and Money*. New York: Harvest-Harcourt.
King, Michael. 2001. "The politics of central bank independence." *Central Banking* 11, no. 3: 50–57.
Konings, Martijn. 2018. *Capital and Time: For a New Critique of Neoliberal Reason*. Stanford: Stanford University Press.
Kriesi, Hanspeter, and Edgar Grande. 2016. "The euro crisis: A boost to the politicization of European integration?," in Sven Hutter, Edgar Grande, and Hanspeter Kriesi, eds., *Politicising Europe: Integration and Mass Politics*. Cambridge: Cambridge University Press: 239–276.
Krippner, Greta R. 2005. "The financialization of the American economy." *Socio-Economic Review* 3, no. 2: 173–208.
    2011. *Capitalizing on Crisis: The Political Origins of the Rise of Finance*. Cambridge: Harvard University Press.
Krugman, Paul. 2020. *Arguing with Zombies: Economics, Politics, and the Fight for a Better Future*. New York: WW Norton & Company.
    2021. *Arguing with Zombies: Economics, Politics, and the Fight for a Better Future*. New York: WW Norton.
Kydland, Finn E., and Edward C. Prescott. 1977. "Rules rather than discretion: The inconsistency of optimal plans." *Journal of Political Economy* 85, no. 3: 473–491.

Latour, Bruno. 2007. *Reassembling the Social: An Introduction to Actor-Network-Theory*. Oxford: Oxford University Press.

Lawson, Tony. 2006. "The nature of heterodox economics." *Cambridge Journal of Economics* 30, no. 4: 483–505.

Leonard, Christopher. 2022. *The Lords of Easy Money: How the Federal Reserve Broke the American Economy*. New York: Simon and Schuster.

Lepers, Etienne. 2018. "The neutrality illusion: Biased economics, biased training, and biased monetary policy testing the role of ideology on FOMC voting behaviour." *New Political Economy* 23, no. 1: 105–127.

Levitsky, Steven, and Lucan A. Way. 2010. *Competitive Authoritarianism: Hybrid Regimes after the Cold War*. Cambridge: Cambridge University Press.

Levy, Jonathan. 2021. *Ages of American Capitalism: A History of the United States*. New York: Random House.

Lindblom, Charles E. 1959. "The science of "muddling through." *Public Administration Review* 19, no. 2: 79–88.

Lowenstein, Roger. 2015. *America's Bank: The Epic Struggle to Create the Federal Reserve*. New York: Penguin.

Lütz, Susanne, and Matthias Kranke. 2014. "The European rescue of the Washington Consensus? EU and IMF lending to Central and Eastern European countries." *Review of International Political Economy* 21, no. 2: 310–338.

MacKenzie, Donald. 2008. *An Engine, Not a Camera: How Financial Models Shape Markets*. Cambridge: MIT Press.

MacKenzie, Donald, Siu Leung-Sea, and Fabian Muniesa, eds. 2007. *Do Economists Make Markets? On the Performativity of Economics*. Princeton: Princeton University Press.

Majone, Giandomenico. 1994. "The rise of the regulatory state in Europe." *West European Politics* 17, no. 3: 77–101.

Mallaby, Sebastian. 2016. *The Man Who Knew: The Life and Times of Alan Greenspan*. New York: Bloomsbury Publishing.

Mandelkern, Ronen. 2016. "Explaining the striking similarity in macroeconomic policy responses to the great recession: The institutional power of macroeconomic governance." *Comparative Political Studies* 49, no. 2: 219–252.

Mankiw, N. Gregory, and Ricardo Reis. 2018. "Friedman's presidential address in the evolution of macroeconomic thought." *Journal of Economic Perspectives* 32, no. 1: 81–96.

Mann, Geoff. 2017. *In the Long Run We Are All Dead: Keynesianism, Political Economy, and Revolution*. London: Verso.

Marcussen, Martin. 2009. "Scientization of central banking: The politics of A-politization," in Kenneth Dyson and Martin Marcussen, eds., *Central Banks in the Age of the Euro: Europeanization, Convergence and Power*. Oxford: Oxford University Press: 373–390.

Marsh, David. 1992. *The Bundesbank: The Bank That Rules Europe*. London: Heineman.

Massoc, Elsa Clara. 2020. "When do banks do what governments tell them to do? A comparative study of Greek bonds' management in France and Germany at the onset of the Euro-crisis." *New Political Economy* 26, no. 4: 674–689.

——— 2022. "Banks' structural power and states' choices on what structurally matters: The geo-economic foundations of state priority toward banking in France, Germany, and Spain." *Politics & Society* 50, no. 4: 599–629.

2025. "Two degrees versus two percent: How central bankers and members of the European Parliament developed a common pro-climate narrative." *Journal of European Public Policy* 32, no. 3: 634–664.

Matthijs, Matthias, and Mark Blyth. 2017. "When is it rational to learn the wrong lessons? Technocratic authority, social learning, and Euro fragility." *Perspectives on Politics* 16, no. 1: 110–126.

Matthijs, Matthias, & Kathleen McNamara. 2015. "The euro crisis' theory effect: Northern saints, southern sinners, and the demise of the eurobond." *Journal of European Integration* 37, no. 2: 229–245.

McNamara, Kathleen R. 1998. *The Currency of Ideas: Monetary Politics in the European Union*. Ithaca: Cornell University Press.

2002. "Rational fictions: Central bank independence and the social logic of delegation." *West European Politics* 25, no. 1: 47–76.

Meade, Ellen E., and David Stasavage. 2008. "Publicity of debate and the incentive to dissent: Evidence from the US Federal Reserve." *The Economic Journal* 118, no. 528: 695–717.

Mehrling, Perry. 2001. "An interview with Paul A. Volcker." *Macroeconomic Dynamics* 5, no. 3: 434–460.

2011. *The New Lombard Street: How the Fed Became the Dealer of Last Resort*. Princeton: Princeton University Press.

Meltzer, Allan H. 2009. *A History of the Federal Reserve: Volume 2, Book 2, 1970-1986*. Chicago: University of Chicago Press.

Meyer, Lawrence H. 2004. *A Term at the Fed: An Insider's View*. New York: Collins.

Micossi, Stefano. 2015. The Monetary Policy of the European Central Bank (2002-2015), CEPS Special Report 109.

Mirowski, Philip. 2020. "The neoliberal Ersatz Nobel Prize," in Dieter Plehwe, Quinn Slobodian, and Philip Mirowski, eds., *Nine Lives of Neoliberalism*. London: Verso: 219–254.

Mirowski, Philip, and Dieter Plehwe, eds. 2015. *The Road from Mont Pèlerin: The Making of the Neoliberal Thought Collective*. Cambridge: Harvard University Press.

Moravcsik, Andrew. 1998. *The Choice for Europe: Social Purpose and State Power from Messina to Maastricht*. Ithaca: Cornell University Press.

Moschella, Manuela. 2024. *Unexpected Revolutionaries: How Central Banks Made and Unmade Economic Orthodoxy*. Ithaca: Cornell University Press.

Mourlon-Druol, Emmanuel. 2012. *A Europe Made of Money: The Emergence of the European Monetary System*. Ithaca: Cornell University Press.

2025. "Accidental Neoliberalism: Democratic Accountability in the Making of the Euro, 1957–92," Contemporary European History. doi:10.1017/S0960777325000207.

Mudge, Stephanie L. 2018. *Leftism Reinvented: Western Parties from Socialism to Neoliberalism*. Cambridge: Harvard University Press.

Mudge, Stephanie L., and Antoine Vauchez. 2016. "Fielding supranationalism: The European Central Bank as a field effect." *The Sociological Review* 64, no. 2: 146–169.

Mundell, Robert A. 2002. "Monetary unions and the problem of sovereignty." *The Annals of the American Academy of Political and Social Science* 579, no. 1: 123–152.

Murphy, Liam, and Thomas Nagel. 2002. *The Myth of Ownership: Taxes and Justice*. New York: Oxford University Press.

Nakamura, Emi, and Jón Steinsson. 2018. "Identification in macroeconomics." *Journal of Economic Perspectives* 32, no. 3: 59–86.

Newman, Abraham. 2015. "The reluctant leader," in Matthias Matthijs and Mark Blyth, eds., *The Future of the Euro*. Oxford: Oxford University Press: 117–135.

Obama, Barack. 2020. *A Promised Land*. New York: Crown.

Offer, Avner, and Gabriel Söderberg. 2016. *The Nobel Factor: The Prize in Economics, Social Democracy, and the Market Turn*. Princeton: Princeton University Press.

Offner, Amy C. 2019. *Sorting out the Mixed Economy: The Rise and Fall of Welfare and Developmental States in the Americas*. Princeton: Princeton University Press.

Orphanides, Athanasios. 2004. "Monetary policy rules, macroeconomic stability, and inflation: A view from the trenches." *Journal of Money, Credit and Banking* 36, no. 2: 151–175.

——— 2017. ECB Monetary Policy and Euro Area Governance: Collateral Eligibility Criteria for Sovereign Debt, MIT Sloan Research Paper No. 5258-17.

Ostry, Jonathan D., Prakash Loungani, and Davide Furceri. 2016. "Neoliberalism: Oversold?" *Finance & Development* 53, no. 2: 38–42.

Padgett, John F., and Christopher K. Ansell. 1993. "Robust action and the rise of the Medici, 1400-1434." *American Journal of Sociology* 98, no. 6: 1259–1319.

Padgett, John F., and Walter W. Powell. 2012. *The Emergence of Organizations and Markets*. Princeton: Princeton University Press.

Park, Gene, Saori N. Katada, Giacomo Chiozza, and Yoshiko Kojo. 2018. *Taming Japan's Deflation: The Debate over Unconventional Monetary Policy*. Ithaca: Cornell University Press.

Parsons, Craig. 2003. *A Certain Idea of Europe*. Ithaca: Cornell University Press.

Paul, Ron. 2009. *End the Fed*. New York: Grand Central Publishing.

Paulson, Henry M., Jr. 2013. *On the Brink: Inside the Race to Stop the Collapse of the Global Financial System*. New York: Business Plus.

Phillips-Fein, Kim. 2017. *Fear City: New York's Fiscal Crisis and the Rise of Austerity Politics*. New York: Metropolitan Books.

Pickering, Andrew. 1995. *The Mangle of Practice: Time, Agency, and Science*. Chicago: University of Chicago Press.

Piketty, Thomas. 2020. *Capital and Ideology*. Cambridge: Harvard University Press.

Pistor, Katharina. 2017. "From territorial to monetary sovereignty." *Theoretical Inquiries in Law* 18, no. 2: 491–517.

Plehwe, Dieter, and Philip Mirowski, eds. 2009. *The Road from Mont Pèlerin: The Making of the Neoliberal Thought Collective*. Cambridge: Harvard University Press.

Plehwe, Dieter, Quinn Slobodian, and Philip Mirowski, eds. 2020. *Nine Lives of Neoliberalism*. London: Verso.

Plosser, Charles I. 1989. "Understanding real business cycles." *Journal of Economic Perspectives* 3, no. 3: 51–77.

Polanyi, Karl. 2001. *The Great Transformation: The Political and Economic Origins of Our Time*. Boston: Beacon Press.

Polillo, Simone, and Mauro F. Guillén. 2005. "Globalization pressures and the state: The worldwide spread of central bank independence." *American Journal of Sociology* 110, no. 6: 1764–1802.

Pontusson, Jonas. 2018. "The Fed, finance, and inequality in comparative perspective." *PS: Political Science & Politics* 51, no. 4: 743–746.

Popp Berman, Elizabeth. 2022. *Thinking Like an Economist: How Efficiency Replaced Equality in U.S. Public Policy*. Princeton: Princeton University Press.

Prasad, Monica. 2012. *The Land of Too Much: American Abundance and the Paradox of Poverty*. Cambridge: Harvard University Press.

2018. *Starving the Beast: Ronald Reagan and the Tax Cut Revolution*. New York: Russell Sage Foundation.

Prasad, Monica, Andrew J. Perrin, Kieran Bezila, Steve G. Hoffman, Kate Kindleberger, Kim Manturuk, Ashleigh Smith Powers, and Andrew R. Payton. 2009. "The undeserving rich: 'Moral values' and the white working class." *Sociological Forum* 24, no. 2: 225–253.

Quaglia, Lucia. 2005. "An integrative approach to the politics of central bank independence: Lessons from Britain, Germany and Italy." *West European Politics* 28, no. 3: 549–568.

Quaglia, Lucia, and Amy Verdun. 2023. "Explaining the response of the ECB to the COVID-19 related economic crisis: Inter-crisis and intra-crisis learning." *Journal of European Public Policy* 30, no. 4: 635–654.

Quiggin, John. 2012. *Zombie Economics: How Dead Ideas Still Walk among US*. Princeton: Princeton University Press.

Quorning, Stine. 2024. "The 'climate shift' in central banks: How field arbitrageurs paved the way for climate stress testing." *Review of International Political Economy* 31, no. 1: 74–96.

Reisenbichler, Alexander. 2020. "The Politics of Quantitative Easing and Housing Stimulus by the Federal Reserve and European Central Bank, 2008–2018." *West European politics* 43, no. 2: 464–484.

Riles, Annelise. 2018. *Financial Citizenship: Experts, Publics, and the Politics of Central Banking*. Ithaca: Cornell University Press.

Rilinger, Georg. 2023. "Conceptual limits of performativity: Assessing the feasibility of market design blueprints." *Socio-Economic Review* 21, no. 2: 885–908.

Rodgers, Daniel T. 2011. *Age of Fracture*. Cambridge: Harvard University Press.

Rogoff, K. 1985. "The optimal degree of commitment to an intermediate monetary target." *Quarterly Journal of Economics* 100, no. 4: 1169–1189.

Romer, Christina D., and David H. Romer. 2004. "Choosing the Federal Reserve chair: Lessons from history." *Journal of Economic Perspectives* 18, no. 1: 129–162.

2013. "The most dangerous idea in Federal Reserve history: Monetary policy doesn't matter." *American Economic Review* 103, no. 3: 55–60.

2024. "Lessons from history for successful disinflation." *Journal of Monetary Economics* 148: 103654.

Rostagno, Massimo, Carlo Altavilla, Giacomo Carboni, Wolfgang Lemke, Roberto Motto, Arthur Saint Guilhem, and Jonathan Yiangou. 2019. A Tale of Two Decades: The ECB's Monetary Policy at 20, ECB Working Paper, No. 2346.

Ruggie, John Gerard. 1982. "International regimes, transactions, and change: Embedded liberalism in the postwar economic order." *International Organization* 36, no. 2: 379–415.

Sabel, Charles F., and Jonathan Zeitlin, eds. 2010. *Experimentalist Governance in the European Union: Towards a New Architecture*. Oxford: Oxford University Press.

Salines, Marion, Gabriel Glöckner, and Zbigniew Truchlewski. 2012. "Existential crisis, incremental response." *Journal of European Public Policy* 19, no. 5: 665–681.

Samuelson, Paul. 1955. *Economics*, 3rd ed. New York: McGraw-Hill.

Sandbu, Martin. 2015. *Europe's Orphan: The Future of the Euro and the Politics of Debt*. Princeton: Princeton University Press.

Saurugger, Sabine, and Clément Fontan. 2019. "The judicialisation of EMU politics: Resistance to the EU's new economic governance mechanisms at the domestic level." *European Journal of Political Research* 58, no. 4: 1066–1087.

Schäfer, Armin, and Wolfgang Streeck. 2013. Introduction, in Armin Schäfer and Wolfgang Streeck, eds., *Politics in the Age of Austerity*. Cambridge: Polity Press: 1–25.

Schelkle, Waltraud. 2017. *The Political Economy of Monetary Solidarity: Understanding the Euro Experiment*. Oxford: Oxford University Press.

Schimmelfennig, Frank. 2015. "Liberal intergovernmentalism and the euro area crisis." *Journal of European Public Policy* 22, no. 2: 177–195.

Schmidt, Vivien A. 2016. "Reinterpreting the rules 'by stealth' in times of crisis: A discursive institutionalist analysis of the European Central Bank and the European Commission." *West European Politics* 39, no. 5: 1032–1052.

2020. *Europe's Crisis of Legitimacy: Governing by Rules and Ruling by Numbers in the Eurozone*. Oxford: Oxford University Press.

Schmidt, Vivien A., and Mark Thatcher, eds. 2013. *Resilient Liberalism in Europe's Political Economy*. Cambridge: Cambridge University Press.

Schneiberg, Marc, and Elizabeth Clemens. 2006. "The typical tools for the job: Research strategies in institutional analysis." *Sociological Theory* 24, no. 3: 195–227.

Schönfelder, Wilhelm, and Elke Thiel. 1996. *Ein Markt-Eine Währung*. Baden-Baden: Nomos Verlagsgesellschaft.

Schonhardt-Bailey, Cheryl. 2013. *Deliberating American Monetary Policy: A Textual Analysis*. Cambridge: MIT Press.

Schorkopf, Frank. 2009. "The European Union as an association of sovereign states: Karlsruhe's ruling on the Treaty of Lisbon." *German Law Journal* 10, no. 8: 1219–1240.

Segers, Mathieu, and Femke Van Esch. 2007. "Behind the veil of budgetary discipline: The political logic of the budgetary rules in EMU and the SGP." *JCMS: Journal of Common Market Studies* 45, no. 5: 1089–1109.

Shenk, Timothy. 2023. "Taking off the neoliberal lens: The politics of the economy, the MIT School of Economics, and the strange career of Lawrence Klein." *Modern Intellectual History* 20, no. 4: 1194–1218.

Shonfield, Andrew. 1965. *Modern Capitalism: The Changing Balance of Public and Private Power*. New York: Oxford University Press.

Siderius, Katrijn. 2023. "An unexpected climate activist: Central banks and the politics of the climate-neutral economy." *Journal of European Public Policy* 30, no. 8: 1588–1608.

Silber, William L. 2012. *Volcker: The Triumph of Persistence*. New York: Bloomsbury Publishing.

Simon, Herbert A. 1947. *Administrative Behavior*. New York: Simon and Schuster.

1991. "Bounded rationality and organizational learning." *Organization Science* 2, no. 1: 125–134.

Sinn, Hans-Werner. 2014. *The Euro Trap: On Bursting Bubbles, Budgets, and Beliefs*. Oxford: Oxford University Press.

Slater, Dan. 2010. *Ordering Power: Contentious Politics and Authoritarian Leviathans in Southeast Asia*. New York: Cambridge University Press.

Slobodian, Quinn. 2018. *Globalists: The End of Empire and the Birth of Neoliberalism*. Cambridge: Harvard University Press.

2025. *Hayek's Bastards: Race, Gold, IQ, and the Capitalism of the Far Right*. Princeton: Princeton University Press.

Smeets, Sandrino, and Derek Beach. 2023. "New institutional leadership goes viral EU crisis reforms and the coming about of the covid recovery fund." *European Journal of Political Research* 62, no. 2: 377–396.

Stanovich, Keith E., and Richard F. West. 2000. Individual differences in reasoning: Implications for the rationality debate? *Behavioral and Brain Sciences* 23, no. 5: 645–665.

Stein, Judith. 2010 *Pivotal Decade: How the United States Traded Factories for Finance in the Seventies*. New Haven: Yale University Press.

Steinberg, Marc W. 1999. "The talk and back talk of collective action: A dialogic analysis of repertoires of discourse among nineteenth-century English cotton spinners." *American Journal of Sociology* 105, no. 3: 736–780.

Stock, James H., and Mark W. Watson. 2002. "Has the Business Cycle Changed and Why?" *NBER Macroeconomics Annual* 17: 159–218.

Stoltenberg, Gerhard. 1997. *Wendepunkte: Stationen deutscher Politik 1947-1990*. Berlin: Siedler Verlag.

Streeck, Wolfgang. 2017. *How Will Capitalism End? Essays on a Failing System*. London: Verso Books.

Suskind, Ron. 2011. *Confidence Men: Wall Street, Washington, and the Education of a President*. New York: Harper Collins.

Swidler, Ann. 1986. "Culture in action: Symbols and strategies." *American Sociological Review* 51, no. 2: 273–286.

Tadle, Raul Cruz. 2022. "FOMC minutes sentiments and their impact on financial markets." *Journal of Economics and Business* 118. https://doi.org/10.1016/j.jeconbus.2021.106021.

Taylor, John B. 2013. *Getting Off Track: How Government Actions and Interventions Caused, Prolonged, and Worsened the Financial Crisis*. Stanford: Hoover Institution Press.

Thelen, Kathleen. 2010. "Beyond comparative statics: Historical institutional approaches to stability and change in the political economy of labor," in Glenn Morgan, John L. Campbell, Colin Crouch, Ove Kaj Pedersen, and Richard Whitley, eds., *The Oxford Handbook of Comparative Institutional Analysis*. New York: Oxford University Press: 41–62.

2014. *Varieties of Liberalization and the New Politics of Social Solidarity*. Cambridge: Cambridge University Press.

Thiemann, Matthias, Carolina Raquel Melches, and Edin Ibrocevic. 2021. "Measuring and mitigating systemic risks: How the forging of new alliances between central bank and academic economists legitimize the transnational macroprudential agenda." *Review of International Political Economy* 28, no. 6: 1433–1458.

Thornton, Daniel L., and David C. Wheelock. 2014. "Making sense of dissents: A history of FOMC dissents." *Federal Reserve Bank of St. Louis Review* 96, no. 3: 213–227.
Thygesen, Niels. 2016. "Why did Europe decide to move to a single currency 25 years ago?" *Intereconomics* 51, no. 1: 11–16.
Tilly, Charles. 1978. *From Mobilization to Revolution*. Reading: Addison-Wesley.
  2008. *Contentious Performances*. New York: Cambridge University Press.
Timiraos, Nick. 2022. *Trillion Dollar Triage: How Jay Powell and the Fed Battled a President and a Pandemic – And Prevented Economic Disaster*. New York: Little, Brown, and Company.
Tooze, Adam. 2018. *Crashed: How a Decade of Financial Crises Changed the World*. London: Penguin.
  2021. "The gatekeeper." *London Review of Books* 43, no. 8.
  2022. *Shutdown: How Covid Shook the World's Economy*. New York: Viking.
Trichet, Jean-Claude. 1992. "Dix ans de désinflation compétitive en France." *Les Notes bleues de Bercy*, October 16.
  2010. "State of the union: The financial crisis and the response between 2007 and 2009." *Journal of Common Market Studies* 48, Annual Review: 7–19.
Truchlewski, Zbigniew, Waltraud Schelkle, and Joseph Ganderson. 2021. "Buying time for democracies? European Union emergency politics in the time of COVID-19." *West European Politics* 44, no. 5–6: 1353–1375.
Tsoukalis, Loukas. 1977. *The Politics and Economics of European Monetary Integration*. London: George Allen and Unwin.
Tucker, Paul. 2018. *Unelected Power: The Quest for Legitimacy in Central Banking and the Regulatory State*. Princeton: Princeton University Press.
Ullmann, Owen. 2022. *Empathy Economics: Janet Yellen's Remarkable Rise to Power and Her Drive to Spread Prosperity to All*. New York: PublicAffairs.
Vail, Mark I. 2014. "Varieties of liberalism: Keynesian responses to the Great Recesion in France and Germany." *Governance* 27, no. 1: 63–85.
Van der Zwan, Natascha. 2014. "Making sense of financialization." *Socio-Economic Review* 12, no. 1: 99–129.
Van't Klooster, Jens. 2021. "Technocratic Keynesianism: A paradigm shift without legislative change." *New Political Economy* 27, no. 5: 771–787.
  2023. "The politics of the ECB's market-based approach to government debt." *Socio-Economic Review* 21, no. 2: 1103–1123.
Varoufakis, Yanis. 2017. *Adults in the Room: My Battle with the European and American Deep Establishment*. New York: Farrar, Straus and Giroux.
Verdun, Amy. 1999. "The role of the Delors Committee in the creation of EMU." *Journal of European Public Policy* 6, no. 2: 308–328.
  2017. "Political leadership of the European central bank." *Journal of European Integration* 39, no. 2: 207–221.
Véron, Nicolas. 2015. "Europe's radical banking union." *Bruegel Essay and Lecture Series* 5.
  2024. "Europe's banking union at ten: Unfinished yet transformative." *Peterson Institute for International Economics Working Paper* 24-15.
Volcker, Paul A. 1976. Reconciling our Short and Long-Run Goals in Economy Policy, a speech delivered to the Boston Economic Club, December 15. Personal Papers of Paul Volcker, pp. 11–12.

Volcker, Paul A., and Christine Harper. 2018. *Keeping At It: The Quest for Sound Money and Good Government.* New York: Hachette.
Volcker, Paul A., and Toyoo Gyohten. 1992. *Changing Fortunes: The World's Money and the Threat to American Leadership.* New York: Crown.
Waas, Lara, and Berthold Rittberger. 2024. "The Berlin puzzle: Why European solidarity prevailed in the adoption of the Corona recovery fund." *European Journal of Political Research* 63, no. 2: 644–663.
Wansleben, Leon. 2018. "How expectations became governable: Institutional change and the performative power of central banks." *Theory and Society* 47, no. 6: 773–803.
  2023. *The Rise of Central Banks: State Power in Financial Capitalism.* Cambridge: Harvard University Press.
Warlouzet, Laurent. 2018. "Le spectre de la crise financière française de 1983." *Vingtième Siècle* 138, no. 2: 93–107.
Wells, Wyatt C. 1994. *Economist in an Uncertain World: Arthur F. Burns and the Federal Reserve, 1970-78.* New York: Columbia University Press.
Whelan, Karl. 2014. "Ireland's economic crisis: The good, the bad and the ugly." *Journal of Macroeconomics* 39: 424–440.
Widmaier, Wesley. 2016. *Economic Ideas in Political Time: The Rise and Fall of Economic Orders from the Progressive Era to the Global Financial Crisis.* Cambridge: Cambridge University Press.
Wiener, Antje. 2007. "Contested meanes of norms: A research framework." *Comparative European Politics* 5, no. 1: 1–17.
Williamson, John. 1990. *Latin American Adjustment: How Much Has Happened?* Washington, DC: Institute for International Economics.
Williamson, Vanessa, Theda Skocpol, and John Coggin. 2011. "The Tea Party and the remaking of Republican conservatism." *Perspectives on Politics* 9, no. 1: 25–43.
Woll, Cornelia. 2014. *The Power of Inaction: Bank Bailouts in Comparison.* Ithaca: Cornell University Press.
Woodward, Bob. 2000. *Maestro: Greenspan's Fed and the American Boom.* New York: Simon and Schuster.
Yellen, Janet Louise. 2009. Minsky Meltdown: Lessons for Central Bankers. Federal Reserve Bank of San Francisco Economic Letter, no. 15 (May 1).
Young, Brigitte. 2014. "German ordoliberalism as agenda setter for the euro crisis: Myth trumps reality." *Journal of Contemporary European Studies* 22, no. 3: 276–287.
Zackin, Emily, and Chloe N. Thurston. 2024. *The Political Development of American Debt Relief.* Chicago: University of Chicago Press.
Ziblatt, Daniel. 2017. *Conservative Political Parties and the Birth of Modern Democracy in Europe.* Cambridge: Cambridge University Press.
Zimmermann, Hubert. 2014. "A grand coalition for the euro: The second Merkel cabinet, the euro crisis and the elections of 2013." *German Politics* 23, no. 4: 322–336.

Index

AfD party (Alternative für Deutschland), 1, 40, 155
Angell, Wayne, 69–70
Asmussen, Jorg, 160
Asset Purchase Program (APP). *See* quantitative easing
austerity
   after 2008, 13, 16, 19, 39, 105, 148–149, 184
   neoliberalism and, 13
   popularity in 2010s, 189

Baker, James, 67 68, 70
Balladur, Edouard, 90
Banca d'Italia, 85
Bank of England, 183–185
Bank of International Settlements, 79–80
Bank of Japan, 182–183
Banque de France, 79, 82, 91
Basel-Nyborg agreement, 77
Bérégovoy, Pierre, 82, 95
Bernanke Fed
   dissenting votes, 122–124
   distributive effects of monetary stimulus, 125
   fiscal policy and, 118–119
   inflation target, 129
   Keynesian approach, 14
   political constraints on, 126
   retreat from neoliberal policies, 104
Bernanke, Ben, 71
   on bailouts, 115
   as dove, 107–108
   on Fed mistakes, 111
   fiscal policy and, 118
   on Japan, 182
   Lehman Brothers and, 112–113
   neo-Keynesianism and, 11, 127
   on Republican Party, 134
   as target of Tea Party movement, 1
Biden, Joe, 171, 179
Black, Robert, 50
Blair, Tony, 184
Blanchard, Olivier, 181
Blinder, Alan, 2, 22, 42–43, 56, 67, 128
Bloom Raskin, Sarah, 179
Bretton Woods regime, 82–83, 90, 180
Brown, Gordon, 184
Brussels-Frankfurt consensus, 17, 137, 139, *See also* Frankfurt consensus
Bullard, James, 108
Bundesbank (Germany), 90–91, 93–94
   ECB and, 158–159
   Economic Monetary Union (EMU) and, 97
   as inspiration for the ECB, 1, 18
   success in fighting inflation, 18
Burns, Arthur, 48–49, 53, 57

capital controls, 83
capital liberalization, 83–86
capitalism, 11, 25, 49
CARES Act, 171
Carter, Jimmy, 48–50, 60
central bank independence
   democratic legitimacy and, 186
   political manipulations and, 190

central bankers
  agency, 25
  as agents of financialization and neoliberalism, 17, 24
  as cautious creatures, 186
  common portrayals of, 2
  as counterweight to fiscal policy, 16, 19, 101, 184
  as defenders of the status quo, 2, 5, 16
  as economic experts, 15
  economics perspective on, 15–16, 24
  growing power, 7, 15, 36
  hawks versus doves, 35
  independence, 2
  Keynesian policies after 2008, 14, 16
  political economy perspective on, 16–17, 24
  pro-finance bias, 17
  retreat from neoliberalism, 8, 38
  role in the waxing and waning of technocratic neoliberalism, 3, 25
  role in ushering in neoliberalism, 8
  role reversal, 1, 38, 186
  support of neoliberal policies in the 1980s, 25
  as technocrats, 2
central banking
  as area of overlap between economics and politics, 15
  democracy and, 189–190
  historical overview, 3
  relationship to mainstream economics, 33–34, 36
central banks
  archives, 28
  as arenas, 4
  economics, 30–31
  evolving relationship with neoliberalism, 4
  hierarchy among, 180
  insulation from electoral politics, 17, 25
  policy contests within, 29, 34–35
  as political institutions, 16
  as sites of organizational innovation, 27
  transparency, 19–20
Chicago School of economics, 32–33
Chirac, Jacques, 90
Ciampi, Carlo, 85
Clinton, Bill, 72
Coeuré, Benoît, 165
Committee of Governors (Europe), 19, 76, See also European Monetary System, See also ECB Governing Council
comparison of similar cases, 179

conservatism
  central banking and, 104
  relationship with central banking, 1–2, 24, 36–37, 39
  relationship with the ECB, 143
  relationship with the Fed, 134–135
conservatives
  as defenders of neoliberalism, 7–8
  ECB and, 155
  relationship with the Federal Reserve, 106
Constancio, Victor, 165
COVID pandemic
  ECB response, 171–172
  inflation and monetary tightening, 174
  inflation and tight monetary policies after, 168
  Japanese response, 183
  monetary stimulus, 168
  normalization of unconventional monetary policies, 177
  UK response, 185
cross-cutting alliances. See also politics of money
  central bankers' participation in, 37
  defined, 6, 35
  in Europe, 94, 96, 138
  political-economic regimes and, 9, 37
  in related arenas, 6, 35
  transatlantic variation in, 102, 141
  understudied, 7
  in the United States, 44, 72, 135

de Larosière, Jacques, 79, 81–82, 84–86, 92, 181
Delors Committee, 75
  as community, 76
  disagreement on the, 86–87
  divides within, 77, 79
  on European fiscal policy and sovereignty, 87–89
  first meeting, 82
  technocratic neoliberalism and, 81
  vision of common European budget, 87
Delors, Jacques, 79, 82, 84, 87
Delors Report, 76, 79, 83, 92
  price stability and, 94
denomination risk, 159
deutschmark, 77, 90, 189
dirigisme, 91
dollar (US), 180
Doyle, Maurice, 87

Index

Draghi ECB
  conflict within the, 165–166
Draghi, Mario, 137, 148, 157–158
  criticism of, 1
  on fiscal space, 163–164
  Jackson Hole speech, 161, 164
Duisenberg, Wim, 79, 84–85, 87, 100

ECB Governing Council, 19, See also European Central Bank (ECB)
  hawks versus doves, 151
  methodology for analyzing the records of the, 21–22
  request for minutes, 20
Economic and Monetary Union, 83
Economic and Monetary Union (EMU), 74–76, 81, 92
  France and, 97
  Germany and, 97–98
  liberalization and, 81, See also capital controls
  membership requirements, 95
  as ordoliberal, 99
  transition to, 75–99
economic evolution since 1945
  economics perspective on, 13–14
  political economy perspective on, 12–13
economic governance
  contrasting perspectives, 11
  regimes, 6, See also political-economic regimes
  status of economics in, 10
economics. See also economics perspective
  as central bankers' language, 30
  expertise and influence, 31
  labels and terminology, 189–190
  Nobel Prize, 31
  as scholarly field, 2
economics perspective
  on 1980s monetary regime change, 18
  on 2010s monetary regime change, 19
  on Bernanke Fed, 112, 125–126
  on central bankers, 2, 15–16
  on the ECB after 2008, 138, 153
  on the ECB in the Eurozone crisis, 149
  on economic evolution since 1945, 13–14
  on Europe's Economic and Monetary Union, 76
  on global financial crisis, 105
  on monetary regime change after 2008, 187
  truncated, 2, 24

economics profession
  as an arena, 1, 4–5
  Bernanke Fed and, 131
  ECB after 2008 and, 143, 159
  Economic and Monetary Union and, 89
  hierarchy within, 187
  IMF and, 180
  mainstream versus heterodox divide, 30
  politics of money and, 29, 36
  post-1945 theoretical synthesis, 14
  representation within central banks, 31
  rise of neo-Keynesianism within, 11–12
  Volcker Fed and, 56–57
Emanuel, Rahm, 116
embedded liberalism, 13
EU Treaty
  European Stability Mechanism and, 154
  less fundamentalist interpretation, 157
  no-bailout clause, 145, 150, 153–155
euro (currency), 74, 180
  scholarly perspectives on its origins, 76
European Central Bank
  Outright Monetary Transactions (OMTs), 158
European Central Bank (ECB)
  conservative base, 155
  Delors Committee and, 87
  evolution under Trichet, 144
  Executive Board, 20
  fiscal austerity and, 147
  fiscal conservatism, 100–101
  on fiscal space, 162
  growing power, 15
  inflation targeting, 172–173
  left-wing opposition to, 137
  legal challenges to, 160–161
  legitimacy, 155
  Long-Term Refinancing Operations (LTRO), 157
  market discipline and, 153
  monetary policy strategy, 172
  origins, 38, 74
  pandemic response, 171–172
  price stability and, 99–100
  Securities Market Program (SMP), 145–147, 150–153
  shift to quantitative easing, 157–158
  sources on, 142–143
  on structural reforms, 165
  support for COVID fiscal stimulus, 173–174
  transparency, 20
  unconventional policies, 160

European central bankers
  cleavage between weak- and strong-currency countries, 77–79
  role in creation of Europe's Economic and Monetary Union, 76–77
European Commission, 80, 96, 99, 148
  on fiscal flexibility, 163–164
European Community, 84, 94
European fiscal policy, 99
European Monetary Institute, 96, 98
European Monetary System (EMS), 74, 76, 82, 184
  Committee of Governors, 89
  crises, 95–96
  currency hierarchy within, 77
  deutschmark and, 90
  France and, 90–91
  Germany and, 92
  sovereignty and, 91–92
European Stability Mechanism (ESM), 154, 158
European Union (EU), 74, 94
Eurozone
  difference with the United States, 152
  recovery from global financial crisis, 141
  sovereign debt, 142
Eurozone crisis
  German response to, 155–156
  political backlash to, 154–155
exchange rate crises, 77, 82

Federal Open Market Committee (FOMC)
  disagreements on, 109
  dovish majority after 2008, 111, 113–114, 130–131
  hawks versus doves, 46–47, 107–109, 121–122
  meeting minutes and transcripts, 19–21
  methodology for analyzing minutes and transcripts, 21–22
  monetary strategy, 170
  response to pandemic crisis, 170
Federal Reserve
  as counterweight to fiscal policy, 119
  dual mandate, 50, 178
  global financial crisis and, 111
  growing power, 15
  inflation targeting, 128, 172
  influence on other countries, 179–180
  leadership in pandemic response, 169
  lessons from the 2010s, 170
  neo-Keynesianism and, 128

  transparency revolution, 19
Federal Reserve Reform Act (1977), 50
financialization, 7, 185
  narratives, 17
  neoliberalism and, 13
  Volcker Shock and, 61
fiscal conservatism, 71, 96
Fordism, 12–13
forward guidance, 126–127
Frankfurt consensus, 137–138, 142, 147, 166, See also Brussels-Frankfurt consensus
Friedman, Milton
  1967 address to the American Economic Association, 14, 32
  as advisor to Reagan, 68
  criticism of Paul Volcker, 52
  criticism of the Federal Reserve, 36, 54
  monetarism and, 3, 32, 41
  Mont Pelerin Society and, 6
  neo-Keynesianism and, 127
  Paul Volcker and, 54–56
  Robert Lucas and, 56

Geithner, Tim, 114, 116
  on bailouts, 115
George, Esther, 131
German reunification, 93–94
Germany
  fiscal policy after 2008, 162–163
  opposition to fiscal stimulus, 161–162
Giscard d'Estaing, Valery, 82
global financial crisis, 7–8, 13–14, 104
  bank bailouts, 115, 144–145
  European austerity after the, 148–149
  fiscal retrenchment after, 117–119
  waning of technocratic neoliberalism and, 38
Godeaux, Jean, 89
gold standard, 189
gouvernement économique, 95
Gramm–Rudman Act, 69
Great Inflation, 14, 18
Great Moderation, 12, 14, 16, 71–72
Great Recession, 121, See also global financial crisis
Greece
  debt crisis, 149–150, 164
  German-French response to debt crisis, 154
  sovereignty, 164
green central banking, 178–179
Greenspan, Alan, 64, 112, 128
  Bill Clinton and, 38
  Great Moderation and, 16

Index

neo-Keynesianism and, 128
Paul Volcker and, 72
reputation of, 1

Hayek, Friedrich, 6, 75
Hoenig, Thomas, 122–124

Internal Market (Europe), 91
International Monetary Fund (IMF), 148, 180–182
politics of money at, 181

Japan, 182–183
politics of money, 182
Johnson, Manuel, 69
Juppé, Alain, 97

Keynes, John Maynard, 16
Keynesian economists
ECB and, 159
Keynesianism, 73
usefulness as label, 189–190
Kocherlakota, Narayana, 109, 132
Kohl, Helmut, 93, 96
Krugman, Paul, 36, 105, 116, 160

Lacker, Jeffrey, 120–121, 129–130
Laffer curve, 67
Lagarde, Christine, 137, 178, 182
Lagarde ECB, 178
Lamfalussy, Alexandre, 79, 85, 88
Lautenschläger, Sabine, 162
Lehman Brothers, 105, 112–113
Leigh-Pemberton, Robin, 183
liquidity trap, 125
Lucas, Robert, 56

Maastricht Treaty, 93–95, 97
machine-assisted analysis, 4
of central bank archives, 1
Manchin, Joe, 179
Martin, Preston, 68–70
Merkel, Angela, 156, 173
Mitterand, François, 82, 97
monetarism
in the 1970s and 1980s, 3, 18
avatars, 106
decline, 177
rise within economics profession, 15
theory, 58
monetary easing
waning of technocratic neoliberalism and, 2

monetary policy
as counterweight to fiscal policy, 38
transmission mechanism, 152
monetary policy committees
as arenas, 1
monetary regime change, 26–28
in the 1980s and 2010s, 18–19
Delors Committee and, 94
monetary regimes, 5, 22
Mont Pelerin Society, 6, 75
moral hazard, 120–121, 160, 163
Mundell, Robert, 91
Mundell–Fleming model, 76, 89

neo-Keynesianism
Ben Bernanke and, 11
central bankers and, 72
in the economics profession, 14
IMF and, 181
as mainstream economics, 30
microfoundations and, 188
monetary policies, 107
as neoliberalism, 17
rise within economics profession, 11–12, 32–33
synthesis, 188
neoliberalism. *See also* technocratic neoliberalism
austerity and, 13
central bankers' response to global financial crisis and, 19
characteristics of, 13
as elite project, 6
Europe's Economic and Monetary Union and, 19
financialization and, 13
in France, 82
narratives, 17
as political-economic regime, 6, 94
political economy versus economics perspectives on, 12
populist recombination, 8, 39–40, 104, 166, 189, *See also* populist neoliberalism
renewed interest in, 6
strange non-death, 7, 11, 13
subjectivity, 39, 186, 189
technocracy and, 7, 23, 189
usefulness as label, 189–190
Next Generation EU, 173
Nixon, Richard, 16, 180

Obama, Barack
  Economic Recovery Act, 115–116
  Keynesianism and, 116
open market operations, 27
ordoliberalism, 19, 88, 99, 138, 155–156, *See also* neoliberalism

paradigm, 27–28, 48
parallelism, 81, 84, *See also* capital liberalization
  as linkage method, 84
  origins, 83
Paul, Rand, 115
Paulson, Hank, 112, 115
Plosser, Charles, 109
Pöhl, Karl Otto, 79, 81–82, 84–86
  deficit ceiling and, 95
  miscalculations, 92–93
Polanyi, Karl, 13, 23
political economy. *See also* political economy perspective
  empirical terrain, 19
  labels and terminology, 189–190
  plea for agnostic approach, 188
  as scholarly field, 2, 6
political economy perspective, 7
  on 1980s monetary regime change, 19
  on 2010s monetary regime change, 19
  on Bernanke Fed stimulus, 125
  on central bankers, 2, 16–17
  on Europe's Economic and Monetary Union, 76
  on financialization, 187
  on global financial crisis, 105–106
  on late-20th century history, 11
  on quantitative easing, 124
  on the ECB after 2008, 138–139, 153
  on the ECB in the Eurozone crisis, 149
  truncated, 2, 24
political-economic regime
  analogy with political-constitutional regime, 8
  broadly neoliberal but less technocratic, 39
  central bank policies and, 22
  change, 2, 5, 25
  monetary regime and, 18, 22, 26, 28–29, 35, 188
  neoliberal, 7, 23
  post-neoliberalism as, 168
  standard scholarly chronology, 12
  technocratic neoliberalism as, 25, 37, 186
politics of money. *See also* cross-cutting alliances

beyond the book's case studies, 169
defined, 35
across different arenas, 4–5, 25
historical evidence, 4
inside central banks and the economics profession, 25
as internal to central banks and the economics profession, 26
overview of the, 4–5
submersed, 1
tilted toward Germany, 94
Volcker Fed and, 67, 72–73
within central banks, 29, 35
within economics profession, 29, 36
populism
  backlash against Wall Street bailouts, 114–115
  conservative strand, 7
  in history of central banks, 23, 136
  rhetoric, 39
populist neoliberalism, 135, 173, 184, 189
  demand for sound money, 189
  as factor of resilience for neoliberalism, 39, 105
  overlooked by scholars, 40
post-neoliberalism, 185
Powell Fed
  support for fiscal stimulus, 171
  technocratic neoliberalism and the, 177
Powell, Jerome, 127, 133–134, 171, 174, 177
  Donald Trump and, 134
pragmatist theory, 27, 33, 188
primary and secondary sources
  overview of, 3–4
public arena
  as site of monetary contests, 1, 5, 24

quantitative easing, 3, 27, 113–114, 119, 121, 124–125, 130, 158, 182
  during COVID pandemic, 168

Reagan administration, 65
  economic factions within, 67–68
Reagan, Ronald, 6, 13, 40
  Paul Volcker and, 67
Regan, Donald, 68
regime of political economy, 6–7, *See also* political-economic regime
Republican Party, 7, 107, 117, 134–135
Rice, Emmett, 70
Romer, Christina, 116, 131
Roos, Lawrence, 51, 63
  as supporter of monetarism, 51, 62

Index

Samuelson, Paul, 14
Sanders, Bernie, 115
Santelli, Rick, 121
Sarkozy, Nicolas, 154
Schäuble, Wolfgang, 160
Schmidt, Helmut, 82
Schnabel, Isabel, 172, 178
Schröder, Gerhard, 101
Schwartz, Anna, 113
science studies, 8
Seger, Martha, 68–69
Solomon, Anthony, 63
sovereignty, 75, 84, 87, 143, 155, 180
  European Monetary System and, 91–92
  fiscal policy and, 88, 164
  France and, 91
  Germany and, 160
  Greece and, 164
  as source of division, 88, 168
Stability and Growth Pact, 74, 98–99, 101, 153, 163
stagflation, 46
Stockman, David, 68–69
Stoiber, Edmund, 98
Strauss-Kahn, Dominique, 181
structural adjustment, 181
structural reforms, 101
Summers, Larry, 116, 177
Sunak, Rishi, 185
supply-side economics, 67–68

Taylor, John, 132–133
Tea Party movement, 40, 104, 117, 121
  criticism of the Fed, 1, 7
  neoliberalism and, 7
technocratic neoliberalism, 72
  defined, 6, 25
  Delors Committee and, 81
  different elements, 37
  as political-economic regime, 8–9
  prevalence of, 179
  transatlantic variation in, 102
  Volcker Fed and, 72–73
  waxing and waning, 2–3, 7, 25
technocratic style, 40
Teeters, Nancy, 50, 63, 66, 68
  as critic of monetary targeting, 58, 60–62
Thatcher, Margaret, 6, 13, 40, 183
Thygesen, Nils, 76, 79
Tooze, Adam, 17
Trichet ECB, 144
  internal divisions, 150

Trichet, Jean-Claude, 1, 137, 143–145
  support for austerity, 148, 150–151
troika, 154
Troubled Assets Relief Program (TARP), 115
Trump, Donald, 40, 104, 133–134, 171
  Jerome Powell and, 134

unconventional monetary policies
  economic turmoil and, 27
  monetary regime shifts and, 27
United Kingdom, 183–185
  parallel trajectory to the USA and the EU, 183

Volcker Fed, 18
  assertion of independence, 55–56
  bipartisan political support, 47
  in comparison with Europe, 75
  conflict within, 50
  dissent within, 44–46, 60, 68–69
  economics perspective on, 72
  economics profession and, 56–57
  end of monetary targeting, 62–65
  financialization and, 43
  hawks versus doves, 51
  monetarism and, 15, 47–48, 53–54
  opposition to budget deficits, 65–66
  political economy perspective on, 72
  politics of money within, 44
  support of neoliberal agenda, 25, 41–42
  technocratic neoliberalism and the, 72–73
Volcker, Paul
  air traffic controllers and, 67
  Alan Greenspan and, 72
  appointment of, 49
  exit from the Fed, 70–71
  as favorite of Wall Street, 49
  Federal Reserve independence and, 63–64
  as fiscal conservative, 65
  as hawk, 46
  legacy, 41, 71–72
  Milton Friedman and, 54–56
  monetarism and, 53
  political skills, 18, 56, 72–73
  on price stability, 71
  Reagan administration and, 67–71
  Ronald Reagan and, 48, 67
  support for Reagan policies, 41
Volcker Shock
  American economy after, 65
  economic effects, 61–62, 71–72
  economics versus political economy perspectives, 42–44

Volcker Shock (cont.)
   financialization and, 61
   neo-Keynesianism and, 42
   political economy perspective, 43
   political response to, 57–60
   political support for, 50
   rationale, 53
   timeline, 50

Wallich, Henry, 50, 55, 62, 66, 69–70
Washington consensus, 17, 181
Weber, Axel, 154, 156
Weidmann, Jens, 157, 159–160, 165, 178

Yellen, Janet, 107, 128, 130, 132

zero lower bound, 144

For EU product safety concerns, contact us at Calle de José Abascal, 56–1°, 28003 Madrid, Spain or eugpsr@cambridge.org.

www.ingramcontent.com/pod-product-compliance
Ingram Content Group UK Ltd.
Pitfield, Milton Keynes, MK11 3LW, UK
UKHW041027160426
469997UK00012B/171